Yahweh before Israel

Yahweh is the proper name of the biblical God. His early character is central to understanding the foundations of Jewish, Christian, and Islamic monotheism. As a deity, the name appears only in connection with the peoples of the Hebrew Bible, but long before Israel, the name is found in an Egyptian list as one group in the land of tent-dwellers, the Shasu. This is the starting point for Daniel Fleming's sharply new approach to the god Yahweh. In his analysis, the Bible's "people of Yahweh" serve as a clue to how one of the Bronze Age herding peoples of the inland Levant gave its name to a deity, initially outside of any relationship to Israel. For 150 years, the dominant paradigm for Yahweh's origin has envisioned borrowing from peoples of the desert south of Israel. Fleming argues in contrast that Yahweh was not taken from outsiders. Rather, this divine name is evidence for the diverse background of Israel itself.

Daniel E. Fleming is Ethel and Irvin A. Edelman Professor of Hebrew and Judaic Studies at New York University. Along with other books and numerous articles, he is the author of *Democracy's Ancient Ancestors: Mari and Early Collective Governance* and *The Legacy of Israel in Judah's Bible: History, Politics, and the Reinscribing of Tradition*.

Yahweh before Israel

Glimpses of History in a Divine Name

DANIEL E. FLEMING
New York University

CAMBRIDGE
UNIVERSITY PRESS

CAMBRIDGE
UNIVERSITY PRESS

Shaftesbury Road, Cambridge CB2 8EA, United Kingdom

One Liberty Plaza, 20th Floor, New York, NY 10006, USA

477 Williamstown Road, Port Melbourne, VIC 3207, Australia

314–321, 3rd Floor, Plot 3, Splendor Forum, Jasola District Centre, New Delhi – 110025, India

103 Penang Road, #05–06/07, Visioncrest Commercial, Singapore 238467

Cambridge University Press is part of Cambridge University Press & Assessment, a department of the University of Cambridge.

We share the University's mission to contribute to society through the pursuit of education, learning and research at the highest international levels of excellence.

www.cambridge.org
Information on this title: www.cambridge.org/9781108799614

DOI: 10.1017/9781108875479

First published 2021
First paperback edition 2023

A catalogue record for this publication is available from the British Library

Library of Congress Cataloging-in-Publication data
NAMES: Fleming, Daniel E., author.
TITLE: Yahweh before Israel : glimpses of history in a divine name / Daniel E. Fleming, New York University.
DESCRIPTION: Cambridge, United Kingdom ; New York, NY, USA : Cambridge University Press, 2021. | Includes bibliographical references and index.
IDENTIFIERS: LCCN 2020023805 (print) | LCCN 2020023806 (ebook) |
ISBN 9781108835077 (hardback) |
ISBN 9781108799614 (paperback) | ISBN 9781108875479 (epub)
SUBJECTS: LCSH: God (Judaism)–Name.
CLASSIFICATION: LCC BM610 .F55 2021 (print) | LCC BM610 (ebook) |
DDC 296.3/112–dc23
LC record available at https://lccn.loc.gov/2020023805
LC ebook record available at https://lccn.loc.gov/2020023806

ISBN   978-1-108-83507-7   Hardback
ISBN   978-1-108-79961-4   Paperback

for Mark Stratton Smith, my friend,
without whom my scholarly life would not be the same
and life generally far duller

Contents

Figures

Preface

My students and I have a running joke about speculation. I am against it, I say. New ideas, new possibilities, are essential, and uncertainty is unavoidable. We must learn to describe precisely what we propose, the evidence and arguments for it, along with the gaps and soft spots in the resulting interpretation. Speculation launches into unfounded guesswork, refusing the rigors of proof and disproof. This is not the same as identification of novel explanations, measured carefully against failed alternatives.

For all my determination to eschew speculation, the accusing word hangs over scholarly work as a plague waiting to infest it. When I took on Yahweh, the special god of the Hebrew Bible and ancient Israel, I entered a realm where ancient history and contemporary religion meet in a cacophony of convictions and conclusions. I offer my own, and their interest to me lies in their novelty, the hope that I have pushed down paths that will prove productive even to those with differing solutions. At every point in the discussion that follows, I will be elaborating what I perceive as a new framework for understanding the earliest evidence for Yahweh, even as I build on the work of others and try not to underplay the uncertainties.

I mean the last in specific terms. My acceptance of the notion that Yhwꜣ of the Shasu people in old Egyptian evidence reflects the same name as the famous god is widely shared but capable of valid doubt. My treatment of the opening hymn in the Song of Deborah (Judges 5) as a later elaboration began as an effort at caution, to avoid reading the name Israel as original to all the peoples of the battle account (vv. 12–23) when the pattern of appearance suggested otherwise. Yet others make the equation without hesitation. These two interpretive choices are essential to the history I reconstruct here, and they are debatable from the start.

Yet I am determined to avoid speculation, and I hope that my interpretations and discussion are thought-provoking and as often as possible persuasive, worth the read, and worth having written. I begin my offering with this acknowledgment of what such an effort involves. My first higher education was in the natural sciences (geology), and I still carry with me the ideals of scientific pursuit. Progress is made by the construction of interpretations that are capable of testing and susceptible to improvement or disproof. There is no fixed destination, because reality always presents new questions with every conceptual advance. For all that readers may prefer certainties to probabilities, and solutions with alternatives may look like speculation, historical reconstruction always inhabits such conceptual space, the more so when peering at obscure first appearances. Possibilities and probabilities are what we have, and they warrant weighing. Through this work I will construct my argument with as much nuance and precision as I can muster, taking account of degrees of certainty along with what appear secure landmarks. It is my hope that readers will find my caution appropriate to the material and measured carefully, even where their own may lead them differently.

My ruminations on Yahweh before Israel build on generations of insightful study, and so far as they contribute to future work, they will themselves be corrected and improved. This is as it should be. These questions take us back to the hazy horizon of the evidence, where the available facts are well known and the issue is how to situate them in the expanse of what we do not know properly. With what follows I propose to rearrange these facts, convinced that the arrangement is new and interesting, plausible and yet tentative, calling for the reflection of others. It is this reflection to which you are invited.

Acknowledgments

The roots of this book lie in a conversation with Rachel Angel, a New York University doctoral student at the time, who asked me what I considered the oldest biblical evidence for Yahweh. This led me to the Song of Deborah in Judges 5, which I had recently recognized to have been recast in a way that made all the peoples of the battle with Canaan a unified "Israel" – when, as I saw it, they had originally been "the people of Yahweh" (v. 13). In this reading, verse 13 would be older than the lines that had Yahweh come from Seir and Edom as "God of Israel" (vv. 4–5), older than the connection with a land far south of Israel and Judah. The geography of the people of Yahweh in the Song of Deborah would overlap with the later kingdom of Israel, and this made me wonder whether Yahweh's connections to a foreign southern space might not provide a straightforward origin story after all. Soon afterward, at the annual meeting of the Society of Biblical Literature (2015), I found myself talking with various colleagues about Yahweh, and in particular, a conversation with Brendon Benz led to a collaboration at the 2016 meeting, to which Benz contributed an evaluation of all the biblical evidence for "the people of Yahweh."

By the end of the summer of 2018, I had completed a full second draft of a book, which I both gave to various generous readers and submitted to Cambridge for review, with appreciation for the editorial interest of Beatrice Rehl. In the last phases of production, the volume benefited especially from the careful copyediting of Eric Christianson. My hope was that the book would benefit from serious response before one last revision, and I am in the particular debt of numerous readers who approached the manuscript from many angles, which I will not elaborate here. The list includes Betsy Bryan, Quinn Daniels, Mahri Leonard-Fleckman, Ted Lewis, Adam Miglio, Lauren Monroe, Jaime Myers, Stephen Russell, Thomas Schneider, Mark Smith, and Michael Stahl. From the sum of my readers' efforts, I have not merely added observations and refined arguments; I have restructured the whole book and reconceived the problem that it treats. These are scholars at every career stage, including current doctoral students, and this diversity of perspective has represented a benefit in itself. All the pleasure of my scholarly work lies in such shared scheming over the mysteries of the distant past, along with the friendships formed in the pursuit.

In the final stage of work on the book, I have benefited from the support of four who served in a variety of roles as research assistants. Quinn Daniels reread the whole for flow – within the limits of what my prose and publication calendar allowed. Spencer Elliott, new to NYU and to the project, offered generously to help with the indices and in the process added polish to the text. Elizabeth Knott stepped in to guide me through the steps necessary to incorporate images and to help with the preparation of the two maps, which were created by Kyle Brunner. She also recruited Ogden Goelet to draw the writing of Yhw₃ from the Soleb appearance, for reference. Jaime Myers ran down material from Soleb to help me refine my treatment of the Egyptian evidence. Nancy Fleming collaborated in the measurement and calculation of space available for prisoners and their identifications on the temple columns at Soleb.

Although the idea for this book began with doubt regarding the Midianite Hypothesis and its expectation of a foreign southern origin for Yahweh, the project shifted as I moved more deeply into the Egyptian evidence, beginning with a full review of all the evidence for the Shasu "nomad" population, as gathered in Giveon (1971). The further I progressed, the more I was convinced that Yhw₃ and the other named Shasu entities in the lists from Soleb and 'Amarah West required new interpretation in social and spatial terms. As part of my final round of rewriting, I benefited from the Egyptological expertise of Thomas Schneider first, in both extended conversation and then response to a chapter draft, and more recently of Betsy Bryan. The interpretation of the Shasu entities remains very much my own, with hope that it makes sense of both the Egyptian scribal perspective and the Asian social and political realities, with which I am more familiar.

I have dedicated this book to Mark Smith, who was my closest colleague at New York University between 2000 and 2016. Together, we worked with an exciting cohort of doctoral students in Hebrew Bible and enjoyed offices with facing open doors across a hallway. This project was just getting under way when he moved to Princeton Seminary, and I began telling people that I had to write on Yahweh because he had bequeathed to me responsibility for the study of God. In fact, this has been an opportunity to walk in Mark's steps for a period, to appreciate more fully how complex, how subtle, are the problems of God's "early history," and the poise and generosity he has added to mastery of evidence and rigor of evaluation. Our years teaching together were a privilege never to be forgotten, including a trust and friendship that undergirded every endeavor. In the last rewriting of this book, your voice has been first in my head, from your reading comments and from these many years of respecting your critical, and self-critical, mind. Thank you for it all.

Finally, I cannot finish a project of this scope without acknowledgment of Nancy, my wife now for years counted in decades, in everything my companion and anchor as I intend to be hers, still.

Abbreviations

BASOR	*Bulletin of the American Schools of Oriental Research*
BN	*Biblische Notizen*
CBQ	*Catholic Biblical Quarterly*
COS	William W. Hallo and K. Lawson Younger (eds.), *The Context of Scripture*, 3 vols. (Leiden: Brill, 1997–2000)
FM	*Florilegium Marianum*
HBAI	*Hebrew Bible and Ancient Israel*
HTR	*Harvard Theological Review*
HUCA	*Hebrew Union College Annual*
IEJ	*Israel Exploration Journal*
JANER	*Journal of Ancient Near Eastern Religion*
JBL	*Journal of Biblical Literature*
JNES	*Journal of Near Eastern Studies*
JQR	*Jewish Quarterly Review*
JSOT	*Journal for the Study of the Old Testament*
NEA	*Near Eastern Archaeology*
PEQ	*Palestine Exploration Quarterly*
RA	*Revue d'assyriologie et d'archéologie orientale*
RlA	E. Ebeling et al. (eds.), *Reallexikon der Assyriologie* (Berlin: de Gruyter, 1928–)
SEL	*Studi epigrafici e linguistici sul Vicino Oriente Antico*
Soleb IV	M. Schiff-Giorgini, *Soleb IV. Le temple: Bas reliefs et inscriptions* (Cairo: Institut français d'archéologie orientale, 2003)
Soleb V	M. Schiff-Giorgini, *Soleb V. Le temple: Plans et photographies* (Cairo: Institut français d'archéologie orientale, 2002)

TA	*Tel Aviv*
UF	*Ugarit-Forschungen*
VT	*Vetus Testamentum*
WO	*Die Welt des Orients*
ZAW	*Zeitschrift für die alttestamentliche Wissenschaft*
ZDPV	*Zeitschrift des Deutschen Palästina-Vereins*
ZThK	*Zeitschrift für Theologie und Kirche*

I

Introduction

Going back to the 19th century, scholars observed that if Israel had an origin, its God must as well. In particular, the divine name peculiar to Israel, written with the consonants Yhwh, must have come from outside this people, and the only question was where. Yet there is no certain evidence for a god named Yahweh before the name's first appearance in a mid-9th century BCE royal inscription from Jordan, where the desecration of his sanctuary at Nebo follows its destruction by the king of Moab.[1] This victory was part of a campaign to expel the rival kingdom of Israel from the region north of Dibon, and Yahweh is identified with that enemy. The question remains nonetheless: How did Israel come to regard Yahweh as its divine patron, to share only with its immediate southern neighbor, the kingdom centered at Jerusalem? To the extent that we could peer behind the biblical tapestry, which renders Yahweh both Israel's special god and a deity with worldwide reach, we might catch a glimpse of the social landscape within which Israel took form.

This project begins in dialogue with the "origins" search, occupied with much of the same evidence and concerns, even as I decline to make the origin of Yahweh my object, preferring instead the idea that the name indeed existed outside the context of Israel and before it. I pursue "Yahweh before Israel" in two principal directions, one more obvious than the other. Reference to Yhw₃ of Shasu-land in New Kingdom

---

[1] For the ancient concern of this project, all relevant evidence comes from before Roman times, and all dates are BCE ("Before the Common Era") unless obviously modern, related to 19th- or 20th-century scholarship, from the "Common Era" (CE). I will not generally mark the dates as one or the other.

Egyptian texts predates any evidence for the name Israel and is most likely older, certainly without connection to Israel. This Yhw₃ is "before Israel" by simple chronology. Equally important, however, is the likelihood that the god Yahweh and the people called Israel coexisted for some time in adjacent and eventually overlapping circles – or populations – so that the Bible itself preserves hints of this situation, where the deity must be understood "before" any relationship to Israel.

Throughout, this project is historical, not just as the history of religion but concerned with the whole landscape of populations in space and time. "History" recognizes the contingent character of identities, ideas, social forms, and practices on the constantly shifting conditions of those populations. As objects of historical investigation, both Yahweh and Israel are moving targets, each with character that changes through time. Approached historically, the names must be taken literally. By Israel, I mean any body that took this name in real time and place, not a catchall for what became the kingdom, the people of the Bible, or the Jews. Lauren Monroe and I have developed an analysis of biblical usage that recognizes expansion of its geographical application both in real time and in the Bible's literary conception. Our distinctions are partial and exploratory, but they are intended to push forward a discussion also current among archaeologists.[2] We begin by separating "greater Israel" from what we call "little Israel," neither one to consider a fixed entity, in recognition of a decisive move from a more limited geographical and political scale toward more ambitious expressions (Monroe, forthcoming a; Fleming forthcoming).[3] Little Israel certainly excludes Judah, but its specific location and extent remain elusive. We propose that earliest Israel is first visible in the Bible linked to distinct kingdoms identified with Saul and David in the southern central highlands and with the town of Tirzah further north. The identity of Israel with land north of the Jezreel and Kishon Valleys and east of the Jordan River was probably limited to particular regions and centers, beyond current reach to reconstruct. For the purposes of pursuing the early history of Yahweh, I mean Israel in this precise sense, so that peoples who eventually became part of Israel could have been associated with Yahweh before identification with Israel.

---

[2] One recent example is the volume of *Near Eastern Archaeology* (82/1 [2019]) devoted to "The Rise of Ancient Israel," most notably the contribution by Israel Finkelstein (2019).

[3] Based first of all on archaeological evidence, Finkelstein (2019) likewise considers Israel to have grown in geographical extent, finally reaching what he calls "united (northern) Israel."

THE SEARCH FOR YAHWEH'S ORIGINS

At the foundations of monotheism stands the Jewish God, first of all the God of the Tanakh, the Christian Old Testament, named in two principal ways, as "(the) God" Elohim and by a proper name rendered with the consonants Yhwh, vocalized something like Yahweh. Both names present historical conundrums, but Yahweh is particularly difficult, the god of no people and no place before or outside Israel and Judah in the early first millennium BCE. The oldest non-biblical reference to Yahweh is found in a royal inscription of Mesha, king of Moab, around 840.[4] These days, the dates of biblical writing are severely disputed, with many in continental Europe attributing most of the text to formative Judaism, after the fall of both kingdoms, in the 6th through 3rd centuries. Who was Yahweh, in his early days, before he became the divine sponsor of Israel and the Jerusalem-based kingdom to its south? Is the question simply impenetrable?

As I began this project I had the sensation of having entered a completely new conceptual space, having discovered an entirely new way to think about Yahweh at the beginning, in the early days. I perceived the field of religious history as it relates to biblical studies to have reached a settled conclusion about Yahweh, that his absence from other peoples and their pantheons could be explained by his origin in the deserts south of Israel and Judah. This explanation has its own long history, beginning in the late 19th century with contemplation of the Kenites and their friendly relations with Israel and Judah, becoming more Midianite with focus on Moses and his father-in-law Jethro, "the priest of Midian" in Exodus 2 and 18. Modern formulations of the approach have little in common with the earliest ones and certainly approach the biblical texts with far greater hesitation.

I undertook my own contribution with what I perceived as a consensus as my target, what I will call for simplicity the Midianite Hypothesis of Yahweh's southern desert origins. In fact, there is no consensus and never was. There have always been serious outliers to this interpretation of Yahweh, and a new wave of these has gathered recent momentum from

---

[4] Thomas Schneider (2007) published a West Semitic personal name found in New Kingdom Egypt of the late 14th or 13th centuries, which he vocalized as *'adōnī-rō'ē-yāh*, "My lord is the shepherd of Yah." In this name, the theophoric (divine) element is *'adōnī*, "My lord," not *yāh*, and this does not represent convincing evidence for the divine name. We will return to this personal name in Chapter 2, in discussion of the Egyptian evidence. For systematic review of all the inscriptional evidence from the earliest alphabetic material, see Theodore Lewis (2020b), chapter 6, "The Origins of Yahweh."

a challenge by Christoph Levin, Reinhard Müller, and others. Rather, I realize that I have long considered Yahweh's origins in the southern steppe to be by far the best explanation for the evidence, for all the varieties of reasoning. My quarrel is with the system that I already find most plausible, and my own proposal takes form against the backdrop of that system. I will set out to repudiate the contemporary Midianite Hypothesis even as my undertaking will betray a kinship to it more marked than to any alternative. I do not think Yahweh began as any form of "The God" El, and I do not think Yahweh was first of all a local highland storm god of the Hadad type.

My own approach shares with the Midianite Hypothesis a focus on the back country and populations not identified by cities and towns. The Egyptian evidence is decisive to my analysis: the name Yhw₃ designates a Shasu group, a Yhw₃-people. So far as this ancient people-name from the early 14th century is in fact to be identified with the later divine name Yahweh (Yhwh), we must begin our interpretation of the deity with the reality of this alignment, or even equation, of god and people. I suggest that the Bible preserves traces of these roots in its designation of a "people of Yahweh" in the Song of Deborah (especially Judg 5:13). In the end, the Midianite Hypothesis and the conclusion that Yahweh originated in the desert south represent less a target than a context, the right point of reference, badly in need of reconception. Along with so many before me, I still find this the right place to start.

Scholars in the late 19th and early 20th century relied on the Bible alone to prove that Yahweh was first worshipped among the peoples of the southern wilderness: the Kenites, the Midianites, and others. This may seem obvious for the time, when we may imagine an absence of evidence for the larger ancient context. On the contrary, the 19th century was a time of rapidly accelerating knowledge on all fronts, including the decipherment of Egyptian hieroglyphs and Mesopotamian cuneiform, and the very endeavor to understand the early religious history of Israel responded to a torrent of information about the ancient Near East. Scholars turned to the Bible for reliable direction because the name Yahweh was so difficult to find elsewhere – and the efforts to do so were myriad. The problem with reliance on the Bible to prove that Yahweh was first worshipped by other peoples is that the texts themselves, unsurprisingly, do not see things that way, and an outside origin has to be found in what are imagined to be embedded traditions that carry older realities. Returning to the material that has been brought to bear on the question, I do not find such old religious tradition.

Generally, the biblically grounded Midianite Hypothesis has presented a thoughtful alternative to generations of unconvincing proposals that the name of Yahweh can be found in other Near Eastern evidence. With all its laryngeal consonants and glides, the divine name can sound like a sigh, and the malleable spellings of cuneiform in particular may produce forms that could be read as this god. For all the many attempts, either the phonology or the context fails to convince, and Yahweh remains unknown outside Israel and Judah.[5] As already observed, there is one crucial exception, from 14th- and 13th-century Egypt, which though mysterious and open to debate, can be disposed of only by convenience and demands explanation in relation to Israel's god. Given the absence of Yahweh from god lists and god references for Canaan and Syria in the second millennium BCE, it is expected that Israel's god came from a region outside what is most settled and best documented. The Egyptian references suit such a requirement, and the Bible's account of Israel with Moses in the wilderness would do so as well. Thus the hypothesis of Yahweh's origins in the deep south of Sinai and Midian, Edom and Seir, still survives, for all that the older expressions of this approach have demanded considerable revision and refinement.[6]

And yet it should give pause that an interpretive framework for explaining the foundational character of Yahweh, the particular god of Israel, derives from and still displays the main outlines of ideas set in place in the 19th century.[7] At that time, the questions that inspired this solution and the evidence available for consideration were embedded in a different intellectual landscape, and it is worth weighing how the changing times

---

[5] Thomas Römer (2015: 35–38) gives particular attention to proposals from the texts of Ebla, Ugarit, and Mari, concluding that none of these persuades. In the late 8th century, it is more plausible that Azri-yau and Yau-bidi of Hamath bore theophoric personal names with Yahweh, as first proposed by Dalley (1990). If this analysis is correct, the names would not derive from pre-Israelite Syrian worship of Yahweh but rather from Israelite influence (cf. Younger 2016: 492–93).

[6] The most recent major statement is in Römer's monograph, along with the articles collected in van Oortschot and Witte (2017); see also Blenkinsopp (2008), Smith (2012), Tebes (2017); cf. Kitz (2019). Note that efforts to explore the religious possibilities of the southern desert in the second millennium, even if focused on noteworthy archaeological data, take for granted the framework of the Midianite Hypothesis, as with Amzallag (2009) and Tebes (2017); cf. Anderson (2015: 100–2).

[7] In this sweeping allusion to scholarship on ancient religion I evoke terminology that Michael Stahl (2020) examines in precise terms, through the "god of Israel" title. He observes in his introduction that "scholars regularly employ the appellation 'god of Israel' as a kind of transhistorical or universalizing identity to refer to the god of the Hebrew Bible, of ancient Israel and Judah, and of earliest Judaism."

might require more sweeping critique. In Germany, beginning with a challenge issued by Christoph Levin when he took a new position at the University of Giessen in 1996, the post-monarchic dating of much biblical writing has generated its own doubt of southern origins. If the Bible's recollection of Yahweh in the southern wilderness must be explained by early Jewish ruminations that offer no threads of real religious history, there is no reason to seek the god's origins anywhere but the land of Israel itself, even if no evidence survives.[8]

My own critique does not derive from the same interpretation of compositional dates, though the settings and associations of the key texts are essential concerns. Instead, my attention was drawn initially to the potential antiquity of Yahweh's presence in other biblical texts that link him to the lands of Israel and Judah.[9] For all that El is a major god known far beyond the geographical space eventually occupied by these kingdoms, it has never been necessary to imagine the borrowing of his worship from distant peoples. El could have been part of the religious landscape before Israel, not the unique possession of that people. What would it mean to take seriously the relative antiquity of Yahweh's presence in this same space?

Read as a unity, the Song of Deborah (Judges 5) locates Israel by its identification with peoples who join to fight or were expected to do so, according to verses 14–18, and the list lacks any interest in Jerusalem or what became the kingdom of Judah. Yahweh goes to battle as "god of Israel" from lands much further south, Seir and Edom (v. 4), but the people who worship him overlap solidly with the geography of the later kingdom of Israel. What struck me above all was the contrast between the geographies of Yahweh's mysterious residence in the distant southern wilderness and of the peoples who worshipped him, obvious though it may seem, in what became the land of Israel. Why should the Song sustain an interpretation of Yahweh's origin in that southern region, when it displayed no notion of his worship there?

---

[8] See first of all Levin (2000). In the recent collection devoted to *The Origins of Yahwism* (van Oorschott and Witte, 2017), the resulting "Berlin hypothesis" is represented by Henrik Pfeiffer and Reinhard Müller, both of whom have produced monographs that develop key elements of this critique (Pfeiffer, 2005; Müller, 2008). In the judgment of Martin Leuenberger (2017), the new approach suffers from a relative lack of positive evidence for the alternative, depending mainly on Müller's analysis of Yahweh as storm god in monarchic psalms.

[9] This entire line of reevaluation began in conversation with Rachel Angel, a doctoral student at New York University, who has my appreciation for her provocative questions.

By the time when I began to reconsider the early history of Yahweh, however, I could no longer regard the named groups of the battle account in Judg 5:14–18 as Israel in their initial conception (Fleming 2012: 64–66). All eight references to Israel in the Song of Deborah appear in the opening hymn (vv. 2–11) and thus reinterpret the battle by what Sara Milstein (2016) terms "revision through introduction." This observation, which Mark Smith affirmed and built into his own detailed studies of Judges 5, has become one element in ongoing work with Lauren Monroe on how peoples and space were named in the early Iron Age (Monroe and Fleming 2019).[10] The significance for Yahweh lies in the possibility, not preferred by Smith, that the peoples of the battle account would still share a common identity, as simply "the people of Yahweh" ('*ām Yhwh*, v. 13).[11]

Renditions of the Midianite Hypothesis over generations have shared the notion that Israel must have come to worship Yahweh as a deity that existed before itself – without adequate consideration of how "Israel" related to other named groups that eventually became part of the kingdom. It is one thing to consider Midianites and Kenites, or Esau and the people of Edom, kin to Israel, but what about Ephraim or Gad? According to the Mesha inscription of the mid-9th century, "the men of Gad" ('*īš Gad*, line 10), had occupied the land of 'Aṭarot "since forever" (*mi'ōlam*), without and before evident connection to Israel. The same could be said of Ephraim, Benjamin, and Amalek as first participants with the people of Yahweh in Judg 5:14, and the relationship to Israel of the other parties to this alliance against the kings of Canaan remains unclear.[12] It is therefore possible that Yahweh could have played a role among groups that came to be part of the Israelite kingdom before this identification.

It is time to reassemble all the pieces of this familiar puzzle in a fresh framework, not seeking a god foreign to Israel but one that belonged to a

---

[10] My first articulation of the observation about Israel in the Song of Deborah was in a draft of *The Legacy of Israel in Judah's Bible* (Fleming 2012a), and Smith (2009) acknowledged it with citation of that work, and took it up again in his extended treatment of the Song in his *Poetic Heroes* (Smith 2014: 245 n.57).

[11] Note that the Masoretic vocalization separates the "people" from Yhwh, where the genitival combination would give us '*am Yhwh*. For Smith (2014: 245–46), with Fritz (2006), the main account of the battle does not involve Yahweh. The '*am Yhwh* in both verses 11 and 13 belong to introductory revision, and Yahweh's curse in verse 23 is a quotation from a separate source that identified the god with a similar conflict (240–41).

[12] This question has dogged Lauren Monroe in her ongoing work on the Song, articulated in two initial forms in her articles on " greater Israel" (forthcoming) and on *mērôz* (2019).

political landscape in which Israel played a relatively small role. In
searching for Yahweh outside what the Bible presents as a large regional
Israel, we are driven far afield, into the wilderness, including the deep
southern spaces of the Midianite Hypothesis. As many have found previously, the wilderness is indeed relevant, and the south remains one part of
that realm, but the retrojection of later Israelite geography onto older
settings has distracted us from peoples who lived cheek to jowl with Israel
in lands long central to the biblical narrative. This landscape before
the kingdoms of Israel and Judah opens up space to consider "Yahweh
before Israel," both in the 14th-century Yhw3 of Shasu-land and in the
"people of Yahweh" of Judges 5.[13]

Much that appears historically true and biblically interesting has been
observed in pursuit of the Midianite Hypothesis, but the Bible's fascinating attraction to back country pastoralists can offer only an indirect
indication of potential cultural and religious affinities, not a straight line
to Yahweh. This conclusion does not repudiate the past generations of
research on Israelite religion but rather embraces it with an enthusiastic
push to abandon the interpretive clothes into which it has been stuffed.
The research itself gives us something new and opens up lines of future
inquiry still not even imagined.

THE MIDIANITE HYPOTHESIS

In a recent elaboration, Joseph Blenkinsopp (2008) conveniently characterizes the Midianite Hypothesis as argued from four lines of evidence:

- stories of Moses and Midian in Exodus 2 and 18;
- references to Yahweh coming from the south in old poetry such as
  Judges 5;
- the name Yahweh in 14th- and 13th-century Egyptian texts, identified
  with Seir;[14]
- and interpretation of Cain as ancestor of the Kenites, with first
  worship of Yahweh in Genesis 4.

---

[13] I have preferred not to define the object of this study by "origins," a category that can be
entangled with problematic assumptions and that tends to stand out of reach, though the
term offers a clear objective. On the broader preoccupation with origins in relation to
Yahweh, see the final article in *The Origins of Yahwism* (2017), by Friedhelm Hartenstein.

[14] More precisely, the Egyptian texts name Yhw3 as one unit of Shasu-land; Blenkinsopp
does not hesitate to equate the Shasu name with the divine name.

The first and last of these were integral to early generations of discussion, and all the evidence pertains to biblical prose. The other two were added in the mid-20th century, not just as novel arguments but also representing completely different categories, with biblical poetry that many understand to be older than the prose and with Egyptian texts that provide essential non-biblical evidence from before the period of the kingdoms. These three bodies of material give form to Chapters 2–4 in my own reconsideration, and a brief review of their combination will give a sense of the current state of affairs.

In 1872, Cornelis Tiele proposed a new direction for understanding the first worship of Yahweh, sharing the common expectation that this should not have begun in Israel by divine revelation. The question was where to look for a historical source. Tiele saw two previous alternatives: that Yahweh came from Egypt by way of Moses; and that he was a Canaanite god picked up by Israel after arrival in the land, and against these he proposed that Yahweh was a desert god, associated especially with biblical peoples called Rechabites and Kenites (see Chapter 3). With time, though the Kenite connection remained, this interpretation of Yahweh's origins came to be associated with Moses and his father-in-law Jethro, the priest of Midian, at the center of the Bible's own account of how Israel came to have a particular god by this name. This approach has been called both Kenite and Midianite, as well as Midianite-Kenite, but for the sake of simplicity and in recognition of the frequent focus on the Exodus narrative, I will call it the Midianite Hypothesis, as a proper noun.[15]

When the Midianite Hypothesis was first proposed, the archaeology of the land of Israel was in its infancy, or perhaps only a twinkle in some mother's eye, and little beyond the Bible could provide illumination. Nonetheless, the ancient Near East was beginning to emerge as a concrete reality, accessible through the monuments of Egypt and Mesopotamia, with the scripts of both deciphered by 1822 and the 1850s, respectively.[16]

---

[15] Mark Smith (personal communication) would even add "Shasu" to the Midianite-Kenite combination, maintaining continuity with the long-standing interpretive approach.

[16] Each story is more complicated. In 1822 Jean-François Champollion deciphered the hieroglyphs of the Rosetta Stone, a single decisive breakthrough that marks the first availability of Egyptian writing, though the hieratic script is equally important for the language; the decipherment of the Old Persian and Akkadian inscriptions at Behistun in Iran began a process that took longer, from the 1830s through the 1850s. For the decipherment of hieroglyphs starting with the Rosetta Stone, see Parkinson (1999); and for cuneiform, with references, Peter Daniels (1995) and Cathcart (2011).

Along with more easily comprehensible alphabetic inscriptions known by the mid-19th century, as well as old lore from Classical sources, the rising tide of new sources from Egypt and Mesopotamia were what motivated Tiele's comparative history of ancient religions, including his fresh effort to locate Yahweh and Israel in the midst of these. It was apparent that the Bible would have to be read in the company of independent evidence from its world. God may always have had a past, but with the emerging Near East, he would have to have a history.

Tiele's initial Midianite (Kenite) Hypothesis shared with earlier proposals the determination to abandon all explanation of Israelite and biblical religion by special divine revelation, in favor of a historical framework and what were judged rational arguments for discerning the merits of all ancient religious ideas and practice. It was taken for granted that the biblical, and eventually Christian though unavoidably Jewish, religion of the Hebrew Bible could be considered superior to all others on purely rational grounds, a perspective that is easily dismissed today. Yet the adaptable character of the project in its historical aims explains how the Midianite Hypothesis could remain viable through substantial transformations of its formulation. Contemporary versions of the Midianite Hypothesis take their form from discoveries after the time of Tiele, with two principal contributions.

First, with the newly discovered "Ugaritic" language as primary reference point, a trend led especially by William Foxwell Albright and his students isolated a selection of biblical poetry that could be regarded as directly ancient, transmitted without linguistic updating or narrative adjustment. As such, it provided a treasury of historical information that could be exploited without dependence on the contested results of literary-historical research on biblical prose, the ongoing effort to reconstruct the composition and revision of each book and combination.[17] The

---

[17] Albright (1922) already identified certain biblical poems as very old based in part on the expectation that they were composed close to the time of the events portrayed, especially the Song of Deborah in Judges 5 and David's lament over Saul and Jonathan in 2 Samuel 1. Excavations at Ugarit began in 1929, with decipherment of its alphabetic cuneiform script following quickly. Albright (1945) took the evidence from Ugarit to confirm his earlier judgments on biblical poetry generally, without focus on older material in particular, though he identified individual texts that could be analyzed afresh in light of the new language evidence (1944). The work of making a systematic argument fell to two of his students, Frank Moore Cross and David Noel Freedman, whose joint Johns Hopkins dissertation (1950) was defined as *Studies in Ancient Yahwistic Poetry*, eventually published without change in 1975 with a second edition in 1997. Cross and Freedman remark the availability of two new techniques for evaluating biblical language and

longer representatives include the sayings of Jacob (Genesis 49); the Song of the Sea (Exodus 15); the Balaam poems (Numbers 23–24); the Song of Moses and Blessings of Moses (Deuteronomy 32; 33); the Song of Deborah (Judges 5); David's lament over Saul and Jonathan (2 Samuel 1); the war poem in Habakkuk 3; and a number of Psalms (e.g. 18 [= 2 Samuel 22]; 29; 68).[18] Two of these poems celebrate the power of Yahweh as he emerges from the southern wilderness: from Sinai, Seir, and Mount Paran in Deut 33:2; and from Seir and Edom in Judg 5:4. Two more attach the motif to "God" as Elohim (Ps 68:8–9) and as Eloah (Hab 3:3), repeating Sinai from Judges 5 in the psalm and adding Teman to Mount Paran with the prophet.

With Ugarit and the early biblical poetry in hand, Cross (1973: 60–75) developed a hybrid form of the Midianite Hypothesis, arguing with great sophistication but general lack of success – as measured by later evaluation – that the name Yahweh originated as a title of the chief god El. Yet the desert south nevertheless held a central place: "If Yahweh is recognized as originally a cultic name of 'Ēl, perhaps the epithet of 'Ēl as patron of the Midianite League in the south, a number of problems in the history of the religion of Israel can be solved" (71). Even where more recent interpreters have not followed Cross (and Albright) in their identification of Yahweh with El, they give notable authority to the poetry and its references to Yahweh coming from the south to fight for his people.[19]

The second new contribution came from Egyptology by way of Nubia, along the Nile River upstream in the Sudan. Two textually interdependent lists of geographical names include Yhw₃ as a constituent of the "Shasu-land" (t₃ Š₃św), not otherwise a known political entity or place, but here a way to render a type of population in terms that could make sense of the individual proper names to be identified together as Shasu. The Shasu

---

literature: orthographic analysis based on the expanding corpus of first-millennium inscriptions; and linguistic analysis that "derives from the study and decipherment of the Canaanite cuneiform texts from Ras Shamrah, their linguistic structure and vocabulary, their poetic style and metrical forms. The application of this knowledge to biblical poetry is perhaps the most significant factor in new studies" (Cross and Freedman 1997: 2–3). They begin the project with the Song of Deborah as point of reference and then develop a core set of texts with chapters on Exodus 15, Genesis 49, Deuteronomy 33, and 2 Samuel 22 (Psalm 18).

[18] Albright (1950–51) had already described Psalm 68 as "A Catalogue of Early Hebrew Lyric Poems (Psalm LXVIII)."

[19] See especially the work of Mark Smith (in Chapter 4 of this volume).

were people of the uncultivated back country, associated with mobility and subsistence by their herds, placing Yhw3 among what the Egyptians considered nomads, dangerous and distasteful by their life beyond Egyptian capacity to control and outside Egyptian norms, associated with all the territory behind the settled Levant, from Arabia north through Jordan and Syria.[20] The first discovery of the Egyptian evidence appears in a short 1947 note by Bernhard Grdseloff, followed by Raphael Giveon with publication in 1964 of new evidence from Soleb.[21] Because the later of these lists, from the reign of Ramses II (ca. 1279–1213), includes a name that many have read as Seir, matching the first site for Yahweh's advance in Judg 5:4, the Egyptian evidence has been understood to confirm further the southern origin of Israel's Yahweh, however the Shasu name may relate to the later god.[22]

By now, all of the main lines of the Midianite Hypothesis are scholarly antiques, familiar furniture in the eccentric club of historical inquiry into Israelite religion. Although each element must be interpreted in a conceptual context very different from the one that first accommodated it, the essentials have remained undisturbed. The biblical texts in question have undergone waves of reevaluation for their compositional histories and chronological settings, but the notion that Moses married into Midian is still widely considered an odd and somehow archaic tradition, and Albright's old poetry is still difficult to dismiss, in spite of new caution and more modest claims for its antiquity.[23] The dates and readings of the Egyptian texts remain fixed. For the many who are inclined to regard Yahweh as originally a god of the southern desert peoples, the question then becomes what kind of deity he was and how he achieved

---

[20] The primary reference on the Shasu people and the sources for their study remains Giveon (1971).

[21] According to Adrom and Müller (2017), the new effort to find the name Yahweh in Egyptian topographical lists followed the proposed identification of the name in Ugaritic texts.

[22] These dates are taken from the "List of Rulers of Ancient Egypt and Nubia" on the site metmuseum.org.

[23] One reason for abandoning the Midianite Hypothesis would be the systematic downdating of this poetry. This is a significant element in the reasoning of Pfeiffer (2005, 2017), with his extremely late, even post-Persian, dates for most of the contents of Judges 5, Habakkuk 3, Deuteronomy 33, and Psalm 68. For Pfeiffer, the oldest material (the 9th/8th century) in the set is the core of the Song of Deborah, which combined the heroism of Jael with (brief) celebration of a victory by Zebulun and Naphtali over Sisera and the kings of Canaan (2017: 125). In general, the historical background for Yahweh coming to war from the south is the Babylonian king Nabonidus's conquest of Edom (126).

identification with El, the senior god at Ugarit and apparently in some larger swath of Syria-Palestine.[24]

What is remarkable is that transformations in how the Bible is understood and in how the history of Israel is reconstructed have not dislodged the common conclusion about the southern origin of Yahweh. The Midianite Hypothesis of the late 19th and early 20th centuries depended on expectation that the Bible could preserve direct access to history through secondary themes and perspectives that coexist with the main narrative. For Tiele and those who followed him, the exodus of Israel from Egypt was a historical event, and the question was how it was told, understanding the Bible to show Moses and Israel meeting Yahweh as a new and unfamiliar god. Yahweh was truly the god of the Midianites, with the Bible's book of Exodus the proof.

Since the 1970s, the dates for biblical writing have shifted later across a spectrum of specialists, and these later dates have required a comparable adjustment in how to explain the Bible's relationship to history. Where many earlier systems envisioned considerable monarchic writing and remnants of tradition if not text from Israel before kings, in the last centuries of the second millennium, increasingly the Bible has appeared to be shaped by writers after Judah's demise in 586, with its sources spanning little more than the two preceding centuries.[25] Recent focus on inscriptional evidence, which blossoms in the 8th century, has been understood to confirm the early end of this range, though in continental Europe, interest often moves toward even later periods.[26] For all

---

[24] Mark Smith (1990: xxiii) includes this identification in his larger category of "convergence," which "involved the coalescence of various deities and/or some of their features into the figure of Yahweh. This development began in the period of the Judges and continued during the first half of the monarchy. At this point, El and Yahweh were identified, and Asherah no longer continued as an identifiably separate deity." For further discussion, see "Yahweh and El" in his second edition (2002: 32–43).

[25] While this trend was pushed forward vigorously in the United States by John Van Seters (1975, 1983), it has taken a more enduring and broadly collegial form in continental Europe over the past decades (e.g. Levin 1993; Kratz 2000; [English 2005]). For moderate positions that share much of the new European trend with more consideration for possible monarchic writing, see Römer 2005; Schmid 2008 (English 2012).

[26] This is the biblical end-point of Seth Sanders's *Invention of Hebrew* (2009). In seeking a context for locating biblical writing in history, William Schniedewind (2004: 61) arrives at the transformation of epigraphic finds in the 8th century: "Whereas the discovery of monumental inscriptions is a matter of pure chance, the relative paucity of mundane writing from early Israel is telling of the limited role that writing played during the twelfth through ninth centuries B.C.E." Seals, seal impressions, and inscribed ostraca are only found in abundance for Israel and Judah in the 8th–6th centuries (62).

involved, the Bible remains a collection of writing from antiquity, and it is both relevant to and illuminated by ancient history, insofar as the settings for its composition and revision can be retrieved. The Bible could have historical interest in this sense even if no single detail from its contents proved relevant to the events directly portrayed. The Midianite Hypothesis requires a relationship between the Bible and history that is focused immediately on neither the settings of writing nor the times and participants portrayed, yet it presents a different kind of ambitious demand on biblical connection to circumstances long before dates of composition. Can we use texts that were written centuries after Yahweh came to be worshipped by Israel or its constituents to identify the people from whom such worship was transmitted, whether as Midianites or Kenites? The methodological stretch becomes more and more tenuous.

Nevertheless, a large proportion of contemporary biblical scholars and specialists in Israelite religion have affirmed a judicious approval of the Midianite Hypothesis that Yahweh was first worshipped by peoples of the southern wilderness from whom Israel somehow adopted him. Certainly these scholars have responded with careful thought to the evidence at hand, and yet there are larger considerations that have contributed to the survival of this approach. At the same time as literary-historical analysis was yielding substantially later dates, archaeologists began to lay claim to the priority of their material and consequent analysis for the reconstruction of history in the lands of Israel and Judah.[27] One early element of this archaeological reevaluation was the argument that in sweeping material cultural terms, the Israelites of the Iron Age could not be distinguished in any absolute terms from the "Canaanites" of the Late Bronze Age and as early Iron Age neighbors.[28] The Canaanite category could be taken from

[27] William Dever's call for an archaeology of "Syria-Palestine" rather than "biblical archaeology" (1981) represented a leading instance of a wider trend. Dever produced a series of books (2001, 2003, 2005; cf. 2017) reevaluating major topics with biblical interest related to history and religion, all with the idea that archaeology would reshape the interpretive ground, all aimed to convince a general public beyond the professional realm. This historical effort has been taken up in equally public though somewhat different terms by Israel Finkelstein, who has accounted for the Bible in collaborations first with Neil Asher Silberman (2001, 2006) and more recently with Thomas Römer (2014a, 2014b), and by Finkelstein alone (2017).

[28] An essential conceptual element of Mark Smith's *Early History of God* is "Israel's cultural identity" (1990: xxii): "Despite the long regnant model that the Canaanites and Israelites were people of fundamentally different culture, archaeological data now cast doubt on this view. The material culture of the region exhibits numerous common points between Israelites and Canaanites in the Iron I period (ca. 1200–1000). The record

ancient texts reflecting New Kingdom Egyptian dominance of the southern Levant, not simply borrowed from the Bible.[29] A list of features such as the four-room house, the collared-rim store jar, and plastered cisterns for communal water collection could not be considered markers of Israelite population and their appearance and use rather followed environmental and historical trends that would have crossed identity boundaries.[30] If archaeology could not isolate material indicators of early Israel, then the people of Israel could not be understood as foreign to the existing cultural landscape. However the name came to be connected to the groups behind the eventual kingdom of Israel, such groups would have to be regarded as culturally Canaanite and probably local, emerging from shifts in population and social organization in the immediate region.[31]

For those working on Israelite religion, this meant that the Bible's God must also emerge from shifts in the immediate region, so that the roots of biblical religion were likewise culturally Canaanite. Here, the absence of Yahweh from Ugarit and other early evidence for the region called for explanation in terms that envisioned nothing unique to Israel, nothing that would suppose a break between Israel and the world around it. Perhaps oddly, the Midianite Hypothesis suited well the constraints of this vision. "The God" of early Israel as El or Elohim could be explained

would suggest that Israelite cult largely overlapped with, and derived from, Canaanite culture. In short, Israelite culture was largely Canaanite in nature."

[29] For the basic evidence, see the volume by Niels Peter Lemche (1991) and the vociferous response from Anson Rainey (1996).

[30] Even at roughly the time of Mark Smith's assertion that Israelite cultural identity could not be distinguished decisively from Canaanite, archaeologists were discussing the question with caution. In an extended treatment of the "origin of pillared four-room houses," Israel Finkelstein (1988: 258) warned that "The most important considerations are quantitative (and not simply whether or not this type occurs at a given site) and chronological." Amihai Mazar (1990: 354) imagines that the early settlers of the Iron Age I, who came to be identified as Israel, "Having no traditions of their own ... utilized the pottery, arts, crafts, and some architectural features of the Canaanite culture – a culture which continued to flourish in various areas of the country." More recently, Avraham Faust (2006) set about resurrecting the old list of identifiable material features of Israelite people. The effort is hampered by an expansive definition of "Israel" that does not consider the likely diversity of names and affiliations in the Late Bronze and early Iron Ages that render problematic the overarching category of "Israel," aside from the Canaanite alternative.

[31] The origins of Israel remain contested and difficult to disentangle, but solutions that require substantial migration have been increasingly abandoned or qualified. For one overview, see Killebrew (2005: chapter 4). In the recent volume devoted to "The Rise of Ancient Israel," see in particular the contributions of Finkelstein (2019) and Gadot (2019).

in local terms as Canaanite, simply carried over from long-standing practice. Yahweh was not part of that Canaanite religious realm, but he could not begin as particular to Israel. Origin among neighboring peoples of the desert south offers a way to leave Israel in its Canaanite environment with an essentially Canaanite culture – and religion – while partaking of contact with its nomadic neighbors.

With the reconsideration and critique of the Midianite Hypothesis undertaken in this book, I do not mean to overturn this conception of Israel as a product of indigenous forces and at home in its environment. Rather, I find that these forces and this environment, along with the identities of the peoples related to and neighboring early Israel, have been conceived too simply. The last stages of the Late Bronze Age and the beginning of the Iron Age in the southern Levant and the regions adjacent to it further inland had no central political power except the retreating New Kingdom of Egypt. In literal terms of the names themselves, both Israel and Yahweh appear to have belonged to the landscape of southern Palestine while Egypt was still present, not yet connected in any evident way.

I will propose that the two names – Israel and Yhw3 – and the populations associated with them were probably embedded in nearby spaces in the Levantine highlands and inland east, whatever their backstories. The notion that Yahweh was first worshipped by peoples of lands much further south depends above all on the deity's identification with that region in the old biblical poetry and as "Yahweh of Teman" in inscriptions from Kuntillet 'Ajrud (ca. 800).[32] The possible reading of Seir in the Ramses II list for Shasu-land would locate the name Yhw3 in the same area, though without clear relationship to deity. In my analysis, Yahweh's residence in distant southern realms and his worship as Yahweh of Teman attribute to the god a power in the southern wilderness without attaching his worship to a population there. The only indication of a population would come with the earlier Yhw3 group in the company of Seir in the 13th century, and we will see in Chapter 2 that this geography is far from secure. What is clearer is the orientation of the Shasu to the eastern back country, away from substantial towns, including lands south into Arabia and north into Syria, and this geographical and social character remains central to the roots of Yahweh, with or without Seir in the Egyptian lists.

---

[32] This material will be addressed in more detail in Chapter 4.

In a way, my effort to push past the Midianite Hypothesis pursues the logic of Canaanite and indigenous cultural foundations to its natural conclusion. Rather than explain Yahweh as foreign to what became Israel, needing importation of the kind imagined in constructions of Israelite origins by conquest or migration, this approach transforms the social landscape into which both Israel and Yahweh were embedded so that both the "foreign" and the specifically southern become unnecessary. Yahweh could be "before Israel" and yet closer to hand. He could be part of the prior fabric of regional society and culture while representing a set of alignments separate from those of Israel and El, somewhere in the highlands of the southern Levant.[33] So far as Yahweh can be identified with the name of the Shasu subgroup Yhw3, part of what the Egyptians characterized as pastoralists whose herds and kinship bonds allowed movement across the political and geographical frontiers defined by city-based kingdoms, the god represents the Shasu world in what would become Israelite religion, filtered through centuries of intervening history.

With such social interaction in view, this book has an ultimate concern and a potential utility not defined by religion, for all that Yahweh is its object. In discussion of the social ingredients in early Israel, there remains a set of tensions that could be named by classical oppositions: between settled and mobile ways of life; subsistence from agriculture and from flocks; large towns and villages; the lowlands and more remote country of the high hills; land west and east of the Jordan River and Dead Sea. These dualities are most likely an obstacle rather than an aid to understanding the character of the region before the kingdom of Israel. Rather, the relationship between El and Yahweh may reflect one expression of a social fabric that bound the peoples who became Israel across realms of greater and lesser accessibility.[34] Yahweh represents the world away from Egypt, away from the cities and the sea.

REBUILDING FROM OLD MATERIALS

It is impossible to construct a fresh analysis of Yahweh before Israel without revisiting the principal data from the generations of analysis,

---

[33] Again, the specific location of early Israel remains uncertain, for all that it must have been smaller than the eventual kingdom and the biblical geography of the territorial allotments in Joshua and of "Dan to Beersheba"; see Finkelstein 2019, Monroe forthcoming; and Fleming forthcoming, both in *HBAI*.

[34] For a vision of such a "social fabric" at the foundation of early Near Eastern society, see Porter (2012).

and Chapters 2–4 are defined by the main divisions of this data. Cornelis Tiele introduced his hypothesis of Yahweh's wilderness origins with focus on biblical prose references to Rechabites, Kenites, and Midianites, an approach that took a more decidedly southern aspect with later emphasis on Moses, Midian, and Sinai. With the passage of time, the Midianite Hypothesis then incorporated Albright's old biblical poetry and the Egyptian evidence from the 14th and 13th centuries. Rather than follow the chronology of scholarship, we will begin with Yhw₃ of Shasu-land (Chapter 2) before turning to the biblical prose (Chapter 3) and poetry (Chapter 4).

Fresh examination of the Egyptian evidence changes everything. Whether or not Yahweh could already have existed as a divine name near 1400 BCE, the reference here is not first of all to the god but to a specified unit of what an Egyptian scribe designated "Shasu-land."[35] The Egyptian evidence derives from a single military encounter, and the older version, from the reign of Amenhotep III, lacks any indication of a southern setting, leaving this to be reconstructed from the later Ramses II text. What is most important in any case is not the geography but the identification of Yhw₃ as part of the Shasu. This material is by far older than all other evidence, and if the name indeed matches the divine name, as many have concluded, no account of Yahweh's roots can begin elsewhere. Further, my interpretation includes new observations that point discussion in previously unimagined directions, and the reader will benefit from knowing from the start what I have done with Yhw₃. This is indeed "before Israel."

Biblical prose and poetry have been invoked to explain Yahweh's worship before Israel among peoples of the wilderness in the distant south. As with the Egyptian evidence, this biblical material, along with reference to Yahweh of Teman at Kuntillet 'Ajrud, has too quickly been understood to confirm Yahweh's southern origin, yet it constitutes one instance of phenomena that link the biblical favorites to inland peoples

---

[35] The distinction between Egyptian scribal-bureaucratic conceptions and indigenous social and political realities is delicate and difficult to reconstruct. This matter will form an important part of the analysis in Chapter 2, on the Egyptian evidence. I am not a specialist in ancient Egypt and Egyptian, and my questions about space, population, and naming reflect extensive work on other materials from the Near East. For orientation to the Egyptian material and conception, I have benefited greatly from the counsel of Thomas Schneider and Betsy Bryan, at the same time as my interpretation of Shasu naming is decidedly my own, an effort to make the most of my questions with the anchor of accurate accounting for Egyptian practice.

not identified by prior occupation of the same space – the Canaanites, Amorites, and such. This material calls for a fresh look, for all the challenges to incorporation of the Bible into historical inquiry. In each case there is both a caution and a benefit, prior interpretation to set aside and a contribution to the context.

My reinterpretation of the two biblical categories begins in Chapter 3 with what launched the Midianite Hypothesis as such, the prose narrative of the Bible, with the most compelling material attached to Moses, the mountain of God, and marriage to the daughter of "the priest of Midian." In the pursuit of early formulations of the approach, I found that its creator was not Friedrich Ghillany but Cornelis Tiele (1872) and that Tiele's interpretation was much less concerned to validate the accounts of Moses as founding figure than the work of many who followed. The next step is Yahweh in the poetry that has been treated as especially old and therefore of particular weight (Chapter 4). In a way, the contemporary Midianite Hypothesis depends first of all on the Egyptian texts and this old poetry, not requiring Midian for its coherence, and the force of Midian in Exodus follows from the framework offered by more clearly ancient evidence.

Once we have addressed the main elements of the Midianite Hypothesis, another age-old interest warrants renewed attention (Chapter 5). Interpretation of Yahweh in relation to a cognate verb is invited by the Bible itself when Moses asks God for a specific name and is told to say, "Ehyeh sent me" – from the verb "to be, become" (*hyh*). Through generations of modern biblical study, as knowledge of the ancient Semitic languages expanded and improved, much effort and considerable exasperation have accompanied this etymological analysis.[36] Without needing to establish a secure solution to the etymological problem, the form of the name as a finite verb is important to finding a social location for the name, all the more when we let its earliest appearance in Egyptian writing be our starting point.[37]

---

[36] Both Albright and Cross open their discussions with disclaimers: "The long debate over the original meaning of the name *Yahwêh* shows no sign of abating, and the most incredible of etymologies are still advanced by otherwise serious scholars" (Albright 1968: 168); "The discussion of the meaning and origin of the name Yahweh constitutes a monumental witness to the industry and ingenuity of biblical scholars. Fortunately, there is no space to review it here" (Cross 1973: 60).

[37] Not everyone considers the name Yahweh to originate in a verbal construction: Manfred Görg (1976: 182; 2000: 12) raises the possibility that the name reflects a kind of bird. In his contribution to *The Origins of Yahwism*, Josef Tropper (2017: 21–28) concludes that it must be a noun ending in the accusative -*a*, regardless of what that noun may be.

While the Midianite Hypothesis has taken its force from Yahweh's surprising association with the south, beyond any version of Israelite people and borders, plenty of biblical material indicates early connection to the land itself (Chapter 6). Even Jerusalem's temple, if it goes back to the 10th century and Solomon, would be as old as the Bible's archaic poetry.[38] Shiloh, which excavation shows to have been destroyed in the 11th century, has a place in biblical lore as a one-time center for worship of Yahweh, gone before the kingdom was established.[39] Yahweh appears in the archaic poetry beyond the references to movement in the south; the Song of the Sea opens as a hymn to Yahweh (Exod 15:1–3).[40] For locating Yahweh in relation to Israel, however, the most important text is the Song of Deborah, with acknowledgment once again of the conscious individuality of my reading, which drives my historical conclusions from it. The central battle narrative evokes the god first to identify the "people of Yahweh" who will win victory and then to curse those who stay at home (Judg 5:13, 23).[41] This "people of Yahweh" name the alliance of groups to follow without reference to Israel, which is only linked to the battle by addition of the opening hymn in verses 2–11.

---

[38] This remains open to challenge. There is no clear way to demonstrate the temple's date of construction, but it seems to have been present in the late 8th century, without question of its recent construction (cf. Isaiah 6). We will return to Jerusalem in discussion of Yahweh and El in Chapter 7.

[39] See Joshua 18 for allotment of land by a ritual of casting lots; Judges 21 and 1 Samuel 1 with local festivals and a temple; and 1 Samuel 4 as the starting point for the ark before its return to Beth-Shemesh (Fleming 2018). Choon-Leong Seow (1989) argued that the Bible's representation of Yahweh at Shiloh covers an original association with El, though Römer (2015: 86–88) treats it as "an important Yahwist sanctuary." We will return to the site in Chapter 7, in combination with Jerusalem.

[40] I do not simply assume early dates for this poetry, and European scholars in particular have pushed to lower the dates radically, regarding the archaic linguistic features as poetic archaism or idiosyncrasy and contrasts to the prose as late recasting (e.g. Pfeiffer 2005, above). Some understand the Song of the Sea as exilic based on vocabulary it shares with Isaiah 40–55 and many psalms. There nevertheless remains a strong case for a much older date, though indeed with a Jerusalem connection: for literature and detailed discussion, see Stephen C. Russell 2009: 127–78. Yet as Mark Smith has observed to me (personal communication), we expect a Jerusalem composition to present some clear reference to the city's institutions, whereas such is notably lacking. I will return to this text in Chapter 6.

[41] Lauren Monroe (2019) has proposed a radical and attractive new reading of "Meroz" in verse 23, a hapax legomenon that has been read since early translation as a place name, though no external evidence shows it to be such. Monroe considers *mērôz* a common noun for the alliance committed to fight on one another's behalf, so that Reuben, Gilead, Dan, and Asher of verses 15–17 are indeed cursed for their disloyalty, rather than chided mildly as might otherwise be assumed. Her work remains in progress.

Evidence for "Yahweh before Israel" therefore includes two principal items: the Egyptian texts long before all biblical writing; and the core narrative in the Bible's Song of Deborah. The people of Yahweh in Judg 5:13 then bring us back to Exodus 15, where the only identification of the rescued people is as "your people, Yahweh" (v. 16), evoking the same combination of noun and divine name.

In a way, my construction of a framework for understanding the early character of Yahweh, outside the framework of Israel, takes the easy way out by identifying only two essential pieces of evidence – or three, if we include the name itself. Yahweh is an immense topic, even when limited to historical study and something like the biblical period. This is not my object.[42] It is difficult, however, to dare reconsider Yahweh before Israel without taking account of his eventual position as god of the Israelite kingdom, capable of identification with the great god El. Though the Midianite Hypothesis may envision a god from the desert margins, these origins are not understood to bestow on Israel a marginal god. One solution is to consider the name itself to derive from an epithet of El, so that the identification is original.[43] The other most plausible set of associations aligns with Near Eastern storm gods, whether Baal/Hadad of Syria or a distinct manifestation suitable to the dry southern back country.[44] For Mark Smith, this makes Yahweh a "second-tier" god in that El alone occupies the first level, with his consort Asherah (or Ilu and Athiratu), but he is absolutely a major figure, capable of promotion just like Haddu as corresponding "Lord."[45] The modest cluster of evidence for Yahweh before Israel does not settle the question of how he could have become a major deity to rival or merge with Baal and El. It nevertheless limits the

---

[42] While much has been written on Yahweh in relation to other deities relevant to ancient Israel, Theodore Lewis (2020b) has undertaken something more ambitious in his study of "God." In the footsteps of Albright's *Yahweh and the Gods of Canaan* (1968) though without his "contrasting faiths," see Smith 1990 and Day 2000.

[43] This is most influential in the interpretation by Cross (1973: 60–68, etc.); and note de Moor's idiosyncratic solution of naming Yahweh as "God of the Fathers," who is also El (1997: 323–44, etc.). Van der Toorn (1999: 914–15) cites Albright on this and says that Dijkstra considered the identification to be original.

[44] Note that van der Toorn (1999: 914) acknowledges the problem of explaining Yahweh as a major deity, discusses the principal alternatives in El and Baal, and then declines to settle on one solution. Reinhard Müller's contribution to explaining a local origin for Yahweh depends on a Syrian and early first-millennium set of comparisons (2008; 2017).

[45] For the four "tiers" of the "divine council" at Ugarit and Yahweh as belonging originally to the second tier below El, like Baal at Ugarit, see Smith 2001: 45–49.

terrain for conceptual points of departure, and I will conclude this study by considering the implications of my core analysis (Chapter 7).

The principal purpose of this project is to recast the current debate over the place of Yahweh in relation to early Israel and the older landscape of peoples in the southern Levant. Israel itself cannot be the essential name that identifies the character of Yahweh as indigenous or foreign to those who came to consider him their particular god. As I understand it, Yahweh is not to be evaluated first of all by the measure of El as father of many gods or Baal-Haddu as warrior storm god; these considerations were secondary. The Bible remains relevant to the evaluation of Yahweh before Israel, but not because Israel got him from desert peoples recalled as Midianite or Kenite and not because his going to war from the southern wilderness preserves the places of his earliest worship. At the center of any evaluation of the early divine name must stand the Yhw3 subset of Shasu-land in the geographical vision of Amenhotep III, in the early 14th century. I will argue that the subdivisions of what the Egyptians fought as a unified "land" of the pastoralist Shasu population are most easily understood as defined by kinship, which does not preclude territorial associations. Whatever the connections of the name Yhw3 in this New Kingdom setting, it is above all a major group of the Shasu, so a population, a people. Old identification of the divine name Yahweh with a people rendered Yhw3, earlier or later, offers a markedly different direction for probing the roots of the deity.

I perceive this interpretive direction to warrant detachment from the Midianite Hypothesis, with its framework of cultural borrowing from peoples foreign to Israel, based on a dichotomy that does not likely reflect the actual social and political landscape of the Late Bronze and early Iron Ages. The notion of specific origin in the distant south, identified variously in biblical poetry by Sinai, Seir, Edom, Paran, and Teman, or in biblical prose by Midianites, Kenites, and Rechabites, depends on tenuous threads of affinity that provide little historical solidity. Much of my own reconstruction could be adapted to the southern reference point of the Midianite Hypothesis, yet the preponderance of the evidence simply does not point there. My new interpretive framework leaves many questions open, and there will be much to pursue, even where my arguments have carried weight. It is my hope that even where I fail to persuade, the Midianite Hypothesis will be reevaluated in more thoroughgoing terms, and the relationship of Yahweh to Israel will be better understood.

2

Yhw3 of Shasu-Land

At the center of any evaluation of early evidence for Yahweh must stand a pair of related texts from New Kingdom Egyptian sites in northern Sudan: one from Soleb, during the reign of Amenhotep III (ca. 1390–1352); and the second from 'Amarah West, during the reign of Ramses II (ca. 1279–1213). Both are monumental inscriptions for display on temples, lists of places and peoples that create a map of Egypt's world. This material is far older than any potential reference to Yahweh, and if the name Yhw3 does match the deity rendered as Yhwh, even if it did not yet identify a god, it becomes the chronological starting point for all historical evaluation (Figure 1). Two questions remain essential at every stage of the discussion, neither of which can be answered with absolute certainty:

1) Does the Egyptian name indeed match the Israelite divine name phonologically and socially in a way that requires historical connection between the two to explain the match?
2) If the match is historically grounded, what is the relationship between the Egyptian name, which does not have deity as its primary identification, and the later deity Yahweh?

In agreement with a significant majority of scholars, I conclude that the first question demands with high likelihood an affirmative response: the names are truly the same.[1] Recognizing that this remains a probability, not a

---

[1] It is too much to speak of "consensus," but the list of those accepting the identification is long. Because any decision requires both Egyptological precision and the interpretation of Semitic and biblical texts, each analysis brings with it a greater capacity on one side or the

FIGURE I Soleb name-ring showing the writing *yhwȝ*
(Drawing by Ogden Goelet)

certainty, the second question then warrants inquiry, which will occupy one
part of Chapter 6, on the "people of Yahweh." One nagging tendency in
treatment of the Egyptian evidence has been the hasty introduction of the
Bible's Midianite Hypothesis into its interpretation, and the object of this
chapter is to redefine the character of the Egyptian evidence on its own
terms.[2] Taking up the charge offered by Faried Adrom and Matthias Müller
in their Egyptological contribution to the 2017 volume on *The Origins of
Yahwism*, I propose a new evaluation of the name that both acknowledges
the likely relationship to the god Yahweh and the equal likelihood that we
are not dealing with the god in this much earlier setting. At least, nothing
requires such a conclusion.[3] For me, the relationship of Yhwȝ to Yahweh is
most convincing because of the phonological similarity and Yhwȝ's

---

other and must then survive scrutiny from specialists from the other domain. In calling the
Egyptian evidence for the name Yahweh "not ... particularly strong," Mark Smith
(2001a: 25) cites two in particular who resist the connection: Goedicke (1994);
Ahlström (1986: 57–60). Among the many more who affirm the identification, after the
broad early agreement, note Weippert (1974); Astour (1979); Redford (1992: 272–73);
van der Toorn (1999: 911–12); Schneider (2007).

[2] One notable exception, developed with just this complaint in view, is the northern
interpretation of the Egyptian evidence by Astour (1979).

[3] Cast in cautious terms as a simple review of proposed Egyptian evidence, without stake in
the results of any application, Adrom and Müller discuss the reading of *Yhw* without
objection to either the interpretation of the orthography or the correlation of form with the
Hebrew divine name (2017, especially 98 and n.36 for this reading in the 'Amarah West
text). Given the plausibility of the phonological match, they offer the following proposals
for future work: to beware associating these with proto-Israelites; to avoid treating these as
proof for southern location (more below); to consider further the type of category indicated by all the Shasu-land names; and to be more careful with the Seir identification (112).

occurrence as a major identity among the Shasu people, the name given by Egyptians to West Semitic speaking pastoralists who inhabited large parts of the Levant and lands further south. My reasoning must follow review of the material itself.

Because the Egyptian texts very likely do present the oldest evidence by far for the name Yahweh, albeit in a form still not clearly identified with the deity, they will represent the beginning of my own reconstruction of Yahweh before Israel. Approach to the Egyptian material may be clarified by consideration of the biblical material in the following two chapters because the Bible and the old Midianite Hypothesis of Yahweh's southern origins have influenced how Egyptological specialists have interpreted the two texts from the Sudan. In particular, the name from the Egyptian texts has been located with reference to the very biblical writing that has been adduced as support for the Midianite Hypothesis, especially the references to Seir and Edom in Judg 5:4. A fresh evaluation of the Egyptian texts will offer an alternative to the southern location of Yahweh in this oldest evidence for the name. Even more crucial to my analysis is the identification of all the named entities in the Egyptian lists as units within a larger "land" that royal scribes identified with the Shasu population – neutral terminology that will be developed with further discussion.[4]

THE SHASU-LAND: YHWʒ IN TWO LISTS

In 1947, Bernard Grdseloff published a piece on Edom in Egyptian sources that observed a reference to the name Yahweh in a list from the reign of Ramses II (1279–1213) found at 'Amarah West in Nubia up-river in Sudan.[5] With the permission of Michela Schiff Giorgini, the excavator

---

[4] Given the importance of the Egyptian evidence to my reconstruction of "Yahweh before Israel," and the fact that I have undertaken a review of this evidence that is more thorough than generally found in discussion of Yahweh's "origins," it is important to recognize that I am not an Egyptologist. In an effort to represent accurately the ancient Egyptian perspectives on display in this material, I have consulted Thomas Schneider and Betsy Bryan – in that sequence – and have benefited enormously from their observations. Both of these specialists approach the naming evidence with particular sensitivity to Egyptian language, administration, and attitudes in literature, and I have tried to incorporate their guidance. My own previous work on the social and political landscape of the early second-millennium Mari archives (Fleming 2004; 2009) informs the questions I bring to the definition of populations not defined by a single settlement or territory, and my view of the Shasu is colored by this experience.

[5] Grdseloff (1947: 79); Astour (1979: 18) observes that Grdseloff discovered the name by working through the hand copy in Fairman (1939).

of the Amun temple at nearby Soleb, Raphael Giveon (1964) published
another reference to the same name from the reign of Amenhotep III,
roughly a century earlier (1390–1352).[6] With the final publication of the
texts from the Amun temple, two of the names from Giveon's published
set were shown to appear again on separate blocks of stone, without
apparent integration into a larger list. One of these was the name that
resembles Yahweh.[7] In his publication of the Soleb list, Giveon (1964)
brought attention to a third source, a long list from Medinet Habu, dating
to the reign of Ramses III (1189–1153), where the name *Yh* comes just
before *Tr*, recalling *Trbr* of the Soleb list. The equation with Yhwꜣ is
plausible, developed by Astour (1979) as separate from any southern
connection, and taken seriously by Adrom and Müller (2017). Aside from
the names mentioned here, however, there is no extended combination to
replicate the lists from 'Amarah West and Soleb, so that these appear to
be selections merged with other sources rather than any basis for reconstructing a longer form of an original text.[8] In the end, we have two
principal texts, the lists from 'Amarah West and Soleb, and discussion of
the Egyptian evidence must be oriented first of all to these contexts.

The Shasu

After their initial identifications, the principal two texts with the Yhwꜣ
name were then examined together as part of a 1971 study by Raphael
Giveon that remains the primary reference for the Shasu, a class of people
attested particularly in documentation from Egypt's imperial period,
between the 15th and 12th centuries, when Egypt established a settled
presence in Syria and Palestine in the Levant, Nubia up-river in Sudan,
and the margins of Libya (Figure 2).[9] For Egyptian scribes, the Shasu
category somehow served to define one important population in Asia, to

---

[6] Aside from the reference to what appeared to match the divine name Yahweh, the Soleb
topographical lists as a whole were at least partly related to another Ramses II list found at
Aksha, also in Nubia (Giveon 1964: 240).

[7] See the account of the Soleb collection in Adrom and Müller (96), and see below for detail
and discussion. For the finished publications of the Soleb material, see Schiff Giorgini
(2002: 179, pl. 206–207). For initial reports on the Soleb excavations, along with other
French archaeological work, see Leclant (1963, 1964, 1965).

[8] The analyses of Astour (1979), Adrom and Müller (2017), thus overestimate what can be
known of the Amenhotep III set from this source. Note that the Medinet Habu list omits
the unique and crucial identification of these names with "Shasu-land" (see below).

[9] Following publication of Giveon (1971), Manfred Weippert (1974) produced an important set of reflections on the same data, including fresh readings of certain texts.

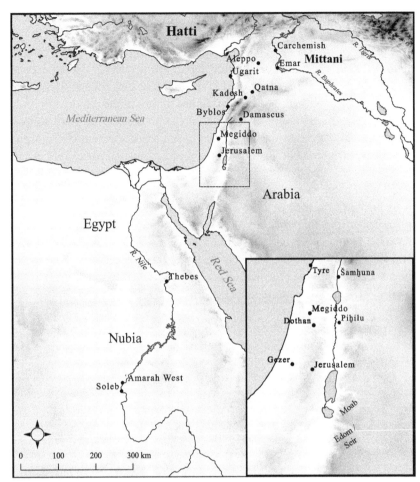

FIGURE 2 Egypt and the Levant in the Late Bronze Age
(Map by Kyle Brunner)

their east, at a time when Egypt was carving out a great kingdom from the land on every side. One key motivation for the political innovation of conquest as buffer was the division of Egypt between the Delta and the south during the late 18th through early 16th centuries, when populations with eastern Mediterranean Levantine background became so powerful that they came to dominate the Nile Delta.[10] The Hellenistic Egyptian

---

[10] On the growing presence and role of Semitic speaking and Levantine population in Egypt during the Middle Kingdom and Second Intermediate (Hyksos) period, see Schneider (2003).

historian Manetho is cited as having called the 15th Dynasty in particular the "Hyksos" period of foreign rule in Egypt, which ended when rulers of Upper Egypt at Thebes defeated the separate northern kingdom and reunified the land under traditional Egyptian auspices.[11] In the second half of the 16th century, Ahmose I and Thutmose I invaded Palestine and Syria and initiated long-term Egyptian hegemony in the region.

Perhaps with enduring territorial interests to secure, Egyptian sources touching affairs in lands to the east and north, especially in modern Jordan and Syria, begin to coin the term Shasu ($\check{s}$₃$\acute{s}w$),[12] first attested in the reigns of Thutmose II and Thutmose III (ca. 1492–1479 and 1479–1425).[13] The word itself presents rival possibilities from Egyptian and Semitic verbs: "to wander" from the former; and "to plunder" from the latter, with particular reference to the Biblical Hebrew $\check{s}$-s-h.[14] These choices are provokingly reversed from expectation, with the Egyptian seeming simply descriptive and the supposed Semitic carrying the prejudice and antipathy that might be associated with the potential targets of such violence, stereotyped into a name.[15] Lacking Levantine evidence for such a Semitic category, which might be found in Middle and Late Bronze Age cuneiform writing, and given the aptness of the simple description in the Egyptian etymology, this is surely preferable: the Shasu were "nomads."[16]

---

[11] For an overview of the "Second Intermediate Period," see Ryholt (1997).

[12] Land that served mobile pastoralists in the second half of the second millennium would have wrapped around the coast and highlands of the Levant, as identified today with Israel and Lebanon. Along with Jordan and Syria directly to the east, such space would also include the Sinai Peninsula, the Negev of southern Israel, and even parts of Arabia.

[13] There is only one document each for these two kings, texts 1 and 2 in Giveon 1971.

[14] Giveon (1971: 261–64) and early references on both sides.

[15] My choice regarding the Shasu etymology does not affect my larger interpretation of the name Yhw₃. Nevertheless, we must keep in mind that the alternatives are the work of modern philology, not ancient perceptions, and only one of them should be correct. In its violent stereotype, the Semitic etymology would thus reflect a modern, mid-20th-century misconception of the Egyptian category, perhaps by influence of common reading of the 'Apiru, especially as known from el-Amarna.

[16] Redford (1992: 271) adopts the Egyptian etymology without question: the word "meant basically to move on foot, and it is often used of journeys or of the daily motion of the sun," then taking on associations with "speed and furtiveness," so messengers and refugees. Grandet (1994: 2.244 n.921) prefers the Semitic etymology without argument, though he renders them as "Bédouins." Note the question of potential relationship to the Akkadian (or Semitic) category *sutû*, already attested in the Old Babylonian period (Heltzer 1981) and likewise applied roughly to "nomads." This term comes up also in relation to the 14th-century evidence from el-Amarna, where letters to the Egyptian court show use of the Akkadian category in regions and settings where the Egyptians would apply their own term, Shasu.

In Giveon's collection, which includes all the known written citations of the name as well as pictorial depictions with what come to be typical apparel and features, 62 "documents" from the New Kingdom reflect the period of interaction with living Shasu.[17] These references to the Shasu are concentrated in the later periods, with only 14 from the 18th Dynasty (ca. 1550–1292), three from Seti I (ca. 1290–1279), and the rest from Ramses II (ca. 1279–1213) and later. Extended narratives mentioning the Shasu come only from the time of Ramses II and beyond.[18] This is to say that the preserved portrayals of the Shasu depend heavily on texts from the later period: the 13th and 12th centuries rather than the 15th and 14th. The character and circumstances of the Egyptian empire in Syria and Palestine changed considerably during the later period, especially after the battle of Kadesh in ca. 1274 and the treaty with the Hittites completed ca. 1258. While the Hittite expansion in itself pressed Egypt southward and back to its secure city centers at Byblos and Sumur, the peace brought a shift in Egypt's military concerns toward the southern part of their Asian holdings.[19] Egypt's conflicts no longer concerned

[17] This number may not be precise; it reflects the addition of 18 entries with extra identification (usually "a," "b," etc.) to the 44 numbered items. There are surely more texts accumulated since 1971; note the Balu'a Stela from the Kerak district of Moab (Mattingly 1992; cf. Tebes 2006; Routledge and Routledge 2009). This object was already known at the time of Giveon's 1971 work, found in secondary use from an Iron Age II context, but the connection with the Shasu had not been made. Routledge and Routledge (2009) conclude that the object can only be dated to a range between the end of the 14th and the mid-12th centuries, and whether it was carved by an Egyptian or otherwise, it can best be interpreted by analogy to other objects in "provincial" style. The central theme of the object is investiture of a figure associated with kingship. "He is clearly represented as a foreign 'Asiatic,' probably a *Shasu* by Egyptian convention, yet he wears clothes and occupies a position in the scene that could not happen in Egypt." It is intriguing to find such an object, with ambiguous composition and unknown context, in a region that could have been associated with Shasu population.

[18] Document 1 (Thutmose II) is a single sentence in the biography of Ahmose; Document 2 (Thutmose III) is one sentence from the royal annals, defining the king's 39th year by the king's visit to Palestine (Retenu) after defeat of the Shasu; Document 3 (Amenhotep II) includes a number of Shasu among prisoners taken from Retenu; and Documents 7–10 are all pictorial.

[19] For detailed discussion of Egypt's military activities in the Levant, weighing both the archaeological and the written evidence for forts and fortified towns from the 18th through the 20th Dynasties, see Morris (2005). Egypt's initial gains in Syria occurred in the late 16th and 15th centuries, when the principal power opposing them in greater Mesopotamia was Mittani, with its center far to the northeast in the Habur River drainage. When the Hittites began to build a large territorial kingdom with interest in northern Syria, Egypt began to lose control over elements of their northern Levantine vassals, most notably the land of Amurru. This evolving confrontation took place over the middle decades of the 14th century, during the reigns of Amenhotep III and Akhenaten (268–9). Morris (368) concludes that for Ramses II, "it may have been only

Syria, where the lines of great-power interest were drawn in relation to Hatti, but likewise shifted southward. Egyptian interaction with mobile populations in the highlands and inland steppe was then colored by the more southern geographical sphere that now required consolidation of power in a more intensely administered Canaanite domain.[20]

Soleb

Evaluation of the Egyptian texts with the Yhwʒ name has both allowed the biblical question of divine origins too much weight and given the historical context of their occurrences too little. Both of the two principal texts derive from lists, each inscribed on highly visible surfaces in major temples, lacking context that would explain the basis for scribal knowledge of the names, valued for what they display of Egyptian dominance. The older comes from Area IV of the hypostyle hall in the royal temple at Soleb, inscribed on a column along the northern external wall, furthest from the central aisle (Figures 3 and 4).[21] The temple is the larger of two new temples built in Nubia (Sudan) by Amenhotep III, the other further north at Sedeinga (Goedicke 1992: 17), with the Soleb site focused on attention to a statue of the king himself as "lord of Nubia" (19). Bryan (in Kozloff and Bryan 1992: 104–10) has proposed that the temples of king and queen at Soleb and Sedeinga represented the southern anchor in a construction program with Thebes at center and sites in the Delta for the north, intended to map divine and cosmic mythology onto the Nile Valley. In the words of O'Connor (1998: 148), reflecting on Bryan's proposal, "to some degree,

in the southern and easternmost regions of his northern empire that this warrior pharaoh could hope to make good on the ever-present pharaonic goal of extending the boundaries of Egypt." Archaeological finds display an "intensification of Egyptian investment in the province of Canaan" during the 19th Dynasty (ca. 13th century).

[20] Redford (1992: 190–91) characterizes the situation after the treaty with Hatti as follows: "Two centuries of fighting for a northern empire had come to an end. But was Ramesses aware of the cost? For when the border was drawn again, all the gains of the Ramesside kings were for nought. Ugarit and its southern coastal neighbor Siyannu remained Hittite; Amurru returned to the Hittite fold, its king Benteshina reinstated, and was granted control over Arvad. Kadesh too became Hittite once again, with close ties to Ugarit. As in Amarna times, Amki remained Egyptian as well as Upe to the south, and the Egyptian headquarters at Kumidi was rechristened 'Ramessesburg, the city that is in the midst of Upe.' Nothing had changed."

[21] The designation of Area IV comes from Schiff Giorgini (1998). Giveon (1971) identifies this as "Room C," citing Leclant (1962: 328) for the description.

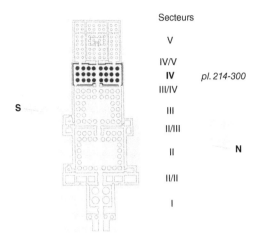

FIGURE 3 The temple at Soleb and the Area IV hypostyle hall
(*Soleb V*, pl. 213)

Egypt – at least under Amenhotep III – was being transformed into a
cosmogram, that is, that the pharaoh was tracing out on the map of
Egypt and Egyptian Nubia diagrams that reflected cosmic processes involving deities, the pharaoh, and his subjects." This role in defining Egypt's
central position in the divine and human worlds provides a context for the
grand geographical claims presented on the columns of Area IV, before
entry into the ultimate sacred center of the temple.

The list with Yhwȝ is part of an extended set of decorations on the
lower part of large columns, where the assemblage as a whole could be
readily seen in procession, with bound prisoners and written insignia to
identify them (Figure 5).[22] Traces of a copy appear on a wall of the entry
portico, without evidence for any text but indicating that the columns

---

[22] Each column in the hypostyle hall consists of six drums ("tambours"), which the excavators designated A through F, starting from the bottom (Schiff Giorgini 1998: 92). The
lowest section (A) of each column was decorated with images of bound prisoners, along

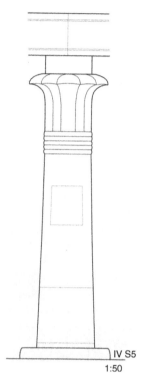

IV S5
1:50

FIGURE 4 Hypostyle hall, column S5, for sample dimensions
(*Soleb V*, pl. 215)

were not the only context for this geographical and military vision (Schiff
Giorgini 1998: 179). Inside the temple, Area IV, just outside the sacred
center, has twenty-four columns, twelve on each side of the central aisle,
in three rows of four. The two sides of the space were apparently intended
as rough mirror images in terms of layout, though the southern side seems
to have been left partly unrealized, in some cases with insignia set up to go
with the bound prisoners but not inscribed.[23] As seen by the adornment
and faces, the two sides of the hall represented separate geographical

with names to label them in what the excavators (p. 93, *passim*) call "escutcheons" or
shields ("écussons"). Kozloff and Bryan (1992: 57) use the term, "name-rings."

[23] In the description of Schiff Giorgini (1998: 114–59), the following column decorations
from the southern set were fully visible but left incomplete: S2 decoration; S3 with panels
of bound prisoners set in place, but the insignia left empty ("les écussons ont été laissés
vides, les noms des peuples n'étant pas gravés," p. 149); S4 same.

FIGURE 5 Hypostyle hall column N5, prisoners from set β
(*Soleb IV*, fig. 97b)

spheres: all the figures on the northern columns have beards and belong to
the Asian world north and east of Egypt; and those on the southern
columns have short hair, with no beards or close-cropped ones, evidently
belonging to the African continent.[24] The Shasu are naturally part of the
Asian sphere and therefore the northern portion of the hall. Although
the excavators promised a new translation of the Soleb column lists in the
forthcoming *Soleb VI*, the actual volume was devoted instead to the
memory of Schiff Giorgini, without this crucial contribution (Beaux and
Grimal 2013). The most complete rendition of the full geographical list
therefore remains that of Giveon (1964).[25]

In order to grasp adequately the context for the Soleb reference to
Yhwȝ, the full set of column decorations calls for consideration. First
of all, each name is matched with a bound prisoner, and the images
of these prisoners vary to match the Egyptian vision of different

[24] This is the observation of Elizabeth Knott, as we examined the drawings of prisoner sets
published in *Soleb V* (Schiff Giorgini 2002).
[25] Edel (1980) provides a partial rendition of the Soleb column list, so far as this is paralleled
in the later lists from ʿAmarah West and Aksha. Where relevant, I have made reference to
this work in the description below.

stereotyped populations.[26] Egypt is thus imagined to have subdued a whole surrounding world of diverse peoples, with their soldiers now paraded before Egypt, its king, and perhaps the whole divine world. The reality behind these portrayals may vary, and the peoples named are organized according to a broad pattern of prominence.[27] In the context of procession up the central aisle, with participants moving toward the sacred center of the temple at its rear, the three columns along each side of the aisle would take priority, first the standard representation of world powers as Nine Bows on column N1, then Babylon and Mittani on column N5, and finally a selection of significant centers on column N9 (Figure 6).[28] In relation to the processional aisle, three more sets of three columns each would be increasingly less visible, with columns 4, 8, and 12 the most obscure. Yhwȝ and Shasu-land appear on column N4, in this furthest tier. The name-rings on the corresponding column S4 were left empty. If the names on the individual columns were to be read at all, it would have required departure from the processional aisle for circulation among the towering pillars. Such circulation, with attention to the contrasting representations of the prisoners or, for a person with scribal training, to the name-rings that identify each one, suggests an occasion other than public ritual. Figure 6 offers a schematic display of the column prisoners and labels, with Giveon's (1964) specific readings in Figure 7.[29]

---

[26] The detailed column descriptions of Schiff Giorgini (1998) include the varying forms of hair, beard, clothing, and jewelry.

[27] Various scholars emphasize the contrast between the apparent world dominance presented in these geographical lists and the obvious independence and prominence of major powers on view in the Amarna correspondence, which highlights especially Mittani, Babylon, and Hatti (e.g. Kozloff and Bryan 1992: 57; Berman 1998: 19).

[28] The choice of the last of these is most difficult to follow, and it is not my goal to interpret the entire hall. There does appear to be a progression from greater to lesser importance, even for the three columns that line the aisle. Giveon lays out his sense of the structure in 1964: 239–40 and 1971: 24. On the Nine Bows, see the review in (Anthony 2016: 37–41) and Uphill (1967). The idea of "nine bows" representing the sum of Egypt's potential enemies goes back to the Old Kingdom, but by the New Kingdom it had developed into a standard list, not a map of the contemporary world but a set of earlier names for what was understood to lie behind current power.

[29] These are provided for context, not as updated readings for the Soleb evidence, a task that belongs to the specialists. I cite Edel (1980) for useful readings and parallels from 'Amarah West and Aksha. Both of these later sites begin with names from Soleb columns N5, N9, and N10. The relationship between 'Amarah West and Soleb is then more extensive but also complicated (see Edel 1980). After different material in 'Amarah West 29–45, 'Amarah 46–49 overlaps with Soleb N11 before a broken section that is difficult to evaluate. 'Amarah West 59–82 then aligns at least in part with Soleb N6, N7,

FIGURE 6 Schematic rendering of columns on the north side of the aisle in the hypostyle hall (Diagram by Daniel Fleming and Elizabeth Knott)

Column N1: 7 names, 5 as the Nine Bows, perhaps plus Mitanni
  *Ten names in two sets of five; only α3, α4, β2, β3, and β4 clearly legible for N1.
  **Only four are visible in each group, leaving less than one meter for fifth prisoner in both α and β sets (other units of prisoner plus separator take between 0.50 and 0.58 meters); too much space would be left if only nine, however.
Column N2: α1 (missing); α2 *swḥ* (Shuah); α3 *ꜣnw*; α4 ... *w* ...
  β1 (empty cartouche); β2 *nrb* (Nirib, near Aleppo); β3 *ḏnir*; β4 *twir*ꜥ; β5 *iwiny*
  *Nine names in sets of four and five. α2 has remains of the name's beginning.
Column N3: α1 *rḫ(b)* (Rehob); α2, α3, α4 (missing); α5 *mkti* (Megiddo)
  β1 *bq*ꜥ*t* (Biqꜥat, from the valley); β2 *iꜣmt* (Yarmuta?); β3 irtiti (Ardata?); β4 *r*?
  *Nine names in sets of five and four. α2, one sign; α3, traces of beginning.
Column N4: α1 *tꜣ šsw trbir*; α2 *tꜣ šsw yhwꜣ*; α3 *tꜣ šsw smt*
  β1 *bt* ꜥ... (Beth A(nath)); rest of β missing
  *Expect count by two sets – no count by two sets, no explanation of basis for expectation.
  Measurement indicates room for nine prisoners, neither more nor less. The four preserved prisoners, with adjacent separators, measure as follows, from the 1:10 scale, checked against the distance between compass points for the inscribed circumference: β1=0.57; α1=0.56; α2=0.56; α3=0.57; average span 0.565. Nine prisoners require 5.085 meters, vs. 4.52 for eight and 5.65 for ten, each far too small and large for columns of roughly 5.00 – 5.20 meters, as rendered to scale by representation of compass points and calculation from column diameter (1.55 meters at top of drum; 1.70 at bottom; see Pl.215 in *Soleb V*).

Column N5: α1 *sngr* (Shinear/Babylon); α2 *nhryn* (Naharina/Mitanni); α3 *ḫt* (Hatti); α4 (effaced)
  β1 *qdš* (Kadesh on the Orontes); β2 *tnp* (Tunip); β3 (effaced); β4 *ꜥkrt* (Ugarit); β5 *kftiw* (Keftiu=Crete)
  *Ten names in sets of four and six. β6 is said to have a legible name.
  **The β set has five names with one location skipped over, between β3 and β4, so there is no β6.
Column N6: α1 *bbr* (Babel); α2 *knn*ꜥ*n* (Canaan); α3 *rpwḥ* (Raphiah); α4 *srḥn* (Sharuhen)
  β1 *ꜥw...*; β2 *rqt* (Raqat); β3 *ḫw...*; β4 *tnpiršmšm* (Tenpirshemshem, cf. Beth Shemesh?)
  *Nine names in sets of five and four. α2 name left "unrealized"; so, the four names from Giveon?
Column N7: α1 *t*ꜥ*nk* (Taanak); α2, α3 (missing); α4 *ꜥsqrn* (Ashkelon)
  β1 *...w...*; β2 (effaced); β3 *swk* (Soko); β4 *i...*
  *Nine places in sets of four and five; β4 omitted.
Column N8: only a fragment of a group of signs in one cartouche
  *Places for ten names in sets of six and four; traces for α1 only.

---

1 Column numbers follow the designations in Schiff Giorgini, with N1, N2, etc. marking the northern (right) side of the central aisle, with procession toward the back. Giveon's A and B sets for each column are rendered in Schiff Giorgini as α and β respectively. Both the Egyptian transliterations and the translations are adapted from Giveon (1964), without effort to update them. Where Schiff Giorgini offer further enumeration of the individual column lists, I add these in a second entry marked by (*). The double asterisk (**) marks indications from examining the drawings and measuring available space for the given circumference.

**Where the description in *Soleb III* indicates the destruction of α3-5, the compass points drawn for this nearly effaced decoration provide no more than half the circumference for this α set, which could not fit six prisoners. There can only have been five. The one measurable prisoner plus separator occupies 0.49 meters, indicating space for ten prisoners (roughly 5.0 meters total).

Column N9: α1 *pḥ(r)* (Pehal/Pihilim); α2 *pwnt* (Punt); α3 *šsw* (Shasu); α4 *tyt*; α5 *'rrpḥ* (Arrapha)

β1 *qdn* (Qatna); β2 *(q)₃(t)₃r* (Gezer); β3, β4 (missing); β5 ...*t*...*2*...*q*

*Ten names in two sets of five.

Column N10: α1 *qrqmš* (Carchemish); α2 *'swr* (Ashur?); α3 *tnr(s)*; α4 *ipṯṯn*

β1 *mrknš*; β2 *ḏr* (Ṣur/Tyre); β3 *ḏtw(kr)*; β4 *kpny* (Gebal/Byblos)

*Eight names in two sets of four.

**Seven prisoners offer usable measurements, occupying space that would nicely fit two more: 4.03 meters for the seven, with each occupying between 0.55 and 0.59 meters.

Column N11: α1 *m(qd)* (Maqed, in Gilead); α2 (effaced); α3 ...*₃yw*; α4 *ps*...; α5 *p₃iwnbn*

β1 (effaced); β2 *'q(r)* (Iqrit); β3, β4 (missing)

*Nine names in sets of five and four.

Column N12: α1 ...*w*...; α2 (traces); α3 ...*rn*; α4 ...*nb'r*; α5 ...*rbt*...; α6 ...*r*

β1 *swḥy* (Shuah); β2 ...*sḥw*; β3 ...?; β4 (effaced, with foreign lands determinative)

*Places for eleven names, distribution not stated.

**It appears that one prisoner has been double counted; there are six in α, four in β. The six in the α set, the only example of such unequal counts with ten prisoners, are proven by the traces of the binding rope on α1, in front of the remaining five.

FIGURE 7 Overview of names in the hypostyle hall column inscriptions (Table by Daniel Fleming)

The Shasu appear on two columns in very different contexts: on column N9 (Giveon Document 6), they join in an odd mix of geographical names from the Levant (Piḫilu, Gezer), Syria (Qatna and Arrapḫa), and Africa (Punt); and on column N4 (Giveon Document 6a), repeated as "Shasu-land" (or, "land of the Shasu") with three distinct subcategories, including Yhw₃ (Figure 8). Nothing about either the set of names on column N4 or the larger pattern of geography and focus locates the Shasu-land names in any particular region, except that the very specificity suggests some direct encounter in relation to Egyptian expansion in Asia. Placement in the row of columns farthest from the central aisle at the least distances them from Egypt's geographical priorities, though it may be the

and N3, followed by a section in 83–91 with contents related to elements of Soleb N9, N6, and N7. Then 'Amarah West 92–100 has been understood to match Soleb N4, the central question in my own analysis; and 101–104 include two repeated names and two novel insertions. It is evident from this description that the 'Amarah West list is textually related but by no means a full rendition of the same geographical composition.

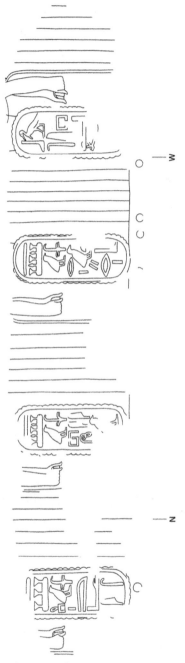

FIGURE 8 Column N4, drawing of name-rings
(*Soleb V*, pl. 221)

Column N4[a]

Set α

1	*t₃ š₃św trbr*	Shasu-land:[b] Trbr[c]
2	*t₃ š₃św yhw₃*	Shasu-land: Yhw₃
3	*t₃ š₃św śmt*	Shasu-land: Smt[d]

(damaged)

Set β

| 1 | *bt* '[...] | Bet '[xxx][e] |

FIGURE 9　Column N4 names

[a] The readings of the Egyptian text here follow the text presented by Adrom and Müller (97), with the vowel marker after the last sign, as *w₃*. Thomas Schneider (personal communication), observes, "the hieroglyphic writing of *y-h-w₃* is clearly syllabic. <*y*> (double reed leaf) always renders /ya/, <*h*> is a single consonant without a vowel marker, <*w₃*> is almost certainly /wa/." Schneider could not think of another instance of the word-final <*w₃*> sign, but reading as /wa/ would be indicated by names such as *t₃-w₃-t₃-s₃* for "Hittite" (*Zuwassaš < *Zuwanzaš). It is possible that final <*w₃*> here could represent /we/. In any case, the name ends in an open vowel. I am grateful for this careful evaluation.

[b] Betsy Bryan (personal communication) renders the construction, "The Land of the Shasu: [or of] Trbr," etc., with each individual name offering further administrative detail. By my streamlining of the genitive as "Shasu-land," I do not intend a different conception.

[c] Astour (1979) simply states that two villages in Lebanon are named Turbu and are situated next to hills called Gabal Turbul, as one part of his search for more northern alignments. Görg (1976) reads the division of two different names *tr* and *br* in lines 116 and 112 of the Ramses III Medinet Habu list as the original state, with the older lists artificially combining them – a forced reversal of the natural chronology of the evidence.

[d] Astour (1979) finds a village called Šamat, "12 km south of Beiṭrūn on the Phoenician coast." In his programmatic search for names that could derive from animal features, Görg (1976) compared the Akkadian *sāmtu*, "redness." The Akkadian noun is not well attested and not found with animals but most often with the sky (*CAD* s.v. *sāmtu* B). Following Giveon (1971), Redford (1992: 272) recalls the Kenite clan Sam'ath (the Shim'ethites) from 1 Chr 2:55, one of the texts familiar from the Midianite Hypothesis discussion (see Chapter 3). Ahituv (1984: 169) rejects the connection as phonologically impossible and simply guesses the location as the northern Sinai, evidently based on his understanding that Yhw₃ must be there.

[e] Giveon reads Bet Anat, which appears in Document 20, a list of toponyms from the reign of Ramses II. In Simons's collection of topographical lists relating to Asia, Bet Anat is by far the most common: see his lists XV, XVI, XIX, XX, XXI, XXIV, and XXXIV; also note *b-t '-r-m* in list XXXIV (Simons 1937). None of these precedes the 19th Dynasty, with XV and XVI from the reign of Seti I (1294–1279); XXXIV is from after the New Kingdom.

specificity of the list that renders it more peripheral, since the generic "Shasu" warrant a position on the aisle with column N9 (Figure 9).

Rather than begin consideration of what may have been missing from the damaged α set on column N4, we turn first to the longer and later list from 'Amarah West, which has been invoked repeatedly as the basis for restoring the Soleb text (e.g. Edel 1980).

'Amarah West

The text from 'Amarah West in the reign of Ramses II was also inscribed in a prominent location on a sacred edifice, in the hypostyle hall of the temple to Amun(-Ra).[30] This particular list begins to the east of the northern gate and follows the entire northern wall, keeping company with the main Asiatic list on the southern and eastern walls of the hall – recalling the situation of the copy traces on the Soleb temple entry (Schiff Giorgini 1998: 179).[31] As with Area IV of the Soleb temple, the hypostyle hall at 'Amarah West was decorated with images of prisoners, calculated to create a similar impression of Egyptian domination manifest in military victories.[32] The 'Amarah West temple preserved evidence of document storage going back to

---

[30] For extended description of the Amun temple at 'Amarah West in political context, see Spencer (2014). The town was founded by Seti I, and two commemorative stelae were found in it from the reign of Ramses II. "Moving further into the temple one entered the hypostyle hall, a space densely packed with three rows of four columns and originally roofed, designed to evoke the primaeval marshes at the time of creation. The decoration in both halls included scenes of pharaoh offering to the gods, but also representations of victorious military campaigns, such as the capture of a Syrian town. Images of bound prisoners – Asiatics, Libyans and Nubians – decorated the base of the walls, further emphasising Egypt's desire to control these chaotic, foreign lands" (15). Morris (2005: 681) characterizes the move by Seti I as relocation of the "deputy of Kush" from Soleb to 'Amarah, explaining the continuity of temples and decoration.

[31] This description comes from Giveon (1971: 75), with reference to Fairman (1939: 141, pl. XIV); Grdseloff (1947: 79). According to Spencer (2014: 16), the hypostyle room served the approach to the central sanctuary; its images would thus have prepared the way for entrance into the presence of Amun-Ra, not part of the principal sacred space. Apparently it lacks any reference to the Shasu, or it would have been incorporated into Giveon's study.

[32] As with Amenhotep III, the world domination of Egypt on display in the constructions of Ramses II was focused more on long-standing achievement than on the specific accomplishments of the current pharaoh. Ramses II was active in military campaigning only during the first ten years of his reign, including the celebrated but problematic battle with the Hittites at Kadesh ca. 1274 (Morris 2005: 372).

the early 15th century, showing how the names inscribed for display could have been obtained from texts available on-site (Figure 10).[33]

THE SHASU-LAND: ONE CONTACT IN TWO TEXTS

It is immediately evident that the lists from Soleb and 'Amarah West are somehow copies, though the first is more than a century older than the second. The three Shasu-land names in Soleb's N4 αι–3 appear in reverse order as the last three lines (96–98) at 'Amarah West (Figure 11). However the related lists found their way to the two nearby temples in Nubia, they must originate in a single text, or text and image together, as representations of Egyptian supremacy by the display of bound prisoners. Given that the Soleb set is certainly incomplete and the 'Amarah West text offers six names, the older Soleb list is routinely restored from the longer, later one. Yet the reversed sequences suggest some further manipulation of the original, beyond simple copying, and the distinct spelling of Soleb's αι Trbr as 'Amarah West's Wrbr could suggest some intermediate text.[34] Elmar Edel (1980: 64) proposed that these two reflect a single Ur-list, which he restored from the longer Ramses II text, in spite of the later date.[35] Given the proximity of the two Sudan sites and the comparable application as temple decoration, it is possible that the 'Amarah West list derives directly from Soleb as its source, and that all differences can be attributed to the work of a single act of copying. Even if so, the reversed order produces a different effect, with different priorities in what appears first and last. Here, S'rr leads the group.

In spite of the definite relationship between the Soleb and the 'Amarah West lists for Shasu-land, the earlier text has too quickly been restored from the later one. Textual variation is a well-known phenomenon, and where one copy is longer than another, it is the longer text that more

---

[33] The temple included a set of what Spencer (17) calls "magazines": "These narrow rooms, with vaulted roofs and stone doorways, were presumably designed to store offerings, archives, cult equipment and other temple property. In one magazine, Egypt Exploration Society (EES) excavators encountered over 400 clay seal-impressions, with the names of Tuthmosis III and Hatshepsut, pharaohs who reigned over 150 years before Amara West was created. Such sealings were probably attached to papyrus archives, or boxes and other containers for storing precious items."

[34] Note that if the sequence of Yh and Tr in a Ramses III geographical list from Medinet Habu reflects Yhwȝ and Trbr from the Shasu-land set, this 12th-century text would share the reversed order of the 13th-century Ramses II setting at 'Amarah West.

[35] Edel also included a third similar geographical list from Aksha, cited already by Giveon. The Aksha list lacks the section with the Shasu-land, rendering it less useful for this specific comparison.

93	*tꜣ šꜣśw š'rr*	Shasu-land: Seir[b]
94	*tꜣ šꜣśw rbn*	Shasu-land: L(?)-b-n?[c]
95	*tꜣ šꜣśw pyspꜣys*	Shasu-land: Pyspys[d]
96	*tꜣ šꜣśw śmt*	Shasu-land: Smt
97	*tꜣ šꜣśw yhwꜣ*	Shasu-land: Yhwꜣ
98	*tꜣ šꜣśw (t)rbr*	Shasu-land: (T)rbr[e]

FIGURE 10 'Amarah West lines 93–98 [a]

[a] Again, readings follow Adrom and Müller (98), the most recent specialist treatment. My comments on potential readings are selective, not exhaustive.

[b] Weippert (1974: 430) observes that *tꜣ* ("land") is in the hieroglyphic text for each line, though Giveon does not transcribe it. Giveon's transcribed text itself displays Weippert's reading (cf. Adrom and Müller). On the crucial question of reading this name, see below.

[c] It is likely that this spelling represents the ubiquitous Semitic root *l-b-n*, but there are too many possibilities for any convincing identification. Grdseloff (1947: 80; cf. Ahituv 1984) invoked the biblical Laban/Libnah from Deut 1:1/Num 33:20–21. Redford (1992: 272) again follows Giveon (1971) in suggesting Libona in Jordan, south of Amman. As throughout, Astour looks further north, based here on reference to a similar name found in connection with Thutmose III, where he sees a clear connection with ᵘʳᵘ*La-bá-na* in EA 53 and 54 from el-Amarna. The parallel with anything from Thutmose III is not demonstrated by any cluster of names to match the two Shasu-land lists, and the Semitic root is far too common to carry the weight of this identification. In Görg's scheme of animal traits and colors (1976), it is no surprise to find here the Hebrew term for "white."

[d] This duplicated form resists any identification with settlement sites, though Astour discovered a spring in the Beqa' Valley called 'Ayn Fišfiš, which he reads all the way back to New Kingdom Egypt, making *pyspys* "a spring frequented by nomads and their flocks" (Astour 1979: 30). Görg connects the name with Akkadian *paspasu* ("duck"), at least more common than the *pispisu* (smelly insect) attested once in Esarhaddon's treaty text. Neither creature offers a particular association with the life of herdsmen in the back country.

[e] The 'Amarah West writing is *wrbr* (so, Grdseloff). Although the sequence and close similarity to α1 in the Soleb list make the identification with *Trbr* unavoidable, it remains uncertain which would represent the error. Because the name *Tr* comes right after *Yh* in the Medinet Habu list (lines 115 and 116), the Soleb writing seems more likely correct, as concluded by many others, including Giveon (1971), Astour, and now Adrom and Müller.

likely reflects elaboration, by the standard of *lectio brevior*. Because of damage to column N4, we do not know securely the number of names in set α. Continuing the reversed text from 'Amarah West, the fourth name would be Pyspys, and an isolated block from the Soleb temple site attests to Pysp[ys] with the same "Shasu-land" connection.[36] Only one of the

[36] Giveon (1964: 245) describes these as "two blocks," one with what he reads as *šsw yh* and the other with *šsw gys*, which he matches with *pyspys* of 'Amarah West, noting the similarity of /g/ and /p/.

Soleb Column N4 Inscription (Set α)	'Amarah West Wall Inscription (lines 93–98)
tȝ šȝśw trbr	*tȝ šȝśw š 'rr*
tȝ šȝśw yhwȝ	*tȝ šȝśw rbn*
tȝ šȝśw šmt	*tȝ šȝśw pyspȝys*
pyspȝys	*tȝ šȝśw šmt*
	tȝ šȝśw yhwȝ
	tȝ šȝśw (t)rbr

Note that readings follow Adrom and Müller (97 and 98)

FIGURE 11 Shasu-land lists from Soleb and 'Amarah West
(Table by Daniel Fleming)

Soleb columns (N12) could have one set of six names, and the rest of the columns have combinations of four or five (see Figures 6 and 7). Giveon (1964: 245) concluded that "it is doubtful that there was room for six cartouches on the column pertaining to a single set; this would leave too little space for the second set" (my translation).[37]

Although the publication includes no measures for the columns' diameter and circumference, and the drawings for each column offer only the cardinal directions and a scale of 1:10, it is possible to examine the available space more closely (Figure 12).[38] Given the consistent horizontal extent occupied on column N4 by the one figure from the β set and all

---

[37] Based on the drawings for the individual columns in Schiff Giorgini (2002), both N8 and N12 have ten prisoners each, with only the latter in a combination of six and four. Thus, format could allow a similar count for N4 and the question is rather one of specific spacing on the different columns.

[38] Work on measurements began in consultation with Elizabeth Knott, then carried out in extended work with Nancy Fleming. In order to count the number of prisoners capable of fitting in the space available in the circumference of each column, we must measure the combination of horizontal extent occupied by the panel for the prisoner himself and the separating fill in the form of vertical lines that produce the effect of a column. Calculation of available space depends on reconstruction of the circumference, which is possible by measurement of the column diameter from Plate 215 in *Soleb V* at 1:50 scale and by measuring the distance between compass points marked on the individual column drawings in the same volume. Neither of these measures can be precise, in part because the variation in compass-point measures shows some degree of inaccuracy in their placement. Also, the lower drum of the columns, on which the images were cut, is tapered slightly, so that the circumference decreases from 1.70 to 1.55 meters, as indicated in Plate 215. The circumferences indicated by the compass points varies from 4.96 meters (N2, at 1.24

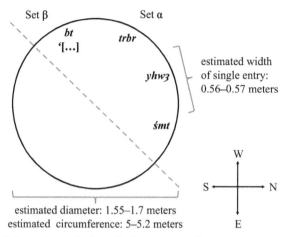

Set β Set α

bt
ꜥ[...] *trbr*

yhwꜣ

śmt

estimated width
of single entry:
0.56–0.57 meters

W

S ——————— N

estimated diameter: 1.55–1.7 meters
estimated circumference: 5–5.2 meters

E

FIGURE 12 Schematic rendering of column N4 and its inscriptions
(Diagram by Elizabeth Knott)

three preserved from the α set, there is little doubt that there were nine
prisoners (see Figures 6 and 7). We cannot tell whether the α or the β set
had five prisoners, but it is highly unlikely that they were divided into six
and three, given the consistent division of nine into four and five on
columns N2, N3, N5, N6, N7, N10, and N11, with no preference for
which set was the larger. Even considering error introduced by measurement from drawings and calculations for scale, each additional prisoner
represents a quantum increase in needed space, almost always between
0.5 and 0.6 meters.

These calculations, tentative as they are, confirm Giveon's conclusion
that six Shasu names do not fit the space for the α set on column N4. Four
names would include the three preserved in place and another from the
separated block: Trbr, Yhwꜣ, Smt, and Pyspys. If the α set included a fifth
prisoner, it would be Rbn (Lbn?). There is no room for Sꜥrr as a sixth, so
that aside from the debate over identification of *śꜥrr* from ꜥAmarah West,
to which we will return, the published drawings for the Soleb temple
make it difficult to restore "Seir" to the older Shasu list. This name is the
one familiar geographical reference, to us and perhaps to the ancient
Egyptians, that could give the Shasu-land any particular location within
the broad inland steppe.

meters for one quarter) to 5.22 meters (N5, at 1.30 and 1.31 meters for two compass
quarters).

Shasu Families

Without Seir, we are left completely ignorant of both the geography and the character of the names included in the Egyptian account of Shasu-land. For all the efforts to identify Trbr, Yhwꜣ, Smt, Pyspys, and Rbn, these are ultimately arbitrary, imposed from the prior conception brought to the list. Grdseloff provided the first of these when he discovered the 'Amarah West reference to Yhwꜣ in the list headed by a name that he read as Seir, which with biblical link to Yahweh in Judg 5:4 yielded a location in Edom. Giveon and others maintained the same orientation toward biblical lore.[39] Although Astour's particular identifications often fail to persuade, lacking any demonstrable connection to a coherent ancient geography or conception, he offers an important alternate vision, considering whether the names could be interpreted without a southern bias. Adrom and Müller are at least sympathetic to Astour's approach, though they attempt a distance from the whole debate over Yahweh's origins, available as Egyptian specialists to referee use of this material. With his animal interpretations, Görg abandons the geographical approach entirely, also an important option to keep in view, even as his identifications carry the same feel of speculation – phonological and conceptual possibilities that have nothing substantial to prove them. For my own analysis of the Egyptian evidence, I prefer to give greatest weight to the fact that the names are entirely unknown, not part of any attested landscape for Late Bronze Age (or later) western Asia.

This novelty of the listed names should then be joined to a second crucial detail from the Soleb and 'Amarah West evidence: these are the only references to the Shasu in all the extant evidence that name subdivisions of the category – actual Shasu entities. That is, if we were to attempt a map or a population breakdown of the Shasu, to attach any more particular names to them, no further evidence would be available. The Yhwꜣ entity thus belongs to a very short list of attested Shasu units. Keeping in view this unique combination with "Shasu-land," it is therefore essential to ask how the Shasu would have been constituted as groups, whether in their own eyes or in the eyes of the Egyptians who

---

[39] Ahituv's 1984 geographical study is cautious and essential, though the biblical default is evident in his decisions regarding "Jahu" (121–22) and "Laban (2)" (129). "Laban" (*Rbn*) is "to be identified with Biblical Laban (Deut 1:1) = Libnah (Num 33:20–21)," as well as a Laban that is associated with Egypt in a Sargon II Assyrian text. For "Jahu (Yāhū)," see below, with reference to Mount Sinai.

encountered them. Here, we do best to set aside biblical names and their much later and wholly unrelated contexts, whether as people or places; and equally, we cannot place confidence in a historical geography derived from modern village names, as undertaken by Astour. As already observed, these efforts have not produced convincing results.

The best place to begin is with the Egyptian evidence for the Shasu, the essential category in question. First of all, the name itself defines for New Kingdom Egyptian scribes and administrators a category roughly translated as "nomad," an Egyptian term with a degree of social imprecision similar to its English counterpart. These were people identifiable above all by their mobility, associated with life in tents and with flocks. As already observed, the preponderance of Shasu reference occurs during and after the reign of Ramses II, in the 13th century, and the only narrative accounts of the Shasu are found in this later period, long after Amenhotep III and the Soleb temple. Two of these later literary papyri describe the Shasu with some detail, not from direct knowledge and individual names, but still usefully.[40]

Papyrus Anastasi VI (Giveon Document 37; Merenptah, 1213–1203) 54–56:
We have finished passing the tribes [*mhwt*] of the Shasu of Edom through the Fortress of Merneptah-Hotephirma, L.P.H. in Theku, to the pools of Pithom, of Merneptah-Hotephirma in Theku, in order to sustain them and their herds in the domain of Pharaoh, L.P.H. the good Sun of every land.

Papyrus Harris I (Giveon Document 38; Ramses III, 1189–1153) 76:9–11:[41]
I destroyed the people of Seir, of the tribes of the Shasu [*mhwt šȝsw*]; I plundered their tents [*ihr.w*], their people, their possessions, their cattle likewise, without number. They were pinioned and brought as captives, as tribute of Egypt.[42]

In both of these texts, the Shasu are understood to be subdivided specifically as *mhwt*, a term that has a genealogical rather than a spatial basis, as

---

[40] In his discussion of how the Egyptians interacted with Iron Age I pastoralists in the Negev, Tebes (2006: 78–79) presents both of these texts in translation, which I follow.

[41] The Papyrus Harris I as such dates from the reign of Ramses IV, though it relates events associated with Ramses III. Morris (2005: 691) calls it a "posthumous celebration" of the life of Ramses III. In the long papyrus, there is a cluster at the end of accounts related to events from the reign of Ramses III, including references to wars with the Sea Peoples (76:6–9); the Shasu (76:9–11); and the Libyans (76:11–77:6). These are followed by accomplishments not associated with war and then an account of the king's death and the accession of Ramses IV (79:4–7). Grandet (1994: 1.337) translates the Shasu section as follows: "J'ai réduit en poussière les Sârou, de la tribu des Shasou. J'ai dépouilleé leurs tentes (ou: leurs campements?) de leurs gens, de leurs biens et de leurs (têtes de) bétail semblablement, sans limites. Ayant été liés (par les bras) et amenés prisonniers comme butin de Kémet, je les ai donnés à (chacun des membres de) l'Ennéade, pour être (litt. En tant qu')esclaves de (litt.: pour) son (litt.: leur) domaine."

[42] For *ihr* as "tent," a loan from Semitic (*'hl*), see Grandet 1994 (2.243, n.921).

"families." David O'Connor (1987: 35) observes in relation to the Meshwesh and the Libu of Libya:

> The Meshwesh and the Libu probably lived in Cyrenaica, where climate and environment made a nomadic or semi-nomadic way of life based on herding the most efficient one to follow. They were described by the Egyptians as *mhwt*, a word translated literally as "family"; however, as applied uniquely to these groups and to the nomadic Shasu of Palestine, *mhwt* clearly refers to a larger social group. By using this term the Egyptians were apparently emphasizing the primacy of kinship within the social and political organization of the Meshwesh and Libu, a characteristic shared with modern nomadic tribal societies such as the Bedouin.

Although the two references to "families/tribes of the Shasu" are later than Amenhotep III, they offer an approach to understanding Egyptian expectations of Shasu subunits that leads away from a geography defined strictly by settlements, by fixed topographical features such as mountains or springs, or by fixed sacred sites. Each of these later texts names what the Egyptians consider a territorial space, "Edom" in Papyrus Anastasi VI and "Seir" in Papyrus Harris I, and then locate within that space a Shasu population organized by kinship (*mhwt*).[43] The "Shasu-land" of the early 14th-century Soleb list follows the same logic of kin-based units within a unified territory, except that instead of adopting Edom and Seir, the lands known to late 13th- and 12th-century Egypt, it avoids any regional name in favor of a generic "Shasu" place. Comparison of the two papyri underscores the problem with including Seir in the older Soleb text: in Papyrus Harris I, Seir is not one of the Shasu units but rather the overarching region that locates all of them together.[44] The authors of the Soleb list and its sources chose neither Seir nor Edom as the land of the Shasu, when these appear to have been the regional names available to later Egyptians for just this identification.

The Soleb and 'Amarah West lists envision some territorial expanse, comparable to the upper and lower "lands" that constitute Egypt, by which a mass of defeated Shasu people could be identified and located.[45]

---

[43] Grandet 1994 (2.244, n.921) translates *mhwt* as "tribe" (tribu) and observes "l'importance relative du groupement humain nommé *mhwt*, par rapport à d'autres groupements humains mentionnés dans les sources égyptiennes" ("the relative importance of the human grouping called *mhwt* with respect to other human groupings mentioned in Egyptian sources").

[44] Grandet (1994: 2.244–45 n.921) considers that the reference to Seir in Papyrus Harris I may be associated with new exploitation of the copper mines at Timna during the reign of Ramses III.

[45] For the word *t3* in "Shasu-land," see Faulkner 1962: 292: "earth" (opposed to sky, other world); "land" (opposed to water); in geographical sense; "ground"; Egypt has "two lands"; plural flat-lands as opposed to "hill-countries."

By defining the specific Shasu in question by a geographical "(low)land," the Egyptian scribes also attribute to the distinct Shasu units places within that lowland, though it is difficult to know whether the writers had particular places in mind, based on ongoing Egyptian contact there.[46] Conceptually, these places would share the character of the Shasu "land" as a whole, an extended lowland that could have individual parts named Trbr, Yhwȝ, Smt, and Pyspys.[47] It is central to my analysis that the names for the distinct Shasu units were not assigned by Egyptian scribes but rather are taken from indigenous Semitic identities. With full acknowledgment of the Egyptian interest in controlled geographical space, the notion of Shasu "families" indicates Egyptian consciousness, or stereotyping, of mobile herding communities by a kinship-based social organization. Evidence for Amorite pastoralists in the early second millennium, for Arameans of the early first millennium, for tribal categories in first-millennium South Arabia (see Chapter 7), and even for Israel's tribal tradition (Fleming 2012a), attests to a long pattern of social organization by kinship in Syria, the Levant, and Arabia. We are confronted with two lines of evidence that point to the likelihood that the indigenous Shasu were organized, at least in part, by such kinship-based bodies: the long-standing regional pattern; and the Egyptian perception as represented in the texts from the late 13th and 12th centuries.

I linger on this discussion of social organization and physical space because it is essential to my understanding of Trbr, Yhwȝ, Smt, and Pyspys in the Soleb geographical collection, and because this conception of the Shasu names is not obvious to my Egyptological interlocutors. For Betsy Bryan, the choice would be between a "tribe" and a "locale." As I understand the relationship between social organization and space, these are not mutually exclusive, as decisively true for the kingdoms of first-millennium South Arabia (see Chapter 7). What is unavoidable is that the

---

[46] Betsy Bryan (personal communication) observes, "The knowledge of the local people residing in areas where Egypt operated actively appears to have been left to those who were posted to the Levant and reported back to Egypt on circuits where they could advise based on that information. But the references to external areas that appear in literary sources, and thus monumental sources, are dominated by how Egypt and Egyptians experienced and/or impacted those areas."

[47] Bryan (personal communication) comments that the only version of these names with a determinative is the later list from Medinet Habu (Ramses III, 1189–1153), and this marks "hill country." As I understand the designations, depending on the expertise of Egyptologists, the *tȝ* of the original list represents lowland, so that the Medinet Habu conception appears to be a reinterpretation by association with later experience of the Shasu population.

names represent groups of people not identified by towns, even as the Egyptian scribes located them in a larger "land" that they call simply "the land of the Shasu," which I have rendered as "Shasu-land." In the original Amenhotep III setting, we cannot tell to what degree the Egyptian administrators imposed their own geographical sensibilities on the Shasu population they confronted, but the Shasu category itself and the later references to "families" indicate consciousness of contrast. With or without particular territorial associations, the individual Shasu units are most easily understood to derive from indigenous social and political organization, which Egyptian scribes could render collectively by the kinship term *mhwt*.

In his unique interpretation of the Soleb and 'Amarah West lists, Manfred Görg was therefore correct to pursue names that need not be defined by settlements or landmarks, even as his focus on animal features as tribes was far too narrow. For example, we should not require such a limited range for the names of Israel's biblical tribes.[48] The kinship-based definition of Shasu units is primary, whether or not they were imagined by the Egyptians to reflect spatial subdivisions within the territorial whole. As argued by Anne Porter (2009 and 2012) for greater Mesopotamia through the mid-second millennium, kinship allows the creation and maintenance of social bonds across distance, without the natural face-to-face interaction of life together in settlements or the connecting structures of large kingdoms and their institutions.[49] At every social and political order of magnitude, bonds and identities defined by kinship

---

[48] Think of Asher as "happy"; Dan as "strong"; and Gad as "fortune." Ephraim and Judah are attached to "highlands" (*hār*), perhaps more territorial; Benjamin is the "son of the right hand," like and probably derived from the Binu Yamina of the Mari archives – and so on.

[49] Porter (2009: 201) explains that early Mesopotamian pastoralism has been understood in terms of "fragmentation and dispersal," the breakdown of the social bonds forged by the concentration of population made possible by irrigation agriculture (Lees and Bates 1974). Working from Anthony Giddens's (1981) idea of "time–space distanciation," the creation of social bonds that maintain relationship without regular face-to-face interaction, so that "separation" need not be the result of "fragmentation." Porter (202) summarizes her analysis as follows: "I suggest there is evidence that indicates time and space was transcended in the ancient Near East, certainly in the third and second millennia B.C., by an intricate mesh of social structures, political ideologies, religious beliefs, rituals, and other practices, that, whether consciously intended or not, had the effect of binding disparate, and distant, components of the sociopolitical entity into one. This complex of structure, thought, and practice was constitutive of ideologies of kinship – not kinship as pre-existing in actual connections through birth, although they are both present and implicit, but kinship as created and incorporative of networks of social relations no matter actual birth relations."

could operate effectively, uniting populations that incorporated both agricultural and pastoral modes of subsistence, as well as both long-range movement and fixed settlement, even in large towns and cities.[50] The cuneiform archives of 18th-century Mari on the Euphrates River provide diverse examples of just this sort of integration between kinship and settlement, territorial space and the ability to cross its bounds, that is seen – with only partial comprehension – through Egyptian eyes in their accounts of the Shasu.[51]

These Near Eastern phenomena provide a context for evaluation of the individual names for the units of Shasu-land in the Soleb list and its later variant from 'Amarah West. In the end, it is not necessary to seek out precedents for Late Bronze Age tribal or people names that were not likely defined by settlements or topographical features. "The *mhwt* of the Shasu" provide an Egyptian framework for understanding this unique set of individual Shasu identities, but even if the Soleb scribes were imagining some other basis for defining parts of this "land," they were naming groups of people to confront and to rule, or to wish to do so.

A Landscape from Amenhotep III

Along with Shasu social organization, it is equally important to recognize what lies behind the textual commonality of the Soleb and the 'Amarah West lists: a single moment of Egyptian contact with the Shasu people in circumstances that could generate knowledge of real Shasu group-names.

---

[50] Thus, Porter rejects vehemently the evolutionary division of "tribe" as small and primitive from "state" as large, complex, and advanced. In the conclusion to her systematic study of early pastoralism (2012: 328), she argues, "It is this duality between social and political function and identity – a duality that emerges, splits, and merges again – that is often mistaken for two political forms, tribe and state. The conflation between social interactions, and social identities, and political organization under the rubric 'tribe' has too long muddied the waters."

[51] One illuminating text reminds the king at Mari how his "Ḥana" (Tent-dwelling) people, otherwise identified as the "sons of Sim'al," are distinguished from the "sons of Yamina," their cousins and rivals. "While the land of Yamḫad, the land of Qatna, and the land of Amurrum are the range(?) of the Yaminites – and in each of those lands the Yaminites have their fill of barley and pasture their flocks – from the start(?), the range(?) of the Ḥana has been Ida-Maraṣ" (Fleming 2004: 29, my translation; the full letter A.2730 was published by Durand 2004: 120–21). Each population is defined by a combination of husbandry of flocks and farming of grain, mixing movement and settlement in patterns that allow them to live in multiple "lands" (*mātum*).

Just as the precise attachments of the Shasu-land names remain out of reach, their Semitic language of origin is evident; part of what makes them so elusive is the surfeit of etymological possibilities. The Egyptians would not have made them up, and their recurrence in related Nubian temple displays indicates a single source. Given the earlier appearance in the Soleb temple, both the ultimate written source and the occasion of the specific Shasu contact must come from the reign of Amenhotep III (1390–1352) or earlier. This means that we have to rely on the much smaller corpus of evidence for the Shasu from the 15th and early 14th centuries as a context for this encounter.

We cannot know the date of the contact that generated the Soleb list, whether as a single military confrontation or as a more enduring administrative relationship. Amenhotep III displays an interest in Nubia that was much more intimate than in the Levant, with expression of this in Egyptian construction at the Island of Saï, Sedenga, and Soleb (Goedicke 1992: 13–14). Goedicke (37, 48–9) identifies the construction of the Soleb temple, which gives particular attention to the deified Amenhotep III himself, as having strong political motivation, consolidating Egyptian administrative control and financial demands in Nubia. The documentation of pharaohs from the 15th and 14th centuries gives the general impression that Thutmose III (1479–1425) and Amenhotep II (1427–1400) pursued more intensive military activity in the Levant than Thutmose IV (1400–1390) and Amenhotep III (Bryan 1998).[52] Weinstein (1998: 224 n.5) finds that

The two topographical lists preserved from the king's reign – at Soleb ... and Kom el-Hetan ... – while impressive in their rosters of place-names from Asia (and, in the case of the Kom el-Hetan list, the Aegean), reflect no military conquests and should be looked at in the context of Egypt's wide international relations during the early fourteenth century B.C.

While this may make sense for their sweeping symbolism, we are left to wonder when the details of the "Shasu-land" depicted at Soleb found their way into Egyptian scribal knowledge. If Amenhotep III took no

---

[52] According to Weinstein (1998: 223), "The military and diplomatic achievements of the early Eighteenth Dynasty kings (especially Thutmose III) had made it unnecessary for Amenhotep III's two immediate predecessors – Amenhotep II and Thutmose IV – to undertake more than a few 'mopping up' operations." So, "not once during his nearly four decades on the throne did the king have to lead an Egyptian army onto Asiatic soil" (224). Kozloff and Bryan (1992: 37) comment on the general absence of military interest in the documentation for Amenhotep III, with the only dated campaign in his fifth year, against the "tribes in Kush" (Sudan).

evident initiative in the inland Levantine regions, the exchange that yielded such specific knowledge may precede this king.[53]

It is also difficult to evaluate the character of the contact between Egyptian authorities and specific Shasu entities. At the time of Amenhotep III, the southernmost of Egypt's Levantine administrative districts was governed as "Canaan" (Weinstein 1998: 226–27), with day-to-day administration left to local town rulers (228). Egypt was involved with mining turquoise at Serabit el-Khadim in southwestern Sinai (234). There is no evidence for ongoing administration of Shasu populations in any of the regions with which they are associated in the small number of early documents (see below). It may be simpler to associate the list with a single moment, a military conflict that the Egyptians could claim as victory, with prisoners and more taken – and recorded – from Shasu entities with particular names. The images of bound prisoners represent ideal world domination, but the context of that ideal is military, and the people and products taken in battle could offer a setting for listed origins without requiring long-term administration. In general, the Shasu evidence gathered by Giveon does not depict an ongoing bureaucratic framework for relationship to Egypt.

At the same time as we must give the Soleb list priority in determining the source and setting for the Shasu identities, we also cannot expect the earlier and later forms of the list to provide a complete match. The distance in time between the Soleb and the 'Amarah West lists, followed by another several decades and substantial distance before the Medinet Habu list of Ramses III, should prepare us for the likelihood of textual variation and development. Rather than treat the evident textual relationship between these lists as a basis for reconstructing a single Ur-text that is beyond reach, we do better to expect and to explore the implications of change. With the two lists at the center of our interest here, the relationship is close and clear, clear enough to allow consideration of them as distinct expressions of the list in question. Two traits stand out: the order of the names has been reversed; and the later list from 'Amarah West has most likely been extended by either one or two names. These features

---

[53] This is not to say that the Soleb list as such originated before the reign of Amenhotep III. Cline (1998: 240) considers that the concentration of references to Tanaja as mainland Greece represents one confirmation of this conclusion. Betsy Bryan (personal communication) considers it possible that the individual names in the Soleb list for the land of the Shasu could have represented new information from the period of Amenhotep III's administration, a solution that would separate the names from the portrayal as prisoners from a defeated people.

suggest a connection between them: the reversal has been coordinated with a new introductory name: *š'rr*. It is conceivable, though to me highly unlikely for a set of nine names, that the lists reflect contemporary variants, and that this is an otherwise unknown Shasu group-name missing from the older version. If S'rr was original to the list, the Ramses II scribes would appear to have conflated it with the Seir (*š'r*) they knew and reversed the sequence in order to move it to the first position. The 'Amarah West text is later, however, from a time when Egyptian military conflict had receded from Syria into the southern Levant, and S'rr looms as a potential reflection of these transformed circumstances. If the actual Shasu interaction that generated the Soleb list dated to the reign of Amenhotep III or before, then the recasting of that list for the reign of Ramses II and 'Amarah West would be detached from the specific contact and must be evaluated separately.

Given the unique character of the Shasu-land list of subdivisions, it is impossible to reconstruct with certainty the administrative need that inspired its initial composition, which would not initially have been for monumental display. The Soleb temple was powerfully identified with the king in a way that pushed the bounds of earlier politics and religion, and its decoration with an accumulation of individual bound prisoners, carefully identified by names from the whole world surrounding Egypt, reflected "the display and ritual killing of prisoners of war" (Kozloff 2012: 169–70). Whether or not the groups from Shasu-land were already known and recorded from some previous exchange, this early application of the list assumes military defeat and the identification of specific subordinated peoples. Whereas the Egyptians seem to have coined the term Shasu for the very purpose of stereotype, to flatten one version of the foreign into a single outsider identity, devoid of specificity, this one list produces the opposite effect, acknowledging the known individuality of each named entity. It did not happen again, which suggests all the more that there was some particular purpose to the administrative occasion.[54]

---

[54] Betsy Bryan (personal communication) observes that the sequence of "land" – "Shasu" – Trbr/Yhwȝ/etc. follows the established practice of scribal administration, adding information by moving from the general to the specific, as available. This is indeed how I understand the individual Shasu names, and the question then is whether the administrative occasion is the accounting for prisoners or booty at the time of a particular conflict, or whether it derives from extended Egyptian administration of "the land of the Shasu" under these categories. As I understand the possibilities, both would be defined by groups of people identified as subsidiary to the Shasu made coherent by their

RAMSES II AND SEIR: REINTERPRETATION OF THE SHASU

The one name crucial to understanding the difference between the Soleb and the 'Amarah West lists for the Shasu-land is Sʿrr (*šʿrr*), which Grdseloff identified with the biblical Seir, in spite of the second -*r*. Since this first foray, every study of the material has taken a stand one way or the other on the name: either it cannot be Seir because of the mistaken spelling; or the spelling can be explained variously and is no barrier to the obvious identification. With his assertive turn to the north, Astour sought a specific alternative and proposed it in the city of Šeḫlal, near Ṣumur and Amurru in the most northern part of Egypt's Levantine sphere of interest.[55] More cautiously, but with sympathy for Astour's northern effort, Adrom and Müller (2017: 99–101) express doubt that the doubled final -*rr* could have represented a legitimate spelling of Seir, which should be rendered as *šʿr*. There are strong arguments from the other side, whether for appropriate orthography or as scribal slip. Redford (1992: 272 n.67) observes that the double -*rr* is in keeping with Late Egyptian orthography, "which often sought to distinguish a consonantal 'trilled' *r* from a uvularized *r* by writing it twice." Ahituv (1984: 169) comments, "The duplicated *r* of the 'Amāra-West list is in line with the careless orthography of the whole list (cf. nos. 67, 97, and 103, where the ʿ in the name *Knʿn*, 'Canaan' is duplicated)."

It appears that there are technical arguments for and against the likelihood of reading Sʿrr as Seir, and caution might suggest leaving the question open. The solution is crucial neither to my reading of the Soleb text nor to my conclusion, since both considerations of physical extent and the passing observation of Giveon (1964: 245, above) indicate that the original Amenhotep III list probably lacked the name. Nevertheless, the addition of this name and its placement at the front of a reversed sequence, effectively recasting the list under the heading of Sʿrr, call for explanation. How would this name offer a clarifying rubric? The probability that this name occurs only in the later text is not generally discussed in relation to this issue, and my conclusion on this point would

---

shared "land." I have already observed that the Shasu category is not generally associated with continuous Egyptian rule, with persisting structures.

[55] See the Amarna letters EA 62 and EA 371; Astour accounts carefully for the linguistic considerations of sibilant and laryngeal consonants, but the location itself has no basis in the context of Egyptian contacts with the Shasu as reflected in the evidence gathered by Giveon (1971).

align with a larger pattern in the use of the name Seir: its association with the Shasu only emerges in the 13th century, with Ramses II.[56]

A Ramses II obelisk from Tanis includes the following inscription: "The fierce lion, full of rage who ... plundered the Shasu-land and seized the mountain of Seir by his mighty arm."[57] The section already cited from Papyrus Harris I (Ramses III, 1184–1153) identifies the families of the Shasu with the "people of Seir" (above). These two important references to Seir define Egyptian understanding of the Shasu people during the period beginning in the reign of Ramses II, after Egypt stepped away from its major conflicts in Syria.[58] They identify the Shasu people in broad terms with Seir in a way that is completely absent from earlier Egyptian evidence (see below). The Ramses II obelisk pairs "the mountain of Seir" with "Shasu-land" in a way that recalls and perhaps even interprets the Amenhotep III list, which unifies these people as "Shasu-land" (*tꜣ šꜣsw*), not Seir. Likewise, as seen in the Papyrus Anastasi VI selection, Edom can stand in similar relation to the Shasu as a population.[59]

Another consideration in evaluating the apparent 13th-century revision of an older Shasu-land list is the larger character of geographical representation under Ramses II and his successors. When it comes to toponym lists in particular, the category develops an increasingly stereotyped aspect, and by the 13th century examples, they are understood to require a skeptical approach. Redford (1992: 143) observes, "Apart from the extensive toponym lists of Thutmose III, which derive from itineraries, the lists of later kings decrease in value as reflections of historic events."[60] He gives an example of a text from Seti I (Qurnah; Simons 1937, no. XV), with twelve names (nos. 13–24), "which could plausibly be linked to the Beth-Shean campaign of year 1, only to include in the same list such

---

[56] See the full list of citations in Ahituv (1984: 169), including several from the reign of Ramses II (note texts from Gebel Shaluf and Tanis).

[57] Giveon Document 25; this is translated to English directly from Giveon (1971: 100). In the copy of Giveon, Shasu-land does appear to share the *tꜣ* identifier of the Soleb and 'Amarah West geographical lists.

[58] Giveon (1971: 112) remarks that during the period of Ramses II, the Shasu were especially the inhabitants of southeastern Palestine, so Edom and Seir. This is what one might conclude from the Egyptian texts and their perspective, at least.

[59] Edom is mentioned as the provenance of a clan granted permission to enter the area of Sile with herds under the reign of Seti II (Papyrus Anastasi VII 54–55) – also later (Ahituv 1984: 90). Moab, another eastern name from the southern Levant, also makes a first appearance in the time of Ramses II, in a more extensive part of the 'Amarah West list (Ahituv 1984: 143).

[60] Redford's sources are especially the *Handbook* by Simons (1937); and Edel (1966).

impossible sites as Cyprus, Assyria, Paba(n)hi (in north Mesopotamia – twice!), Takhsy (twice!), and Qatna (ibid., XIV, no.31) no longer in existence" (143 n.61).

Different kinds of geographical adjustments characterize the lists of Ramses II, which I illustrate from texts that include the Shasu and so form part of the systematic collection by Giveon (1971). In some cases, names with specific associations and sources, such as military engagements and their records, may be merged with generic names that reflect an Egyptian sense of the whole world, cast as the Nine Bows. An example is Giveon's Document 20b, starting with Shat, Mentiou-nou-Setet, Peditiou, Tehenou, and Sehet Yam (his orthography).[61] Another type includes pairs of names that represent geographical extremes: north and south, east and west. For the reign of Ramses II, Giveon considers Document 24 (from Bubastis) to be an example, setting Nubia on one hand in opposition to "the land of the Shasu" on the other, as south and north.[62] This would be an interesting choice, not considering the Shasu to be eastern, since these are then represented by Tehenu in the next line, and Giveon (99) expects the missing element to be Libya, which would provide an east–west contrast.

The introduction of Seir into the Shasu-land list would represent something else. In the 12th century, Papyrus Harris I identifies the Shasu population broadly with Seir, not as a subset but for the whole, pairing their defeats. If Sꜥrr was original to the Soleb list, it is not clear whether or not this name matches "Seir" (šꜥr), but in this context the name would represent only one unit of "Shasu-land," side by side with the rest. If this sixth name was added only in the time of Ramses II, it would represent an innovation, the work of a scribe impressed by the unique specificity of the Shasu names, perhaps recognizing the rarity of such information and reveling in the record of Egypt's intrusion into their wilderness world. At 'Amarah West, the scribe would have maintained the particularity of the source while redefining this Shasu-land according to the experience current to the 13th century. Without knowledge of its peoples, Egypt identified the space east of Canaan by regional names: Seir, Edom, and Moab. In the early 14th century, Egypt confronted a Shasu population in space given no further identification, so that we know only

---

[61] Anthony (2016: 39) lists, with Egyptian orthography provided, the full New Kingdom set of the Nine Bows as Haw-nbw, Shat, Ta-Shema, Sekhet-Iam, Ta-Mehu, Pedjtiu-Shu, Tjehenu, Jwntjw-Stj, and Mentiu-Setjt.

[62] Again, the Shasu "land" is indicated by the tꜣ writing.

their way of life as understood by outsiders. Trbr, Yhw3, Smt, and Pyspys, at least, were subunits of a Shasu "land," which the later "tribes/families of the Shasu" suggest may have belonged to kinship structures. Where was this Shasu-land, during or before the time of Amenhotep III? There is no definitive answer, when none of the names can be located convincingly. Was it in the desert south, already aligned with Seir? For context, we must turn to the small set of documents from the 15th and 14th centuries, during the 18th Dynasty (Giveon's Documents 1–10).

THE SHASU IN THE 15TH AND 14TH CENTURIES

There is a chronological clustering of references to the Shasu in Egyptian texts. Not only do the largest number come from the reign of Ramses II in the 13th century but the few early texts are separated by more than 50 years between the latest under Amenhotep III and the reappearance of the name with Seti I (1294–1279).[63] This separation of reference sharpens the geographical contrast between the small earlier and larger later groups of texts. Even if Sʿrr belonged to the older list, the geography of Amenhotep III's Shasu-land remains uncertain. For context, the Shasu references from the 15th and early 14th centuries lack entirely the deep southern orientation of the 13th- and 12th-century texts, with their links to Seir and Edom.

Egypt's empire in the Levant was established above all by Thutmose III (1479–1425), who campaigned all the way to the Euphrates River and aimed to annex much of what he had assaulted.[64] Since the Middle Kingdom, the Egyptians had given the name Retenu to the whole Levant, and after a major battle at Megiddo against allied kings of Canaan, including the key center of Kadesh, the defeated rulers were forced to swear loyalty oaths: "The lands of Retenu shall not again rebel on another occasion."[65] Giveon's Document 2 belongs to the same king: "Year 39. His majesty was in Retenu during his 14th victorious campaign, after he was (over) the defeated Shasu."[66] Although Giveon reads

---

[63] Giveon (1971: 31–38) gathers three visual portrayals of Shasu on two tombs from el-Amarna (Documents 8a–c); two more on the tomb of Horemheb at Memphis (Documents 9 and 10).

[64] For a historical overview, see Redford 1992: 156–62. For further discussion, see Redford (2003); Cline and O'Connor (2006), especially the contributions by O'Connor and Redford.

[65] Redford (1992: 158), from the Barkal stela, line 21.

[66] This is my translation from Giveon (1971: 11).

this text as confirming a southern location for the Shasu, the combination
of Retenu and the Shasu just as easily places the latter in inland regions
further north at a time when Thutmose III was occupied with pushing his
power into the Euphrates in aggressive challenge to the great Mittani
kingdom.[67]

The next reference to the Shasu comes from the reign of Amenhotep II
(1427–1400) and includes them among a list of 89,600 prisoners, headed
by 127 "chiefs of Retenu" and 179 of their "kin" (brothers). The captives
are then grouped as 'Apiru (3,600), "living Shasu" (15,200), Kharu
(36,300), "living Nuḫašše" (15,070), and their families (30,652).
Neither the 'Apiru nor the Shasu designations indicate particular location,
Kharu (from the "Hurrians" of Mittani) could refer broadly to Asiatics[68],
and Nuḫašše is in the northern Levant, east of the Orontes and south of
Aleppo in modern Syria. Without attempting to force the text to offer
geographical information that cannot be extracted from it, the
Amenhotep II list offers only a land far north of Palestine for its one point
of reference.[69]

Beyond the two Soleb texts from the reign of Amenhotep III, we have
only a short list of names on the royal chariot of Thutmose IV (Document
4) and three more Amenhotep III texts, all likewise toponym lists
(Documents 5, 5a, and 7). These appear to divide between geographical
accounts of Egypt's world domination (4, 5, and 7) and the more particular interest of Document 5a, which in this respect resembles the two Soleb
lists. Together, therefore, the three Amenhotep lists with particular focus

---

[67] Redford (1992: 159–60). Note that Giveon's Document 1 comes from the reign of
Thutmose II, with simple reference to prisoners brought back from the Shasu.

[68] The 'Apiru in New Kingdom Egyptian texts, as evident especially from the 14th-century
letters found at el-Amarna, were populations that Egypt could not reliably control. They
were not particularly associated with herding and the movement of flocks. In older use,
the term designated people who had moved from their original residence, still capable of
maintaining ties to that home (Fleming 2012b).

[69] The reign of Amenhotep II appears to have coincided with the early rise of Hittite power
and a reestablishment of Mittani interest in the west, eventually resulting in alliance
between Egypt and Mittani in the face of Hittite expansion (Redford 1992: 162–65). In
the context of a campaign against Nuḫašše, in northern Syria deep inland, it is unlikely
that any deep southern contingent was involved. It is more natural to take the 'Apiru and
Shasu as categories of population not defined geographically and picked up in the same
general undertaking that generated all the Nuḫašše prisoners – perhaps or probably as
allies to Nuḫašše. The Kharu would likewise be allies or others from the region picked up
on the same campaign that had Nuḫašše as its target.

compose the oldest such texts that name the Shasu, and we do not encounter the same approach until the 19th Dynasty and Seti I.[70]

All of these older lists, idealized and particular alike, are oriented especially toward Asia and none of them shows any demonstrable concern for the southern wilderness. The one other focused list (Document 5a), a group of names on the socle of a colossus from the funerary temple of Amenhotep III at Thebes, appears to revolve around northern Palestine, where Thutmose III had won a major victory at Megiddo in the early 15th century. The set includes six names:[71] *ḥps, ʿyn šȝsw, skr, dtn, mt, šmʿn*.[72] While Giveon gives priority to *dtn*, which he identifies as Dothan based in part on its appearance in Gen 37:22, where Joseph finds his brothers with their herds, this reading only becomes convincing in combination with *šmʿn*, which Giveon (23) reasonably equates to Šamḫuna of EA 225:4, evidently in the Jezreel Valley.[73] The second item on the list is the unique "Shasu Spring" (*ʿyn šȝsw*), which names a

---

[70] The *Handbook* by Simons (1937) shows no lack of topographical lists for the 18th Dynasty: five for Thutmose III, including two long ones (one for the Megiddo campaign and Palestine; the other for Naharina and the north); two fragmentary ones for Amenhotep II; two short lists on a chariot for Thutmose IV (as list VIII); and two for Amenhotep III (one long, mostly for Africa, list IX). Then Dynasty 19 begins already with two from the time of Haremheb. That is, there is no gap comparable to the one evident in references to the Shasu. It appears that the Shasu only become a standard part of the listing genre with Ramses II. So far as the Shasu are concerned, the first example of the type focused on a specific region after Amenhotep III does not occur until Ramses II (Document 20) at Karnak, in a list dependent on two lists from Seti I from the same structure (Simons lists XIII and XIV); see Giveon (1971: 85, 87). Simons's list XIV is the source for Giveon's Document 12 (Seti I), which extracts lines 20–36 from a longer text with more ambitious range and perhaps a mix of actual and idealized conquests; Simons identifies lines 20–36 and 51–67 as related to Asia, in a list of 67 entries; Document 20 is also an extract from a longer list (Simons XXIV). Document 12 opens in line 20 with Ḥatti, Naharin (Mittani), Lower and Upper Retenu, and Babylon (*sngr*), imagining a very wide reach, as if prisoners from all these lands and peoples could suffer "immolation" (slaughter) before the pharaoh.

[71] This text was not available to Simons, and it appears in Edel (1966: 25–6; cf. Edel and Görg 2005: 103–18, combining Edel's earlier text with Görg's elaboration). Giveon (1971: 22) says that in general the socle of each colossus bears a series of toponyms, inscribed within ovals below portrayals of Asiatics, with only the upper bodies and heads visible. There are other toponyms listed on the same socle, with 19 missing from the adjacent group.

[72] For the Shasu texts presented in Giveon (1971), I retain his orthography for this discussion of the early documents.

[73] Rainey (1976) identified the site with Tel Shimron at the northwestern tip of the Jezreel Valley; cf. Finkelstein and Naʾaman (2005: 177). Daniel Master is now in the early stages of new excavations at Tel Shimron.

targeted site rather than a region or people, yet not necessarily a settlement.[74] In the company of Dothan and Šamḫuna, two towns in fairly
close proximity, ʿÊn Shasu is easiest to place in some relation to the valley
system that cuts across northern Palestine.[75] As a whole, this set is striking
for its relative obscurity, without names that suggest the grand scope of
Egypt's power and reputation.[76] Here we are offered the fine grain of
Egypt's intrusion into Asia, evidently with focus on a region crucial to the
early establishment of its empire.

The other three older lists display the importance of the Shasu to
Egypt's sense of itself as a world power with reach toward
Mesopotamia. Thutmose IV's chariot (Document 4) includes the Shasu
among six names, beginning with Mittani as Naharin and then embedding the Shasu in a group of key Syrian sites: *nhrn*, *sngr*, *twnp*, *šȝsw*, *qdš*
(*y*), and *tḫsy*; Naharin, Babylon, Tunip, Shasu, Kadesh, and Takhsi.[77]
Tunip and Kadesh were major political centers in western Syria when
Egypt first launched itself into Asia, perhaps gaining from a reduction in
the power of nearby Qatna.[78] Both Tunip and Kadesh were in the
drainage of the Orontes River, east of Lebanon and north of
Palestine.[79] Takhsi was likewise on the Orontes, though further south,
between Kadesh and Damascus.[80] In this context, placement of the Shasu
in sequence with three major capitals of central Syria indicates their
importance for Egypt's effort to win control of this inland region, which
had served as an avenue for the assertion of Mittani's interest in the
region.[81] When Ramses II fought his famous battle with the Hittites at
Kadesh he recorded the presence of Shasu fighters on the city's ramparts
(Document 15; cf. 14), likewise assuming their prominence in the region.

---

[74] Giveon cites Boree (1930: 85–86) for other examples. In Simons (1937), note for sites in
Syria and Palestine *ʿn šw* (list I:5) and *ʿn qnʿm* (list I:113; II:7), both in texts from
Thutmose III and not likely in the deep south.

[75] Tel Shimron and Dothan are roughly the same distance north and south of Megiddo, on
either side of the Jezreel Valley.

[76] Edel (1966: 23–26) otherwise identifies only *mt* from this group, which could match the
town of Mudue in the kingdom of Alalaḫ on the Orontes River in Syria, a considerable
distance to the north of Šamḫuna and the Jezreel Valley.

[77] Giveon follows Gardiner (Onomasticon, I 212 and II 323) for the "controversial"
identification of *sngr* with Babylon. The reading of Sangar as Babylon is now settled
(e.g. Cline 1998: 240).

[78] For the basic situation and geography, see Redford (1992: 147).

[79] The location of Tunip is not certain, but it appears to have been north (downstream) of
Kadesh in the Orontes Valley.

[80] Redford (1992: 162); with reference to Ahituv (1984: 185–87).

[81] See the discussion in Redford (2003).

According to the list for Thutmose IV, therefore, the Shasu were a major factor in subduing opposition to Egyptian ambitions in Syria, and their significance for Egypt depended on involvement in this northern Levantine setting.

The other two idealized lists, both from the reign of Amenhotep III, present an even broader scope, with names from the worldwide scheme of Nine Bows set beside a sampling of powers from the world Egypt knew, whether or not fought or defeated. In a text from the Amun temple at Karnak (Document 5), the Shasu are flanked by Naharin and Lower Egypt on the one hand and Hatti, Irtu/Arzawa, and Assur on the other (lines 4–9).[82] The list lacks any interest in the south, and Egypt's territory in the Levant is represented only at the end by three major cities from the same Orontes region: Tunip, Kadesh, and Qatna (lines 13–15). While the association is not as close as on the chariot of Thutmose IV, the same geography is suggested. One final text, which Giveon characterizes as purely conventional, lacking reference to any military accomplishment of Amenhotep III, begins with Sngr/Babylon and concludes with the Shasu, attending likewise to Kush/Nubia, Naharin/Mittani, and Tehenu/Libya, among others. There is no reference to Egypt's involvement in Syria and Palestine. The names are given in association with bound prisoners, alternating black with non-black for artistic effect (Giveon 1971: plate I), so that figures and names together give the effect of universal domination without link to narrowly conceived details, even to match names to individual prisoners. It is only significant that the Shasu represent a grand type in this Egyptian vision.

This evidence for the geography of the Shasu in the 15th and 14th centuries does not settle the location of "Shasu-land" in the Amenhotep III list from Soleb. The point is that in the earlier phases of Egyptian involvement in Asia, when conflicts were focused on the entire Levant running north to Syria, the geographical associations of mobile Shasu people tended to be more northern. As the Egyptians saw them, the Shasu were people of the wilderness, who could live without cities. This land wrapped around the more settlement-oriented coast and highlands that ran north and south across the Levant, opening into space to the east and south. All the individual units of "Shasu-land" in the early 14th century, including Yhwȝ, can only be placed somewhere in this back country, beyond easy Egyptian reach.

---

[82] The text is restored in part from a much later copy on a statue from the reign of Taharqa in the 25th Dynasty (7th century), likewise found at Karnak.

THE SHASU'S YHWȝ WITHOUT SEIR

For years, scholars in pursuit of Yahweh's origins have returned to the two related Egyptian Yhwȝ citations without reviewing the Shasu material as a whole. They have thereby relied on the longer Ramses II list to restore Seir in the older Amenhotep III text, most often in order to locate Yhwȝ in the southern wilderness of biblical poetry and Midian of Moses.[83] Giveon obviously knew and considered the entire corpus, but he let the Bible guide his interpretation of the Egyptian evidence:

A few toponyms from the combined Soleb-'Amarah West lists can be identified. It may be that Laban is the town mentioned in Deut 1:1 and situated south of Transjordan (see Doc.16a, note 2). This agrees with the mention of Seir. Yahweh's link with these regions is noted, along with other biblical texts, by the Song of Deborah: "Yahweh, when you went forth from Seir, when you marched from the countryside of Edom ..." (Judg 5:4). The toponym Yahweh (originally Beth Yahweh, the house of Yahweh) may therefore indicate a town with a sanctuary in the same region.[84]

Following Grdseloff, Giveon was ready to identify *śmt* by the Bible's 1 Chr 2:55, which offers a Kenite clan that can be interpreted to suit the Yahweh hypothesis. Ahituv had a different object in view, a systematic geography of the southern Levant according to New Kingdom Egyptian sources rather than collection of all the Shasu evidence, yet when he reaches "Jahu" from the two Shasu-land lists, he observes simply,

The *šȝsw*-land of Jahu (Yāhū) is the wandering area of the clan of the worshippers of Yāhū, the God of Israel. It most probably pertains to the region of Kadesh-barnea and Jebel Hilal, which might be the sacred Mt. Sinai.

His comments on the other listed names are similar:[85]

- Pispis: "This obscure name of some nomads and their land might be of non-Semitic origin and may refer to a Horite clan of the Seirite confederacy" (155).
- Simet: "The *šȝsw*-land of Simet is unidentified, but probably should be located in northern Sinai," seemingly only by connection with Jahu.[86]

---

[83] Astour (1979) represents a vigorous alternative; cf. Adrom and Müller (2017).

[84] Giveon (1971: 28), my translation.

[85] On *rbn* as Laban (2) as Libnah, see above. Ahituv (1984: 169) reads *ś'rr* as Seir, against Astour (1979).

[86] Giveon (1971) rejects association with Shammah son of Reuel son of Esau from Gen 36:13 and 17; 1 Chr 1:37 as "linguistically unsupported" (177).

- Twrbr: "The unidentified wandering grounds of *Twrbr*, probably in northern Sinai" (191).

When stripped of circular dependence on the Bible, these units of "Shasu-land" are left without secure geographical identification. Compared with the 12th-century Papyrus Harris I, which aligns the land of the Shasu with "the mountain of Seir," the Soleb list lacks any independent territorial reference point and leaves us only with the "Shasu-land" itself. Yhwȝ is just one group-name among a set of four or five, the principal units of some whole that Egypt knew, and as a coordinated set, perhaps fought and claimed to have defeated. All of these would thus be major Shasu entities, identified for interest in the populations named by them. Nothing in the Egyptian evidence indicates that Yhwȝ reflects a divine name.

One further morsel could contribute to the question: Thomas Schneider (2007) published evidence from New Kingdom Egypt for the West Semitic theophoric personal name, *'adōnī-rō'ē-yāh*, "My Lord is the Shepherd of Yah." Understanding Yhwȝ to be "a mountainous region linked to the worship of a god named Yahweh" (114), he suggests that the personal name would confirm the early identification with deity, with *y-h* an abbreviated form of the divine name. So far as the name *'adōnī-rō'ē-yāh* does preserve a hypocoristic or shortened form of Yhwȝ, the connection could be interpreted simply by the group-name attested for the Shasu.[87] The divine element in the theophoric name would be *'adōnī*, "My Lord," as in the Amorite name Aduna-Addu, "The Lord is Addu."[88] Appropriate to the Shasu as people with primary subsistence from herding, the personal name found in Egypt would mean, "My (Divine) Lord is the Shepherd of (the) Yah (People)."[89] The name occurs in six variants, all dated to the late 18th or 19th Dynasties, ca. 1330–1230, some decades after Yhwȝ appears during the reign of Amenhotep III.

As by far the oldest reference to the name that comes to be divine, the Egyptian evidence must provide a point of departure to examine on its own terms. In fact, the personal name *'adōnī-rō'ē-yāh* would reduce the

---

[87] Reading of Yh as a hypocoristic form of Yhwȝ would be confirmed by the same form Yh in the Medinet Habu list of Ramses III, where it precedes Tr, identified by Giveon (1964) as a reflection of the old pairing of Yhwȝ and Trbr.

[88] In the evidence from Mari, four texts preserve this name: A.1098:21, 26; *FM* II 24:16; *FM* VI 5:38, 44, 62; and TH 72.8+:48. Huffmon (1965: 20) includes this name as the only representative with this noun; Streck (2000) does not analyze the name as Amorite.

[89] In his invaluable comments to a draft of this chapter, Schneider observes that the name from his 2007 publication would suit well my interpretation of Yhwȝ as a people.

plausibility of a conclusion that Yhwʒ already represented the deity Yahweh, identified with a named group, or people. It is the people, not a god, that need a "shepherd." Most simply, Yhwʒ is one subdivision of some association of groups that the Egyptians during or before the reign of Amenhotep III considered to constitute a territorial "Shasu-land." The Ramses II source depends on material at least as old as the Amenhotep III text from Soleb. If the name Sʿrr does represent Seir, it has reoriented the older list by a 13th-century sense of the Shasu, who came to be identified with the wilderness south of settled Palestine. Considerations of space make it highly unlikely that Sʿrr could have been part of the Soleb list, which would then require uniquely mismatched α and β sets of six and three names. As a member of Shasu-land and not an inclusive region, Sʿrr would probably not be the same as the later Seir. The similarity between the two names would then account for the reversal of the listing sequence, to give priority to a name that Egyptians in the 13th century identified with Shasu space.

Aside from the Soleb list for Shasu-land, the entire set of Shasu references from the 18th Dynasty lacks any idea that this population specially inhabits the Sinai Peninsula, Negev, southern Transjordan, or adjacent Arabia. Where the sweeping geographies of Egyptian domination in Giveon's Documents 4 and 5 focus their Levantine interest in the Orontes region of Syria, the two lists with more local focus display awareness of greater Palestine: Dothan and Šamḫuna in Document 5a; Piḫilu and perhaps Gezer in Document 6. So far as the Shasu-land list likewise shares this local focus, association with lands near Palestine may be conceivable, with potential lines of connection to the east as much as to the south.

Even as I consider highly unlikely the identification of Amenhotep III's Yhwʒ with the southern wilderness of Seir, my goal is not to move the name confidently from south to north. Although the context of Egyptian interests in the 15th and early 14th centuries points away from the back country south of Canaan, we cannot locate Yhwʒ of Shasu-land and should focus instead on what we do know. This evidence is the correct starting-point for evaluating Yahweh before Israel and it offers substantial insight. Consider the following:

- Yhwʒ is logically what I will call a "people" – not a city, a topographical landmark, or a sacred site. So far as the name is indigenous to the Shasu population, it would have identified a social and potentially political unit, a body that shared identity and perhaps the capacity to act together. It does not make sense that the Shasu themselves would have regarded these names as purely spatial without reference to population. In later texts the Egyptians understood the Shasu to be organized by "families" as groups defined by kinship (*mhwt*). This character leaves open the question of their relation to territory and the possibility of movement across political boundaries not defined by them and others like them, as attested in evidence from early second-millennium Mari.

- The Yhwӡ people are what the Egyptians identified as Shasu, linked to territory deeper inland and more difficult for the Egyptians to master, associated with reliance on herding for subsistence and with mobility – seen as some sort of nomads, or bound up with them.
- Yhwӡ is attested before Israel, which is not a name linked to the Shasu.[90] As encountered by Egypt, the Israel people from the Merenptah Stele (ca. 1207) and the Yhwӡ group of the Shasu (early 14th century) have nothing to do with each other.

With these concluding statements, I commit myself to key elements of what I have argued as carefully as possible in this chapter. By eschewing any possibility that the names from Soleb are towns or landmarks, I insist that they are groups within the Shasu "land," and that the names only make sense in relation to people. This would be as true with Egyptian assumptions of fixed geographical space or actual sedentary life as it would be for nomads. The Shasu name, however, combined with Egyptian concern for a particular "land" inhabited by them, suggests mobility.

Everything associated with the Yahweh divine name, its potential etymology and early use, must first of all be measured against the Egyptian Shasu group, not by the religious and divine categories. Somehow, the special name of the biblical God preserves historical traces that lead back to a heritage separate from "Israel" by name, the literal entity in history. The important point is not that Yahweh came from some place or people outside Israel and is thus not "Israelite." In historical terms, neither Merenptah's Israel nor the Yhwӡ people of Shasu-land are "Israelite" in what becomes the biblical identity, though of course the former is literally so in more reduced terms. As we will explore further in Chapter 6 with the Bible's "people of Yahweh" ('*am Yhwh*), groups

---

[90] By this conclusion, I diverge from Na'aman (2011), who conflates Israel with the Shasu category.

identified with Yahweh and with Israel may have been affiliated or closely aligned in configurations that are difficult to reconstruct from existing evidence (Monroe and Fleming 2019; Fleming forthcoming). Where Israel belonged to the southern Levantine highlands and could be confronted by Egypt in straightforward terms, the old Yhwȝ identity, evidently surviving in the "people of Yahweh," would have belonged to everything represented by the Shasu category – more distant, elusive, and finally frustrating to the great power.

As we move from Yhwȝ of Shasu-land in New Kingdom Egyptian geography to the heart of the Midianite Hypothesis in biblical writing, this older material will represent a constant call to reevaluate the scholarly status quo. If nothing else, the sheer antiquity of 14th-century Soleb by comparison with biblical writing confronts us with centuries of change. The search for the "origins of Yahweh" might be cast as the question, "Where does the name Yahweh come from?" It seems that the name does not, or at least may probably not, begin as divine. Another origins question could be, "In the beginning, what kind of deity was Yahweh?" The match with Yhwȝ of Shasu-land would caution against measurement by "The God" El (Ilu) at the head of a Levantine divine family or by the dynamic storm god Hadad/Baal. What matters about the name Yhwȝ is its complete identification with a population that the Egyptians linked to mobile herdsmen, some specific group among the Shasu. As a god, Yahweh carries the name of that people forward in time, into a political landscape transformed as Egypt withdrew and new entities emerged. Tied to the inland east or further south, Yahweh was not borrowed by "Israel" from those somehow foreign to it. Yahweh was carried into what came to be the kingdom of Israel by people embraced as fully at home there.

3

The Midianite Hypothesis

Moses and the Priest

In spite of its frequent application, the Egyptian evidence for Yhw₃ does not supply straightforward support for Yahweh's origins among peoples of the wilderness south of Israel and Judah. Yhw₃ identifies a major unit of what the Egyptians confronted as a unified "Shasu-land," a land not yet situated by Egypt in Seir and Edom. As often asserted, nevertheless, the Shasu name does appear to lie behind the deity Yahweh. When Bernhard Grdseloff (1947) discovered the Shasu list, he presented it as confirmation of an already dominant explanation for Yahweh's origins, what I have called the Midianite Hypothesis. In order to reconsider the implications of this oldest Egyptian evidence, we must examine the Hypothesis in its larger form, and the next two chapters address the main material and arguments. The idea that Yahweh was originally a god of desert peoples from whom Israel learned of him was first based on biblical prose (this chapter). Current renditions now give greater weight to biblical poetry that is considered older than and independent from those prose texts (Chapter 4).

Although current expressions of the Midianite Hypothesis draw on all material understood to support and elaborate the notion that Yahweh came to Israel as a god of peoples in the southern back country, it was defined first of all by a selection of biblical prose traditions for Israel's old association with southern peoples. Over time, this collection of evidence came to be dominated by elements from the book of Exodus that portray a special connection between the name Yahweh and Moses as Israel's first great leader. When reading the literature on Israelite religion, one encounters explanations of Yahweh's origin in the south under various names and forms, commonly called the Midianite or Kenite hypothesis. Because the biblical narrative base for explaining Yahweh by the southern steppe has come to be linked especially to Jethro, the priest of Midian and Moses' father-in-law, I will identify the problematic interpretation as the Midianite Hypothesis, a proper noun.

As a first step toward understanding how the Hypothesis works, as well as how it fails, I begin with the biblical narrative around which it was originally constructed. This undertaking involves two distinct elements: consideration of the texts themselves and an attempt to understand the perspectives that governed earlier readings of them. When it comes to the earlier readings, there can be considerable confusion over the details, which turn out to have lost some clarity in the transmission of their own interpretive tradition across more than a century. The supposed creator appears to have done nothing of the kind, and the scholar who seems to have launched the idea of Yahweh's desert origins went largely unacknowledged, as his thoughtful work was taken up and transformed by biblical specialists, especially in Germany. This actual innovator, a scholar of comparative religion named Cornelis Tiele, cast his vision without focus on the south as such and without framing his interpretation by Moses and Sinai. We will return to Tiele in concluding the chapter, to take the measure of what may still be worth considering from this biblical narrative material.

BEFORE SHASU AND OLD POETRY

So far as the first identification of relevant Egyptian texts from Nubia came in 1947, these only became part of a renovated Midianite Hypothesis in the second half of the 20th century. Likewise, the development of the implications for proposed early biblical poetry by Albright and his students came after World War II, and these references to Yahweh going to war from the southern wilderness only became central as they were applied to questions of history and religion, most notably by Frank Moore Cross.[1] This makes the synthesis by H. H. Rowley in 1950 (the 1948 Schweich Lectures) a significant articulation of the Hypothesis in a

---

[1] Albright's work on identifying early biblical poetry began long before (1922), but it was not applied to the question of Yahweh's origins until later. Cross's great synthesis, *Canaanite Myth and Hebrew Epic*, came out in 1973, incorporating and reworking 20 years and more of preliminary research (cf. already, Cross 1962, 1966, 1968).

form still based entirely on the original biblical base, a point of closure for the first age of its existence.[2]

The Midianite Hypothesis was the creation of the later part of the 19th century, when biblical interpretation had established a framework for distinguishing the voices of first-millennium authors from the materials with which they worked, and a burgeoning trove of finds from ancient Egypt, Mesopotamia, and the Levant had begun to yield a completely new historical landscape. The ancient world was emerging in unfamiliar terms that could no longer be defined by the Bible and old lore preserved in Greek and Latin writing. Without attempting a full history of the idea, it is worth revisiting the first formulation of the Midianite Hypothesis, which developed somewhat differently than generally imagined. According to Joseph Blenkinsopp (2008: 132), who gives notable attention to the early discussion, "the earliest formulation has been traced to a German scholar, F.W. Ghillany, writing in 1862, who published his theory under the pseudonym Richard von der Alm."[3] Blenkinsopp characterizes the first appearance of the interpretation as follows:

Not all who subsequently adopted the theory were indebted to Ghillany's work. Most, in fact, appear not to have been, but in any case it was accepted during the remaining years of the nineteenth and the early part of the twentieth century by German scholars of note including Eduard Meyer, Bernhard Stade, Karl Budde, and Hugo Gressmann.

In a note (132 n.1), Blenkinsopp observes, "The hypothesis was advanced independently of Ghillany by the Dutch scholar Cornelis P. Tiele, in *Vergelijkende Geschiedenis van der Egyptische en Mesopotamische Godsdiensten*, I (Amsterdam: Van Kampen, 1872), pp. 558–60."

Although Blenkinsopp treats the origins of the idea as developing independently with several different scholars, it seems more likely that expectations of citation were not demanding and the early lines of transmission are simply obscure. Curiously, Ghillany did not in fact consider the name Yahweh to have come to Israel through Moses or the desert peoples, and it is not clear why Holzinger attributed the idea to him.[4] This

---

[2] Rowley was aware of the new discovery of Egyptian evidence by Grdseloff (1947), but this had not yet become an object of extended study.

[3] He identifies this origin based on an early German commentary (Holzinger 1900: 13–14) and acknowledges that he could not check Ghillany's work directly.

[4] In his reference to the Midianite Hypothesis and Ghillany's role in its origin, Holzinger (1900: 13) identifies Stade as a source, though I cannot confirm the statement. It is possible that Holzinger understood Stade as the origin of his information about Ghillany.

leaves Tiele the oldest proponent, and he advances the interpretation as a self-conscious novelty: there is no reason to locate the origin of the hypothesis anywhere else. Yet reference to Tiele is broadly absent across early advocates.[5] Tiele was a prominent scholar, appointed to a chair for the history of religions at Leiden in 1877 and an associate of the biblical scholar Abraham Kuenen, who completed a book on Israelite religion in 1869–70.[6] The idea must have germinated in this stimulating circle, with Kuenen's study of religion one point of reference, the idea then picked up especially by German scholars in dialogue with the Dutch group.

In the interest of clarifying the origins story of the Midianite Hypothesis, I offer a brief account of both Ghillany and Tiele. What follows constitutes far less than an intellectual history of the Midianite Hypothesis and its early context. My goal is to characterize the development of this approach before the introduction of biblical poetry and Egyptian evidence into this history of religion.

Friedrich Wilhelm Ghillany (Richard von der Alm, 1807–1876)

In 1900, Heinrich Holzinger somehow had the impression that Friedrich Ghillany (as Richard von der Alm) invented the Midianite Hypothesis, even though the text in question makes clear that Ghillany had something else in mind. In 1862, the former city librarian of Nürnberg published under a pseudonym a collection of rambling essays assembled under the conceit of being open letters to progressive Christian readers: *Theologische Briefe an die Gebildeten der deutschen Nation.*[7] With the spiritual

---

[5] In my reading of early literature, the one notable exception is Holzinger (1900: 13–14), who was clearly familiar with Tiele's work in the Dutch original.

[6] In a long appreciation after Kuenen's death, Philip H. Wicksteed (1892) included the following characterizations of his work and stature: "he shared with Wellhausen the acknowledged leadership in the field of Old Testament criticism and the Religion of Israel, as interpreted by the newer school of which he, himself, was practically the founder" (571). On his *Historico-Critical Inquiry into the Origin and Collection of the Books of the Old Testament* he comments, "Apart from its great intrinsic merits, Kuenen's book did for Holland all and more than all that the first part of Colenso's Pentateuch did for England. It made it impossible for instructed persons henceforth to ignore or deny the fact that the Bible bears upon its face the evidence of growth and compilation, in accordance with the ordinary laws and subject to the ordinary errors of the human mind" (587). Wicksteed considered that the history of Israel's religion was of equal weight, irreversibly transforming the pursuit of these questions from rehearsal of the biblical narrative to reconstruction of human development.

[7] "Theological Letters to the Educated of the German Nation"; volume 1 is devoted to the Old Testament.

development of humankind in view (iii), he undertakes a rational rumination aimed to consider what Christians are to do with an imperfect Bible (vii).

Letter 14 is devoted to the pre-Jehovist (Yahwist) religion of the Hebrews, a category applied to the people from whom Israel emerged. The Bible tells nothing of the Hebrews' religion in Egypt, though we can expect natural adaptation to Egyptian ways, with particular attention to fire and the sun (477–79). Moses was evidently a runaway priest of On, and he married into the family of the priest of Midian, who worshipped the sun god at Mount Sinai, where the deity appeared in connection with the storm (480). Jehova was only later identified with this god, which Moses would not have known. Instead, "Moses probably named his god by the common Semitic divine name El" (482).[8]

In letter 15, on Jehova and his worship, Ghillany envisions the later arrival of Yahweh in Israel, not from Midian, the wilderness, or the south but through the Phoenicians and their god Yao. Although Exod 6:3 assumes that Moses knew the name Yahweh, "we have reason, however, to suspect that the name Jehova first came to the Hebrews from Phoenicia in the time of Samuel" (524).[9] Ghillany thus understood the attribution of Yahweh's revelation to Moses as secondary, and though he gave Sinai and the south a significant role in Israel's early religion, this had nothing to do with the divine name in question.

Cornelis Petrus Tiele (1830–1902)

If Friedrich Ghillany did not come up with the idea that Yahweh was first worshipped in the southern desert, the next earliest date associated with this interpretation belongs to Cornelis Tiele's 1872 Dutch work on "The Comparative History of the Egyptian and Mesopotamian Religions: Egypt, Babel-Assur, Yemen, Harran, Phoenicia, Israel."[10] In contrast to

---

[8] "Moses nannte seinen Gott wahrscheinlich mit den allgemeinen semitischen Gottesnamen El."

[9] "[M]an hat aber Ursache, zu vermuthen, dass der Name Jehova erst in Samuels Zeit von Phönizien her zu den Hebräern gekommen." Ghillany regards Sanchuniathon's god Yao as Phoenician (525).

[10] *Vergelijkende geschiedenis von de Egyptische en Mesopotamische godsdiensten: Egypte, Babel-Assur, Harran, Fenicië, Israël* (1872); translated into French as *Histoire comparée des anciennes religions de l'Égypte et des peuples sémitiques* (1882). My reading is based on the French, which covers the entire original work, whereas the English translation only covers the first volume of the Dutch.

Ghillany, Tiele certainly proposes a new way to understand the origin of Yahweh in relation to the peoples of the inland deserts, including the Bible's Rechabites, Kenites, and Midianites. Moreover, he advances the idea with consciousness of its novelty: only two alternatives had been considered before him, that Yahweh came from Egypt and that Ya(hweh) was a Canaanite deity acquired after conquest (347–49). Given that the Dutch biblical scholar Abraham Kuenen (1869–70) had just published a groundbreaking history of Israelite religion, it appears that Tiele developed his ideas in some kind of dialogue with his colleague, whom he cites as an authority for the Bible and history (331).[11] After Tiele's arrival at the University of Leiden in 1877, he and Kuenen would share the same academic setting until the latter's death in 1891. It is at least clear that Kuenen knew and followed the work of his younger colleague, which he cites in the preface to the 1882 English edition of his own work on the religion of Israel.[12]

Tiele himself was not a biblical scholar, and what he brought to the problem of early Israelite religion was a thorough and sympathetic knowledge of ancient religion more broadly. He began his working life as a pastor, but starting with a major volume on Iran (1864), Tiele made himself a specialist in comparative religion, as embodied in an 1876 handbook, translated into English, French, and German. His extensive research on Mesopotamia resulted in a two-volume history (1886–88).[13] In the Dutch title of the 1872 book, Israel is the last of a long list of names, and the scale of attention devoted to it suits its place – indeed a destination but not an overwhelming preoccupation. While it may be easy to write off 19th-century religious analysis as hopelessly biased toward, in this circle, a Christian culmination shared by Tiele, what impresses me is how much he respects the religions he compares. Egyptian religion was not idolatry. It combined a lively spirituality united from the material representations of different deities, even of the crudest type, and an

---

[11] Citing Kuenen and Julius Wellhausen in that order, Tiele distinguishes biblical religion of the 9th century and later, the system developed by the authors who created the texts as we have them from various prior traditions (330). The stories they used are not pure invention, but in order to find history, we must look for what lies below these authors' own ideas.

[12] Kuenen (1869–70: 278–79): "According to Tiele, l.c. pp.558 seq., Jahveh was originally the god of the Kenites. Comp. with this what I wrote on pp. 179–182, 358 seq., 403: thus his opinion is not absolutely opposed to mine." Kuenen himself (398–403) had argued against the notion that Yahweh was a Canaanite god, in favor of an Israelite origin.

[13] For the full bibliography of Tiele's work, see Molendijk (2000: 102–109).

equally lively sense of the unity of God (133). Though we might find their visual representation of deity repulsive, they respond "to a notion of divinity purer, more spiritual, than the handsome and noble forms of the gods of the Hellad" (136) – the Greeks. The benefit of attending to Babylonian and Assyrian religions (his plural) is that Israelite religion is ultimately cut from the same cloth. The Mesopotamian peoples are of the same Semitic race as the Hebrews (no Sumerians known yet) (146), and there is so much new cuneiform evidence. Evidence for Canaan and the Phoenicians will then bring us closest to Israel, from which its religion separated. The Phoenicians were the apostles of Mesopotamian civilization in the west (261), even as their inscriptions present us with El and Baal, obviously relevant to Israel. Ugarit had not yet been excavated.

For the early history of Israelite religion, with the Bible as the repository, we must look beneath the authors' own ideas, which come from the 9th century and later, in this case for "Hebrew tradition" of times before life in the land. The Bible's insistence that Moses gave Israel its national god, as asserted in Exod 6:2–3 with reference to the ancestors and El Shadday, contradicts the historical requirement of "the organic development of religion" (341). With notable caution, Tiele precedes his investigation with the comment that "we must not forget that we are in terrain here absolutely before history," with no monument, no direct attestation, so that we can only approach the question by way of analogy.

From wider biblical portrayals, Tiele concludes that Yahweh is shown by origin a god of nature, connected easily to phenomena such as light and wind. The most ordinary manifestation of Yahweh is the storm, so that Yahweh is a god of the sky, the source of heat and life, a major type common to all ancient peoples (343). In this judgment, Tiele is not far from long-standing and still current notions. Yahweh's major festival was in the fall, the time of grape harvest and wine, as in Canaan generally, though Samson and the Nazirites represent "strict Yahwists" who resist the licentious associations of these (347). The question then becomes where the Israelites learned of Yahweh.

Against the two existing options of Egypt and Canaan, including Yao as a Canaanite god, Tiele begins not with the divine name but with divine character: neither the "sensuous god" of Canaan nor a god of wine and oil, so of settled agriculture, but a warrior, a god of the desert, and mobile (349). Launching his new proposal, he observes, "There is in the story [histoire] of Israel a fact that can put us on the track of the true origin of the worship of Yahveh, for it was basically only an attempt to restore this worship in all its primitive purity" (350). This is the sect of the

Rechabites, named for its founder, a group that lived in tents and eschewed agriculture and wine, to whom Jehu shows off his "zeal for Yahweh" in wiping out Ahab's royal house (2 Kgs 10:15–17).[14] Tiele then turns to the genealogy for the tribe of Judah in 1 Chronicles 2, which culminates in "the Kenites who come from Hammath, the father of the house of Rechab" (v. 55). Identification of the Rechabites with the Kenites leads back to bits of detail from Israel in the wilderness through the father-in-law of Moses (351). Judges 1:16 has the Kenites settle the southernmost part of the land, with the people of Judah (cf. 4:11, for Jael's husband, Heber the Kenite).[15] The threads of evidence for the Kenites as zealous representatives of the purist Yahwism, allies of Israel, finally incorporated into Judah, and living near Mount Sinai when Moses and Israel arrive, all point to "the historical seed of the Yahvist tradition" (351). It seems that Yahweh was worshipped by the Kenites before Israel. Only after making the case for Yahweh's origin through the character of the Rechabite Kenites and their intimate relationship to Israel does Tiele rehearse the dominant biblical account of Moses and Sinai, which the Bible offers as explanation for Yahweh's name and role as Israel's national god. He even remarks the poetic references to Yahweh coming from the desert, especially Seir and Edom in Judg 5:4, as suitable to the strict Yahweh who is separate from Canaan.

Tiele's explanation of Yahweh's origin displays the careful construction of a new argument, not a passing speculation, and he should be regarded as the creator of what became the Midianite Hypothesis. Most of the biblical references that are repeated with each iteration of its discussion appear already as allusions in this first work. Yet Tiele's proposal contrasts with later renditions in significant ways. His interpretation is Kenite, not Midianite, because he has little interest in the story of Jethro as Midianite priest.[16] More significantly, Tiele's spatial point of reference is not the south as such but the wider desert, which represents a

---

[14] The Rechabites' refusal of wine, along with all agriculture and settled houses, out of loyalty to Jonadab son of Rechab and to Yahweh, is recounted in Jeremiah 35, as a prophetic proof of their fidelity.

[15] It is possible that Tiele got his argument for the close relationship between Israel/Judah and the Kenites from Kuenen's *Religion of Israel*, which develops the same set of connections from the same texts (Kuenen 1869–70: 179–82; cf. 358–59), without reference to how Yahweh came to be Israel's god.

[16] There is passing reference to Exodus 18 as part of Tiele's recounting of biblical high points: "Mais du moment que les chefs des tribus, sous la présidence de Moïse et de Jethro, le prince et le prêtre des Kénites, conclure une alliance avec le dieu du désert, ce dieu dut avoir son sanctuaire au milieu d'eux" (354).

way of life alternative to that of settled Canaan. Moreover, Tiele gave first priority not to the exodus story and its religious priorities but to what he could understand as an ongoing component of Judah's social and religious fabric, the Rechabite clan that represented a desert and nomadic ideal tied to particular religious commitment. He had made himself an early specialist in comparative religion, not a theologian or biblical scholar, and the character of his Kenite explanation contrasts vividly with its development in the decades that followed.

After Tiele

Blenkinsopp makes reference to two major German biblical scholars who published variations of the Midianite Hypothesis in the last part of the 19th century: Bernhard Stade and Karl Budde. In my limited reading, neither of these makes reference to Tiele. Already in 1900, Heinrich Holzinger (13–14) appears to be conversant with the work of Tiele, though his principal point of reference appears to be Stade's history (1887).

Bernhard Stade (1848–1906)

Perhaps the most mysterious step toward the larger adoption of a Kenite-Midianite approach to Yahweh's origins is its movement from Dutch Leiden into the prominent, if not preeminent, German current of late 19th-century biblical scholarship. The earliest elaboration that repeats Tiele's non-Canaanite, wilderness hypothesis is found in the influential "History of the People Israel" (*Geschichte der Volkes Israel*) by Bernhard Stade (1887).[17] This work becomes a standard citation as the idea gained currency, and its authority is evident. One indication of Stade's influence is his founding in 1881 of a major journal specializing in study of the Hebrew Bible, the *Zeitschrift für die alttestamentliche Wissenschaft*. The first two issues included contributions by Karl Budde, Eduard Meyer, and the elder Rudolf Smend.

Stade divides the first volume of his "History" into "books," the second of which is devoted to Israel before the monarchy. Religion is not the focus of the project, and the origin of Yahweh comes up in the context of geographical discussion of Israel in the Transjordan, introduced as "Israel und Kain" (1887: 126). In this section, Stade turns

---

[17] Notice that Stade only begins his history proper with the kingdoms.

quickly to religion, contrasting the Canaanite gods of individual places, like Bethel and Beersheba, with Israel in the Transjordan after exodus from Egypt (127–28). Stade treats Moses as the real agent of religious transformation in ancient Israel. Biblical parallels to Egyptian religious practice show what Moses brought from his Egyptian upbringing, and Moses brought a new worship of Yahweh as a tribal god (129–30). The higher religion of this new worship obscures any traces of what came before.

It is at this point that Stade addresses the origin of Yahweh, without any sense that the interpretation is new or needs particular proof. Stade gathers the same details already presented by Tiele, this time with the object of showing that the worship of Yahweh must have been foreign to Israel. Where Tiele began with the continuity of social connections in Rechabite and Kenite communities tied to Judah, Stade starts with Moses and Midian: Moses and the Levites must represent an old non-Israelite priesthood of Yahweh that derives from Midian, as reflected in his marriage to Jethro the priest. The two essential texts are Exodus 3 and 18, where the mountain of God, Yahweh, and Jethro are brought together. Then he turns to the same list of extended family connections: Num 10:29 for Hobab the Midianite; Judg 1:16 and 4:17, 1 Samuel 30 and 15:6 for friendship with the Kenites, through the same link to Moses (131). It is here that Stade offers his only citations of prior work, with reference to Meyer (1881: 137) for Judg 1:16 and Moses' in-laws, and with a separate reference to Kuenen (1869–70: 179–80) for the alignment of Midianites and Kenites. Given his familiarity with Kuenen and the Leiden center, along with what comes across as a summary rehearsal and recasting of Tiele's meticulous argument, it is remarkable that Stade makes no mention of the man responsible for this innovative idea. Did Stade consider Tiele a less than reliable interpreter because he was not a biblical scholar?

Whatever Stade intended, the result of his failure to credit Tiele was to erase him effectively from continuing discussion and to introduce a subtle shift in its conception, making it more biblical, with a reduced sense of religious context. With Stade, the biblical story of Israel's national origins under Moses is moved to the center of the historical question about how Israel came to have Yahweh as its national god, and with that shift, the relationship with the Kenites becomes less important than the role of Midian. It is this concern to match the Bible's origins story to the history of religion that turns Tiele's Kenite-focused interpretation into a Midianite Hypothesis. Like Tiele, Stade has no particular interest in the south, and the world of the Midianites and the Kenites is defined rather by the Transjordan as a contrast to Canaan.

Karl Budde (1850–1935)

Karl Budde was a contemporary of Stade, who moved in the same intellectual circles, participating in the launch of the *Zeitschrift für die alttestamentliche Wissenschaft* (1882). This early work was on Hebrew lamentation poetry, and Budde wrote an array of commentaries for biblical material, including the Genesis prologue (1:1–12:5), Judges and Samuel, Job, and the Song of Songs. As a senior scholar, he was invited to the United States to give a series of eight popular lectures on the religion of Israel, a topic for which he was well prepared even as it was outside his principal research. Even at this distance, the writing is lucid and engaging, an excellent introduction to the Midianite Hypothesis in an early expression.

Budde gave first place to "The Origin of the Yahweh Religion," which he approached as a problem to address in both historical and theological terms.[18] Budde's account completes Stade's move toward matching the biblical origins story to the history of Yahweh: "The origin of the Yahweh-religion as the religion of Israel coincides with the origin of the nation itself" (1899: 1). As envisioned by Tiele, the "tradition" picked up by biblical writers carries historical information (3).[19] When it comes to

---

[18] It appears that the occasion of these English-language lectures offered Budde a first opportunity to synthesize his views of Israelite religion, which he only published afterward in German (1905; cf. Budde 1912).

[19] So far as Tiele measured the character of the Bible in Kuenen's shadow, it is worth noting that in composing his *Religion of Israel* Kuenen committed himself to a view of tradition that appears more cautious than what Budde confidently asserts, once this is separated from the documentary hand that organized it. Kuenen develops his critique of tradition with careful deliberation: "Suppose that we knew of the latter (a 500-year-old Dutch dispute) only by traditions which had never been committed to writing up to this time; should we have the boldness to trust ourselves to the historian, who now wrote them for the first time, as a safe guide? Surely it is almost inconceivable that a narrative which was not written down until after so long an interval, should yet entirely accord with the reality" (1861–65: 1:17–18). After review of established historical problems in the biblical text, Kuenen continues: "An event does not pass away without leaving any trace, any more than it occurs without preparation. If we succeed in discovering its traces, our conviction of its reality is confirmed. But also, conversely, if we do not find its results in later times, if rather we meet with facts which are incompatible with the supposition that such an event has preceded them, then we reject the accounts which record it, or at least consider them as extremely doubtful" (19). In the context of debate over the viability of stories that involve miracles, Kuenen turns to "tradition": "The probability that a departure from the natural order of things must be placed to the account of tradition,

Yahweh, the Bible itself presents his role as a novelty that confirms the story as history: "the tradition claims that it was *not* Israel's *own* God who performed these great deeds, but a God up to that time completely unknown to the Israelites, whose name, even, they learned for the first time" (14). With Moses and the exodus at center, Budde's interpretation is framed very much in terms of a pentateuchal Documentary Hypothesis, where the Elohist and Priestly sources of Exod 3:13–14 (E) and 6:2–3 (P) preserve a tradition older than the Yahwist (J) source, which assumes knowledge of this divine name from the beginning (16). Budde takes for granted that the portrayal of the mountain as Yahweh's home means a place where people worship him: "The God of Sinai must have been worshipped by the people which dwelt in His territory, at Sinai." Because Moses tended flocks for Jethro, the priest of Midian, Yahweh must be the god of the tribe to which Moses was joined by marriage (19). Like Stade, Budde only then brings up the familiar list of references to the Kenites and Hobab, next citing the Rechabite texts first considered by Tiele. The story of Jethro meeting Moses at the mountain in Exodus 18 should be understood to show the Midianite priest exulting in the power of his own god on behalf of Israel (21–23).

Budde's account of Yahweh is calculated to bring history together with biblical narrative, so that the two align without significant tension. He takes the stance of a theologian, even concluding with (Christian) satisfaction that Jewish religion began as a "conversion" (24). His overall argument is with those who see history in the Bible only back to the time of David or perhaps Saul (1) – a defense of the biblical memory. There is still no special interest in the south, though likewise Budde is not generally occupied with the social landscape of urban Canaan and the mobile peoples of the desert.

Eduard Meyer (1855–1930) and Hugo Gressmann (1877–1927)

Two more notable European efforts to develop particular dimensions of the Midianite Hypothesis came from Eduard Meyer (1906) and Hugo Gressmann (1913), picking up on the work of Stade and Budde, citing them without acknowledgment or awareness of Tiele. Meyer was a

---

or of the narrator, in accordance with analogy, is infinitely greater than the probability that such a departure really occurred, in opposition to all analogy" (21). Tradition in general tends toward exaggeration. The history of early Israel is the stuff of legend (22); "transmitted from mouth to mouth, it gradually lost its accuracy and precision, and adopted all sorts of foreign elements."

historian, also writing on Greece and early Judaism, offering one of the first extended studies of the Elephantine papyri (1912), and he approaches ancient Israel as a historical object, not as a biblical scholar. He pursues the Kenites as "Qainites" sharing the name of Cain, finally attributing the first worship of Yahweh as asserted in Gen 4:26 to the line of Cain, linked to Amalek and preserved in the name of the Kenite people (1906: 89–91, 389–98). Only Stade serves as a prior point of reference for his ideas about Yahweh (91). His treatment of the already classic set of Kenite references regards them as secondary to the older narrative about Moses and his Midianite in-laws in Exodus 2–3 and 18.

Where Meyer was working on Israel's historical relationship to other tribal peoples, Gressmann set himself to explore the Bible's collection of Moses tales on their own terms. A younger associate of Hermann Gunkel, Gressmann developed further application of the new "form criticism," seeking orally based tradition within the written biblical text. Faced with the body of biblical lore attached to Moses, the question of Yahweh's origin arises in the context of the Exodus stories. Following Stade, Gressmann (162–63) understands Moses as a priest through his ties to Jethro, with Jethro already a priest of Yahweh, worshipped as the highest of all gods (Exodus 18). As part of his treatment of Kadesh as a location for exchange between Israel and the desert peoples, Gressmann returns to Jethro and reviews the same group of Kenite references with little new to add and Meyer as authority (431–38). For all that these German scholars return to the same texts introduced earlier by Tiele, and the Kenite theme is elaborated by connection to Cain, the historical priority is the combination of Moses, Midian, and Sinai as the avenue by which Yahweh came to be worshipped by Israel.

H. H. Rowley (1890–1969)

Like the important contribution by Budde, H. H. Rowley's[20] treatment of Yahweh's origins (1950) was incorporated into prominent public presentations, the 1948 Schweich Lectures.[21] Rowley began as a missionary to China and came to biblical studies by way of work on the Aramaic language, followed by books on Daniel and on apocalyptic writing. He

---

[20] I provide dates of birth and death only for the series of figures that represent the early development of the Midianite Hypothesis, for chronological perspective, with Rowley the last of these.

[21] Rowley's three lectures were defined as "extra-biblical evidence"; "biblical traditions"; and "synthesis." The question of religion only comes up with his synthetic review.

was neither archaeologist nor historian, but after World War II he took a leading role in the Society for Old Testament Study and produced a series of books of broad interest (e.g. Rowley 1946, 1951). By this time, excavations in British Palestine had become a major factor in any historical reconstruction of ancient Israel, and the lectures were cast as an opportunity to reflect on the situation to a larger audience. He approaches the question of "extra-biblical evidence" as a representative of biblical scholarship who faces a burgeoning body of outside data, not so much the more distant finds from Egypt, Mesopotamia, and Phoenicia as material coming out of the very space occupied by Israel and Judah.

Rowley reaffirms the Midianite Hypothesis of Stade and Budde, with Holzinger (1900) as authority for its origin with Ghillany.[22] He regards this as the correct and majority view, with the following arguments in its favor: the fact that the Bible considers worship of Yahweh to be new to Israel with Moses (1950: 143–44) connected to Jethro the priest and the Midianites; Jethro's role in advising Moses on matters of justice (Exodus 18); the familiar references to Hobab and the Kenites; and the evident relationship between the Kenites and Cain (150–53). Without effort to evaluate it, Rowley is newly aware of Grdseloff's discovery that Egyptian evidence preserves Yhw₃ as a "place." There is no concern for Yahweh marching from the southern wilderness as found in what Albright and his circle saw as early poetry, still to be applied to questions of early Israelite religion. Nevertheless, the debate over Yahweh's origin had turned to a specifically southern location, with an alternative that the god had long been worshipped by the Hebrews in Judah, as the southern part of Israel.[23] Like the preceding work by Tiele and the rest, Rowley's reconstruction depends almost entirely on biblical narrative, which can still bear the weight of historical consideration.

THE PROSE BIBLICAL TEXTS

With Rowley, we reach a turning point in discussion of Yahweh's origins, after which Albright's notion of early biblical poetry introduces a new set of evidence, the focus of the next chapter. The current chapter is not intended as a history of the Midianite Hypothesis, and the preceding review serves rather to provide a sense of its shape before the poetry

---

[22] Interestingly, Rowley bypasses the citation of Tiele by Holzinger, who displays a rare familiarity with the actual originator of the Midianite Hypothesis.

[23] Rowley (1950: 143) responds in particular to Meek (1920: 212).

began to play a major role. It is important to our reevaluation that many current specialists conceive of Yahweh's origins in a shape that still aligns visibly with the old renditions reviewed above. The old poetry discussed in the next chapter has Yahweh go to war from the southern wilderness, but it offers no notion of social connection between Israel or Judah and peoples who could have shared their religious practice.

In his affirmation of the Midianite Hypothesis, Joseph Blenkinsopp (2008) summarizes it neatly by four categories of evidence, only two of which reflect the decades of early discussion: the Moses narrative linking him to Midian; the old poetry; the Egyptian texts; and the Kenites and Cain. Although this list gives the impression that all of these are of similar character and similar conviction, the reality is that the Midianite Hypothesis has morphed from truly "Midianite," based on the prose story of Moses fleeing Pharaoh, to something more "Seir-ite," having lost much of its reliance on the biblical texts that made the original idea possible. With the poetry of Deuteronomy 33, Judges 5, and Habakkuk 3 now essential, the wilderness of Yahweh's early associations is now decisively south of Israel and Judah, not broadly from the Transjordan and the east. For all of its metamorphosis, the enterprise of seeking Yahweh's original worship among the peoples of the southern wilderness depends deeply on the Moses narrative, not first of all on the geography of Midian and Sinai but rather on the story's assertion that neither Moses nor Israel knew Yahweh by name before meeting him after the exodus. According to the "documentary" analysis of the Pentateuch that dominated biblical scholarship until recent decades, both the Priestly (P) and Elohistic (E) sources understood the name only to be revealed to Moses, in contrast to the Yahwist (J) source, which placed first worship of Yahweh before the Flood (Gen 4:26).[24] With this emphasis on the contrast between pentateuchal sources, we are still dealing with a Midianite Hypothesis bound up with Moses and Jethro the priest. The prose element that matters most is not so much that Yahweh came from the distant south as that he came from a different people, not Israel but neighbors with whom Israel felt an abiding affinity.[25]

According to the updated Midianite Hypothesis, this account of a delayed revelation of Yahweh's name preserves a historical memory of

---

[24] See already Budde (1899: 16) for this evaluation.
[25] The links between biblical Israel and the deep south are peculiar and important, somehow historically significant, though their interpretation is difficult. We will return to the problem in both this chapter and the next, with biblical poetry.

Israel's actual acquisition of Yahweh worship from others, including the southern origin. Yet the antiquity of the texts in question, along with that of the lore they carry, is far from certain and warrants cautious historical evaluation.[26] Whatever its age and earliest interest, the account of Israel's exodus from Egypt envisioned from the beginning a journey that linked the people to the wilderness, and the version in the book of Exodus includes Moses' marriage to a Midianite and movement through the south.[27] But these story elements in no way assume that Israel lacked knowledge of Yahweh and the southern affinities here and elsewhere have nothing to do with learning about this god from others. If a version of the Midianite Hypothesis is to be maintained, it will have to be without the Midianites.

[26] In common European perspective, Exod 3:1–4:18 belongs not to a long monarchic composition (J) but rather to a post-monarchic effort to bind a unified ancestor narrative, now in Genesis, to an extended Moses-exodus story. See, for example, Konrad Schmid (2010: 172–93), who understands this as one of a key set of texts that bridge the Genesis and Exodus material, in contrast to alternative views, especially in the context of the Documentary Hypothesis. Note the response to Schmid by Joel Baden (2012), with reply by Schmid (2012b).

[27] Without reference to a period of wandering as punishment, the book of Hosea envisions a movement from Egypt to Israel's own land through "desert" or "wilderness" (*midbār*). Yahweh promises to lead his faithless wife to or in the desert with agricultural gifts compared to "her youth" when she came up from the land of Egypt (2:16–17). He says, "I found Israel like grapes in the desert" (9:10), an unexpected treat, before they turned to shame at Baal-Peor. After reference to his bond with the people since "the land of Egypt," Yahweh says, "I knew you in the desert, in a land of thirst" (13:4–5). For discussion of these texts and literature, see Russell (2009: 59–63), who sets out uses of the Egypt motif in settings outside the book of Exodus. The desert appears in Hosea as a nebulously defined passage, a space between Egypt and Israel's eventual home, though more than (or different from) a simple obstacle to travel. The exodus complex in the book of Exodus is interpreted in vividly divergent ways, not all of which include Moses' marriage to a Midianite and passage through the desert in any form. For example, Berner (2010: 43–44) constructs the entire exodus narrative from two independent stories: Moses' birth in 2:1–10 and crossing the sea in chapter 14. Considering the whole wilderness interest in any form to be a later development, Berner considers the scene at the well in 2:16–22 an insertion, marked by a doublet of "staying" (verb *yšb*) at the end of verse 15, and carrying with it the whole identity of Moses' wife as daughter of the priest of Midian (56–62). Schmid (2012a: 80–82) envisions an old Moses narrative as anti-imperialist, inspired by the presence of the Assyrians in the late 8th and 7th centuries, and launched by a birth story that casts Moses in terms imitating the Sargon birth legend. Like Berner, Schmid excludes the plague narrative from this tale and envisions a text that moved directly to crossing the sea, but he does imagine a story that includes journey through the wilderness and even bits of the Joshua land occupation (83). Earlier expectations from within a Documentary Hypothesis framework are still embodied in Propp (1998: 162), who treats 2:11–22 as a unit from the Yahwist (J) source.

The Contemporary Midianite Hypothesis and Moses

Blenkinsopp affirms the Midianite Hypothesis without hesitation, and the object of his 2008 study is to extend the traditions attested in connection with Yahweh to what he proposes to be the origins of Judah in a southern league unified by worship of Yahweh – almost like Martin Noth's discredited tribal league for Israel.[28] Moses is linked to Midian through marriage to the daughter of "the priest of Midian" (Exod 2:16), named Reuel in 2:18 and otherwise named Jethro (3:1; 4:18; 18:1–12). The key reference to religion comes in Exodus 18, where Jethro as "priest of Midian" (v. 1) comes to Moses and Israel at the mountain of God (v. 5). Upon hearing all that Yahweh accomplished on their behalf, rescuing the people from Pharaoh and the Egyptians, Jethro worships Yahweh with blessing and a sacrificial feast that is shared by "the elders of Israel" (vv. 10–12). For Blenkinsopp (2008: 135), "Jethro is the principal actor; he initiates the action, and Aaron and the elders come and eat with him in the presence of Yahweh." He cites Budde (1899: 22–23) for his early insight: "He [Jethro] rather gives expression to his proud joy that his God, Yahweh, the God of Kenites, has proved himself mightier than all other gods." Or, according to Rowley (1950: 151), this is no conversion but rather "the first incorporation of the Israelite elders into the worship of Yahweh."[29] We will return to the text. Notice, for the moment, that Blenkinsopp takes for granted the assertion from Exodus 3 and 6 that Israel did not always know the name of Yahweh, a historical reading that was central to many early renditions of the Hypothesis.

Other recent historians of Israelite religion consider Yahweh's origins among southern neighbors a secure conclusion even as they treat the Midianite and Kenite connections with greater caution. It is the Egyptian evidence and the old poetry that now anchor what was once based entirely on the prose accounts of these peoples. Karel van der Toorn

---

[28] Blenkinsopp (2008: 148) includes the Kenites, Kenizzites, Calebites, Jerahmeelites, Judahites, Simeonites, and Levites in the northern Sinai and Negev in the Late Bronze and Iron Age I; cf. Weinfeld (1987), on a southern alliance. For the notion of an Israelite amphictyony, see Noth (1966); and for two important responses, Mayes (1974) and de Geus (1976). In contrast, Norman Gottwald (1979) combined Noth's idea of a tribal league with the notion that Israel formed out of Canaanites throwing off urban rule and joining in the highlands under worship of Yahweh.

[29] It is significant that in his original proposal of Yahweh's desert origins, Tiele did not focus on Exodus 18, which Budde appears to have made central to what with his work became a more Midianite than Kenite hypothesis, focused on the introduction of the name to Moses in Exodus 3.

(1999: 910) maintains the conclusion that Yahweh's origins lie among the peoples of the south, as proposed long ago with different reasoning. He begins with the absence of Yahweh from the god lists of Ugarit and from "the West Semitic world" of the Bronze Age more generally. The compelling evidence for Yahweh and the south comes from Egypt and old biblical poetry (911–12), so that the Midianite Hypothesis is to derive from these, in no way shaping or coloring the southern interpretation by the fact of its original formulation. "If Yahweh was at home in the south, then, how did he make his way to the north? According to a widely accepted theory, the Kenites were the mediators of the Yahwistic cult." The "classical form" of the Hypothesis understood the connection to come through Moses. If the Midianite (Kenite) Hypothesis has as a strength the way it draws together threads of biblical and non-biblical evidence that point outside Israel itself, it disregards the actual Canaanite origins of Israel and neglects the fact that most Israelites were rooted in Palestine (912). "If the Kenite hypothesis is to be maintained, then, it is only in a modified form." So far as Israelites may have been introduced to the worship of Yahweh by peoples such as Midianites and Kenites, it would not have been outside of Palestine but through contacts with such groups in the land, especially by trade (913).[30] Van der Toorn makes no specific claim for the antiquity of specific prose texts about Moses and Midian, though he seems to understand them as having preserved a crucial ancient aspect of Israelite religion.

With an effort to address the issue of the non-poetic material more directly, Mark Smith (2012a: 8) proposes that "the biblical prose story 'narrativized' the ancient tradition of Yhwh's origins in the south, the setting of Yahwistic cult among a southern people other than Israel, and the secondary contact of Israel with this god." The antiquity of the Midianite connection in Exodus 2 and 18 is proven by the old poetry, including the fact that in the Song of Deborah, Jael is the wife of "Heber the Kenite" (Judg 5:24). Smith observes that the Egyptian evidence mentions neither Midianites nor Kenites, and its best links to biblical writing lie instead with Seir and Edom of Judg 5:4: "biblical memory may recall the southern peoples involved as ones that Israel knew, but it does not preserve the memory of the earlier people among whom its deity enjoyed cultic devotion" (10). For more direct glimpses of Yahweh in the south, Smith turns to Judges 5 and Psalm 68, which he regards as the earliest

---

[30] Here, van der Toorn cites the interpretation of the Song of Deborah by Schloen (1993).

poetic material. The resulting interpretation may be called "a more complex form" of the Midianite Hypothesis (8).

In contrast to van der Toorn and Smith, Thomas Römer's recent work on Yahweh responds especially to the new "Berlin" approach that treats the god's arrival in Israel as a first-millennium phenomenon, unrelated to the south or the steppe.[31] Römer begins in familiar territory, reading Exodus 3 and 6 as Yahweh's revelation of his name to Moses, as a previously unknown god: "Is this a trace of the historical fact that this god was not always the god of Israel?" (2015: 2). Again, it is the non-biblical evidence that demonstrates Yahweh's origin in the "south," between the Negev and Sinai, yet the Bible's narratives "may conceal within themselves references to historical facts that a historian may to some extent be able to reconstruct" (4). In his second chapter on "The Geographical Origin of Yahweh," Römer makes his case from the Egyptian Shasu texts and then the poetry that represents Smith's primary proof. He reserves treatment of the prose for the next chapter on "Moses and the Midianites," starting like Budde and Blenkinsopp with Exodus 3 and 18. Where the early scholars went directly to the set of texts that connect Moses' father-in-law to the Kenites, Römer offers a systematic examination of the Midianites as such, beginning with general geographical information and moving through the Bible's accounts of Midianite enemies, before moving toward Moses and the familiar material (54–63). Like Schmid, he regards the story of Moses' call in Exod 3:1–4:18 as an insertion, and this text is not essential to his reconstruction. Rather, what is significant is Moses' link to "some Midianite priest" (63) and the fact that the cult of Yahweh is founded by a Midianite priest in Exodus 18 (64). Although this text has been revised, Jethro is the one who initiates sacrifice to Yahweh (66–67). It is best therefore "to suppose that there was some memory of a Midianite contribution to the cult of Yhwh that it was impossible simply to ignore; so the only way it was possible to include it was by placing it before the 'true' revelation of Yhwh at Sinai" (65).

Yahweh: The Unknown Name

For all that the Midianite Hypothesis and its Kenite antecedent came to depend decidedly on the texts that identify Moses' in-laws, the

---

[31] *The Invention of God* (Römer 2015); this book is defined very much by Yahweh, for all that its title lacks the name.

expectation that Israel got the name from another people is still widely understood to be preserved in divine declaration of the name to Moses in Exodus 3 and 6. These chapters have been central to the reconstruction of literary sources and the process of composition in Exodus and the Pentateuch, and it is impossible to address them without reference to that debate, especially with Exodus 3 and 18. At the same time, the essential question for the issue of Yahweh's relation to Israel is not the particular role played by the two texts in formation of the Exodus narrative. My larger conclusions do not depend on the choice between documentary and non-documentary explanations, though the resulting interpretations of literary context and range of possible compositional dates could diverge.

For the accounts in Exodus 3 and 6 to preserve relevant historical information about the early worship of Yahweh, they must reflect traditions far older than the times of writing, traditions that could be preserved even though at odds with Yahweh's special relationship to Israel. That is, religious realities that likely go back to the second millennium, before the kingdoms of Israel and Judah, would have to survive in texts from centuries later, whether from the 9th and 8th centuries or after the end of Judah, in the 6th century and beyond. Such survival is possible in biblical writing, but its identification must be demonstrated by some combination of external evidence, historical argument, and literary contrast to the primary currents of biblical thought.

The issue of earlier "tradition" embedded in later writing confronts the interpreter of all long compositions in the Bible, texts that are acknowledged to combine numerous once-independent stories and shorter collections into works that would have occupied one or more long scrolls. My own approach to narrative and history, with an eye to the eventual creation of such lengthy texts that constituted the Bible as an archive of book-scrolls, takes particular note of content that reaches beyond the immediate story horizon – or does not – as well as by the degree of that reach. What material elsewhere in the existing biblical book, or in the Bible beyond, does the text at hand assume readers to know? Whether a text like Exod 3:1–4:18, which builds a link between the ancestors now in Genesis and the figure of Moses, preceded the composition of core Deuteronomy and the first Priestly (P) treatise, or reflects knowledge of these as prior texts, it belongs in either case to the creative work of the long composition's author.[32] It is conceivable that the author of such a

---

[32] On the Priestly composition as a learned narrative, with particular focus on the ritual content of Leviticus, see Boorer (2016). My consideration of this work as an extended,

longer text would draw on a truly ancient tradition, known from another source, but in material that clearly serves to bridge distinct narrative parts, such a conclusion calls for even more substantial proof. In the specific case of the ancestors and Moses, I am inclined toward the European model of relatively later connection, though I do not consider myself in a position to arbitrate between the competing systems.[33] In Exod 3:1–4:18, the strongest links to Genesis promises and the Joshua conquest appear in the section where the divine name is revealed (3:6–17), thus entangling the Yahweh introduction in the most visibly bridging content.[34]

I will conclude that no matter the literary-historical system, there is no good case that Exodus 3 and 6 represent such ancient religious realities. The texts contradict the assumption in Genesis that Israel's ancestors knew Yahweh by name, but with Moses' privileged authority at stake, it appears that the writer of this section in Exodus has added the revelation to its already powerful claim that Israel's life with its god was founded in all significant respects through this man. I begin with Exodus 6 in part because its compositional interpretation is less controversial, in part because it has been widely understood to represent a relatively late stage of biblical writing.

Exodus 6

In a text that lacks any link to the mountain of God, Exod 6:2–8 recounts God's command to present Israel an offer of divine deliverance. The passage has long been attributed to Priestly (P) writing, which begins with the creation of the world in Genesis 1 and self-consciously connects an account of ancestors in Genesis with Moses as chosen intermediary in Exodus – setting aside the question of how it concludes.[35] Typical Priestly

---

complex text is informed especially by the work of Liane Feldman, who has examined especially the literary character of the ritual account in Leviticus.

[33] David Carr, an American scholar who does not adopt the documentary solution, nevertheless carefully separates his interpretation of Exod 3:1–4:18 from the "post-Priestly" approaches of Schmid and others. In a cautious argument developed in three different contexts, he ends up envisioning a "post-D" (core Deuteronomy) Hexateuch-building contribution (2011: 118–20, 140–43, 270).

[34] See "the God of your father(s)" (Exod 3:6, 13, 15, 16); (the God of) Abraham, Isaac, and Jacob (3:6, 15, 16); and the peoples of the land to take as Canaanites, Hittites, Amorites, Perizzites, Hivites, and Jebusites (3:8, 17).

[35] Some scholars identify the conclusion of the original Priestly narrative with construction of the tabernacle in Exodus 40, or even with instructions for the cult in Exodus 29: for the former, see Pola (1995); for the latter, Otto (1997). For a conclusion in Leviticus 9, see

language and concepts recur throughout, including the covenant with the ancestors and promise to give them "the land of Canaan" (v. 4).[36] The text opens with a precise and emblematic declaration that Yahweh has reserved communication of his proper name to Israel for this occasion of rescue from Egypt and establishment in their own land:

God (Elohim) spoke to Moses and said to him, "I am Yahweh.[37] I appeared to Abraham, to Isaac, and to Jacob as El Shadday, but by my name Yahweh I was not known to them.[38] And further, I established my covenant with them to give them the land of Canaan, the land where they lived as foreigners."

(Exod 6:2–4)

In literary terms, this passage bridges Genesis and Exodus, the ancestor tales and the Moses story, two contrasting and even rival renditions of Israelite origins.[39] The text could stand as a credo for the founding acts of Israel's God, hearkening back to elements from Genesis. Those who remember can be encouraged both by Yahweh's creation of Israel as his own people in a land of their own and by the fact that he promised this in advance to Abraham, Isaac, and Jacob, by covenant. God only explains to Moses that the ancestors did not worship him by the name Yahweh, evidently so that he can appreciate the enormity of what he now bestows

---

Nihan (2007). Given the Priestly color that permeates the land allotments of Joshua 13–19, which most consider secondary to the original P work, some locate the end of P in Joshua (Lohfink 1978; contrasted with Cortese 1990). Schmid (2010: 47–49) offers a brief overview of the issues with detailed bibliography.

[36] For detailed consideration of the Priestly features in the book of Exodus, see Driver (1911: xv–xvii). In 6:2–8, these include El Shadday (v. 2); establishing the covenant; land of sojourning (v. 4); remembering the covenant (v. 5); "judgments" (v. 6); knowing "that I am Yahweh"; to be to you a God (v. 7); "I am Yahweh" (v. 8); and see the notes to the text on pp. 42–45. Also more recently, see Propp (1998: 266–68), including particular parallels of vocabulary between Exod 6:4, 7–8, and Gen 17:7–8.

[37] See Propp (1998: 262) on the variation in the textual versions between "God"/Elohim and "LORD"/Yahweh. The alternatives were possible because either choice would make sense with the historical statement that follows.

[38] The verb is a niph'al of *yd'*, which suggests a passive or reflexive aspect, so that "my name" appears to be an object with assumed instrument, so Childs (1974: 108), "but by my name YHWH I did not make myself known to them." Propp (261) reads with a double subject, "I, my name Yahweh, was not known to them." Citing Garr (1992), Schmid (2010: 242) translates, "I am YHWH, and I appeared to Abraham, Isaac, and Jacob as *El Shaddai*, but my name is YHWH. I have not made myself known to them."

[39] This is a particular concern of Konrad Schmid (2010); see also his list of "theologically programmatic texts" for the Priestly narrative in 2012: 147, with Genesis 1, 9, 17, and Exodus 6. He observes (148), "if it is true that the patriarchal and Moses-exodus themes were only combined by the Priestly document, then it is the origin of one of the most important literary-historical syntheses in the Old Testament."

on Israel. The message to the people, in contrast, will require no explanation. It begins, "I am Yahweh, and I will deliver you from beneath the burdens of Egypt" (v. 6). As in marriage, Yahweh promises, "I will take you for myself as a people, and I will be for you a God, so you will know that I, Yahweh, am your God who delivered you from beneath the burdens of Egypt" (v. 7). The name goes with the deliverance, and the deliverance will confirm the name. No other introduction is necessary – yet Moses is allowed to understand that revelation of the name is a new gift, not shared by the ancestors who received the promises.

In this setting, the notion that Israel only learned the name Yahweh through Moses by special divine declaration serves the rhetorical weight of a transformative moment in the Priestly account of Israel's beginnings. With this command, Israel's God dislodges his people from what seemed like endless subservience, reminding the reader that this was intended from generations past, perhaps waiting only for the fathers of Israel to grow to their present scale.[40] The commitment to bring the people "to the land I raised my hand (on oath) to give to Abraham, to Isaac, and to Jacob" (v. 8) anticipates the conquest recounted in the book of Joshua, wherever the original Priestly narrative is understood to end.

How do we evaluate the contents of Exod 6:2–8 in relation to "tradition" as a potential carrier of much older historical information? The Priestly writer here offers an interpretation of Israelite religious history that contrasts with much of Genesis, where the name Yahweh is often taken for granted, an early basis for distinguishing a Yahwist (J) document. Yet this eloquent explanation appears just that, an effort to organize the past, integrating the writer's structuring theme of divine covenant, another tool for identifying eras, in an elegant expression of Priestly erudition. Further, the revelation of the name Yahweh through Moses involves no mention of Midian or even of any settings besides Egypt and

---

[40] For discussion of Exod 1:1–8 as the direct bridge between Genesis and Exodus, see Schmid (2010: 62–65). As Schmid sees it, in this section, 1:7 is the one clear Priestly contribution, directly explaining the multiplication of Israel in language familiar from Genesis 1: "The Israelites were fruitful and swarmed and increased and thrived enormously, and the land was filled with them." Even if verse 7 is ascribed to another organizing hand, the Priestly narrative assumes this transformation (e.g. Van Seters 1994: 20). Carr (2011: 275–76) argues that Exod 1:1–6 as a block appears to be Priestly, while the reference to Israel's numbers in 1:8 picks up from Gen 50:26, as part of a non-Priestly but post-Deuteronomy narrative that concluded with the covenant in Joshua 24. In any case, notice the Priestly work in connecting the ancestors to the exodus.

Canaan, and no southern origin for Yahweh could be deduced from Exodus 6.[41]

Exodus 3

I have reserved Exodus 3 for second treatment because it is more difficult, even as I see a clear application to the problem of Yahweh and Israel. Where Exod 6:2–8 is generally agreed to serve a Priestly account of Israel's earliest relationship to God, Exodus 3 is central to current dispute over the viability of the old Documentary Hypothesis, with its model of long parallel compositions before the work of P, known as J (Yahwist) and E (Elohist).[42] At stake is the "call narrative" of Moses, defined either as Exod 3:1–4:17 or to 4:18, depending on assignment of the last verse, where Moses is said to return to Jethro and ask permission to go back to Egypt.[43] As I understand the material, Exodus 3 in any case displays the effort of a writer to bind together elements outside the text itself, most obviously the ancestor lore now in Genesis with the exodus account in a long text. This work appears to represent historiographical interpretation

---

[41] The Priestly narrative avoids using the name Yahweh before this text, with the notable exception of Gen 17:1, in the opening of a text with deep schematic relationship to Exod 6:2–8. Schmid (2010: 239–47) observes a series of close connections between the two texts, along with other Priestly writing. On the statement in verses 2–3, it is worth quoting at length: "The statement in Exod 6:3, however, stands in striking contradiction to the Yahwistic shaping of the ancestor story, which usually, and in my opinion correctly, is seen as older than P. However, the fact that P still stresses as a central point that the revelation of the name of God occurred at a period between the ancestors and Moses makes it highly improbably that the thematic flow from ancestors to Exodus would have already been fixed centuries earlier with the forefathers of Israel and Israel itself. In fact, one can even ask literary-historically how old the 'Yahwisticized' version of the ancestor story really is. Furthermore, the characteristic P concentration on the Abrahamic covenant contrasts too much with the understanding of Exod 6:3 for Exod 6:3 to fit the theology of P. Contrary to its normal word choice elsewhere in Genesis – Exodus 6, it is hardly accidental in Gen 17:1 that P uses יהוה instead of אלהים. Thus, the late introduction of the name יהוה in Exod 6:3 apparently must be explained by the presupposed background knowledge that the ancestor bears a completely different imprint from the Moses/Exodus story" (242).

[42] Knohl (1995) attributes a large part of what has commonly be identified as P in Exodus to a revision of Priestly writing that he calls H (Holiness), including Exod 6:2–7:6 (61–62).

[43] This request stands in tension with 4:19, where Yahweh commands Moses in Midian to return to Egypt, with reference back to his flight in chapter 2, in fear for his life. On 3:1–4:18 as an interruption of a prior account of flight from and return to Egypt, see Carr (2011: 118). Childs (1974: 47–89) reflects frequent delineation of 3:1–4:17 in documentary discussion, even as he acknowledges the problems in what follows, with 4:18 and 4:19 a "clear doublet" and much disagreement over how to explain the documentary attributions for 4:18–27 (94).

rather than preservation of received "tradition." Even by the most restrictive reading of a core account of name-explanation, which would involve something like 3:9–14, this text is a bridge, and the treatment of a name is an ancient scholar's play.

Exodus 3 forges just the link that is missing from chapter 6, envisioning Yahweh's declaration of his name to Moses during a first visit to the sacred "mountain of God" (v. 1, cf. v. 12). In this respect, it anticipates and connects directly to Exodus 18, where Jethro comes to meet his son-in-law Moses at the "mountain of God" (v. 5). As currently organized, the call of Moses in Exod 3:1–4:18 stands before and thus anticipates the historical schema offered in 6:2–3 so that the novelty of Yahweh's declaration of the name is explained as part of Moses' prophet-like calling, and the Priestly passage becomes a review.[44] The call of Moses lacks the language of P and has never been identified as Priestly, which has left it to J and E in documentary analysis, with varied accounts of its composition and adjustment.[45] Because the J writer(s) understood the ancestors to have worshipped Yahweh by this name, Yahweh's self-identification in Exodus 3 was aligned with the E document, which must have shared the perspective made explicit in the P schema of chapter 6.[46] For Propp (2006: 728–29), the notion that Yahweh had to be introduced to Israel by an unfamiliar name constitutes the best basis for distinguishing an

---

[44] Childs (1974: 55–56, 68) emphasizes the location of 3:1–4:17 in the "prophetic office," as displayed in the literary calls of Isaiah (ch. 6), Jeremiah (ch. 1), and Ezekiel (chs. 1–3) and in the demands in Deut 13:1 and 18:20, where the legitimate prophet must speak only in the name of Yahweh. Carr's analysis of Exod 3:1–4:18 as part of a "post-D Hexateuchal" contribution also highlights the identification of Moses with prophecy (2011: 271).

[45] Childs would eventually give up participation in literary-historical analysis of biblical texts, and his commentary already offers a refreshing caution, weighing the narrative coherence of each section against the long history of division into contributing sources and revisions. He represents the ordinary division as 3:2–4a, 5, 7, 8, and 16–22 for J and 3:1, 4b, 6, and 9–15 for E, a starting point for diverse solutions and refinements (1974: 52).

[46] Propp (1998: 190–94) maintains his own rendition of the classic Documentary Hypothesis, addressing chapters 3–4 in the following terms: "distinguishing P from JE remains a subject of near-consensus – but separating J from E will henceforth be difficult, sometimes impossible ... Chap. 3 is harder to analyze than chap.4; Redactor^{JE} apparently manipulated his sources with great freedom. An additional complication is that the Versions often disagree in reading 'Yahweh' or '(the) Deity'." Propp confidently assigns 3:11–20 to E, by its revelation of the divine name and reference to Gen 50:24–25, which he also reads as E. Baden (2009: 234) interacts especially with Propp in his analysis of Exodus 3, where he defends the presence of J in 3:6b–8 as the logical continuation of Yahweh speaking from the burning bush in verses 2–4b and 5.

Elohistic "E" document within the non-Priestly contents of Genesis and Exodus.[47]

In spite of vigorous maintenance and defense of documentary interpretations, especially in the United States, the "Documentary Hypothesis" of pentateuchal composition can no longer be considered a consensus. There has been a weakening of confidence in the possibility of proving separate J and E compositions that bridged Genesis and Exodus, the ancestor and the Moses stories.[48] Moreover, European scholarship from diverse perspectives has doubted the antiquity of any literary combination of these distinct origins stories for Israel, so that the handful of binding passages may be dated even after Priestly writing, probably from Persian times.[49] Schmid (2010: 158–213) identifies Genesis 15, Exod 3:1–4:18, and Joshua 24 as the three principal passages that bind the Genesis ancestor tales to exodus and conquest, as part of the entire history of Israel, so that presentation of Yahweh's name in Exodus 3 is even later than the Priestly effort in Exodus 6 and dependent on it.[50]

Whether or not Exodus 3–4 is still understood in documentary terms, the point to be argued here is that Yahweh's declaration of his name is embedded in schematic explanation that relates the time of Moses to that of the ancestors, as in Exodus 6. In his introduction to Priestly writing, Carr (2011: 292–93) draws attention to the many cases in Genesis and Exodus where "P and non-P" narratives "propose opposing positions," with "virtually no verbal parallels between the strands," including the two call narratives in Exod 3:1–4:18 and 6:2–8. Here and elsewhere, we

---

[47] "Is it just coincidence that a corpus of stories in Genesis exclusively uses *'ĕlōhîm* as the divine name, a corpus that parallels accounts preferring the name 'Yahweh'? It is hard to conceive" (Propp 2006: 729).

[48] For one articulation of this doubt, with reference to earlier discussion, see Carr (1996: 196–202), who begins from the common identification of substantial E material in Genesis 20–22.

[49] The most rigorous and systematic argument is that of Konrad Schmid (2010), with documentation of prior discussion. Erhard Blum (1990: 22–28) identified Exod 3:1–4:18 with his Deuteronomistic pentateuchal composition (K^D); and Eckart Otto (1996) includes this section in his identification of post-Priestly writing in Exodus. On this text having knowledge of the Priestly narrative, see more recently Römer (2006). Also more recently, Blum (2006) distinguishes Exod 3:1–22 as pre-Priestly from 4:1–17 as post-Priestly, both contributing to "compositional" work.

[50] Abandonment of the documentary explanation for pentateuchal composition does not require agreement with these European interpreters on the "post-Priestly" character of Exod 3:1–4:18, as exhibited by Carr (2011: 269–70), who considers the text older than P, which is in dialogue with it. The text nevertheless belongs to the composition of a large-scale text that would conclude with conquest of a Promised Land.

are faced with alternate interpretations of material known to both writers or circles, where neither text displays authority that calls for repetition of the other's words. As previously observed, I would emphasize that Exodus 3 is particularly laden with allusions to the ancestors that bind Moses and the exodus to narrative from Genesis. Further, Yahweh's declaration of his name to Moses is embedded in a "call narrative" that shares a scribal defense of textual authority also found in prophetic writing (Isaiah 6; etc.). My own doubt of the coherence of J and E documents inclines me toward solutions that allow relatively later combinations of narratives and visions that are intrinsically very different, with different notions of how to explain the beginnings of Israel. Yet as part of an E document, perhaps aligned with a related J account of Moses at the mountain without Israel, the self-presentation of Yahweh in Exod 3:14–15 would still display the interpretive work of an author combining far-flung materials (more, below). Either way, Moses' new knowledge of the name is no sign of high antiquity as a survival from Israel's deep past, recalling an origin outside of Israel.

Beyond the debate over the Documentary Hypothesis, what of the text itself? One peculiarity in the book of Exodus is its combination of two visits to the mountain of God. The Pentateuch as a whole, and the Moses story in Exodus through Numbers, make "Mount Sinai" the fulcrum for Israel's establishment under covenant and law (Exodus 19–Numbers 10).[51] Exodus 19 introduces Israel's arrival at Sinai without mention of Moses' previous visit. In Exodus 3–4, Israel's meeting with Yahweh at the mountain is anticipated by a private showing for Moses, with only a burning bush instead of the whole smoking mountain. Most of this first meeting consists of an elaborate conversation, impressive in part for Moses' boldness in confronting his god.[52] The exchange is given a memorable setting in the opening verses (2–3), with the bush that burns

---

[51] The drama of divine display in Exodus 19 revolves around Mount Sinai by name (vv. 11, 18, 20, 23); before the Priestly instructions for tabernacle and priests begin in Exodus 25, the "glory of Yahweh" makes its home on Mount Sinai (24:16); and the Priestly covenant with Israel under Sabbath sign is made on Mount Sinai (31:12–18). Sinai as "mountain" holds less interest in the book of Numbers, which mixes assignments of legal formulations between the periods before and after departure. The people are said to leave "the wilderness/desert of Sinai (*midbar sînāy*)" in Num 10:12.

[52] This boldness and conversational pattern resembles Gen 18:22–33, where Abraham challenges Yahweh's willingness to destroy a whole city in judgment. In recent treatments, many consider that text very late in relative terms. Carr (1996: 171) observes that Gen 18:17–18 and 22b–33 show no clear connection to Deuteronomistic themes and language even as "they address a problem of collective destruction and individual

without being consumed. This event only opens the door to Yahweh's call, "Moses, Moses!" (v. 4), followed by the command to approach barefoot because the ground is sacred (v. 5).[53] Then, "he said, 'I am the God of your father, the God of Abraham, the God of Isaac, and the God of Jacob,'" to which Moses responds by hiding his face in fear of seeing God.[54]

Yahweh says, "I have indeed seen the oppression of my people who are in Egypt and I have heard their cry" (v. 7; cf. v. 9), similar to the cry from servitude heard by God in the Priestly text, Exod 2:23. He will bring them to "a land flowing with milk and honey" (v. 8), the famous phrase repeated in prominent promises of Deuteronomy and elsewhere (e.g. Deut 6:3; 8:8; 11:9), attached here to a list of disposable inhabitants that anticipates land to conquer, like the set promised to Abram in Gen 15:18–21. Moses is dispatched to confront Pharaoh with this promise of success (v. 10). In the face of such divine enthusiasm, Moses demurs: "Who am I that I should go to Pharaoh?" (v. 11). The answer looks toward the looming exchange over the name: "I am (or will be) with you" (*'ehyeh 'immāk*, v. 12), with this very promise cast as a verbal "sign" (*'ôt*).[55] God sets forth the whole exodus program: deliverance from Egypt followed by the main event at the mountain of God.

Moses then presents a second objection: "So I am about to come to the Israelites, and I say to them, 'The God of your fathers sent me to you' – they will say to me, 'What is his name?' What should I say to them?" (v. 13). At this point we have reached "holy ground" with an interpretive accretion that makes it difficult to read the text innocently. We could imagine scenarios whereby Moses himself does not know the names in play; after all, he has spent his life in Egypt and with the Midianites.[56] Some have proposed the reverse, a kind of test or game in which all the

---

righteousness first documented in a broad spectrum of exilic texts." Earlier, see Schmidt (1976: 159–64).

[53] One feature of the text that lent itself to variable analysis of sources is the free use of both Yahweh and Elohim for the divine name, without evident effort to produce a dramatic shift. Moses finds himself at "the mountain of Elohim" (v. 1); "the angel of Yahweh" is in the bush (v. 2); Yahweh saw Moses turn to look and Elohim calls to him (v. 4); Moses was afraid to look at Elohim (v. 6); Yahweh declares his mercy (v. 7); Moses responds to Elohim (v. 11); and so on.

[54] The notion that direct exposure to the face of God is a risk to life reappears in Exod 33:20.

[55] Schmid (2010: 187) considers that the events of the future Sinai encounter in Exodus 19–24 are here "relegated" to the status of a sign, without interest in the law.

[56] This is what appears to be envisioned in older studies, as in Budde (1899: 14).

participants understand the names but require them to be rehearsed.[57] Moses has sensibly chosen the name by which God introduced himself in verse 6, translating "the God of your father" with its attendant list of three into plural "fathers" in verse 13. The question about the name, when combined with the "God of your fathers" identification, does suggest an ignorance like that made explicit by the Priestly writer in Exod 6:2–3. The Israelites have heard of Abraham, Isaac, and Jacob, but they do not have a proper name to specify their God. It is not clear why they should want a better name, or why Moses should think they will. We must keep in mind that the story presents Moses as stalling, hoping to avoid a head-on confrontation with the ruler of Egypt.

Before the question, Yahweh has made no issue of the name, so that whether or not Moses himself knows Yahweh by name, his tactics of avoidance bring down either a gift or a declaration of power: "God said to Moses, 'I am who I am' (or, 'I will be what I will be'). He said, 'You shall say this to the Israelites: I Am sent me to you'" (v. 14). The final statement repeats the terms of Moses' question in verse 13 about "sending," replacing "the God of your Fathers" with "I Am," Hebrew *'ehyeh*. The verbal root is the same from which the name Yahweh could be understood to derive, showing that early readers recognized the divine name as a verbal form. The writer makes no attempt to imagine what the name Yahweh means or meant; rather, he continues the play introduced with God's promised care in verse 12: *'ehyeh 'immāk*, "I am with you."[58] Verse 15 gathers up all the loose ends that could be left by this exchange to make sure the readers understand that all of the names align: Yahweh is indeed the God of the fathers.[59] If this verse is removed as later

---

[57] Given the likelihood that the people were understood to know the divine name already, Benno Jacob (1922: 32) proposed that "what is his name?" should be taken to mean, "what does his name mean?" Blum (2002: 124–27) envisions the question as a test of legitimate authority, not indicating real lack of knowledge. According to Carr (2011: 293), Exod 3:13–15 "featured an interaction surrounding certification of the authenticity of Moses's message through his being able to accurately report Yhwh's name and interpret its significance to Israelites who might not recognize him."

[58] For detailed discussion with bibliography, see Schmid (2010: 190–92). Schmid argues that the presentation of the name in 3:13–16 is shaped by awareness of the Priestly text to come in 6:2–8. The best explanation for the "surprising" statement in chapter 3 is that it "redactionally accommodates itself to the graduated revelation theory in Exod 6:2–3." To avoid contradicting Exodus 6, chapter 3 creates a tension with Genesis.

[59] Berner (2010: 105) takes this as the latest elaboration in a series of post-Priestly adjustments; see also Blum (1990: 24–27); Schmid (2010: 191). Recall that 3:15 would close out the important contribution of E in documentary terms. Working out of a framework for Exod 3:1–4:18 that he shares with Carr, Freidenreich (2019) argues for

elaboration, and our goal was to imagine a text without reference to the three named ancestors from Genesis, we could reconstruct a previous version of Moses' initial confrontation with Yahweh in something like 3:9–14, focused only on Egypt and the mountain. Such a reading would require skipping the old E-source lead-in from verse 6, with Abraham, Isaac, and Jacob, and it is not clear how it would relate to an exodus-story introduction without the ancestors. While this block anticipates "serving" God as in the request to "let my people go" (Exod 7:16; 9:1, 13; 10:3), that demand simply envisioned the "wilderness" (*midbār*, 7:16), whereas this one pictures the "mountain" of chapter 18 (below). Even such a reduced text would still serve to connect a statement of Israel's suffering with the account of plagues and eventual arrival at the "mountain of God" (18:5), which will be identified with divine instruction.

While reluctance to commit to a particular composition and transmission history may be taken as technical inadequacy or failure of nerve, it is crucial to emphasize what I take to be the deeper character of the dialogue set out in Exod 3:6–15, which should remain visible within vastly different literary-historical analyses. The wordplay on the name Yahweh in verse 14, which avoids giving Moses the name itself as a solution, is bound tightly to the God of the fathers, not in this case a general term but specifically evoking Abraham, Isaac, and Jacob, the figures from Genesis.[60] Even if verse 15 is considered an addition, "the god of your [singular] father" in verse 6 is identified with the three Genesis ancestors. This text reflects the same preoccupation of Exod 6:2–3, where the Priestly writer reserves the proper name for the occasion of Israel's covenantal binding to its god under Moses. Exodus 3 shows awareness that a distinct set of ancestor accounts in what we know as Genesis may suggest a religious horizon so different from the carefully managed legal and ritual arrangement through Moses that the God of the fathers could seem – to the audience – almost another character.

Whether we consider Exodus 3–4 to be a mix of pre-Priestly J and E sources in a documentary system or something either aware of P or

---

a dialogue between heirs of the large Priestly and non-Priestly compositions, still before the moment of their combination into something close to our finished books of Genesis, Exodus, and beyond. In a detailed treatment of Exod 3:15 as one example (chapter 3), he understands the verse as an elaboration that is aware of and opposed to the notion from 6:2–3 that Yahweh had appeared to Abraham, Isaac, and Jacob by another name.

[60] For interpretation of the "fathers" in Deuteronomy and Deuteronomistic writing as the direct predecessors of the people rather than as the figures from Genesis, see Römer (1990).

sharing its concerns, this second naming text is schematic, bridging the ancestor and the exodus origins stories, making sure they read well together.[61] As with Exodus 6, chapter 3 presents a picture of naming Yahweh anew that self-consciously navigates the relationship between the Moses and the ancestor stories.[62] Neither text offers a matrix that preserves fixed ancient traditions for religious origins with roots in historical realities. Yahweh must be named because of perceived narrative problems, and Moses has the privilege of bringing the name to Israel because of the prestige he enjoys as the central figure of early Jewish religious tradition at a time when the Torah was the principal project of Jewish writing. We must conclude that the Bible does not preserve an ancient tradition that Yahweh only became the god of Israel at some distinct moment in history, somehow recalled as attached to Moses, yielding a time when the people and its god were attached to the southern wilderness, the location of Yahweh's sacred mountain. When we come next to the specific narrative for the Midianites, as well as other glimpses of friendly relations with southern peoples, we cannot interpret these as hints of old religious affinities, or further, as forgotten sources for the worship of Yahweh. If such were the case, it is not the biblical narrative that tells us so.

Midianites and Kenites

Having just asserted that the Bible's notion of special relations with desert peoples does not demonstrate the borrowing of Yahweh from such groups, the notion is nevertheless important and demands explanation. We will return to this larger question, but first, one more text has played a central role in development of the Midianite Hypothesis from prose biblical texts. Exodus 18 brings together Jethro as "priest of Midian" with Israel's devotion to Yahweh, as celebrated after first arrival at the mountain of God. Exodus 3 and 6 involve Moses in fresh identification of the people's god as Yahweh, without reference to Midian or other groups.

As conceived in relation to the Moses-exodus story, the essential Midianite Hypothesis derives above all from Exodus 18, an encounter

---

[61] Following Kratz (1997: 13–24), Berner (2010: 68–85, 431) pieces together a pre-Priestly account of the burning bush in 3:1–10, a text that would already have had in view the conquest of the land. This solution likewise envisions a schematic role for Exodus 3, even in its earliest form.

[62] This conclusion would apply equally to reading the text as a test or an affirmation of the name.

between Moses and his father-in-law Jethro that is tucked into the story-line just before Yahweh confronts Israel at Mount Sinai and begins setting out the law that will constitute the people as a worshipping community.[63] While the relationship between Moses and Midian is established in 2:11–22, the religious role of Jethro as "priest of Midian" can only be attributed to his appearance at the mountain in chapter 18. The first word of Israel's arrival at "the mountain of God" comes in 18:5, where Moses has set up camp and Jethro brings him his wife and two sons (v. 6).[64] Moses bows to his father-in-law with the respect due an elder, not to take as indication of subservience; they meet in Moses' personal tent, without reference to Israel and his role as leader (v. 7).[65] The narrative then alludes to the mass of what has preceded this meeting, as Moses brings Jethro up to date on what has occurred since their last contact, a celebration of Yahweh's beneficence (v. 8). Few clues are provided regarding the details: "Moses reported to his father-in-law all that Yahweh had done to Pharaoh and to Egypt on behalf of Israel, all the hardship that overtook them on the way, and then Yahweh rescued them."[66] Specification of Pharaoh suggests the ongoing conflict of the plague sequence, whether or not it embraces the Reed Sea as well. The "hardship" is associated with travel and would allude to at least some part of Exodus 15–17 after the Song of the Sea: the bitter water at Marah; manna and quail; water from a rock at Massah and Meribah; and war with Amalek. It is significant in narrative terms that Moses' report in Exod 18:8 assumes knowledge of an

---

[63] As observed earlier, the focus on Exodus 18 is particularly visible in the new synthesis of Römer (2015), like Blenkinsopp before him (2008).

[64] Carr (2011: 118–19) observes the link between Exod 3:1–4:18 and chapter 18 by the specific reference to the "mountain of God" (3:1; 18:5; cf. 33:6), without the close association with the name "Sinai" that appears in 24:12–18.

[65] "The scene depicted is a typical Ancient Eastern greeting ritual. By leaving his tent to meet Jethro, bowing before him and embracing him, Moses shows his respect and affection" (Houtman 1996: 2:406).

[66] Aspects of the wording are unusual, neither standard Priestly nor Deuteronomistic, yet tied to summary of a whole notion of deliverance from Egypt. The compound preposition *ʿal-ʿôdōt* ("because of, on behalf of") appears mainly in texts that suggest late (post-monarchic) prose: Gen 21:11 (Sarah drives out Hagar); Gen 26:22 (etiology for the well Rehoboth); Num 12:1 (Miriam and Aaron); 13:24 (etiology for Eshcol in the spy episode); Josh 14:6 (Caleb's approach to Joshua); Judg 6:7 (prophet in Midianite oppression); and Jer 3:8 (Judah's adultery). The "hardship" (*tĕlāʾāh*) also refers to difficulties in transit in Israel's request to the king of Edom for safe passage (Num 20:14), again as something that "finds" (so, "overtakes") the people (verb *mṣʾ*); otherwise only Mal 1:13; Lam 3:5; Neh 9:32.

extended text that precedes the Jethro meeting, not just divine deliverance as such.[67]

Jethro's response stands at the core of the Midianite Hypothesis, because it is the one religious act associated with him in the Bible. First, "he rejoiced over all the good that Yahweh had done for Israel, in his rescue from the hand of Egypt" (v. 9).[68] It is striking to see such a sympathetic response to Yahweh from a non-Israelite, and while Blenkinsopp (2008: 135) scoffs at the notion that Jethro heard Moses' report "and thereupon became a convert to Yahwistic faith on the spot," the text presents this as appropriate reaction to the full power of Yahweh on display in his provision for Israel. We see a similar response in Rahab, when she acknowledges the power of Yahweh visible in his known deeds, including the Reed Sea crossing after leaving Egypt and defeat of the Amorite kings (Josh 2:9–11).[69]

Jethro's joy generates two acts of ritual recognition, verbal and sacrificial. He says, "Blessed be Yahweh, who rescued you from the hand of Egypt and from the hand of Pharaoh, who rescued the people from beneath the hand of Egypt" (v. 10). Also, "he took a burnt offering and sacrifices to God (Elohim), and Aaron came with all the elders of Israel to eat the meal with Moses' father-in-law in the presence of God" (v. 12). The verbal blessing is defined by recognition of the same divine displays acknowledged in verse 9, and it is followed directly by a specific statement of religious respect: "Now I know that Yahweh is greater than all the gods" (v. 11). In his vigorous defense of much older readings from the Midianite Hypothesis, Blenkinsopp observes (134), "There Moses recounted the great deeds of Yahweh (Exod. 18:8), but it was Jethro the priest who pronounced the blessing on Yahweh and acclaimed this

---

[67] Römer (2015: 66–67) reconstructs the original Jethro narrative here as located in 18:1, 5, 7, 8, 9, and 12. The "confession of faith" in verses 10–11 is a later addition that resembles the portrayal of Rahab in Joshua 2.

[68] The verb "rejoice" is unusual (*ḥdh*), only here and Job 3:6 in the qal stem. For such collective "good" performed by Yahweh, see also the (schematic) speech of Solomon, "because of all the good that Yahweh had done to David his servant and to Israel his people" (1 Kgs 8:66). The verb *nṣl* for "rescue" was the choice of the Priestly writer in Exod 6:6.

[69] With its awareness of an extended exodus account that includes the cited episodes, the Rahab prelude to conquest of Jericho is often considered a late, probably Persian period, text. See the syntheses of Römer (2005: 134), as "a later, non-Deuteronomistic addition"; and Kratz (2005: 201) identifies only Josh 2:1–7, 15–16, and 22–23 as the original account of Jericho and Rahab, without the declaration of faith. On the phenomenon of such recognition of Yahweh by non-Israelites, see Spina (2005).

demonstration of the incomparability of his god." And the reading as conversion "contradicts the most natural sense of the passage: Jethro is the principal actor; he initiates the action, and Aaron and the elders come and eat with him in the presence of Yahweh" (135). Yet it is more difficult to read the text as if Jethro were a priest of Yahweh, confirming Moses' new "Yahwistic faith" after enjoying the benefits of the Midianite god's choice to rescue Israel.[70] Jethro's respect for Yahweh as "greater than all the gods" only comes "now" (*'attāh*), a conclusion drawn from new experience.[71] Rahab likewise responds to what she has seen of Yahweh with a declaration of respect: "indeed Yahweh your god, he is God in heaven above and on earth below" (Josh 2:11).[72]

Without the expectation that the people of Israel only learned of Yahweh by name in connection with the exodus, Jethro's meeting with Moses would never have suggested a Midianite origin for the god. Exodus 3 and 6, the texts that carry this expectation, are schematic efforts to relate the exodus to the ancestor narratives of Genesis, not repositories of hidden religious history. Likewise, the account of Jethro at the mountain of God sanctifies Moses' family after the fact, so that for all his Egyptian upbringing and marriage to a foreigner, he could remain untainted by the potential religious associations, especially by the Midianite wife. It appears that the Midianite marriage was a problem to solve in known narrative, not a creation for (or addition to) Exodus 18.[73] Likewise, the

---

[70] For me, it is more important to understand the text's schematic function than to date it late, though this could be the case. In the recent collection of articles on *The Origins of Yahwism* (van Oortschot and Witte 2017), two of the European contributors respond to Exod 18:1–12 as a post-Priestly composition in its entirety (Pfeiffer, especially 133; and Berner, especially 193). For Berner, this is a post-Priestly "manifesto," to illustrate the "radiant success" of Yahweh worship beyond Israel's borders.

[71] Compare the mother of the boy restored to life by the prophet Elijah: "Now [*'attāh*] I know that you are a man of God and the word of Yahweh is truly in your mouth" (1 Kgs 17:24). She can only say this after the demonstration of power.

[72] With his removal of verses 10–11 from the original composition, Römer (2015: 66) softens the force of Jethro's act as a response to word of Yahweh's power on Israel's behalf, but this interpretation does not change the essential exchange. The fact that Jethro is the one to make the sacrifice does not show him the priest of Yahweh who is instructing Moses and Israel in his worship. This analysis is perhaps confirmed by the fact that Berner (2010: 426) reconstructs the original conclusion of Jethro's offering as almost a mirror image of Römer's text, in 18:1, 5, 6a, 7, 8a, 10a, and 11a (plus v. 27).

[73] Both Berner and Römer remove the elements of Exod 18:1–12 that allude to Moses' marriage to Jethro's daughter, with the notion that she had been sent back to her father (v. 2). Indeed this element of chapter 18 makes reference to the marriage in chapter 2, but by my reading, the marriage is not added in chapter 18 because of Jethro as priest.

specific vehicle of Jethro's priesthood appears to have been inherited rather than carried into the text as part of its scene of sacrifice to Yahweh. Jethro is introduced as "the priest of Midian" in 18:1, picking up the title from 2:16 and 3:1, but the title plays no further role in the exchange with Moses. Moses reports to "his father-in-law" (18:8), and each act of speech and sacrifice is performed by "Jethro" without title (verses 9, 10, and 12), only adding "the father-in-law of Moses" twice in the last verse, with sacrifice and feast. While Exodus 18 consists of two parts, with the arrangement for a judicial hierarchy to assist Moses probably the later contribution, the entire chapter seems to have been added at a relatively late stage to the front of the long Sinai law-giving, resolving the loose end of Moses' marriage to a Midianite.[74]

Both the Midianite marriage and the father-in-law as "priest," however, do come from deep in the exodus narrative.[75] The introduction of Moses in Exodus 2 leads seamlessly into his flight from Egypt into the wilderness. First, we are to understand Moses' Egyptian-sounding name in relation to his true standing as an Israelite of Levite origin, by the ruse of his mother, who introduced him into Pharaoh's household by having

Rather, Jethro shows up at the mountain of God to demonstrate his commitment to Yahweh because of the narrative fact, from chapter 2, of marriage to a foreigner who was identified opaquely as simply "the priest of Midian." For marriage to a Midianite as a problem in early Jewish circles, see Lawrence (2017: 2): "Jethro becomes a locus of anxiety for Jewish interpreters: an apparent idolater, the priest of a foreign religion, who is nonetheless the inventor of the Jewish system of justice and Moses' father-in-law." I conclude that this early sensitivity is already present in the composition of Exod 18:1–12.

[74] On the rendition of Jethro's role in coming up with a system of justice as secondary to the meeting in 18:1–12, see Russell (2015) and Berner (2010: 406–407). The parallel account of developing a system of justice in Deut 1:9–18 has no role for Jethro, who has been inserted into it in Exodus 18.

[75] Berner (2010: 55–62) regards the encounter with the family of "the priest of Midian" in Exod 2:16–22 as secondary to the Moses story, developed from his birth and flight. Nevertheless, it appears to me that, however the early Moses combination took form, the primary writer of 18:1–12 responds to a version of it that already includes particular details and must grapple with them. Two key features in the Jethro-Midian material come from non-Priestly narrative and have nothing to do with Yahweh. One is marriage to a Midianite as part of locating Moses in the wilderness, where an exodus will lead. The second is Moses' father-in-law as "the priest of Midian," evidently a title that renders Jethro/Reuel the leader of the Midianites, with the title a marker of status without carrying religious interest. The marriage is presented in 2:16–22 and then assumed by the accounts of the wife's return to Egypt (4:19–20), of her return to Jethro (18:2–5), and of her role fending off divine assault in an unidentified camp (4:24–26).

her son discovered adrift by the king's daughter (vv. 1–10).[76] Moses' departure from Egypt, necessary for his separation from the land and return as an outsider, is explained by murder in foolhardy defense of a battered Israelite ("Hebrew") laborer, provoking Pharaoh's wrath and so Moses' flight "to the land of Midian," where he "sits" – or perhaps takes up residence – at a well (vv. 11–15).[77] This situation permits Moses to gain the good graces of a man introduced simply as "the priest of Midian," without name (v. 16), when Moses defends the man's daughters from overbearing herdsmen (vv. 16–20). "The man" gave Moses his daughter Zipporah in marriage, with the result of a single son named Gershom (vv. 21–22). What follows is dominated by the burning bush and subsequent conversation with Yahweh at the mountain of God in 3:1–4:18, followed by an account of Moses' return to Egypt that picks up from 2:23 as if he had never been to the mountain of God (4:19–20).[78]

Division of the early Exodus chapters between J and E documentary sources seemed to be supported by the patent doubling of names for Moses' Midianite father-in-law, first as Reuel in the account of the well (2:18) and then as Jethro with introduction of the mountain of God in 3:1 and subsequently (4:18; and ch. 18).[79] Reuel is never "the priest of Midian" and the title may be attached secondarily to Jethro, since it stands alone as the initial introduction of the seven girls' father in 2:16. Without any religious activity or affiliation to accompany the title, the singular office in this text appears to have been carried with the narrative as an expression of social standing and leadership among tent-dwelling

---

[76] Thomas Schneider argues that there is no plausible Egyptian etymology for the name Moses, in spite of the fact that the name is commonly conceived as such (presentation to the Biblical Colloquium, October 2017).

[77] The same verb *yšb* is used both for Moses' arrival at the well and his introduction into Reuel's household (vv. 16, 21).

[78] This logical link between 2:23a, reporting the death of Egypt's king, and 4:19, where Yahweh tells Moses that the men who want to kill him are dead, is one part of the argument by Schmid, Römer, and others that 3:1–4:18 constitutes an insertion (see above).

[79] For the book of Exodus, Propp's commentary represents a careful, if somewhat idiosyncratic, rendition of composition in documentary terms, maximizing the Elohistic content. He begins his identification of E-writing by the very notion that the name Yahweh must be revealed to Moses and Israel in 3:15–17, with its allusion to Gen 50:24–25. Taking Reuel as a mark of the Yahwistic (J) source in 2:18, reference to Jethro in 4:18 indicates E (1998: 50–51). The tension between one and two sons in 2:22 and 18:3 reflects J and E (170). "If the Elohist's Moses was born in Egypt, we must assume that Redactor[JE] discarded E's account of the journey to Midian" (171). This kind of source division has been widely abandoned in recent European biblical scholarship.

herdsmen, not for any interest in its religious function. The tale is notable for its location of Moses among a desert people, without towns, social divisions, or formal leadership, having only a "well" as gathering place.[80] In Gen 14:18, Melchizedek is both "king of Salem" and "priest (*kōhēn*) to El Elyon," a priest as ruler in another tradition of a distant time gone by.[81]

In this context, "the priest of Midian" has no more to do with Yahweh than with any other god, and his religious associations have no interest to the narrative. Throughout the episode at the well and resulting marriage, the man performs no sacred act and expresses no religious commitment. We may expect the text to assume some unnamed deity, but any guess-work risks forcing the identity into a range of biblical possibilities that did not govern its initial use in Exod 2:16. The blessing and sacrifice in Exodus 18 would then derive from the mysterious title in the marriage account, still without concern to identify an imagined deity of his titular service. Neither Exodus 2 nor 18 supplies any basis for finding biblical memory in any form for non-Israelite worship of Yahweh. Even where this is so often imagined in formulations of the Midianite Hypothesis, it is not clear how such an idea of Midianite religious affinity could have been preserved in Israel and Judah as a historical artifact. The peoples of the Bible would have had no notion of desert deities and religion from before Yahweh was worshipped in Israel.

Israel's Southern Kin

Exodus 2 does, however, belong to a cluster of biblical texts that envision friendly relations with peoples on Israel's southern margins, exhibited in diverse texts that attracted much attention in the late 19th and early 20th centuries as part of the work that generated the original Midianite Hypothesis.[82] The collection of such texts represents a separate undertaking, only indirectly relevant to evaluation of Yahweh's supposed southern origins. Some of the peoples in question are attached

---

[80] The name Reuel may evoke the same environment, as the injunction, "Shepherd, O El!"

[81] It is somehow significant that the priest in Exod 2:16 is defined without reference to a deity, unlike Potiphera the priest of On, father-in-law to Joseph in Egypt (Gen 41:45, 50; 46:20). This may add to the impression of nonreligious significance.

[82] See already the long note in Kuenen's *Religion of Israel* (1869–70: 179–82). Tiele's entire proposal worked from this set of texts, then was repeated in various forms by all who followed. In his recent reiteration of the Midianite Hypothesis, Römer also revisits the biblical traditions of links to southern peoples (2015: chapter 3).

to accounts of enmity and conflict, even as other stories picture peace and even kinship, though the division always separates the exodus and conquest on one side from later conflicts on the other. Amalek fights a pitched battle with Israel through a full day at Rephidim, with Joshua as commander (Exod 17:8–16), concluded with a prophecy that Yahweh will always oppose Amalek, yet the battle narrative in the Song of Deborah identifies Ephraim as having its root "in Amalek" (Judg 5:14). The chronological alignments are reversed with Midian, whose relationship to Israel through Moses contrasts with the accounts of war in the time of Gideon (Judges 6–8). In Genesis, Israel is assigned the closest imaginable blood bond with Edom through the definition of Jacob and Esau as twins (25:19–34). Deuteronomy's law defining the community of worship distinguishes the Edomite as "your brother" from Moabites and Ammonites who shall be excluded permanently (23:4–8). Deuteronomy 2:1–5 has the people turn toward (or go around the edge of?) "the highland of Seir" for "many days" (or years), before they are finally instructed to cross "the territory of your brothers the sons of Esau, who live in Seir" (v. 4). At the same time, in the last poetry assembled around the name of Balaam, Jacob's star and staff defeat Moab, the children of Seth, Edom, and Seir in sequence, with Amalek's demise to follow (Num 24:17–20). Israel is both kin to the various peoples of the desert back country and prone to conflict with them. It is hard to date the positive and negative accounts securely and it may be a mistake to treat all positive relations as older, but given the memory of specific and severe battles, the idea of kinship in itself appears old – just the sort of "tradition" that is not suggested for Yahweh by Exodus 3 and 6. These texts offer nothing to locate Yahweh in the southern wilderness, but they do display close and sometimes surprising relations with Israel.

One more southern connection with Israel gives its name to the initial form of the Midianite Hypothesis as "Kenite." The most famous biblical figure attached to the Kenites is, like Moses and Midian, only related by marriage. Jael, who tricks the Canaanite commander Sisera into trusting her and then dispatches him with a tent peg, is identified by marriage to Heber the Kenite (Judg 4:11, 17; 5:24). Judges 4:11 remarks that "Heber was separated from Cain [Qayin; cf. the Qêni or Kenites], from the sons of Hobab, the father-in-law of Moses." This text adds a third name to the set of Reuel and Jethro already known from the book of Exodus. The same family association appears to be envisioned in Judg 1:16, which locates "the sons of the Kenite, the father-in-law of Moses" in the territory of Judah in the Negeb of Arad.[83] In Num 10:29, as Israel departs Sinai, Moses' invitation to "Hobab son of Reuel the Midianite, the father-in-law of Moses" offers a genealogical solution that seems more an attempt to tie up loose ends than a true alternative.

Unlike Midian, which could be remembered as Israel's outright enemy, the Kenites are never envisioned as a threat, perhaps in part because they are not perceived to have existed as a coherent political entity of significant scale.[84] David considers them among his wilderness friends when he lives with the Philistines and ranges through the region south of Israel (1 Sam 27:10; 30:29). Saul is said to spare the Kenites from his assault on Amalek: "You acted loyally with all the Israelites when they came up out of Egypt" (1 Sam 15:6) – a good deed not actually attested in any biblical account.[85] Genesis 15, which serves to bind the ancestor stories to the exodus, begins its long list of peoples to be replaced with the Kenites, the Kenizzites, and the Kadmonites, before getting to the more conventional Hittites, Amorites, and Canaanites, among others (vv. 19–21). And after disposing of Moab, Edom, and Amalek, the last Balaam poetry promises captivity to the Kenites at the hands of the Assyrians, in spite of their rocky refuges (Num 24:21–22).

Here again we have no evidence that Yahweh was a Kenite god – no interest in Yahweh at all, except by extrapolation from Moses' "father-in-law" in Exodus 18. The religious role of the Kenites is drawn from another fragile construction of linked intrigue, propelled by the hope that the Bible should preserve clues to Yahweh's origin outside of Israel. The Kenites share their name with Cain, the ancestor of antediluvian civilization according to Genesis 4, a tradition never visible in the Bible's various

---

[83] Pfeiffer (2017: 136) considers that these two Judges texts reflect post-monarchic uneasiness with the Midianite relatives of Moses and connect them secondarily with the Kenites.

[84] Mark Smith (personal communication) wonders whether the Kenite category could have represented craftsmen who did not represent a threat to those who came to be identified as Israel, with their evident dependence on farming and livestock. Cain is associated with metalwork through his descendant Tubalcain, said to be the founder of forging implements in bronze and iron (Gen 4:22). Citing Dijkstra (1988) for "a potential attestation of Kenite metalworkers near the South Judean desert with which they were associated in an inscription found at a metal mine in the Sinai that refers to a 'chief of the Kenites'," Carr (forthcoming) affirms the possibility of such an interpretation. See also McNutt (1999). I appreciate greatly David Carr's generosity in sharing his manuscript for the Genesis 1–11 project.

[85] This tradition of a bond between Israel and the Kenites during the time of Saul provided one of Tiele's original arguments and was likewise revisited in many early comments on Yahweh's origins in relation to the Kenites and the Midianites.

allusions to Israel's Kenite neighbors.[86] At the end of this account of Cain and his offspring, we are informed that Adam and Eve had another son named Seth, after the loss of Abel to Cain, and that Seth had a son called Enosh. A closing note, before the Priestly genealogy from Adam to Noah in chapter 5, proposes that Yahweh was known to the ancients before the Flood: "Then it was begun to call on the name of Yahweh" (4:26).[87]

Because the only documentary source imagined to assume the worship of Yahweh before Moses was the Yahwist (J), and this was long considered the oldest of the pentateuchal documents, the note in Gen 4:26 could be understood to preserve an early view of Israelite religion.[88] Going back to the 19th century, Gen 4:25–26 has also been explained as a bridge between the Cain and Lamech material of chapter 4 and the Priestly genealogy of chapter 5, thus later than both. Whether or not in the service of a J document, Genesis 4:26 is, however, another schematic text, identifying the first prayer to Yahweh with the earth's earliest human population, before Noah and the great flood. Like the two explanations for Yahweh's special revelation through Moses in Exodus 3 and 6, the interpretation of Yahweh's first worship in Gen 4:26 represents the guiding hand of a fellow scholar, not the passing on of near-forgotten lore – from before the great flood!

So far as there was lore to be passed on, this was perhaps in the mapping of names from the beginning of time. In his coming volume on Genesis 1–11, David Carr continues to develop his long-standing division between Priestly and "non-Priestly" writing, the latter category allowing consideration of reconstructed texts that need not have served J or E documents combining the ancestors with Moses. In the case of Gen 4:25–26, Carr rejects the "post-Priestly" explanation, in part because the

---

[86] Carr (forthcoming) proposes that while written by the same hand as the Eden story, the Cain text of Gen 4:1–24 was based on an etiology of the Kenites that may have been oral.

[87] See above for the introduction of this text into consideration of Yahweh's origins, repeated in Blenkinsopp (2008).

[88] This documentary reading of Gen 4:26 is maintained in Hendel (2017: 251). Blenkinsopp (2008: 141) embraces the traditional/historical value of the line without commitment to a date or assignment to J: "I take Gen. 4.26 (recording the birth of a son to Shem when people first began to invoke the name of Yahweh) to mark a decisively new stage in religious history with the beginning of the line which leads to Israel's ancestors. But this history has a prehistory, a problematic prehistory in the view of the author and the tradition which he reproduces." It is not clear to me that this line about religion had any particular interest in relating the first worship of Yahweh to Kenites as people with direct lineage to an ancestor from before the Flood, when these would seem to have been wiped out.

passage envisions an early approach to Yahweh long before Moses, in contrast to P.[89] At the same time, however, he emphasizes the separate genealogical reasoning in these verses, which set out a line from Adam to Seth to Enosh, from the Cain/Lamech material of 4:1–24. This moment of first prayer to Yahweh has nothing to do with Kenites, in any case, and Carr wonders instead whether it may look to the next non-Priestly morsel in 5:29, now embedded in the last part of P's antediluvian genealogy, where Noah's name is linked to comfort from Yahweh's curse against the "ground" (*'ădāmāh*).[90]

In the end, the old Midianite (or Kenite) Hypothesis was constructed from biblical prose that cannot provide the conceptual scaffolding for historical accounts of early religion. Exodus 3 and 6 do not intend us to understand Yahweh to have been worshipped first by other peoples, however we interpret the literary intent of Yahweh's self-introduction in each case. The figure of Moses looms in Torah imagination as essential to God's establishment of Israel as his people before providing them a land of their own, and both texts make Moses central even to knowing the name by which this god must be approached. Genesis 4:26 casts a completely different vision, locating Yahweh and knowledge of him in

---

[89] This analysis appears to represent an evolution in Carr's thought, now inclined to read 4:25–26 as a whole, with the reference to Yahweh in 26b an intrinsic part of it. In his 1996 exploration of a non-Priestly "proto-Genesis composition" in the "primeval history" of Genesis 1–11, Carr considers the possible shape of the large narrative units created by non-Priestly writers, breaking these into primeval history, Abraham-Isaac, and Jacob–Joseph sections (1996: 215–16). He weighs Gen 4:26 as part of this level of composition, starting with the observation that the theme of "calling on Yahweh's name" occurs for the first time here, before its more prominent role in the Abraham and Isaac stories (12:8; 13:4; 21:33; 26:25). "This theme's distribution in the very sections where the proto-Genesis author seems to have been most active suggests it was important to him. One might suppose that he developed the theme from the notice in 4:26b, but there [are] also indicators that 4:26b may have been added secondarily to its context. It is only loosely connected to the genealogy of Seth (4:25–26a), and the following primeval history narrative does not develop the theme of calling on YHWH's name. Such indicators suggest that this theme of calling YHWH's name was inserted at its appropriate point by the proto-Genesis author." Carr tentatively dates this work to the very end of the Judah kingdom or to its early aftermath (232).

[90] At the end of his discussion of the pre-flood non-Priestly material, Carr ranks the degree of certainty in his proposals, with this one the least secure, mainly because the link between the first human generations in 4:25–26 and Noah in 5:29 must be reconstructed. The idea is attractive nonetheless because it follows directly the non-Priestly content on either side of the P genealogy in Genesis 5 and in the process offers a potential link between two otherwise adjacent non-Priestly texts that both refer to the worship of Yahweh.

the earliest epoch of human history, available to all, without need to identify what peoples did or did not have access to him.

The Midianites and the Kenites themselves are another matter entirely. Jethro – or Reuel, or Hobab – represents just one instance of a recurring theme in biblical accounts of origins and early days, when the predecessors of the biblical peoples manifest diverse lines of affinity and kinship with the inhabitants of the inland back country, often in spaces south of Israel and Judah. This phenomenon constitutes the kind of "tradition" that is no creation of monarchic or post-monarchic scribes, a tradition that creeps into widely varied texts with a panoply of particulars, and we will return to it in consideration of Yahweh and the south in the Chapter 4, on old poetry. There are Rechabites, Kenites, and Midianites, as well as Esau as Jacob's twin, Ishmael and the sons of Keturah – and more. Tiele proposed his hypothesis for the origin of Yahweh as an alternative to two other geographical explanations: Egypt and Canaan. If we shift the question from Yahweh's background to Israel's, the multitude of southern connections suggests at least another element in Israel's past, pointing inland and sometimes south, away from the settled landscape of Canaan.

Biblical notions of nomads tend southward, perhaps displaced from Israel's and Judah's own lands, as well as from Ammon and Moab to the east, by the establishment of kingdoms and capitals in the early first millennium. As observed in Chapter 2, the experience of New Kingdom Egypt seems likewise to have seen a similar southward shift. The mobile pastoralist Shasu population only comes to be identified with Seir and Edom in the late 13th and 12th centuries. Faced with the complex biblical picture of southern affinities, I hesitate to reconstruct a southern alliance in the fashion of Blenkinsopp (2008). Esau is Jacob's twin, relating him to Israel, not Judah. As will be seen in Chapter 4, the texts from Kuntillet ʿAjrud, far south of Beersheba, indicate connections with both kingdoms, but the primary affiliation appears to have been with Israel. Stephen Russell (2009) concluded that the narrative of escape from Egypt was the particular possession of highland Israel, not Judah, and I have argued (Fleming 2012a) that the tradition of tent-dwelling ancestors goes back to peoples of the northern kingdom.[91] It seems somehow significant that

---

[91] Documentary interpretations of the Pentateuch have generally located J at Jerusalem and E in the northern kingdom, so that both Israel and Judah would have shared essentially the same origins narrative, with distinct emphases. When the ancestor collection is seen as more deeply separate from the Moses material, interpreters have given more weight to the origin of entire traditions, with the Jacob lore oldest and associated with the kingdom of Israel (Blum 1984; Carr 1996).

these bonds belong to peoples not identified with cities and kings, envisioned to live more the way the ancestors did in Genesis, with extended family and the possibility to change their settled base as needed. Even the exodus story supposes a long-standing Egyptian base of operations for a shepherding people that must disentangle itself from external demands, resorting to the back country as refuge (Fleming 2015). The Bible's Midianites and Kenites are further manifestations of this same "collective memory."[92]

Although Cornelis Tiele proposed a desert origin for Yahweh with religion in view, his interpretation depended first of all on the notion that Israel began as a desert people, a scholarly interest that was embedded in now untenable conceptions of the Bible in history but that keeps a connection with present historical inquiry. Once Tiele's proposal was picked up by biblical specialists, who turned it toward Moses and the exodus, its power lay in the idea that even the Bible's God, the God of Christianity and Judaism – the sequence reflecting the direction of thought – had a history. The Midianite Hypothesis was proposed before the discovery of Ugarit and its poetry for "The God" Ilu (El), so with much less evidence for pre-Israelite religion in the Levant.[93] Where modern specialists are impressed by Yahweh's absence from the inscriptional record of the Bronze Age and limitation to Israel in first-millennium texts, in contrast to El, Tiele and those who followed had only the compelling certainty that the Bible must preserve more than revelation.[94] In fact, God does have a history, as Karen Armstrong (1993) asserted to a broad audience and Mark Smith (1990) had already suggested to a more

---

[92] I would apply Mark Smith's nuanced and productive analysis of memory and its intriguing cousin, "amnesia," to the complex background of Israel (Smith 2004; especially chapter 4, "The Formation of Israel's Concepts of God: Collective Memory and Amnesia in the Bible," 124–58). These factors in the production of ancient literature influence every dimension of its contents, including religion, but when it comes to Midianites and Kenites, the primary significance attaches to populations and conceived affinities.

[93] Even writing for publication in 1872, Tiele could already conclude from alphabetic inscriptional evidence that El and Baal were prominent Phoenician divine names (1872: 281–85).

[94] Tiele (1872: 328–29) offers a direct argument in favor of a rational basis for evaluating competing religious claims. So far as the best expressions of Israel's religion can be judged superior, "To seek the explanation of this phenomenon in a supernatural revelation – as difficult to comprehend as little satisfying – is to apply arbitrarily to the religion of Israel a method one would reject for other religions." All religions claim the same, so there must be another basis for judgment.

targeted one.[95] The failure of the biblical evidence invoked by the framers of the Midianite Hypothesis to support the particular history they envisioned does not mean that the alternative is a god without history. Both Elohim and Yahweh have roots in worship before Israel. As the literal God, sometimes represented as "The God" (*hā'ēl* or *hā'ĕlōhîm*) like the older father of gods, it is easier to track the ancestry of the biblical God by that name. Moreover, "God" is at home in Canaan, where specialists now expect us to find the cultural ancestry of ancient Israel. It should not be surprising that Yahweh also had a history before Israel, and the evidence still points to such a reality, even without the biblical prose that long sustained the Midianite Hypothesis.

---

[95] Notice that Smith did not pick up the title from Armstrong! Nothing in the notes to Armstrong's book suggests any awareness of Smith's work and title.

4

The Old Poetry

One thing about Mark Smith's work on religion is that his analysis of any individual problem always represents just one part of an effort to understand the whole. He has written synthetic studies but no "history of Israelite religion" or book-length examination of El, or Yahweh, or all the gods of Israel. It is particularly interesting to me that Smith's treatments of Yahweh have the feel of finishing a landscape rather than of isolating a portrait. He has written on Yahweh because he must, in order to address so many different views of biblical and (call it) Israelite religion. I wonder whether he has not made Yahweh his primary object because he has not been certain of having discovered something deeply new about the god, and he is always looking for a fresh line of sight on the material at hand. He tells me, reflecting on what I just wrote, that another factor is "how the biblical material seems to reflect lost knowledge about Yahweh," or even that Yahweh could have been "an unknown god for Israel in some critical respects to which the biblical authors – and we – no longer have access."[1]

With this larger consideration of Mark Smith's oeuvre in mind, I come to the biblical evidence for the new Midianite Hypothesis as seen through the lens of the poetry in Deuteronomy 33, Judges 5, Habakkuk 3, and Psalm 68 – listed here in order of their biblical appearance. For Smith, these are jigsaw pieces in a puzzle not delimited by Yahweh or the notion of early Hebrew poetry, and his judgment as I see it carries the more weight because it belongs to a larger evaluation of the Bible and ancient

---

[1] These are quotations from his reading of the penultimate manuscript of this book.

Levantine religion. More than others who advocate some modern manifestation of the old Midianite Hypothesis, Smith places special weight on these poetic texts, especially the Song of Deborah, in part because he hesitates to force the Egyptian Shasu evidence to accomplish too much, when it does not involve a god and the match of names is probable but not certain. At least the biblical poetry has the god Yahweh as its secure focus, and Smith is ready to let it take the lead in pointing toward Yahweh's southern desert origin. After quick review of the Egyptian evidence that Smith (2017: 25–26) regards as less than secure, he allows it a role only based on its alignment with Judg 5:4:

While the Egyptian evidence for YHWH does not seem particularly strong, it appears consonant with the biblical tradition of YHWH attached to southern locale known by various names: Edom (Judg 5:4; cf. Num 24:18) and Seir (Deut 33:2; Judg 5:4; cf. Num 24:18); Teman (Hab 3:3; cf. "YHWH of Teman," *yhwh tmn/tymn* in the Kuntillet 'Ajrud inscriptions); Paran (Deut 33:2; Hab 3:3); and the best known of these locales, Sinai, attested both as a place name (Ps 68:18; Deut 33:2) and as part of a divine title, "the One of Sinai" (Judg 5:4; Ps 68:8). . . .

Building on these basic features, three related points come into focus. First, from the perspective of the poems and the putative Egyptian evidence, YHWH is grounded in a place outside of Israel.[2]

Throughout his discussion of the biblical evidence for "YHWH's original character," Smith returns to a category that has long held prime place in biblical criticism: the idea of "tradition." For generations of its practice, critical analysis of how the Bible was composed and revised distinguished between the identifiable work of authors or editors and the raw materials accessible to them, whether oral or written. Such freestanding material, stripped of the organizing ideas of the biblical composers, could be understood to carry notions of the more ancient past. Even without non-biblical evidence, history could be reconstructed from this kind of biblical tradition. In the case of the Midianite Hypothesis, the scattered references to Israel's southern associations, interpreted through the Midianite and Kenite names, were received as historically informative tradition.

This separation of organizing narrative and thought from independent underlying material remains a viable method for analysis with historical

---

[2] The second and third points are that "the evidence presently known gives reason to entertain a more complex form of what has come to be known as the 'Midianite hypothesis' or the 'Kenite hypothesis'" (Smith 2017: 26); and finally, in noting the geographical and chronological distance between the Egyptian and the earliest biblical evidence, "the Israelites who composed these relatively early pieces worked with a certain ignorance of their own about the original profile of their God" (28–29).

interest. Where smaller units of writing do not share the perspectives and assumptions of the surrounding text, these provide a prior view of the Bible's conceptual landscape. Different questions can be posed in relation to the settings of their creation. Yet the varied material calls for evaluation with the same caution applied to the compositional work of its organizers. What were the concerns and the knowledge that informed such prior thinking? In the poetry cited by Mark Smith and often essential to new constructions of the Midianite Hypothesis, we are dealing with a cluster of references informed by some shared expectation of Yahweh, truly a "tradition" in the above terms. In the Bible's prose references to friendly relations with Midianites, Kenites, and Rechabites, I see another such tradition that reveals old alignments, even where I conclude that this tradition has only been secondarily associated with Yahweh. In contrast, the tradition of Yahweh going to war on Israel's behalf from different named sites in the southern back country has to do explicitly with religion. Yet it has too quickly been conflated with the prose accounts of Midianites and Kenites to identify a location for earlier worship of Yahweh. As much attention as these poetic texts have received, it is therefore necessary to return to them here.[3]

EARLY HEBREW POETRY

Beginning even before discovery of the new West Semitic language found in the alphabetic cuneiform texts from Ugarit, and then propelled forward by the new evidence, William F. Albright found a way around the endless wrangling over the date and character of literary sources in the Bible.[4] At Ugarit, as in Mesopotamia, the normal vehicle for written storytelling was

---

[3] I will not reproduce the kind of systematic examination of these texts that has been undertaken by many others, including whole monographs on the individual poems. References will be provided with the discussion of each text. In order to maintain a necessary balance between the different elements of my argument, I refrain from detailed readings of the entire poems, the presentation and defense of which would become too much an end in itself.

[4] See the literature cited in the Introduction. Writing on the Balaam poems, Albright offers his analysis based on new knowledge of "early Northwest-Semitic grammar, lexicography and epigraphy," especially from Ugarit (1944: 208). In his study of Psalm 68, Albright notes directly the key impact of Ugarit: "The study of Ugaritic verse has thrown a flood of light on the evolution of Hebrew poetic forms, as I have pointed out in various recent publications" (1950–51: 5). Ugaritic phenomena like "climactic or repetitive parallelism swarm in the Song of Deborah and the Song of Miriam [i.e. Exodus 15], both dating from between 1300 and 1100 B.C.E., but both disappear in such late compositions as Job."

poetry, evidently carried over from oral narration, as long observed with Homer.[5] Whereas the Bible is dominated by prose narrative, there are notable exceptions, in some cases embedded in the prose as a celebratory elaboration: most notably, the Song of the Sea with the Reed Sea crossing in Exodus 14–15; and the Song of Deborah with victory over Sisera in Judges 4–5.[6] Viewed in the light of Near Eastern and Greek patterns, the Song of the Sea and the Song of Deborah offered renditions of victory over Egypt and the Canaanites more archaic in literary mode. Albright concluded that the same could be said of the Hebrew grammar on display in such poems, as measured against the full range of inscriptional evidence for Hebrew, its early first-millennium Northwest Semitic cousins, and the older West Semitic from Ugarit.[7] As he saw them, these poems represented the oldest writing in the Bible, transmitted with little updating of language and no significant revision of content.

Biblical poems like those in Exodus 15 and Judges 5 were also independent of the surrounding prose, or could be taken as such if proved not to be written under inspiration of the narrative now preceding each poem.[8] The poems were not implicated in the debates over potential prose sources and documents, the grist for the mill of literary-historical

[5] The reference to oral composition was developed much further by Frank M. Cross, who had this in view behind the title of his *Canaanite Myth and Hebrew Epic* (1973). Introducing his chapter on "The Song of the Sea and Canaanite Myth" (ch. 6), he turns to the Baal myth from Ugarit: "There can be no doubt that this poetic cycle was orally composed. It is marked by oral formulae, by characteristic repetitions, and by fixed pairs of synonyms (a type of formula) in traditional thought rhyme (*parallelismus membrorum*) which marks Semitic oral literature as well as much of the oral literature throughout the world" (112). For authority, Cross cites "the epoch-making work on the character of oral literature" by Albert Lord (1960). The Ugaritic point of reference is still widely understood to confirm the likelihood that a tradition of Israelite and Judahite narrative poetry must have existed, with only glimpses preserved in the Bible, though little survives of Cross's particular scheme of a massive "Hebrew epic," and the relationship between such poetry and oral composition from standard poetic formulae is much doubted (see Dobbs-Allsopp 2015: chapter 4, "An Informing Orality: Biblical Poetic Style"). Homeric studies have continued to develop increasingly nuanced accounts of composition in this narrative poetic tradition (e.g. Hainsworth 1968; Foley 1991). I thank Zachary Margulies for his guidance on literature related to these questions on both the Greek and the biblical sides.

[6] See first of all Halpern (1983), followed by two systematic works treating the wider phenomenon (Watts 1992; Weitzman 1997). Kawashima (2004: chapter 2) offers a more theoretically informed development of what he sees as Halpern's essential insight.

[7] For Albright, see the references cited in the Introduction. This analytical strategy culminated in the monograph by Robertson (1972), who was influenced by this intellectual stream but wrote his dissertation at Yale under Marvin Pope, not a student of Albright.

[8] In his 1983 article, Halpern sets out to demonstrate the reverse, that the prose narrative of Judges 4 was composed with the Song of Deborah as its principal source.

scholarship, and they could provide a substantial body of evidence from which to begin afresh the construction of Israelite history, culture, and religion. Every name and reference in these poems offered itself as an ancient data-point, plausibly the oldest evidence for the entity in question. One of the important and eye-catching applications was religion: What names appear in the old poetry, and how is the people's god described? What literary forms and active settings are suggested? In my characterization of "early Hebrew poetry," I am certainly reflecting a student's sense of what Frank Cross and his circle deemed plausible and important in the 1980s, even as profound challenges to existing literary-historical syntheses were gaining momentum.

When it comes to Israel itself, the poems present a mix of modes, which we do well to respect for their variety. The Song of the Sea has only a "people" (*'ām*): "whom you redeemed" (Exod 15:13); "your people" (v. 16); and "the people whom you purchased" (v. 16). The Song of Deborah names Israel eight times, all in the opening hymn (Judg 5:2–11), before the call to Deborah and Barak in verse 12, the direct address that offers the effective opening of the battle account: "Awake, awake, Deborah. Awake, awake, recite a song."[9] The Song goes on to list the peoples who fought and those who stayed home (vv. 14–18), providing a roster of constituents for what the hymn identifies as Israel, a penchant reflected in two more old poems, now assigned to Jacob and Moses. Both Genesis 49 and Deuteronomy 33 assemble sayings that sketch the character and destiny of individual peoples, combined under the name Israel in their introductions (Gen 49:2; cf. 16, 24; Deut 33:5; cf. 28–29). These sets of sayings are linked by textually overlapping pronouncements for Joseph (Gen 49:22–26; Deut 33:13–17), which indicate some contact between them in their composition and transmission.[10] The sayings of Jacob consist only of lines devoted to 12 sons, bound to the patriarch by the poem's opening line: "Come together and give heed,

---

[9] "When long hair flows in Israel" (v. 2; for discussion and literature, see Smith 2014: 223–24); "I will sing to Yahweh, the god of Israel" (v. 3); "the mountains shook before Yahweh, he of Sinai, before Yahweh, the god of Israel" (v. 5); "the village-muster ceased, ceased in Israel, until you arose, O Deborah, you arose, a mother in Israel" (v. 7; cf. Smith 2014: 225–26, "village militia," after Albright and Stager); "shield was not seen, nor spear, in the forty thousand of Israel" (v. 8); "my heart belongs to the leaders of Israel" (v. 9); "the victories of his village-muster in Israel" (v. 11). My first publication of this was in *Legacy* (2012a: 64–66), but Smith knew about it from a draft and cited me in his 2009 article, "What is Prologue is Past."

[10] Each poem has been the object of a monographic study (Macchi 1999 for Genesis 49; Beyerle 1997 for Deuteronomy 33). For both, see also Sparks (2003).

O sons of Jacob; give heed to Israel your father" (Gen 49:2). The attribution of Deuteronomy 33 to Moses, in contrast, is supplied only by a prose heading, though each named people is introduced with expectation that we know the attribution: "this he said of Judah" (v. 7); "of Levi he said" (v. 8), and so on.[11] Jacob's sons are equated with Israel through this alternate name of the patriarch (see Gen 32:29), but one saying declares, "Dan shall judge his people as one of the tribes of Israel [*šibṭê yiśrā'ēl*]" (Gen 49:16), and Joseph's military might is upheld by one god under a parade of titles: "the bull of Jacob"; "the shepherd, the rock of Israel"; "the god of your father"; and "El Shadday" (vv. 24–25).[12] The groups named in Deuteronomy 33 are identified as "the tribes of Israel" in the last line of the introduction (v. 5), after the people are presented as a unified congregation at worship under the authority of Moses and Torah: "Moses commanded us the Teaching (*tôrāh*), the inheritance of the assembly of Jacob; and so he became king in Jeshurun, when the heads of the people gathered" (vv. 4–5a). The people are Israel, Jacob, and Jeshurun once again in a closing section (vv. 26–29).

Several more biblical poems were identified by Albright and others as early, ranging from the very beginnings of Israel in the late 13th or early 12th century through the 10th century and the first kings, this in a time when extended narratives in the Pentateuch and the books of Samuel were widely dated to the 10th century and Solomon's reign.[13] These four poems were regarded as particularly old and solidly situated in a pre-monarchic age that archaeologists of the time would call Iron Age I. The three poems with listed groups, understood as "tribes" by their match with the standard list of Israel's member peoples from the Pentateuch and beyond, were particularly useful for their detailed attention to the naming

---

[11] Note that there is a terse saying for Reuben in verse 6, without such introduction, opening the door to doubt about its originality to the poem. In her monograph on Reuben, Ulrike Schorn (1997) finds arguments that every reference in potentially earlier writing is in fact a late (post-monarchic) addition, a conclusion that I find more plausible here than for Judg 5:15–16.

[12] For *'ăbîr* as "bull" see Cross (1973: 4 n.6), with reference to Ugaritic and a general study by Patrick Miller (1971). Notice also the Jacob/Israel pairing in the word against Simeon and Levi (v. 7).

[13] Gerhard von Rad (1966: 1–78) could offer an extended argument for a Solomonic enlightenment in the 10th century. Note also the hypothesis of early written compositions related to David, a "Succession Narrative" (Rost 1926) and a "History of David's Rise" (Nübel 1959). See the contextual discussion in Hutton (2009: 116).

of Israel and its parts, which could thus be confirmed an ancient construction, a tribal confederacy without individual head.[14]

In religious terms, this confederacy could be connected securely to Yahweh, who held a place in each of the texts. The Song of the Sea opens with song to Yahweh (Exod 15:2) and returns repeatedly to the name, his marvelous capacities and deeds, and finally his rule as eternal king from a mountain shrine in the midst of his people (vv. 17–18). The Song of Deborah begins with invitation to "bless Yahweh" (Judg 5:2) and Yahweh stands behind the victory of Israel throughout the opening hymn.[15] Deuteronomy 33 leads with the name Yahweh (v. 2) and concludes with confidence in Yahweh's deliverance (v. 29). The tribal sayings are sprinkled with references to the name, with Judah (v. 7), Levi (v. 11), Benjamin (v. 12), Joseph (v. 13), Gad (v. 21), and Naphtali (v. 23). Jacob's poetic words contrast vividly by their relative failure to mention deity in any terms, with the colorful Joseph blessing an exception that draws attention to this people and suggests it as the text's destination.[16] Genesis 49 therefore carries its own religious interest by the absence of

---

[14] As one example outside the American context but before the influence of Martin Noth abated in Germany, see Claus Westermann (1986: 222) on Genesis 49: "Vv. 8–14 of Judg. 5 indicate the original *Sitz im Leben* of the tribal sayings. It is not the battle as such (so H. J. Kittel), but a convention following it, a debriefing or a more accurate critique of the strategy." Judg 5:14–18 reflects a specific occasion, while Genesis 49 and Deuteronomy 33 are general. "The setting in which they arose and were handed down is no longer the briefing after the battle, but the various occasions when the representatives of a number of tribes came together."

[15] The name is invoked in verses 2, 3, 4, 5, 9, and 11. The limited further references are the focus of discussion at a later point in this chapter.

[16] Benjamin is the last son (v. 27), falling back into a pattern by which the first four and last two names match the birth order in Genesis 29–30 and 35, against the six sons from Zebulun to Naphtali (vv. 13–21). Macchi (1999) regards these six as the original set around which the larger poem was extended. This compelling conclusion should be modified to include the complex Joseph saying in verses 22–26, so that the collection would share with the birth story of chapters 29–30 a preoccupation with Joseph as the most important group. So far as Joseph could be identified with Israel as such (e.g. Ps 80:2), he becomes the patriarch of a more geographically limited "little Israel," before expansion under ambitious royal rule, probably in the 9th century. These are issues and materials that have occupied me for several years, partly in collaboration with Lauren Monroe, who is now developing a book-length study of the House of Joseph. I address the Genesis material in general in chapter 5, "The Family of Jacob" (2012a: 72–90). On the birth narrative of Genesis 29–30, where Joseph represents the audience for the story, most easily understood as Israel, see Fleming (2020). Monroe and I develop the distinction between little and greater Israel in companion articles to appear in a forthcoming volume of *HBAI* (Fleming forthcoming; Monroe forthcoming a).

Yahweh and identification instead with El Shadday in association with other titles.[17]

The notion of old biblical poetry had potent impact on the old question of Yahweh's origins, a question answered by the Midianite Hypothesis that still provoked substantial opposition.[18] Although these texts made no mention of Midianites, and the Kenites were only represented by Heber, husband of Jael, they offered fascinating confirmation that Yahweh could literally "come" from the southern wilderness, not by redundant reference to Mount Sinai but rather by a series of distinct geographical identifiers. Of the three old poems devoted to Yahweh, only the Song of the Sea lacks interest in the south, focused instead on Yahweh's mountain dwelling in the midst of his people.[19] Among the early poems that list individual peoples within Israel, the sayings of Moses and the Song of Deborah incorporate into their opening praise of Yahweh a different kind of procession. After his defeat of Egypt in the Song of the Sea, the people themselves are on the move, "crossing" (verb *'br*) to the land where Yahweh "plants" them (Exod 15:16–17). As the Moses sayings begin, it is the god who moves: "Yahweh came from Sinai" (Deut 33:2); and in the Song of Deborah, "Yahweh, when you came out from Seir" (Judg 5:4). Here is a god who lives in the very southern realm visited by Moses as the exodus narrative gets under way, not at "Mount Sinai" as such but in the same region, capable of identification by the same geographical name.

---

[17] With the Jacob/Israel pairing of verse 24, along with "the tribes of Israel" for Dan in verse 16 and the geographical range indicated by the seven sayings together, I am inclined to locate the text in greater Israel, when the kingdom embraced peoples from north of the Jezreel Valley and east of the Jordan River. Note that Gad is in the list to represent the east, without Reuben and Manasseh (not a son of Jacob), and recalling the 9th-century reference to Gad in the Mesha inscription. Macchi dates his set of six to roughly the same period. Note also that Genesis 49 could be invoked to prove that Israel could still identify specially with El rather than Yahweh. If Yahweh came to be "god of Israel" through the greater Israel monarchy, then the role of El in Jacob's sayings would attach more narrowly to Joseph, who may represent Israel in its older and more modest scope (so, "little").

[18] It appears that the application of the poetry to the problem of Yahweh's origins did not occur until the generation of Frank Cross and his students. In a volume dedicated to Albright, Roland de Vaux (1969) was able to undertake a systematic refutation of the Midianite Hypothesis, including text-by-text treatment of all the principal prose evidence and the Egyptian Shasu references, without mention of Yahweh's movement from the south in the poetic texts.

[19] This detail could align with Jerusalem's identification with a sacred "mountain" as Zion, the site of a temple for Yahweh, as in Isa 8:18 and Ps 78:68–69, though such alignment could be secondary. I will return to this text and its discussion in Chapter 6.

With these texts, the Midianite Hypothesis could seem to have been confirmed by other means. Mark Smith already affirmed the likelihood of such an interpretation in 2001 (140), with the same poetry as the essential evidence.[20] If the poetry would not on its own show Yahweh to have originated as a god of the southern peoples, it complements what the prose accounts of Midianite and Kenite religious connections to Moses have been understood to convey. With heavy dependence on Erhard Blum's compositional analysis of the Pentateuch, Rainer Albertz (1994: 51) cautiously affirms an origin of Yahweh in the south from a combination of old poetry and prose:

a series of partially old poetic texts indicates an original local link between Yahweh and this region, which here is called Sinai, Se'ir, the fields of Edom, Teman, or the mountains of Paran. Yahweh sets out from there to come to the aid of his people in Palestine (Judg.5.4f.; Ps.68.8f.; Deut.33.2; Hab.3.3). In an early epithet Yahweh can even be termed "the one from Sinai" (Judg.5.5; Ps.68.8f).

Albertz and Blum represent an approach to biblical writing that embraces the preservation of much older tradition in texts finished and combined at late, often post-monarchic dates. It is nonetheless noteworthy that on this matter, Albright's influence reached continental Europe.[21]

Yet here again, interpretation of these poetic texts has been colored by the expectation that the Bible recalls vaguely that Yahweh only came to be known to Israel through contact with southern peoples, articulated in the Moses narrative by marriage into a Midianite family. Likewise, because the idea of Yahweh's foreign and southern origin is seen as intrinsically ancient, rooted in real religious history, the texts that relate

[20] Smith has worked on problems related to early Israelite religion over many years, and his analysis continues to evolve fruitfully. With this evaluation, Smith follows the spirit of much American analysis in the generation after the pioneering work of Albright and Cross. Note that Cross endorses the southern origins of Yahweh, even as he merges these origins with two major themes of traditional religion. For Cross, the name Yahweh derives from a liturgical formula in the worship of El, so that Yahweh's connection to the south would represent a particular custom for El (1973: 68–71). Cross (99–103) then conflates all the references in the old poetry to Yahweh's southern movement as variations on the prose account of exodus from Egypt and entry into a Promised Land, so that the god's victorious progress belonged to a "ritual conquest."

[21] A more recent example might be the 2015 study of Yahweh by Römer, who affirms the capacity of the Bible to preserve tradition that is much older than the time of writing. For Römer, the references in these poetic texts reflect "an old tradition according to which Yhwh is a divinity associated with a mountain in the desert, to the east or to the west of Araba" (47). He comments further that Pfeiffer's (2005) date of these texts to the period after destruction of Jerusalem and its temple creates an unlikely anachronism.

Yahweh to the south tend to be identified with the earliest levels of composition. If we reconsider the notion that Yahweh's southern connections reflect the peoples who first worshiped him, and we allow the dates and settings of each poetic text to be reevaluated without the Midianite framework, alternative interpretations emerge. The texts are indeed relatively old, though I will conclude that the specific references to Yahweh coming from the south probably fall within the horizons of established Israelite, and perhaps Judahite, religion during the period of two kingdoms (9th and 8th centuries).[22] They attribute to Yahweh a sacred range of movement, almost like that of mobile pastoralists with their flocks, across a swath of southern steppe, which the writers, at least, linked in no way to places of worship or peoples devoted to this god.

Each text warrants a closer look. I will address Judges 5 first, to reflect its particular antiquity as well as its primary place in discussion of Yahweh's origins. This text requires consideration alongside Psalm 68, which shares elements of the crucial text and yet lacks interest in Yahweh's movement from the south. Deuteronomy 33 is the other text that explicitly attributes this war-march to Yahweh, also attached to a poem that identifies Israel with an assembly of members, this time as "the tribes of Israel" (v. 5). Finally, Hab 3:3 offers another variant on the theme of march to battle from the south, but it is linked to "God" as Eloah, not to Yahweh. This text is attached to a book of prophetic writing concerned with the last days of the Judahite kingdom, so the late 7th or early 6th centuries. Although Albright (1950) understood Habakkuk 3 to include material going back to the 11th century, Eloah's movement from the south suggests only continuity with poetry that may come from the

---

[22] In recent years, there have been a number of thoughtful reevaluations, still sympathetic to the idea of early biblical poetry. Smith (2014: chapter 8) revisits the whole approach with Judges 5 in view, listing seven "points" that provoke caution, including a small sample size; the existence of old features in later poetry; inconsistent "density" of supposed old features; dispute over specific types; methodological complications; the need to consider "cultural" factors; and "perhaps most critically, all arguments in any direction turn on arguments from silence" (218). It would be better to build each case for an archaic feature "on a narrow base of evidence that combines three criteria" (219): dissimilarity from later features; demonstrable replacement in later language; and indications of older cultural-linguistic combination. Examples of the last in Judges 5 include long hair for battle (root *pr'*, v. 2); "routes" (*nĕtîbôt*, v. 6); and "village militia" for *pĕrāzôn* (vv. 7, 11) – all in the introductory hymn. Schniedewind (2013: 70–72) accepts the category of "Archaic Biblical Hebrew" with the caveat that this is based only on a "relative chronology," so that "there are few objective criteria by which we could date the Song of the Sea from Exodus 15 to the thirteenth century B.C.E. as distinguished from the tenth century B.C.E." Further, there is a tendency for later scribes to normalize archaic language.

kingdom of Israel (Judges 5; cf. Psalm 68), with nothing to demonstrate composition before the 9th or 8th centuries.[23] Each of these texts has received overwhelming scrutiny, and my purpose is only to reevaluate their references to Yahweh and places south of Israel and Judah. I will limit the discussion to the details at stake in the Midianite Hypothesis of Yahweh's southern origins.

In what follows, I conclude for each text that we cannot derive from the content any location for the worship of Yahweh, as in a people or community who served Yahweh as a god in the given place: Edom, Seir, Paran, Teman, or Sinai. Regardless of date and setting, this is not what the names either bear with conscious intent or reflect by unwitting transmission. Further, the combination of texts for Yahweh coming from the southern wilderness to fight for Israel does represent a "tradition" in hymnic writing and performance, but this is not a tradition that carries information about Yahweh's geographical origin or identification before Israel. We will return to the character of the tradition after discussion of the individual poems. Finally, the particular lines that express the idea of Yahweh coming from the south either do not date to the earliest level of the poems in question or belong most likely to the period of the two kingdoms, in the 9th and 8th centuries.

JUDGES 5:4–5 AND PSALM 68:8–9

The Song of Deborah in Judges 5 has proved durably plausible as a piece of old writing, independent of the various biblical systems into which it is embedded.[24] While the entire poem is saturated with unusual vocabulary, archaic grammatical features, and other odd details that suggest

---

[23] Mark Smith (2014: 219) observes that the poem in Habakkuk 3 makes reference to "the monarchy" in verse 15. For systematic treatment of the poem in the framework of Cross's perspective, see Hiebert (1986); also note Haak (1992).

[24] Even Henrik Pfeiffer (2017: 125), whose express objective is to lower the dates of the supposedly early poetry that has buttressed the contemporary Midianite Hypothesis, makes a stripped-down version of the Song of Deborah his one deeply monarchic text, from the 9th or 8th centuries: Judg 5:12*, 13a, 18/19–21a, 22/24*, 25, 26*, 27/28*, 29–30. Römer (2015: 43–44) calls the Song a "patchwork" without committing to a particular setting and date; the Hebrew "is either archaic or consciously archaizing." For methodical consideration of these questions, in favor of a finished date in the 10th century, see chapter 8 in Smith (2014). Quinn Daniels (personal communication) wonders whether scribes from the late monarchic or post-monarchic periods would conceive of texts in Judges as particularly old in comparison with the Torah and especially Genesis. Should Genesis show the most effort to "archaize," if this was a significant scribal preoccupation?

independence if not antiquity, the strongest case for substantial age comes from the battle account in verses 14–22, leaving its immediate frame (vv. 12–13, 23) open to discussion that will become central to my evaluation of Yahweh beyond reference to the south. Verses 14–18 consist of an intense geographical review, constructed as praise and condemnation of groups that fought and those that did not. We are clearly in the landscape of Israel, with most of the groups familiar as "tribes" from the Genesis family of Jacob and standard lists. Yet various aspects of the list present different angles of vision, all within a framework that is so north-oriented that even the central highlands are rendered southern. This effect is generated especially by the battle itself, which occupies the valley of the Kishon River, in the lowlands between coastal Mount Carmel and the Jezreel Valley.

Consider the following:

- The central highlands (between Jerusalem and the Jezreel Valley) are represented by Ephraim and Machir, with Benjamin as one of "your peoples," in address to Ephraim (v. 14). Ephraim itself has its roots in Amalek (Daniels 2018), a people principally associated with the region south of Judah.[25] None of this fits the more common biblical picture, where Benjamin is a separate tribe and the highlands between Ephraim and the Jezreel Valley would be occupied by Manasseh.

- Machir is a special case, difficult to locate geographically, especially in relation to the space east and west of the Jordan River (Fleming forthcoming). Its genealogical association with Manasseh at least places it north of Ephraim.[26]

---

[25] Amalek is named among the clans of Esau in Gen 36:12, 16; Israel fights Amalek at Rephidim, just before arrival at the mountain of God (Exod 17:8–16; cf. Deut 25:17–19; the conflict under Saul in 1 Samuel 15, with reference in 1 Sam 28:18); the spies locate them in the Negev (Num 13:29); after refusal to enter, Canaanites and Amalekites bar Israel from a direct southern entry into the land (Num 14:25, 43, 45); the last of the Balaam poetry associates Amalek with Seir and the Kenites in their downfalls (Num 24:20; cf. Judg 6:3, 33; 7:12, linked to Midianites and Qedemites in raiding Israel); Amalekites are near the Negev and David's southern base at Ziklag (1 Sam 30:1, 13, 18; cf. 27:8; 2 Sam 1:1). Some passages could be understood to place Amalekites in more northern territory, perhaps still with inland associations: Eglon king of Moab is said to have united Ammonites and Amalek under his rule (Judg 3:13); an Amalekite tells David that he killed Saul, but it is not clear whether we are to understand a Philistine connection (2 Sam 1:2–16); there is a "Mount Amalek" in Ephraim, where the leader Abdon is buried (Judg 12:15).

[26] In Num 26:29; 32:39–40; and Josh 17:1, 3, Machir is identified with the east.

- The rest of the active participants inhabit the hill country north of the Jezreel Valley: Zebulun, Issachar, and Naphtali – all tribes from the lists of 12, though a key element in defining the northern center of the Song's battle account (vv. 15, 18).[27]
- The east is represented by Reuben, a familiar name as firstborn of Jacob and first in most tribal lists yet oddly absent from individual narratives about separate Israelite peoples; and Gilead, the regional name that was never incorporated into the Bible's tribal lists (vv. 15–17).[28] This is an idiosyncratic eastern political landscape.[29]
- Dan and Asher are both associated with the sea, with the complaint about Dan particularly unexpected and intriguing (v. 17).[30]
- The assembled coalition fights a similarly plural coalition identified as "the kings of Canaan," where the Canaan name can be identified with inhabitants of the northern lowlands long after an imagined conquest under Joshua. The geography of the battle mentions two confirmed old cities, Taanach and Megiddo, and the Kishon River (vv. 19–21).
- Taken as a geographical name by even the earliest translators, "Meroz" would be unknown from any other context (v. 23). Lauren Monroe (forthcoming b) now proposes to understand this as a common noun. In either case, the reference is strange and striking.[31]

---

[27] In her recent treatment of "greater Israel," Lauren Monroe (forthcoming a) proposes that the call to battle comes from Machir, Zebulun, and Issachar, the last of which is aligned directly with Deborah and Barak in verse 15. Zebulun is named twice (vv. 14 and 18), first to describe its role in enlisting the Ephraim combination as allies and then to emphasize its own engagement in battle, together with Naphtali, as in the prose of 4:6 and 10. In the prose of Judges 4, this combination stresses the northern focus of the conflict, which is also visible in the Song.

[28] Note, for example, Amos 1:3 and 13, in the cycle of oracles against Israel's neighbors, with Gilead a target for Damascus and for the Ammonites.

[29] Mutually exclusive interpretations of Reuben are found in Cross (1988), who proposes the group's historical antiquity, and Schorn (1997), who removes all references to Reuben as hypothetical and secondary. The section in the Song of Deborah is particularly difficult for Schorn's effort, even as Cross's biblically based historical reconstruction is impossible to evaluate properly without further evidence.

[30] Note Lawrence Stager's (1989) proposal that the criticism of Dan reflects a trading relationship with the coast.

[31] The word represented as *mērôz* in Judg 5:23 has resisted interpretation through the ages, already treated as a place name in Greek and Latin translations, though no one has been able to identify it. Monroe observes that in a text otherwise completely concerned with collectively defined groups, on both sides, a city or town is unexpected. A key barrier to interpretation of *mērôz* as a common noun is the lack of a Hebrew or other Semitic root from which to derive it. In a careful and cautious review, Monroe revisits the Akkadian

This list of geographical oddities does not by itself establish a date for the Song of Deborah's battle account, but it indicates a vision of the land and its peoples vastly different from anything encountered elsewhere in the Bible. Equally, it presents a major conflict affecting much of what became the kingdom of Israel without the involvement of any king or centralized government. Judah and Jerusalem are off the radar, not a consideration in any form. Deborah makes her peculiar appearance as a woman in leadership, paired with and preceding Barak in a unique configuration (v. 15). Even the name Israel, which is sprinkled liberally through the opening hymn (see above), never appears in the battle account. The core battle account does suggest the pre-monarchic, Iron Age I date that was attributed to it by Albright, Cross, and those in their wake.[32]

Revised Introduction in Judg 5:2–11

At the same time, elements of the poem suggest revision on one hand and later writing on the other. In an analysis that developed from my effort to identify biblical writing that was composed and transmitted in the northern kingdom, I retreated from allowing the name Israel from the introductory hymn to provide a collective identity for the listed peoples in

middle-weak verb *râṣu*, which can mean "to come to the aid of," "to be allied with." Biblical Hebrew does attest verbs expressed in both /z/ and /ṣ/, such as ʿlz and ʿlṣ ("to exult"), an example with Akkadian cognate *elēṣu*. Monroe's bold proposal offers satisfying advantages for interpretation. The curse now would have an intelligible target: the four non-participating peoples of verses 15b–17 (Reuben, Gilead, Dan, and Asher), who failed to come to Yahweh's "help" in their role as *mērôz*, a force committed to come as reinforcements. Intriguingly, the double call to Deborah and Barak in verse 12, "awake, awake," would have a corresponding repetition in verse 23, with "curse." Monroe translates the verse, "Curse the auxiliary force, curse bitterly its leaders, for they did not come to the help of Yahweh, to the help of Yahweh among the warriors." I very much appreciate the generous access to Monroe's work in a stage before completion, and readers must refer to the finished article for the polished argument.

[32] Albright essentially assumed a pre-monarchic date from the combination of literal setting and level of detail, before the availability of Ugaritic and the language-based argument. At verses 17–18, he observes, "We seem to have a most important chronological datum in this line. Dan's residence on the sea-coast preceded the Philistine occupation. On the other hand, our poem dates from after the career of Shamgar, who beat off – or assisted in warding off – the first Philistine irruption, presumably that of the year 1190 B.C. The date of the battle of Taanach will then fall between about 1180 and 1170 or a little later, when the successful invasion occurred, after the death of Rameses III" (1922: 82 n.1). Cross and Freedman (1997: 3) set aside any extended discussion of the text. For the undertaking to follow, "The proper starting point is the Song of Deborah, a victory hymn, the occasion of which is known, and the approximate date quite certain, i.e., ca. 1100 B.C."

verses 14–18. As already observed, Israel is named eight times in verses 2–11, before the call to Deborah and Barak to "awake" in verse 12, and this identification of the groups that follow unifies the hymn as a single literary creation.[33] It may seem futile to suggest a new distinction of literary components and compositional process for a text that already has dozens available, but my crucial choice to refuse the equation between Israel and the individual participants makes such a solution unavoidable.[34]

With this pattern at center, it is impossible to include any part of the introductory hymn in the original poem, as do Hans-Peter Müller (1966), Neef (2002: 59–69), and Römer (2015: 43), all of whom look for an introduction in verses 6–8. Israel is the repeated concern of these verses: the village muster ceased in Israel (v. 7a); Deborah arose, a mother in Israel (v. 7b); and Israel is the measure of 40,000 fighting men (v. 8). My separation of the hymn from what follows resembles the solution of Volkmar Fritz (2006: 2:692–3), who locates the foundational text in verses 12–22 and 24–30.[35] Where Fritz approaches these two very different parts of the poem as one composition, I conclude that they more likely represented separate poetic reflections on the same victory over Sisera. This figure is mentioned in passing in the first poem (v. 20), with "the kings of Canaan" the primary definition of the enemy (v. 19), but he is the focus and antagonist in the second, killed by Jael while awaited by his mother (vv. 26, 28, 30).[36] Approached this way, the Song of Deborah was composed as a unity from two known sources (oral or written), binding them by a hymn placed in front of them in a version of what Sara Milstein (2016) calls "revision through introduction." One indication of the combination is the dating to "the days of Shamgar son of Anath" and "the days of Jael" (v. 6), not a signal of original continuity but rather of recasting. In verses 6–8, which provide a chronological setting otherwise lacking from the Song, the reference to Jael is followed directly by observation of the moment when Deborah "arose" (v. 7), so that this section brings together the two women who are central to each episode.

[33] See my discussion in Fleming (2012a: 64–66).
[34] A long list of previous schemes is assembled by Neef (2002), and note also the bibliography in Smith (2014: chapter 8).
[35] Pfeiffer (2017) follows Fritz in finding the start of the original poem in verse 12, though he strips down that text to a much more reduced form (see above).
[36] Milstein (2010: 174–75) raises the possibility that Sisera could have been added to the battle account, while leaving the main part of the verse in place; cf. Stahl 2020.

Jael and Deborah do not otherwise overlap; only the introduction joins
them.

My analysis differs slightly, at least, from that of Mark Smith, who
shares, I think, my sense of unified creation from older materials but who
declines to define a coherent whole that lacked the entire introduction in
verses 2–11. Smith (2014: 243–44) proposes to understand verses 2–13 as
a "double introduction" to the remaining body in 14–30. Like me, he
identifies his analysis with that of Fritz, with the comment that "Fritz may
be right that v. 12 was the original beginning of an older poem," but in its
present form, Deborah's own song does not begin until verse 13. Where
I would consider only verses 2–11 as setting up the combination to
follow, Smith includes verses 12–13 in that project (245), with one result
being the separation of "the people of Yahweh" in verse 13 from the
initial composition. Perhaps with an eye to the Midianite Hypothesis,
Smith grants verses 4–5 special status as another old component (247),
though this text shares the larger hymn's use of Israel, and more specifically, the naming of Yahweh as "god of Israel" (vv. 3 and 5).[37]

The apparent act of joining two distinct Sisera texts by itself would
raise the question of later perspectives in Judges 5 – later than the pre-
monarchic impression given by the battle account. Particular details from
the introductory hymn (vv. 2–11) offer further basis for identifying later
elements in the finished Song. Above all, the repetition of the name Israel
eight times both contrasts vividly with the political geography to follow
and transforms the coalition into terms with major significance in a
monarchic setting. An association of allies without fixed institutions of
individual leadership is by this revision translated into an anticipation of
the later kingdom. The text remains a celebration of unity and victory
from before the time of kings, so a natural fit with the collection that
became the book of Judges, even as these groups are recast by the name of
that kingdom. Given that the expanded kingdom of Israel in the 9th and
8th centuries did encompass the peoples named in the Song's battle
narrative, the translation to render them "Israel" would make sense.

---

[37] On the difficulty of this epithet in the Song of Deborah, see the treatment by Michael Stahl
(2020), who discusses Judg 5:2–11* as "the earliest programmatic identification of
Yahweh as the 'god of Israel'," an innovation from the original role of El. In Stahl's
analysis, the new naming of Yahweh as "god of Israel" refocused the collective social and
political identity of Israel, which had regarded El as "god of Israel," with a corresponding
shift of sacral/political center from Shechem to Samaria, in the 9th century.

The introduction both salutes the old alliance and coopts it subtly by naming the whole as Israel and Yahweh as "god of Israel" (vv. 3, 5).[38]

Despite the archaic terminology scattered through the hymn, certain other features raise the possibility of later settings – during the separate northern kingdom, if not later. The audience of kings in verse 3 makes most sense in a landscape of kingdoms: "Hear, O kings; give ear, O princes." These are not the allied city-rulers envisioned with "the kings of Canaan" as enemy but represent a larger stage, more like the "kings of the earth" set against Yahweh in Psalm 2 (vv. 2, 10). The scale is suggested by Yahweh as "god of Israel," a whole people and logically at the time of writing a major kingdom.[39] In verse 8, we are told that Israel was left defenseless after having "chosen new gods," or "a new god" (*'ĕlōhîm ḥĕdāšîm*), a phrase not otherwise found in the Bible. These are not the stereotypical "other gods" of Deuteronomistic writing, but the phrase does point to individual commitments between peoples and deities, perhaps of the sort envisioned in Elyon's apportionment of nations to gods in Deut 32:8–9, with Yahweh taking Israel.[40] In the Song of Deborah's opening hymn, it seems we have entered a world of kingdoms and the competing divine powers attached to them, not the concern of the battle account and tribute to Jael in the rest of the poem.[41]

---

[38] Stahl (2020) presents an extended argument for a 9th-century date, under Omride rulers, even if verses 4–5 (with Smith) could have been reworked from older sources. "I claim that the Omride royal house 'invented' Yahweh as the 'god of Israel' in a political act, at a particular historical moment, as part of the process of forging an expanded, more centralized Israelite political identity, one grounded in the mutual interdependence of Israel, Omri's royal house, and Yahweh(-El) as the 'god of Israel'." Stahl weighs the following factors: the geographical range for the ten named peoples that likely matches the kingdom of Israel only beginning in the 9th century; the audience of kings and kingdoms in verse 3; archaeological evidence for expansion of Israel in the 9th century; the Mesha and Tel Dan inscriptions for Israel pushing east and north in the 9th century; and Kuntillet 'Ajrud for Yahweh in the deep south, with Israelite interest, by the late 9th century.

[39] Smith (2014: 245–46) includes this "invocation of kings" in verse 3 in his list of new "interpretive parameters" for verses 14–30, with the observation that it anticipates the kings of Canaan in verse 19. If there is any such conscious connection, the effect is to diminish the defeated kings by contrast to a much larger audience of surrounding monarchs.

[40] The closest comparison may be Deut 32:17, also calling gods "new," perhaps confirming the context suggested by Deut 32:8–9 (observation courtesy of Michael Stahl). Along with Psalm 82, this text is central to Mark Smith's delineation of separate roles for El and Yahweh in a tiered pantheon, before their eventual identification (2001: 48–49).

[41] Smith (2014: 223–26) concludes that the Song's introduction would suit the 10th century, before the expansion of Israelite monarchic scale, because of the long hair for battle in verse 2 (*pĕrā'ôt*), and the "village militia" (*pĕrāzôn*) in verses 7 and 11. As I understand

Before we turn to Yahweh's movement from the south in Judg 5:4–5, it is worth pausing to acknowledge the choices I am making in developing this part of a larger argument regarding the history of religion. Where possible, I have tried to leave interpretive options open. In two crucial instances, I have made decisions that thoughtful specialists have declined and may refuse again: the historical connection between the god Yahweh and Yhw₃ of Shasu-land in early 14th-century Egyptian writing; and the argument here for "revision through introduction" in the Song of Deborah (Judg 5:2–11). I did not reach this second conclusion as part of this project but rather several years earlier, as I worked to grasp the character of Israel and the biblical content that came through the northern kingdom (Fleming 2012a). In joint research since the completion of my book on *The Legacy of Israel*, Lauren Monroe and I have probed ways in which the Bible may preserve hints of the political landscape from periods not explicitly recognized in finished biblical writing, especially with respect to the name Israel itself (Monroe and Fleming 2019; Monroe forthcoming a; Fleming forthcoming).[42] As we see it, no historical evaluation of the land of Israel and Judah before the 9th century can proceed without interrogating the basic biblical names potentially in play – even when the result yields greater uncertainty and caution.

With my current reconsideration of "Yahweh before Israel," it is as important to reevaluate "Israel" as it is to revisit the familiar evidence for early Yahweh, and my conclusion regarding the Song of Deborah is essential to that reevaluation. This is not a consensus interpretation, and I invite ongoing discussion. In broad terms, my reading of Judges 5 belongs to the stream of scholarship that understands certain poems to contain some of the oldest biblical writing. I am inclined to read connected works as coherent until there is compelling reason to identify revisions, and my reconstruction of two poems joined by "revision through introduction" is simple compared to some more layered interpretations. What matters most to my argument is the decoupling of "Israel" from the battle account in verses 12–22/23 and its peoples. On this issue, there are large historical implications to reading the poem as a whole. Based on verses 3 and 5, Yahweh would then have to be

---

the monarchic recasting of a non-monarchic poem, the whole idea is to embrace a prior political tradition of allied or confederated peoples and to redefine them as Israel, the entity led by kings. This terminology would therefore suit entirely a 9th-century compositional project.

[42] For the application of "political landscape" to ancient settings, see Adam Smith (2003).

understood as *the* "god of Israel," taking the place of or identified with El, who appears to have been the first and logical bearer of the title (Stahl 2020). Further, we would have to consider all ten named peoples in verses 14–18 to have been identified already as somehow members of "Israel," evidently before any continuous monarchy. The geographical scale of this Israel would incorporate lands well north of the Jezreel/Kishon Valleys, south to Ephraim/Benjamin, east to Gilead, and west to the sea – before kings. Some will embrace these two historical implications, but there is danger of reading a later and imaginative map back onto much earlier settings. In my own reading of history, the Song of Deborah will attest to "Yahweh before Israel" because the battle poem of Judg 5:12–22/23 contains Yahweh and not Israel. This conclusion does not change my understanding of the Egyptian evidence for Yhw3 as a subset of Shasu-land, but when it comes to the god Yahweh, this interpretation of Judges 5 is my starting point.

Yahweh from the South

In the opening hymn to the Song of Deborah, the focus turns to the specific occasion for conflict in verse 6, with a chronological introduction: "In the days of Shamgar son of Anath, in the days of Jael," leading to the Song's particular heroine, "until you arose, O Deborah" (v. 7).[43] In the few lines before the battle is brought into view, Yahweh is named as the essential power, "blessed" (v. 2) and "sung" (v. 3), under the particular title "god of Israel" (vv. 3, 5). Yahweh's departure from the south is bound to the singing by repetition of the shared object as "god of Israel" at the end of that section (vv. 4–5):

> (4) Yahweh, when you went out from Seir,
> when you walked from the open country of Edom,
> the earth quivered,
> as the heavens dripped,
> as the clouds dripped water.
> (5) The mountains gushed

---

[43] One implication of the compositional analysis shared in its main thrust by Fritz, Smith, and me is that the explanation for the conflict in verses 2–11 would not be original to the battle account. Instead, this would constitute a reinterpretation of what might provoke military engagement in the Kishon Valley, probably assuming the conditions of the Israelite monarchy. Where David Schloen's (1993) explanation for the historical context takes for granted a Late Bronze and Iron Age I chronology, the same concern for caravan trade could apply to the early first millennium.

> from before Yahweh, he of Sinai,
> from before Yahweh, god of Israel.

Where Yahweh "comes" (*bw'*) from Sinai in Deut 33:2, the Song of Deborah employs two other verbs with distinct associations. First, he "goes out" (*yṣ'*), what the sun does every morning and armies do (e.g. 1 Sam 8:20, of kings; 17:20, of armies).[44] Then he "marches" or parades (*ṣ'd*), a verb attached to the ritual procession by David and the ark in 2 Sam 6:13. In contrast to Deut 33:2, the southern location represents a single land, named by a known biblical pairing as Seir and Edom. Although only Edom is assigned to the eventual kingdom, Judah's inland eastern neighbor south of the Dead Sea, Seir may represent the same whole. See in particular the Balaam poetry of Num 24:18:

> Edom will be a possession,
> and Seir will be a possession – (for) its enemies,
> while Israel flourishes.[45]

It is notable that Seir precedes Edom in Judg 5:4, in contrast to the Balaam text, undermining any expectation that the kingdom has priority in the identification of this land.[46] Both names are very old, going back to 13th-century references from New Kingdom Egypt, and Egyptians associated both with the Shasu people, as noted in Chapter 2.[47] Yahweh's very movement generates a response in the natural world, first defined by the merism of heaven and earth, encapsulating all space, and then identifying representatives of power attributed to each domain: clouds in the sky and mountains on earth. There is forward motion to the sequence, so that the result is water where it would not ordinarily be found, in the arid south. We are not told of stormy clouds, wind, or explicit rain; we see only the

---

[44] By this action, Judg 5:4 may evoke the brilliant "dawn" explicit in Deut 33:2, so indirectly introducing the image of light.

[45] Levine (2000: 202–203) interprets the rare form *yĕrēšāh* as a "land depopulated," a "dispossession" rather than a "possession." For all the difficulties in these lines, the equation of Edom and Seir is clear.

[46] Note that the particular "back country of Edom" (*śĕdēh 'ĕdôm*) occurs otherwise only in the account of Esau's location in Gen 32:4, defined as "the land of Seir, the back country of Edom," in the same order.

[47] These southern locations only appear in texts from the time of Ramses II and beyond, beginning in the 13th century. According to Ahituv (1984: 90), the one reference to Edom is from the Papyrus Anastasi VI text cited in Chapter 2, from the reign of Ramses IV (1153–1147). Aside from the contested reference in the 'Amarah West list, Seir appears in two other Ramses II (1279–1213) texts, along with the Papyrus Harris I reference cited in Chapter 2 (Ahituv 1984: 169).

water running from the sky and then flowing from the mountains. The image here is commonly linked to the "storm god" as a type, with Haddu/Hadad in view, though we are not in Hadad's terrain and these are not the thunderstorms of the northern mountains.[48]

In the last segment of the section, the thought turns back to Yahweh, "from" whose movement and presence nature responds, as if recoiling before his power. Yahweh is given two titles: "he of Sinai" (*zeh sînai*) and "god of Israel." As will be seen also with Deut 33:2, Sinai is the one southern reference that has no association with a population; it is purely the sacred place of Yahweh. It is significant, therefore, that in the Song of Deborah, Yahweh moves out of Seir, the territory of a people well known to Israel and related to them in the book of Genesis by the bond of Jacob and Esau as twins, but he carries only Sinai as a title. Yahweh moves through the inhabited lands of various southern peoples, here focused on just one, as Israel's close kin, but he is attached to a place not defined by population.

The Midianite Hypothesis has cobbled together a diverse set of southern identities by which to derive the origins of Yahweh, before attachment to Israel. In the exodus narrative, it is noteworthy that Edom and Seir are treated as clearly separate from the region where Moses and Israel encountered Yahweh in the wilderness. Moses is linked to the Midianites up to his arrival at the mountain of God, and the mountain marks an abrupt divide in the experience of the people. Israel does not attempt an incursion into Canaan until it reaches Kadesh in the back country south of the land, a site treated as directly accessible to southern Canaan.[49] In Numbers 20–24, Edom is the first kingdom encountered in southern Jordan, before Moab and the extended episode of the diviner Balaam, and the writer considers that with Israel's peaceable approach to Edom, they have reached the frontiers of the world they will inhabit. In Deuteronomy 2–3, Israel is considered to have lived side by side with the people of Seir (2:1), so that "the sons of Esau" in Seir would provide the first

---

[48] Smith (2014: 238) compares the anticipated return of Baal from the underworld in CAT 1.6 III 6–13, where "the heavens rain oil, wadis run with honey." The climate and conditions for the southern steppe would be quite different from the setting in the north, where Baal lives on Mount Ṣapan, whatever the original location of the myth's composition, and the analogy remains partial. If Hadad was indeed in view, Damascus of the 9th and 8th centuries could offer a context for rivalry over such a god.

[49] The role of Kadesh in what was considered the shaping of Israelite culture and religion in a desert context was particularly important in early writing; see especially Meyer (1906: 60).

contact with the social order of the new land (2:2–4). So far as Yahweh "goes out" from Seir in Judg 5:4, this represents a place and a people entirely separate in the exodus narrative from the experience of Yahweh at his sacred mountain and equally distant from Moses' relationship with a Midianite leader.

Yahweh's movement from Seir and Edom in the Song of Deborah serves the monarchic context of the opening hymn, and it shares deeply in the recasting of the battle as Israel's, granted victory through Yahweh as "the god of Israel." Whatever their source, verses 4–5 contribute to the monarchic program undergirding the whole "revision through introduction" (Milstein 2016), and this identification of Yahweh with Israel would be central to that program. In its attachment to "the god of Israel," therefore, the tradition of Yahweh coming from the south in Judges 5 is old relative to most biblical writing, but it does not represent the earliest material in this poem. Rather, it has been added from a social and political context vastly changed from the one that produced the account of battle with Canaan, with the emergence of a powerful monarchy based at Samaria. The question then is how the notion of Yahweh coming from the south on Israel's behalf would have served an ambitious kingdom, when this notion may not have been part of Israel's prior religious sensibility.

One further piece of evidence contributes to our analysis of Judg 5:4–5: the text shares substantial wording with Psalm 68:8–9. Based on this shared content, Mark Smith (2014: 238; cf. 2012: 16) has proposed that the segment depicting Yahweh's movement from the south in the Song of Deborah "was drawn upon by the composer as a building block in the introduction (vv. 2–13), fronted to the body of the poem (vv 14–30)." The two texts align as follows:

Judg 5:4–5	Ps 68:8–9
(4) **Yahweh,**	(8) **Elohim,**
when you went out from Seir,	**when you went out** before your people,
when you walked	**when you walked**
from the open country of Edom,	in the wasteland,
the earth quivered,	(9) **the earth quivered,**
as **the heavens dripped,**	indeed **the heavens dripped,**
as the clouds dripped water.	
(5) The mountains gushed	
from before Yahweh, he of Sinai,	from before Elohim, he of Sinai,
from before Yahweh, god of Israel.	from before Elohim, god of Israel.[50]

---

[50] For more detailed treatment of the two texts in combination, see Smith (2012a: 11–17).

Smith (2012a: 11) concludes that neither text is best explained as direct borrowing and revision of the other; rather, the small contrasts in wording found in the lines on earth and heavens indicate what Frank Cross (1973: 101 n.35) called ancient oral variants. While it is indeed possible that the partially overlapping content suggests that both texts drew on a familiar hymnic fragment, the contrasting elements cannot be read with confidence as equally ancient variants. The demonstrably oldest material should be what both have in common.[51] This shared text would look something like the following:

*Yahweh, when you went out,
*when you walked,
*the earth quivered,
*the heavens dripped,
*from before Yahweh, he of Sinai,
*from before Yahweh, god of Israel.

The shared Judges 5/Psalm 68 text is certainly a short hymn to Yahweh, with the psalm confirming the hypothesis of an Elohistic portion of the psalter.[52] Before the title "god of Israel," Yahweh is identified in the shared material as "he of Sinai," which appears to assume a southern geography, though not tied to any polity or population known to biblical narrative – a "Sinai people." Both Judg 5:4 and Ps 68:8 choose a wilderness reference with *śādeh* ("open country") attached to Edom and *yĕšîmôn* ("wasteland"), perhaps to complement a southern Sinai.

The most important difference between the two texts is the feature most central to evaluation of the Midianite Hypothesis. Psalm 68:8 lacks Seir and Edom, and instead, it develops Yahweh's movement without reference to the south. In other contexts, the "wasteland" (*yĕšîmôn*) can be the harsh country in Moab visible from Mount Pisgah and Peor (Num 21:20; 23:28), as well as the imagined terrain between Babylon and Judah when Yahweh returns his people from exile

---

[51] This is a textual critical mode of analysis that is not generally applied to this combination of texts. In this pair of texts, all of the divergent material is extraneous to what is shared: the two verbs of movement match and are elaborated differently to orient the movement; and Judg 5:4–5 adds two more lines to the description of the elemental response to Yahweh's movement, already expressed in parallel, yielding an A:B::B:A construction of earth and sky while bringing heaven's water to earth. None of the elaborations to either text is necessary to its basic sense.

[52] On the Elohistic Psalms collection, see Hossfeld and Zenger (2003), with references to previous work.

(Isa 43:19, 20). According to Deut 32:10, Yahweh "found" his people in the wilderness (*midbār*) and the wasteland (*yĕšīmōn*) – only the back country, not specifying the south. However we resolve the problem of this difference between Judg 5:4 and Ps 68:8, it is likely that Seir and Edom were invoked specifically for the Song of Deborah introduction, and the psalm does not demonstrate the higher antiquity of a shared hymnic fragment. If there was such a fragment, it included "he of Sinai" but not the march from Seir and Edom.[53] It may be easier to explain the textual interdependence by the priority of Judges 5:4–5, with Psalm 68 drawn from that text and molding it to suit a Jerusalem setting and an exodus story that had God accompany Israel in the wasteland on its way to the Promised Land.[54] If the new hymnic introduction to the Song of Deborah drew on an older bit of known praise, the case is best made from Judges 5 alone.

However old the poetic tradition of Yahweh's arrival from the southern wilderness, it does not describe the god's historical origin. Seir and Edom are not presented as peoples who worship Yahweh, and they are not related to the Midianite tradition of Moses' marriage in the exodus narrative. In the shared material of Judg 5:4–5 and Ps 68:8–9, Yahweh is "god of Israel" and "he of Sinai," the latter a location in the southern desert that has no associated population, evidently a divine dwelling, a category to which we will return after discussion of the biblical texts. It appears that Seir and Edom are elaborations on the wilderness association of Yahweh with Sinai, though they could also display a less targeted and equally ancient Israelite conception of the god's southern home.[55]

---

[53] On the antiquity of a shared hymnic fragment, see also Day (2000: 15–16) and Lemaire (2007: 21–23). Smith's argument depends above all, it seems, on the antiquity of the names Seir and Edom, as found in New Kingdom Egyptian geography, combined with the surprise of these locations as a point of departure for Yahweh (2014: 237).

[54] This is a widely held interpretation, including Coogan (1978: 161–62); Hossfeld and Zenger (2005: 162); Rofé (2009: 445); and Römer (2015: 42). In Stahl's most recent version of the argument (2020), the following features are decisive. Psalm 68 displays composition in Judah at a relatively late date (as Smith would agree); the "god of Israel" title should originate in the Israelite setting of Judges 5, where it also occurs in verse 3; Psalm 68 removes Seir and Edom so that Yahweh/Elohim can inhabit Jerusalem; and the psalm has been widely observed to reference other biblical texts.

[55] Identification of Sinai in the Moses narrative with the "mountain of God" is likely to be a secondary combination, but it is a reading of both the Sinai and mountain traditions in tune with their older intent.

DEUTERONOMY 33:2

While Judg 5:4–5 and Ps 68:8–9 are variants of the same short hymnic strophe, Deut 33:2 shows that the motif of Yahweh's movement from a southern base had a range of expression not bound to any individual form or compositional setting. Even as it repeats the same motif, the imagery and the geographical references are entirely distinct from the other texts and thus display the work's independence. Like Judg 5:4–5, where the motif of Yahweh and the south contributes to a vision of many peoples unified as "Israel," the poem in Deut 33:2–29 salutes the named members of Israel by sayings and blessings. The opening begins with Yahweh and the south (v. 2) and concludes with assembly of "the tribes of Israel as one" (v. 5), imagining an occasion that gathers all the tribes of Israel in a sacred context that would have suited Martin Noth's idea (1966) of an Iron Age I "amphictyony" or confederacy.[56] Yahweh's power is introduced by a point of departure from a land with three, or perhaps four, names:

(2) Yahweh came from Sinai and dawned for them from Seir;
he blazed from Mount Paran and proceeded from Revivat Kadesh;
flashing fire for them from his right hand;[57]
(3) who adores his people indeed.[58]

---

[56] It is notable that Deuteronomy 33 levels all the constituents of Israel as equal "tribes," as in the saying for Dan in Gen 49:16, so the individual groups are ordered by, and perhaps conceptually subordinated to, the overarching identity as Israel. The Song of Deborah undertakes no such classifying of the Israel peoples by a single type, possibly in deference to the received poem in verses 12–22/23, which lacks any common category.

[57] For literature, see the works already cited by Beyerle (1997); Sparks (2003); and Pfeiffer (2005). In context, Revivat Kadesh should be a geographical name in the tradition of a southern wilderness site called Kadesh. On the translation issues here, see Tigay (1996: 319–20). The term that I have translated as "flashing fire" ('*ēšdāt*) has a long history of discussion with recent entries by Steiner, Leiman, and Lewis, who propose to read "fire" plus a 3fs form of the verb *d'y*, "to fly." Most recently, Lewis (2013: 798) reads, "With him were myriads of holy ones, from his right hand *fire flies forth*"; cf. Steiner (1996); Steiner and Leiman (2009). Lewis (793 n.3) concludes that what I have rendered as "for them" most likely represents a secondary addition in two parts of the verse.

[58] The MT has "who loves (the) peoples" ('*ammîm*); HALAT s.v. *ḥbb*, reads "his people" ('*ammô*), with the Greek. If the plural, the traditional Jewish reading as the constituents of Israel would make most sense in the context of the whole poem (Tigay 1996: 321), though this would require understanding '*ām* as an equalizing social and political category set in parallel with *šēbeṭ* ("tribe"), which is likewise unexpected.

All its holy ones are in your hand,[59]
and they, having bowed(?) at your feet,[60]
carry your decrees.
(4) Moses commanded us the Teaching [tôrāh],
a legacy (for) the assembly of Jacob.
(5) And there was a king in Jeshurun,[61]
when the heads of the people gathered,
the tribes of Israel as one.

Deuteronomy 33 and Genesis 49

The above text serves as introduction to a poetic collection of tribal sayings that has as its closest formal cousin the list of sayings for the sons of Jacob in Genesis 49. Only Deuteronomy 33 includes the motif of Yahweh coming from the south, part of a unifying frame not provided for Genesis 49. Aside from the separate introduction and conclusion in Deut 33:2–5 and 26–29, both poems appear to have been massaged to suit the biblical tradition of 12 Israelite tribes, so that neither can be understood to have taken its current form from first composition. In their sequence and detail, the two lists do not match and the procedures by which the number was achieved appear to have been separate.[62] Each poem relates to the preceding prose narrative, again in varying ways. Genesis 49 introduces Reuben, Simeon, and Levi by reproaches that contrast both with the tone of the other sayings and by their reference to earlier narrative (Gen 35:22 and Genesis 34). It is striking that the order of Jacob's sons follows exactly the narrative sequence for Reuben,

---

[59] The MT of this verse has address to Yahweh in the second person, and any effort to resolve the unevenness of reference becomes entangled in the possibility that early transmission and translation undertook a similar task.

[60] The verb is uncertain and the solution is contextual (Cross and Freedman 1997 [1975]).

[61] In the context of praise to Yahweh, the evident king would be divine, though the title evokes political monarchy as well.

[62] Deuteronomy 33 has ten sayings, identified with Reuben, Judah, Levi, Benjamin, Joseph, Zebulun, Gad, Dan, Naphtali, and Asher. Twelve tribes may be counted by replacing Joseph with Ephraim and Manasseh (v. 17), and by counting Issachar with Zebulun (v. 18). Simeon is missing. Genesis 49 has eleven sayings, for Reuben, Simeon and Levi together, Judah, Zebulun, Issachar, Dan, Gad, Asher, Naphtali, Joseph, and Benjamin. Ephraim and Manasseh are not named, to suit a list of blessings for Jacob's sons, and the one double saying easily brings the number to 12, matching the sons named in the birth narratives of Gen 29:31–30:24 and 35:18 (Benjamin). I am persuaded by recent arguments that the biblical scheme of 12 Israelite tribes is artificial and post-monarchic, simply because no text, above all including these two poems, can demonstrate its antiquity (e.g. Schorn 1997).

Simeon, Levi, and Judah at the beginning and for Joseph and Benjamin at the end, while the remaining six diverge completely. In Deuteronomy 33, only the saying for Levi evokes prose narrative, not Deuteronomy but especially Exodus.[63] The compositional histories of both poems are much discussed, but these narrative connections suggest some process of growth, especially for Genesis 49.

Jean-Daniel Macchi (1999) has made a cogent case that the sequence of six simple sayings from Zebulun to Naphtali in Gen 49:13–21 were combined as one text in 9th-century Israel, and the pattern of naming supports identification of these as a distinct group. I would add the Joseph encomium in verses 22–26, which close by calling Joseph "the one dedicated [*nāzîr*] of his brothers," reflecting the region of the northern kingdom's capital.[64] Deuteronomy 33 offers no such neat contrast of types, though it is tempting to consider the whole Levi saying an addition, since even the characterization of Levi as a "tribe" involves a conception very different from the political association imagined for the rest, and the poem alludes to the prose narrative only here. Otherwise, the poem includes both short and longer sayings, some of which could certainly be as old as the early sayings from Genesis 49. While Deuteronomy 33 shows an interest in Yahweh that is missing from the Jacob series, this interest need not prove later composition. Among the sayings for the same six peoples of Macchi's Gen 49:13–21 core, clustered in different order in Deut 33:18–25, only the words devoted to Gad and Naphtali (vv. 21, 23) invoke Yahweh – or any divine name. Where the set of six is followed by Joseph in Genesis 49, it is directly preceded by Joseph in Deut 33:13–17, maintaining a similar sense of connection. Benjamin is separated from those six by Joseph in both poems, after him in Gen 49:27, before him in Deut 33:12. In both texts, the tribes from the first set of Leah's sons in Gen 29:31–35 are clustered at the beginning: the entire foursome of Reuben, Simeon, Levi, and Judah in Gen 49:3–12; and just Reuben, Judah, and Levi in Deut 33:6–11. As shaped by these names, Genesis 49 gives priority to Judah as ruler (vv. 8–12, especially v. 10), and Deuteronomy 33 highlights Levi as link to Moses and representative of Yahweh (vv. 8–11).[65]

---

[63] See Exod 17:7 for Massah and Meribah together (cf. Num 20:13 for Meribah); 28:30 for the Urim and Thummim (cf. Lev 8:8); and 32:25–29 for Levites slaughtering even their own "children and brothers" in support of Yahweh. These references combine non-Priestly (Exodus 17 and 32) with Priestly (Exodus 28) material.

[64] See my interaction with Macchi in Fleming (2012a: 86–88).

[65] Both the Judah section in Genesis 49 and the Levi section in Deuteronomy 33 have inspired proposals that they were revised. As one example for Deut 33:8–11, Mayes

Admitting the impossibility of finding absolute dates for these laconic tribal sayings, the larger idea of joining such tidbits for Zebulun and Issachar, Gad, Dan, Naphtali, and Asher, with Joseph as "one dedicated of his brothers" (so also Deut 33:10), has its own chronological logic. Just as "the tribes of Israel" in Gen 49:16 included Dan, north of Hazor along the line of the Jordan Rift Valley, Yahweh's "judgments with Israel" in Deut 33:21 are located in Gad, east of the Jordan River. The 9th-century inscriptions from Tel Dan and Mesha of Moab suggest Omride competition for these locations, at some distance from all the capitals of Israel listed in the biblical narrative of Samuel and Kings.[66] The eastern expansion of the 9th century is recalled in the Mesha text as the specific accomplishment of Omri (lines 5–8).[67] According to the geography of Joshua 19, late as it is, Zebulun and Issachar occupy the space just north of the Jezreel Valley; Naphtali and Dan reach further north along the Jordan Rift, and Asher stretches along the northern coast between modern Haifa and Tyre of Lebanon. Gad is an eastern people, confirmed by reference in the Mesha inscription (line 10).[68] Combination of Joseph with these six peoples represented a systematic extension of the Israelite kingdom north and east of its political center in the central highlands.

While the pattern of names in Genesis 49 suggests an Israelite (northern kingdom) text that was extended to match Jacob's 12 sons, so the sayings could become his blessings, Deuteronomy 33 is more difficult to parse for settings. Reuben remains first, treated as endangered ("let him live and not die," v. 6), and Judah is now second, but without any notion

(1981: 402) proposes that 8–9a represents the oldest and most archaic claim for Levi, with 9b–10 an elaboration and 11 originally the end of the Judah saying picked up from 7.

[66] Taking all on the biblical terms, these are Gibeah (Saul), Jerusalem (David), Shechem/Tirzah (Jeroboam, Baasha), and Samaria (Omri), divided into two geographical groups with Gibeah and Jerusalem in the south and Tirzah and Samaria in the north, all sites in the upper highlands.

[67] Among the extensive bibliography on Mesha, note especially the collected articles in Dearman (1989); chapter 7 in Routledge (2004); and the articles by Grabbe, Lemaire, Na'aman, and Thompson, in Grabbe (2007).

[68] Confirmation, and in some cases complication, of the Joshua geography can be found in other sources, though the outlines are less precise. In the north-oriented Song of Deborah, the battle against "the kings of Canaan" takes place in the Jezreel/Megiddo Valley, identified with the Kishon River and the cities of Taanach and Megiddo. According to Monroe's new reading of the conflict (forthcoming a), Ephraim is praised for coming to help the peoples most immediately concerned, Zebulun and Issachar, adjacent to this Canaanite region. It seems, then, that those who remain aloof are furthest from the fight: Reuben and Gilead east of the Jordan River; and Dan and Asher further to the north. Naphtali does participate.

of dominance (v. 7). To call the list Levite would not locate it in either kingdom or region, north or south, and the Levite cast may in any case be secondary. One solution would be to imagine Reuben, Judah, and Levi all to be added onto a cluster of sayings that began with Benjamin and Joseph – or with Joseph alone – each of the first names representing a nod to different constituencies in the reception of the text.

Deuteronomy 33 and Greater Israel

As we explore the interpretation of Deuteronomy 33, the lingering issue for the history of Yahweh is the antiquity of the poem, whether as a whole or with potential renovation into its finished shape. Examined in combination with Genesis 49 as a tribal list, Deuteronomy 33 cannot date to the 11th century and is not likely to come from the 10th, even in its earliest form.[69] Whatever the answer, it is important to recognize the unlikelihood that the Deuteronomy 33 poem is extremely old as an unrevised entirety, a conclusion that is clearer for Genesis 49. The two poems are constructed from sayings that only make sense with knowledge of monarchic Israel. In the 9th and 8th centuries, this meant the northern kingdom, which was constructed from peoples such as those found in the battle account of the Song of Deborah, groups with identities that did not dissipate with inclusion in the kingdom (Fleming 2012a: 90).[70] Both Genesis 49 and Deuteronomy 33 share a core of Joseph (with or without Benjamin) and the six tribes of the north and east: Zebulun, Issachar, Gad, Dan, Naphtali, and Asher (Deut 33:18–25). The geographical scope of these peoples alone suggests the expanded Israelite monarchy of the Omrides, which Monroe and I call "greater Israel," in contrast to

---

[69] Cross (1973: 123) dates both Genesis 49 and Deuteronomy 33 to the 11th century; see Cross and Freedman (1948). For all that David Robertson became the final reference for the identification of a corpus of early poetry, he proposed a much later date, in the 8th century (1972: 49–55).

[70] As Monroe and I understand the situation, Omri and Ahab would have cast themselves as advocates of tribal identities, welcoming long-time allies into direct participation in the kingdom with promises that they would maintain their traditional character under the new regime. Even as the Israelite kings grasped for power and hoped to increase its centralization, they would have built their ambitions on deeply held traditions of political decentralization. This decentralization of old Israelite political tradition, both under the name Israel and as a broader association of peoples or "tribes," represents the essential political character of Israel, in contrast to Jerusalem-centered Judah (see Fleming 2012a: 23–27).

"little Israel."[71] Interpreters do not expect the first reference to Israel in the Merenptah stele (ca. 1207) to match the geography of the kingdom, and yet few have probed the precise scale of Israel by name in the earlier periods.[72]

Biblical writing offers glimpses of earlier landscapes, which I have assembled into an album for "little Israel" in Fleming (forthcoming). One text that indicates the contrast is the notice for what the house of Saul ruled in the days of Ishbosheth (Eshbaal), in 2 Sam 2:8–9:

> Abner son of Ner, military commander to Saul, took Ishbosheth son of Saul, brought him across to Mahanaim, and made him king toward Gilead, toward the Ashurite, and toward Jezreel; and over Ephraim, over Benjamin, and over Israel, all of it.

Only the second group of three is ruled "over" (*'al*), the standard idiom that binds king to population: Ephraim, Benjamin, and Israel, "all of it." Gilead in the east and Jezreel of the major northern valley appear to be regarded as separate from the principal domain, even when viewed from a base at eastern Mahanaim. "Israel" in this context may be distinguished from Ephraim and Benjamin, the two peoples merged in the Song of Deborah (Judg 5:14) as first to respond when called to fight.

The gathered list of Deuteronomy 33, rendered parts of a whole as "the tribes of Israel" (v. 5), represent a larger, and almost certainly later, historical and political reality. Solomon offers no plausible setting, if such a large realm existed, without highlighting Judah or Jerusalem, and Israel of the 9th and 8th centuries offers a more likely origin for this kind of unified tribal list. As for the poem framed by "Jeshurun" in verses 2–5 and 26–29, I cannot identify a convincing context, north or south,

---

[71] Archaeologists grapple with the rise of "states" in north and south, with particular concern for the extent of monarchic influence. One approach, most visibly represented by Israel Finkelstein, identifies the first notable expansion with the Omrides of the northern kingdom, with excavated evidence for Omride presence in monumental architecture, listing the following sites (2013: 87–103): the acropolis and lower platform at Samaria; fortifications at Jezreel; fortifications at Hazor; Jahaz and Ataroth in Moab, known from the Mesha inscription, identified with Khirbet el-Mudeyine eth-Themed and Khirbet Atarus; Tell er-Rumeid in the Gilead; Gezer; En-Gev on the east shore of the Kinneret; and Har Adir in the Upper Galilee. These evaluations are informed by his proposal of a later chronology, so that others would date some of the finds to the 10th century instead. William Dever (2017: 408, 416) would date the fortifications at Hazor and Gezer to the earlier period, so that Hazor Stratum X would not reflect Omride construction.

[72] There is increasing archaeological and historical interest in this question, as reflected in the issue devoted to "The Rise of Ancient Israel" in *NEA* 82/1 (2019).

monarchic or post-monarchic. The introduction to the Song of Deborah demonstrates the antiquity of Yahweh's procession from the south. The framing introduction and conclusion to the sayings of Moses could be older than the tribal expansions (potentially Reuben, Judah, and Levi), perhaps even composed to go with the earliest version of the sayings, which could belong to the 9th or 8th centuries.

Little from the conclusion (Deut 33:26–29) illuminates the question. The people are Jeshurun (v. 26), which Yahweh rules as king in the introduction (v. 5), otherwise found only in two more poetic texts, condemned as faithless in Deut 32:15 and chosen in Isa 44:2, paired with "my servant Jacob."[73] Israel is paired with Jacob (Deut 33:28), as in the Balaam poetry (Num 23:7, 10, 21, 23; 24:5, 17, 18–19).[74] While Israel is delivered by Yahweh (Deut 33:29), Jeshurun is first told "there is no one like El" (v. 26), and "the God of the ages [*'ĕlōhê qedem*] is a shelter" (v. 27). Yahweh and El are also named together in the Balaam poetry (Num 23:8, 21–22; 24:4–8).[75] The material could be monarchic, even from the northern kingdom, but such placement is not secure.

Deuteronomy 33 opens with Yahweh's arrival from Sinai, and the poetry itself sets no expectation that what follows will be words of Moses for the individual peoples of Israel, whether as blessings (v. 1) or anything else. This contrasts with Genesis 49, which invites the ambiguous "sons of Jacob" themselves to "come together and give heed . . . give heed to Israel

[73] The name Jeshurun has a secure 6th-century date in the Isaiah text, with the two Deuteronomy poems left uncertain. Certainly it does not necessarily signal an older and monarchic setting, though this is not to be excluded. Horst Seebass (1977: 158) considers that the Isaiah text, along with Sir 37:25, does suggest that the term is quite late.

[74] On the combination of Jacob and Israel as a particular feature of the Balaam poems, see Levine (2000: 211–12). Levine takes the combination as referring to Israel and Judah together, east and west. "The combination Jacob/Israel may have originated in northern Israel, although it was used by Judean, Israelite and Transjordanian poets as well. A blatantly northern Israelite reference to Jacob/Israel comes in Genesis 49:24, in the blessing addressed to Joseph . . ." To my mind, the inclusion of Judah in the Balaam poems is not clear.

[75] Levine (2000: 219) argues that the Balaam poems display the conscious identification of Yahweh and El, aware of their character as distinct deities: "we would hypothesize that texts like the Balaam poems, though possibly originating in archives of the cult of El, the regional deity, were adapted by Yahwistic writers and reinterpreted to refer to YHWH, the God of Israel. Theologically, we would say that El merged with YHWH, with YHWH absorbing El." The same phenomenon would be on display in Deut 33:25–29 as well: "Deuteronomy 33:29 serves as a commentary on Deuteronomy 33:25–28, and identifies YHWH as the redeemer of Israel in place of El" (220). Mark Smith endorses Levine's conclusion, with comment that "Yahweh and El were likely identified at an early point in the monarchy, if not earlier in many parts of ancient Israel" (2004: 110).

your father" (v. 2). Moses does appear in the introduction to the sayings of Deuteronomy 33, but without reference to the text's apparent purpose: "Moses commanded us the Teaching [tôrāh], a legacy (for) the assembly of Jacob" (v. 4). Instead of preparing the audience to hear what Moses has to say about the individual peoples of Israel, the introduction turns to his stock role as mediator of divine instruction. In combination with the notion of Jacob as a "congregation" (qĕhillâ) using a term found otherwise only in Neh 5:7, this treatment of Moses could be considered post-monarchic, though we also face the possibility of revision or combination.[76]

We are left with an introduction to the sayings of Moses that lacks secure connection to the original poem, which probably was composed during the 9th or 8th centuries either in Israel or in Judah with knowledge of Israel's tribal tradition. It appears to have been revised in post-monarchic times to fill out the eventual standard of 12 tribes. At the earliest, Yahweh's movement from Sinai, Seir, and the Paran highlands could have been written during the flourishing of the northern kingdom of Israel. As with the statement about Moses and "teaching," Yahweh's arrival from Sinai fits awkwardly with the sayings that follow. The Song of Deborah, Psalm 68, and Habakkuk 3 are all concerned with Yahweh at war, so that the image of Yahweh or Eloah coming from the southern wilderness is tied to the promise of victory in battle. In Deuteronomy 33, no military conflict inspires the collection of sayings, and even the introductory lines have no concern for Yahweh's defeat of enemies.[77] Rather, the ultimate object is his rule as king (v. 5), setting out a rule of law through Moses (vv. 3–4), with his arrival from the south a matter not of storm or plague but of brilliant light (v. 2), the metaphor of magisterial justice in the ancient Near East.[78] This shining appearance seems adapted

---

[76] Mayes (1981: 400) raises the possibility that the first half of the verse could be a gloss, but this does not address the terminology in the second half. Seebass picks up the prior notion that the framing hymn in 2–5 and 26–29 could represent a separate text and argues that this is particularly true of 2–3 and 27–29, which read together as the remains of a battle poem like the Song of Deborah (1977: 159–60). This solution leaves Jeshurun an epithet for Judah (161), part of the introduction to a tribal list that was defined as 4–26 (164). From this period of biblical scholarship, Seebass is thinking of compositional dates from the time of the two kingdoms.

[77] This is a problem with Seebass's attempt to reconstruct a framing hymn that resembles the Song of Deborah.

[78] As the god of justice, Shamash "shines" his authority; see the well-known Shamash hymn in Lambert (1960: 121–38), throughout. The Akkadian adjective šūpû(m), "brilliant, shining, splendid," is attached to gods and kings. For Yahweh and solar imagery, see

to the rest of Yahweh's introduction, so that the whole notion of his starting point in the south no longer envisions a long-standing desert residence but a one-time move to a new royal capital "in Jeshurun."[79] Listeners would perhaps call to mind the military context of Yahweh's approach from Sinai and Seir, even as the rest of the introduction turned their thoughts elsewhere.

Because the construction and context of Deuteronomy 33 leave us uncertain of its date and place of composition, and we cannot be sure when it was framed by the introduction, set in motion by Yahweh's blinding arrival, this motif cannot be dated by the text around it. The lines themselves are notable for the combination of likeness and contrast to Judg 5:4. The great commonality is the verb of movement, this time "coming" instead of "going out," defined by a distant starting point, "from" Sinai, Seir, and Mount Paran, at the least, in place of Seir and "the open country of Edom." In Deut 33:2, there is only the brilliant light of the newly risen sun, without response from heaven and earth. Interestingly, the metaphor of sunrise evokes appearance from the inland east, though the wilderness names are identified with terrain south of Israel and Judah. It is significant that like all of the references to Yahweh and the south in the old poetry, the plural geographical names are not simply alternatives for a single place. Without an allusion to the mountain of Moses, Sinai is left an apparent territory, linked to neither population nor known geography, in contrast to Seir and Paran.[80] As with Seir and Edom in Judg 5:4, the locations in Deut 33:2 are not understood in relation to

Mark Smith (1990: chapter 4); and Taylor (1993). Keel (2006) identifies the principal god of early Jerusalem as solar.

[79] Ted Lewis (personal communication) observes that the typical military context for Yahweh's march from the south works well with some of the sayings themselves, including help against Judah's enemies (v. 7), crushing Levi's enemies (v. 11), protecting Benjamin (v. 12), and Gad as "commander" (v. 21). In the conclusion, Yahweh is shield and sword against enemies.

[80] In Genesis 14, the Elamite Chedorlaomer establishes his power in the west by victories over peoples that include the Horites "in their highlands, Seir as far as the Oak of Paran, which is on the wilderness" (v. 6). Here, the place name with Paran is commonly read as "El-Paran," though the first element does derive from the word for a large tree (cf. Seebass 1997: 52). Paran is most commonly defined by the "wilderness" (*midbār*), where Hagar raises her son Ishmael (Gen 21:21), where the Israelite camp at Kadesh is located when they send spies into Canaan (Num 13:26; cf. 12:16; 13:3), and where David encounters Nabal and Abigail (1 Sam 25:1). An early Edomite king named Hadad is said to have taken refuge in Egypt as a boy, and his party picked up a group from Paran on the way out of Midian (1 Kgs 11:18). Like Seir, Paran is known territory, populated, though the two are distinct from each other.

peoples and not as places where Yahweh receives worship. If he comes from them, he must live there, or circulate there, when not brought forth by his people's need. How this notion relates to Yahweh's "origins" must remain a separate question, to which we will return after addressing a final biblical text.

HABAKKUK 3: ADDING TEMAN

The Bible provides one more apparently old poem that incorporates an expression of the tradition that Yahweh may join his people from a starting point in the distant south. In the short book of Habakkuk, the first two chapters are devoted to the last days of Judah before its fall to Babylon. Whatever the distance between time portrayed and date of composition, the contents of these chapters would be no earlier than the classical period of biblical writing, between the 8th and 5th centuries.[81] The third and last chapter of Habakkuk represents something else entirely, attached to the book for no clear reason, though praise of Yahweh's power and prowess in war may always offer a ray of hope. In his search for old poetry in the Bible, Albright found features of Habakkuk 3 that predated "Standard Biblical Hebrew," but neither content nor context supplies evidence to date the text, a hymn to Yahweh at war that does not name his people.[82] Yahweh fights alone, with only (divine) plagues in his retinue (v. 5), turning his wrath against Sea (Yam, v. 8), the victim of Baal's victory in the Ugaritic myth. The result is deliverance for "your people" and "your anointed," the latter indicating one of the two kingdoms, to composition in the 9th–7th centuries, whether in Israel or Judah.[83] Cushan and "the land of Midian" provide enemies or audiences to be shaken (v. 7), with Midian a figure from the past more than

---

[81] This definition is calculated to match "Standard Biblical Hebrew" as measured against inscriptional Hebrew, which offers a sizable collection (in early alphabetic terms) of texts from the 8th through 6th centuries. Oddly, as observed by William Schniedewind (2013: 148–49), there is almost no Hebrew inscriptional evidence from roughly 500 to 350 BCE. During much of the Persian period, the existing finds are in Aramaic, as for the Jewish/Israelite community at Elephantine in Egypt. The pattern of inscriptional finds highlights the concentration of biblical writing explicitly dated to this period, as with most of the writing in the prophet books, and various features of Biblical Hebrew align well with the inscriptional Hebrew of this period, including orthography and syntax.

[82] See Albright (1950: 8–10); cf. Hiebert (1986: 119–21). For the casting of an old hymn (3:3–15) in the context of Habakkuk as a book of prophecy, see Watts (1996).

[83] Smith (2014: 219) also draws this conclusion from verse 13. For comments on verses 2–7, see Ahituv (2008).

any monarchic threat and Cushan only here.[84] The hymn seems to require no current antagonist, perhaps to suit its application beyond a single circumstance.

After an opening declaration of awe, addressed in the first person to Yahweh (v. 2), the actual account of the god at war avoids the name until concluding with another promise to worship (vv. 18–19).[85] This distinct text in 3:3–15 begins with the familiar motif of movement from the south, initiated with the name Eloah, the singular form from which Elohim derives.[86] If we read the war poem without its framing focus on the worshipful observer (vv. 2, 16–19), it comes to us without reference to Yahweh, an equation that can only be made by argument that the content requires specific allusion to this deity. Judges 5:4–5 and Ps 68:8–9 offer one example by the substitution of Elohim in the psalm, and travel from the south shows every sign of being a motif particular to Yahweh. Further, the title "Holy One" (*qādôš*) has extensive association with Yahweh.[87] We will see that the representation of Yahweh by a form of El, assuming their identification as one, appears to occur in the one poetic text from Kuntillet 'Ajrud. With strong likeness to Deuteronomy 33, the composition opens with the divine appearance, constructed almost exactly the same way: the name leads, followed by "from" and a place, with movement as "coming" (verb *bw'*).

> (3) Eloah came from Teman,
> and the Holy One from Mount Paran.[88]
> His majesty covered the heavens,
> and his praise filled the earth.
> (4) And the shining was like the sunlight ...

In Hab 3:3, the god's arrival first of all displays "majesty" (*hôd*), and "praise" (*tĕhillāh*) is shouted or sung aloud, so that we have performance and audience. As the poem continues, Eloah's movement is

---

[84] The great conflict is associated with Gideon in Judges 6–8; cf. Ps 83:10.

[85] Yahweh appears otherwise only in verse 8, with anger at River/Sea, and the BHS would prefer to delete it. Ahituv (2008: 225) treats the introduction of Yahweh here as marking the transition to a new section of the poem, about war with the sea (8–16).

[86] The short form Eloah occurs occasionally, mainly in poetry, including Deut 32:15, 17, and Ps 18:22. Watts (1996: 221) identifies 3:3–15 in particular as the block of older material adapted for use in the book of Habakkuk.

[87] Lewis (2020b) devotes an entire chapter of his book on "God" to "Yahweh as the Holy One" (chapter 10).

[88] The verb is prefixed, which Cross (1973: 102) understood as an old preterite – perhaps supported by the suffixed past for the same verb in Deut 33:2, if they envision the same completed action.

accompanied first by brilliant light (v. 4), then pestilence (v. 5). The earth shakes and shifts (v. 6) and eventually water is everywhere – out of the ground (v. 9), as rain, and as a thundering ocean (*tĕhôm*, v. 10), extending elements found in both Judg 5:4–5 and Deut 33:2. Among the set of texts for Yahweh coming from the south, only this one lacks Sinai, the place of which is occupied by Teman, with Mount Paran adding to the impression of replacement by its position in Sinai's supporting cast in Deut 33:2. As in the Judges 5/Psalm 68 fragment, the divine presence imposes itself on all space, as heavens and earth, including a production of water that does not seem to require the vehicle of storms, as something more like the breaking forth of creation waters past all barriers. The initial focus on light recalls the shining in Deut 33:2, though in this case the brilliance brings terror, in the ancient tradition of divine radiance.[89]

For consideration of the Midianite Hypothesis, the most important contribution of Hab 3:3 is the new appearance of Teman, seemingly in place of Sinai.[90] Teman comes in the Bible to refer broadly to the "south," as a common noun, though its use can be ambiguous.[91] As a particular people or place, Teman is situated in the genealogy of Esau, representing a clan in the line of Eliphaz (Gen 36:11, 15). In prophetic poetry, it is paired with Edom (Jer 49:20) and Bozrah as part of Edom (Amos 1:11–12); it is clustered with Edom and Mount Esau in Obadiah 9 and with Dedan and Esau in Jer 49:7. Like Seir and Edom of Judg 5:4, Teman can assume a people, in contrast to Sinai. From Habakkuk alone, we might conclude only that a monarchic-period praise of the warrior Eloah (for Yahweh) has taken on a geographical interest that appears also in prophetic writing suitable to the book of Habakkuk. Considering the other appearances of Teman in these books, there could be no reason to date Hab 3:3–15 substantially earlier than Amos 1, which appears to date to the late

---

[89] See the various terms associated with Huwawa, guardian of the Cedar Forest in Gilgamesh tradition. In particular, the Sumerian texts alternate words for brilliance and terror, meaning the same thing. The Sumerian terms are ni_2 or ni_2-te for "terror" and me-lam$_2$ for "(brilliant) aura," the latter reflected in the Akkadian *melammu*, associated with divine presence. On Huwawa's possession and loss of these, see Fleming and Milstein (2010: 57–58, 79–81).

[90] In a completely different analytical framework, Ahituv (2008: 232) concludes that Hab 3:2–7 as a whole culminates in a reference to the Sinai theophany by mention of Midian and Kushan.

[91] The general use is clearest in combinations of directions, as with south and north in tabernacle construction, according to Exod 26:15–25, especially v. 18 for the south.

8th century.[92] This would fit the "anointed" king of Hab 3:13, who could belong to Judah as well as to Israel. Unlike Sinai, Teman has no connection at all with the early history of Israel as measured by exodus from Egypt, life in the wilderness, or meeting with God at a mountain. In this context, the southern residence of Yahweh can hardly replay a "ritual conquest" (Cross) with any meaningful connection to biblical origins stories.

Teman and Kuntillet ʿAjrud

Yet the greatest interest of Teman reflects new evidence from outside the Bible, found in the eastern Sinai Peninsula at a place called Kuntillet ʿAjrud, dug by Israeli archaeologists during the brief period of occupation between 1973 and 1982, relevant because the site is no longer accessible to the excavators.[93] Several short inscriptions, found on two enormous store-jars and on plaster from separate spaces in the fortified enclosure, include multiple invocations of "Yahweh of Teman."[94] One further blessing is addressed to "Yahweh of Samaria," showing that in spite of the southern desert location, Kuntillet ʿAjrud was the particular concern of Israel, not Judah, and this reference opens up new questions for the activity of Israel in the south.[95] Although the biblical texts with Yahweh coming from the south are not all demonstrably from the northern kingdom, in both Judges 5 and Deuteronomy 33 the association of peoples united as Israel and under the god Yahweh is best understood to originate there, rather than in the southern kingdom of Judah and Jerusalem. The book of Habakkuk expressly reflects the fears of Judah in the face of Babylonian assault, and we cannot know the original setting for the composition in 3:3–15, with its older sacred poetry. In spite of its location far south of both Israel and Judah, the site's alignment with

---

[92] Large parts of the book of Amos remain most plausibly dated to before the fall of the northern kingdom in 720, though there are unsurprising hesitations. For a reflection on the problem with Amos 1–2 as focus, see Barstad (2007).

[93] The site was excavated in 1975/76; my reference to the inaccessibility of the primary data reflects conversation with Bill Schniedewind, who has been working on its inscriptional finds.

[94] There are three: 4.1.1 (ink on plaster), from an inside room; and 3.6 and 3.9 (Pithos B), outside this room. The first two are benedictions, and the last is broken and more difficult to characterize, though the text also includes blessing. See first of all the publication with photographs and drawings in Ahituv, Eshel, and Meshel (2012); and note the recent discussion in Allen (2015: 264–65).

[95] Text 3.1, on Pithos B.

Samaria means that interest in Teman need not indicate a Judah perspective in Habakkuk. Kuntillet 'Ajrud is nevertheless essential to understanding the association of Yahweh with Teman, and to that end, the site bears further consideration.

On a rise beside a road connecting Kadesh-barnea with the Gulf of Aqaba, the extent of construction at Kuntillet 'Ajrud was limited and its visitors or residents were isolated from any large settlement. Pottery and other material finds have been taken to indicate that the site was only in use for several decades at most, at the beginning of the 8th century, but Schniedewind (2017) raises the possibility that it was founded generations earlier.[96] Debate over the essential purpose of the buildings has simmered since their discovery, without decisive conclusion. Any attempt to treat it as primarily or exclusively religious (so, Meshel) would seem to require understanding it as a site for pilgrimage, when nothing about the location indicates a destination in itself.[97] Lacking a significant long-term population, Kuntillet 'Ajrud is best investigated in terms of travel, and we must be prepared to tolerate overlapping functions. Considerable resources were invested in building the site, and it is reasonable to imagine that royal funds were disbursed, making this in some sense a public construction.[98]

Two important reasons for travel to, or by way of, Kuntillet 'Ajrud appear to be trade and the projection of power, which need not be mutually exclusive.[99] There may have been people stationed at Kuntillet 'Ajrud for extended periods, and the isolated location would have

---

[96] According to Meshel and his collaborators (2012) the ceramics, paleography of the inscriptions, and Carbon-14 all point to the same period ca. 800 and just after. One reason to consider the possibility of earlier use is the notably older script on two of the stone vessels, including the enormous basin KA 1.2 (Cohen 2019). Singer-Avitz (2006) proposed a date in the late 8th century and Judahite association, without general agreement (e.g. Freud 2008).

[97] Several studies emphasize the role of the Kuntillet 'Ajrud site as a stopping point for travelers: e.g. Hadley (1993); Brian Schmidt (2002); Schniedewind (2014, 2019).

[98] This interpretation is based especially on the quality of the ink-on-plaster writing and drawings from the inside "bench room" (Keel and Uehlinger 1998: 245–46; developed by Hutton 2010: 199–200). See also the proposal by Ornan (2016) for sketches before painting on the walls, all in the context of royal involvement.

[99] Schniedewind (2014: 293) concludes: "In sum, the inscriptions at Kuntillet 'Ajrud need to be assessed holistically. First of all, this begins with understanding the natural function of a remote desert fortress on the trade route from the Red Sea to the Mediterranean. The site was chosen because it provided access to water for travellers in the desert. The fortress was part of state-run caravanseries – apparently, operated by the kings of Samaria judging by the personal names and the reference to 'Yahweh of Shomron'."

demanded the capacity for defense against small forces or banditry. Even if soldiers constituted some part of the population that flowed through Kuntillet 'Ajrud, the larger question is what they were intended to protect, or to project.[100] If Israel had interests in the eastern Sinai, they were almost certainly financial, tied up with long-distance trade.

The textual finds are abundant and varied, especially considering the site's small size and remote location. The official publication divides them into four types: incised in stone (KA 1.1–1.4); incised in pottery (2.1–2.28); ink on pottery (3.1–3.17); and ink on plaster (4.1–4.6). The first group consists of four stone vessels inscribed with personal names, evidently to record who gave them. The incised ceramic vessels are divided between those inscribed before firing and those done after, all relating somehow to the administration of stores, incoming or assigned. Most of the ink on pottery was found on two enormous "pithoi" (A and B), storage jars that came to serve as writing boards for repeated use. More than one space, including the "bench room" (4:1–4.3) and the entries to the western storeroom (4.4–4.6) were decorated with inscriptions and drawings on plaster, found in fragments on nearby floors. Writing was not a casual activity at this desert site, and it was exercised regularly and with sophistication. Together, the writing and the elaborate visual art communicate wealth and significance – again, considering the location and distance from population centers.

There is also controversy about the purposes and perspective of the writing at Kuntillet 'Ajrud, and the role of religion remains disputed. Hutton (2010: 202) suggests that the "bench room" in Building A was devoted to Yahweh of Teman by this title, though it is not obviously a temple or place for performing animal sacrifice. In his series of studies, Schniedewind argues directly against Meshel's interpretation of Kuntillet 'Ajrud as a religious center for a community of priests, and he downplays the possibility of any specifically sacred space or personnel associated with it. Recently, Noam Cohen (2019) has observed the importance of an enormous stone "basin," with a diameter of roughly 1 meter and which the excavators estimate to weigh 150 kilograms or more, inscribed with some of the older letter-forms remarked by Schniedewind: "From Obadiah son of Adnah; be he blessed of Yahweh."[101]

---

[100] Schniedewind (2019: chapter 2) develops at length the notion of the "soldier-scribe" as the most likely participants in the scribal exercises practiced at Kuntillet 'Ajrud.

[101] KA 1.2, *l'bdyw bn 'dnh brk h' lyhw*. Cohen emphasizes the likely association of the name with the person who donated the object, which means that the opening preposition

With the closest comparison for the object a cuneiform-inscribed basin from Late Bronze Age Hazor, part of a monumental podium in the royal complex, the Kuntillet 'Ajrud basin appears an expensive donation for ritual use, unlikely to have been moved again after initial installation.[102] The basin was found complete but in pieces, perhaps fallen from a second floor, near the entrance to the southern storeroom, so not in the bench room discussed by Hutton. Cohen argues that such an object, with the inscription binding the donor to Yahweh, very likely served a regular ritual purpose, given not simply to draw attention to his support but to serve the activity of the building as a whole, an activity that would thus include some essential sacred aspect.[103]

It seems in any case that the Kuntillet 'Ajrud building complex incorporated a formal religious dimension defined by the title "Yahweh of Teman."[104] This conclusion need not contradict the direction of Schniedewind's analysis. Such a combination of cultic and military infrastructure could find a comparison in the roughly contemporary fortress at Arad, with the remarkable sanctuary that occupied a significant portion of the space without rendering the whole construction a "temple" or priestly residence.[105] The spelling of theophoric personal names, matching the Samaria Ostraca, indicates that the compound at Kuntillet 'Ajrud was erected especially for travelers from the kingdom of Israel, probably at the initiative of the administration itself.[106] This means that the written evidence for Yahweh of Teman does not display the religious practices of populations from the southern wilderness and especially of the Edomites,

---

(*l*-) should indicate the source, not a recipient or ongoing possession. The independent pronoun for "he" (*hū'*) produces an effect distinct from the prefixed jussives in the blessings on the pithoi, suggesting a result deriving from the donation, whether or not to be read as a request.

[102] The text is published as Hazor 13 in Horowitz and Oshima (2006: 85–86), with further information and photograph in Horowitz and Oshima (2002: 179–83).

[103] With appreciation to the author, I describe Cohen's proposal at some length because it undertakes an argument for a sacred function at Kuntillet 'Ajrud without focus on the blessings or on the supposed presence of priests. He considers the large basin in the context of three more inscribed rims from smaller stone vessels, along with the finds from the building as a whole.

[104] Such compound divine names constitute the entire focus of Spencer Allen's 2015 book, with one chapter devoted to this deity. I am not persuaded that the terminology of "first names" and "last names" provides a compelling analogy for ancient worship of gods at different sanctuaries and with second naming elements. The problem is not my concern here.

[105] See especially Herzog (2002).

[106] See the discussion and references in Allen (2015: 267–68).

who lived some distance to the east.[107] Rather, we have here evidence for devotion by Israelites to their own god Yahweh in identification with his southern presence.

If we begin with the notion that there was ritual practice at Kuntillet 'Ajrud in the name of Yahweh of Teman, the next question would be where else we might find worship by this divine designation. The whole discussion of divine "multiplicity" follows the reality that the names of prominent gods could be qualified with supplementary titles that distinguished a separate worship site and divine representation. In some circumstances, these combined titles, with their more particular associations, could be duplicated in turn when transported to different communities.[108] Are we to imagine such duplication for "Yahweh of Teman," so that there would have been multiple sacred sites devoted to worship of Yahweh by this compound name? It is certainly possible, and existing evidence will not answer the question. Nevertheless, it is equally possible that the Kuntillet 'Ajrud site specially represented "Yahweh of Teman" as the particular sanctuary identified with the name. This would then have been the sanctuary of reference for the name. In either case, Yahweh of Teman was a manifestation of Israelite worship, joining the perception that Yahweh somehow inhabited the wilderness far from Israel (and Judah) to the projection of Israelite, Samaria-based, presence into that very space.

Yahweh's March at Kuntillet 'Ajrud

The predominance of perishable writing materials in ancient Israel and Judah probably explains the general lack of literary inscriptions, hard-

---

[107] Allen (2015: 271) refers to Yahweh of Teman as "the local Temanite Yahweh" and says, "The two unofficial texts that invoke Yahweh-of-Teman (*Meshel* 3.6 and 3.9) reinforce the idea that Israelite travelers would be inspired to revere the local Yahweh." Yet he clarifies that we have no evidence for non-Israelite worship of this deity: "the divine name Yahweh-of-Teman and his shrine have confidently been interpreted as the result of Israelite initiative. No native Temanite community need be assumed. It could have existed, but it need not be assumed." It may be that the very name (and divine name) reflects a northern perspective in relative terms: it is not clear that local residents would consider themselves to live in a region called "South." Note that Jeremias (2017: 155) understands Seir and Teman not as precise places from which Yahweh comes "but rather the direction from which he comes," further south than Edom.

[108] For nuanced discussion of the phenomenon in the context of Samsi-Addu, his upper Mesopotamian kingdom, and ritual texts found at Mari from the 18th century BCE, see Elizabeth Knott (2018).

copy counterparts to most of what found its way into the Bible. Here once again, the unlikely site of Kuntillet 'Ajrud, with its sophisticated practice of writing, offers an exception, fragmentary as it is. Recognizing the unique character of this lacework of Israelite literature, Lewis (2020a) has devoted an extended study to sifting possible readings of its mottled several centimeters of ink on decorated plaster (Meshel 2012: 110–14, KA 4.2). The surviving lines evoke the poetry of Yahweh's arrival from the south, especially the god's blinding sunrise appearance for war and the physical response of the earth. Lewis translates, with two preferred options for line 4:

2   ...with/during the/an earthquake,   ...*brʿš.wbzrḥ.ʾl b*[*ʾš*] [*y*]*hw*[*ḥ*]
    when El shines forth (or, buffets) [with fire?];
    [Ya]hwe[h] ...
3   The mountains melt, the hills are crushed ...   ...*r.wymsn.hrm.wydkn.pḥnm*
4   [(*m/b*?)]ʾ*rṣ.qšdš.ʿly.ʾtn/m.ḥz.kr/s*[
(a) ...earth. The Holy One at/over/against the ever-flowing waters. He gazes
    like ...
(b) [From/in] the land of Qadesh at the ever-flowing stream he looked upon
    (with favor) ...
5   ...?? to bless the (war-)lord [El? Yahweh?]   ...*kn lbrk.bʿl.bym.mlḥ*[*mh*]
    on a day of war
6   ...[to prai]se the name of El   ...[*lhl*]*l šmʾl.bym.mlḥ*[*mh*]
    on a day of wa[r] ...

Linking this text with Deuteronomy 33:2 in particular, Lewis comments (2013: 591),

The poem in which this verse is found is often assigned to the corpus of archaic Hebrew poetry. The opening describes YHWH coming from the south/south-east with cosmic vocabulary and topographic allusions that resonate with other archaic biblical passages (Judg 5:4–5; Ps 68:8–9, 18 [Eng 68:7–8, 17]; Hab 3:2–7). The antiquity of these motifs was underscored when they were found in the late-ninth- to early-eighth-century B.C.E. inscriptions from Kuntillet Ajrud.

Leaving aside the obvious likenesses that put this text in dialogue with the old poetry of Yahweh on the warpath, we should note first of all the absolute difference of the word-for-word text from any biblical comparison. After having seen something more like a recast quotation in Ps 68:8–9, KA 4.2 reminds us of the creative variability visible in such poetry, even when carrying well-worn motifs that were colored by ritual reuse. The ideas and images are familiar, but the wording and details are new to us. El "dawns" (*zrḥ*) like Yahweh in Deut 33:2, but it is not from any preserved location, and his rising is announced by an earthquake (cf. Judg 5:4). Mountains "melt" (verb *mss*), where they "gush" (*nzl*) in Judg 5:5.

Lewis generously acknowledges Erhard Blum's (2013: 32–34) reading of the place name "K(Q)adesh" as a second "preferred" reading for line 4, but his argument that *qšdš* does in fact add a /š/ to the important word for "holy" highlights its occurrence in Hab 3:3 with reference to the deity, not to a place. Among the three principal biblical instances of the journey from the south, Habakkuk 3 lingers by far the longest, giving a sense of how the motif could be developed as a full-blown battle hymn, in contrast to what feels like citations of such material in Judges 5 and Deuteronomy 33. Like KA 4.2, Habakkuk 3 brings together brilliant light (v. 4), quaking earth (v. 5), mountains in movement (vv. 5, 10), and water (vv. 9, 10). Among the biblical texts, Hab 3:3 stands out by the unique designation of Teman as point of departure, by the substitution of Eloah for Yahweh, and by the parallel epithet *qādôš*, the Holy One. Teman is not named in the text, but Yahweh of Teman is the special deity of Kuntillet 'Ajrud. Lewis argues convincingly, in part by analogy to the very texts that occupy this chapter, that KA 4.2 has Yahweh in view, like Hab 3:3–15, another particular connection between the texts. And finally, only in Hab 3:3 do we find the deity as "Holy One." These details suggest a continuity of settings between Habakkuk 3 and Kuntillet 'Ajrud that may be closer than with the other biblical texts, which would confirm the impression of a monarchic inspiration for that expression of Yahweh and the south.

YAHWEH'S DISTANT HOME

Working from decades of familiarity with the Midianite Hypothesis, itself developed as an answer to the question, "Where did Yahweh come from?," this poetic motif seemed to provide the most straightforward of solutions. According to Judg 5:4 and Deut 33:2, Yahweh literally lives in the distant southern wilderness, a region identified variously with Sinai (not as mountain), Seir, Edom, and Mount Paran. Habakkuk 3:3 adds Teman, the literal "South." With increasing availability of written and iconographic evidence for the second and early first millennia, especially from Ugarit, Yahweh's absence becomes the more impressive. The old advantage of the Midianite Hypothesis is that it looked away from the great kingdoms and major cities, the first object of archaeological interest, toward elusive peoples of the inland wilderness who left behind little writing and nothing so ancient. Here in the old poetry can seem to be confirmation of that line of sight.

Yet like the prose texts of Exodus, these poems do not expressly identify non-Israelites who worshipped Yahweh. Even where names like Seir and Edom were associated with people by biblical writers, they were also associated with great empty spaces and the possibility of free movement without the constraint of cities and farmed land. Before we reconsider the south as such, it is useful to inquire further about divine residence, especially when removed from the homes of those who worship. In the poetry of Judg 5:4–5 (Ps 68:8–9), Deut 33:2, and Hab 3:3, Yahweh moves out of some large cross-section of the southern steppe. He is bound to no people and no particular space, but when he "comes" to Israel it is from outside their own realm. In the more recent renditions of the Midianite Hypothesis, this starting point for divine movement toward Israel is interpreted as recollection of the peoples who first worshiped Yahweh. Without the Bible-oriented question of divine origins, however, such movement has nothing to do with the peoples identified with deity.[109]

In the corpus of Near Eastern narrative about the gods, the Baal myth from Ugarit offers a useful point of reference, focused as it is entirely on the gods and their affairs. The gods move across a largely obscure landscape in pursuit of their particular interests, assembling in the company of El (Ilu, The God) as patriarch, traveling from one god's domain to another's for particular transactions, sometimes associated with a mountain dwelling. Note the following:

- The storm god Haddu/Baal is linked to Ṣapan (biblical Zaphon), north of Ugarit just over the Syrian border in modern Turkey, near the Mediterranean coast.[110] It is assumed that whoever takes Baal's place as king after his death will have to sit on his throne at Ṣapan.[111] When Mot confronts Baal after each has suffered humiliation, it is on

---

[109] It is noteworthy that Frank Cross (1973), who acceded to the ubiquitous notion that Yahweh must have originated as a southern deity, a distinct manifestation of the great god El, did not understand the old poetic texts in terms of divine origins. Rather, Cross attached Yahweh's movements to an idea of ritual conquest (see above), where the starting point is defined more by Sinai as sacred wilderness space for Israel's transformation than by any population that could once have worshiped this god.

[110] CAT 1.1 II 5, 18;1.3 III 29, as "my mountain"; also IV 18–19, 37–38; 1.4 IV 18–19; V 23, 55; 1.5 I 11; 1.6 I 15–16.

[111] CAT 1.6 I 58–59, 62.

Baal's turf, at Ṣapan, and this time the outcome is a draw, after a fair fight.[112]

- The gods must travel to their assembly with El.[113] The location of this assembly is named only once as Mount LL, when the sea god Yamm sends his messengers there.[114]

- El himself lives at a separate, second mountain called Mount KS. This is the first destination of Kothar-wa-Hasis in his summons to see El.[115] Kothar "comes" (the same verb as Yahweh in Deut 33:2) to "the mountain of El," where we find "the tent of the king."[116] El resides "at the springs of the Rivers, amid the streams of the Deeps."[117]

- The craftsman Kothar-wa-Hasis is associated with Kaphtor (Crete, or perhaps a part of Cyprus) and Memphis in Egypt – not because his early worshippers are found here but for their association with

---

[112] CAT 1.6 VI 12–13. Mark Smith (1994: 122–23) locates both the conflict involving Anat in 1.3 III 35–47 and the eventual combat between Baal and Mot at Ṣapan. In his more recent work on sacred geography, Smith (2016: 86) observes that in the Baal myth, "Mount Sapan serves as the literary mirror for the city and its patron god. The mountain is the divine site for Ugarit's religious and political reality." Smith observes distinct expressions of this relationship in different genres at Ugarit. Letters and treaties show that it is Baal Ṣapan that is known to the larger world, not Baal of Ugarit, so that Baal Ṣapan is the "political Baal" (85). Ritual texts list the gods separately, with another effect: "In a sense, Baal of Sapan lends cultic power to Baal of Ugarit. It is the mountain outside the city that empowers the city itself" (83). While Smith envisions an origin of this cult on Mount Ṣapan itself (87), it is not clear that the sacred character of the mountain depended on worship there. What is most significant is separation of the location of divine residence from the community of worship. Note that Smith's work is a response to questions about deity and space that have resulted in the discussion of "divine multiplicity" (Allen 2015; Knott 2018).

[113] CAT 1.1 III 2–4; the assembly is invited, including "the distant ones," the very name of which suggests travel. The location is "the house of your lord" (III 6).

[114] CAT 1.2 II 13–14, 19–20. It is not clear where Yamm resides, and it is intriguing that Baal's attack against him is given no location, in a long section that is almost undamaged.

[115] CAT 1.1 IV 11–12, 21–22.

[116] Whereas "Mount KS" is a ǵarru (mountain), "the mountain of El" (Smith's translation) is ḏd. Although some have identified the two mountains as one location, the terminology and larger descriptions suggest two different places (cf. Smith, 1994: 174–75). Note that the "tent" is a qirsu, the same term known in association with large tents in Mari texts and in the framing supports for the biblical tabernacle (qereš); see Fleming (2000b).

[117] CAT 1.2 I 4; 1.3 V 6–8; 1.4 IV 20–24; 1.6 I 32–36; cf. 1.5 VI 1–2. I adopt the translations by Mark Smith in Parker (1997). Note that the "deep" is dual, so that Frank Cross (e.g. 1998: 89) rendered this, memorably, as "double-deep."

skilled artisanship.[118] The god's connection to these places is spelled out with Baal's instructions to his messengers: "Then you shall head for great and wide Memphis, to Kaphtor, the throne where he sits, Memphis, the land of his heritage" – this, having crossed Byblos and QʻL.[119] Kothar's geographical range is also expressed in his contacts for acquiring materials, with cedar for Baal's palace from the Lebanon and Siryon mountain ranges.[120]

- The war-goddess Anat lives at a distance from El's Mount KS.[121] When at war, she is mired in the gore of the slain "in the valley" and "between the two towns," perhaps generic, for the human antagonists.[122]

- Athirat, the divine matriarch as consort of "The God" El, lives apart from El and from the other gods, so that Baal and Anat must travel to visit her.[123] She travels to El on a donkey, also perhaps assuming distance as well as dignity.[124]

- Mot (Death) has a mountain dwelling as well. When Baal sends messengers to convey his boasts, they are instructed to go "to Mount TRGZZ, to Mount THRMG, the two hills at Earth's edge."[125] Mot's "town" (*qrt*) is called "the Watery Place" (*hmry*). No other god is identified with a communal settlement of any kind, and the inhabitants may be the dead themselves.[126] The entrance to the underworld is located at another mountain, called KNKNY, which Baal must lift like a sewer-cover.[127]

---

[118] For Kothar's association with Egypt and Crete (or Cyprus), see Smith and Pitard (2009: 379–80). The first reference in the Baal myth (1.1 IV 1) is entirely restored from later parallels; see afterward, IV 18–19; 1.2 I 2–3.

[119] CAT 1.3 VI 12–16, cf. 7–9.   [120] CAT 1.4 VI 18–21.

[121] CAT 1.1 V restored; V 14–15. On the use of a thousand *šd* and ten thousand *kmn* to describe distance, see Smith and Pitard (2009: 290 n.8), "They are measurements of field-size in Akkadian documents" – not distance measurements as such. These represent "a well-attested formula, used either to indicate long distance traveled by a deity, or the great distance from which someone is seen, as here" (301). This is the distance from Baal's residence in 1.3 IV 38. Baal also must send messengers to Anat, indicating distance between them: CAT 1.3 III 8–9, 18–20.

[122] CAT 1.3 II 5–7, 19–20. While some have proposed particular identities for the two towns, Smith and Pitard emphasize the absence of a specific geography (2009: 130).

[123] CAT 1.4 II 12–16; III 23–24.   [124] CAT 1.4 IV 9–15 (parallel "mule").

[125] CAT 1.4 VIII 1–4; this is Smith's translation.

[126] On *hmry*, see Smith and Pitard (2009: 717–18), evidently referring to the abode of the dead, contrasting with the Mesopotamian notion of its dry character. Mot also has a "land of his inheritance," another reference to a domain with a population, not otherwise attributed to the gods in this text (VIII 14); also 1.5 II 15–16.

[127] CAT 1.5 V 12–13.

- In order to find Baal, Anat must traverse "every mountain in the heart of the earth," "every hill in the heart of the fields."[128] It is expected that the gods will roam and that the range of that roaming will be defined by highlands.

In Ugarit's Baal myth, the landscape of divine residence and travel is overlaid onto known human geography but with places of mystery and power assigned to the gods, especially in less accessible locations.[129] Among the gods of the Baal myth, only the craftsman god Kothar-wa-Hasis is defined by human domains, because his work is bound up with the best human artistry. The four deities who frame the circle of major gods that comes to surround El – El himself, Baal, Anat, and Athirat – all live at distance from each other, detached from human abodes. We are missing large blocks of text to tablet damage, but the names of specific residences survive only for male gods (including Mot) and for the place of divine assembly. While Mount Ṣapan was visible from Ugarit, to the north, the two mountains linked to El and the assembly of gods may not have belonged to the immediate region of those who worshiped them; at least, the names are not known. In any case, Ṣapan is not to be understood as a geographical clue to the people who first worshiped Haddu or the Akkadian Adad, though the mountain may indeed have been associated with rain and violent storms.[130] Similarly, the entire Lebanon range had a reputation at Ugarit and elsewhere as meeting place of the gods (Smith 2016: 89; cf. Ps 29:5–6) – not to be understood as their place of worship.

For comparison of Yahweh going to war from his home in the back country, notice especially the travels of Baal and Anat, the powerful young god and goddess who embody the terrors, exhilaration, and potential glory of battle. Anat has left her home to join in human combat, and

---

[128] CAT 1.5 VI 25–28.

[129] Smith and Pitard (2009: 43) observe regarding the general landscape of the Baal myth: "The gods are not envisioned in Ugaritic mythology as living together in 'heaven,' but rather at different locales around the earth, primarily on the mountains. The gods must make substantial journeys to get from one divine abode to another. Regular communication between them is portrayed as relatively rare and primarily through messengers." There is "virtually no contact with cities on earth."

[130] The site of Mount Ṣapan (Saphon) is the modern Jebel 'el-Aqra', known also from Hittite (Mount Hazzi), Akkadian (from the West Semitic), and Greek (Kasios). "It is fitting that Sapan was known as the mountain of the great storm-god, as this mountain receives the heaviest annual rainfall on the Levantine coast at over fifty-seven inches" (Smith 1994: 122–23; with reference to Hunt 1991).

she likewise journeys to reach El. In search of Baal, Anat sets out for the most remote locales. Baal is willing to leave his new palace in order to confront Mot on the death-god's own terms, a bold and risky move. Both Baal and Anat leave their home bases to visit Athirat.

The motif of Yahweh's march to war casts him in the same role as young god of battle, ready not just to fight but to journey to do so. Like the gods of Ugarit's Baal myth, Yahweh inhabits a land of sacred mystery, distant from Israel and Judah. While biblical writers could look north toward the mountains, including "Ṣaphon" and the Lebanon, Judges 5, Deuteronomy 33, and Habakkuk 3 turned instead to the vast spaces of the south, populated mainly by small communities of herdsmen and their scattered strongholds. In his ruminations on Yahweh, Mark Smith is struck above all by Judg 5:4–5, with its pairing of Seir and Edom as the regions from which the god goes forth as "god of Israel." In this context, the names do not identify the later kingdom of Edom but rather Seir takes priority and Edom is open space (*śādeh*). Recall from our discussion of the Shasu that the two Egyptian texts specifying such people's organization by "families" or "tribes" (*mhwt*) attach them to Edom and to Seir:

- Papyrus Anastasi VI (Merenptah, 1213 – 1203), "the tribes of the Shasu of Edom";
- Papyrus Harris I (Ramses III/IV, 1189–1153, 1153–1147), "the people of Seir, of the tribes of the Shasu."

At the very end of the 13th and in the mid-12th centuries, Egyptian scribes defined the mobile, difficult to manage, Shasu people by the very two names that identify Yahweh's point of departure in Judg 5:4. For the Egyptians, these were not political entities but regions, specific names not available to the earlier scribes of Amenhotep III (1390–1352), to describe the space occupied by back-country pastoralists. This definition of Seir and Edom suits well the context in the Song of Deborah. As argued in Chapter 2, the Shasu unit called Yhw3 predates the Egyptian focus on Seir and Edom as the location of such population, and the appearance of these places in the later 13th century would align with a southward shift of Egyptian military concerns. Whatever the explanation for the emergence of the names, Seir and Edom seem to have served as the primary designations for the mobile pastoralist homeland in the 12th century, at least from an Egyptian perspective. The names themselves are Semitic (Ahituv 1984).

I have already observed that the biblical poetry identifies Yahweh's southern starting point variously, not as a specific sacred mountain or sanctuary but as broad space, in each case identified by more than one name: altogether, Seir, Edom, Sinai, Mount Paran, and Teman. We could conclude based on geography alone that this is the land of pastoralists, though it also could evoke desert mining or the Arabian frankincense trade.[131] The combination of Seir and "the open country of Edom," however, in the oldest of the biblical texts, would confirm the apparent reference to the habitation of mobile herding peoples. The diverse biblical kinship with southern peoples, including the Midianites of Moses, who met his wife by helping their herdswomen, indicates an ancient recollection of the same association. Judges 5 does not reflect the older Egyptian understanding of such people as Shasu, and the writer does not imagine Yahweh to have received worship in Seir and Edom before the time of Israel by the people elsewhere equated with Esau. Yet this poetic motif, however ancient, makes Yahweh at home in the land of pastoralists, the very population that in still earlier times include a group called Yhw3. Cast in Smith's terms of "memory" and "amnesia," the Song of Deborah displays both, as my colleague intends in his use of the combination. Much has been remembered of Yahweh and his associations, even as the location for such people has been confined to the distant south in just the way that came to characterize Egyptian reference to the Shasu. By the early first millennium, the inland east was occupied by other groups – Aramean Damascus, Ammon, and Moab – and the south was the terrain left open for life on the move, life in tents. Like the tradition of southern kinship in biblical prose, therefore, the old poetry draws our eye not just to the south, but behind the geography, to a deep affinity for the pastoralists of the inland steppe.

YAHWEH IN THE OLD POETRY

We cannot discern the origin of this poetic motif, and I do not intend to characterize it as a first-millennium invention, in no way related to older settings, with earlier social and religious implications. Nevertheless, it is important to recognize the possibility, or I would say likelihood, that all of the texts in view were composed to serve monarchic interests.

---

[131] These alternatives came to mind for Thomas Schneider (personal communication). On copper mining in the south, see Ben-Yosef (2010); and for the possibility that pastoralists were involved with mining, see Martin and Finkelstein (2013). These questions about the interests of the kingdom of Israel in the land south of Judah are central to the New York University dissertation of Quinn Daniels, and the references come from him.

Returning to the centrality of "revision through introduction" in my reading of the Song of Deborah, the reimagining of a battle alliance as "Israel" transforms the allies into a permanent polity under this name, most easily understood as an effort serving kings (Stahl 2020). The other three poems also suggest monarchic settings, probably later than the composition of Judg 5:2–11. In the actual texts before us, we see the idea of distant divine residence in the service of rulers, whether Israel's or Judah's. In this early first-millennium vision, Yahweh is a god who fights for Israel as a people under royal leadership. This poetry represents a tradition of monarchy during a time when individual kingdoms of the region could be identified with single gods who took their part, as envisioned for both Kamosh and Yahweh of Moab and Israel in the 9th-century Mesha inscription.

Both the old poetry and the prose Midian-Moses narrative share the notion that Yahweh circulated and had some kind of residence in the southern wilderness in the region south of Israel and Palestine. Even if Exod 3:1–4:18 is a secondary text that adds Yahweh's name play to an older Moses story, the marriage to a Midianite appears intended to bring Moses into the desert, where he and Israel will encounter Yahweh on the god's own terrain at the "mountain of God," in an unknown location.[132] The mountain of God may be envisioned as a divine residence like Mount Ṣapan (Zaphon) or Mount Olympus, but unlike those sacred heights, it is not visible for the worshiping people and is impossibly remote and mysterious, effectively inaccessible. In Exodus 3, Moses finds the mountain only by accident, and Reuel/Jethro seems to have no idea of its existence. In Exodus 18, Jethro only finds Moses at the mountain because he is already there with all the people – and the mountain itself is not a focus of the ensuing feast. The only other biblical figure to visit the site is

---

[132] In the finished form of the exodus narrative, Moses is understood to have lived with the Midianites as a way to encounter Yahweh at the mountain, thus giving him a precise destination for leadership of Israel out of Egypt. Without the preparatory experience at Horeb, it is only Moses' own flight that anticipates that of the whole people; he has his own exodus, which results in establishing a life for himself in the back country with the herding groups of Midian. This relationship appears to lay the foundation for Israel's arrival in the same land, not simply a hostile testing ground (so, Deut 8:15–16) but a space to inhabit until establishment in a land of their own is possible, more like the time spent among the "sons of Esau" in Deut 2:2–4. Such a simpler narrative structure would still portray Israel as having a background in herding life (Fleming 2015; 2012a: 168–71). The other references to friendly relations with desert peoples (see Chapter 3) would reflect the same broad notion of ancient affinity, without intending any explanation of Yahweh's origin or demonstrating this unconsciously.

Elijah, who travels for forty days on the strength of a single meal provided by the angel of Yahweh (1 Kgs 19:5–8), without landmarks, so that he can only go there by divine appointment. It appears that the mountain of God can only be found if revealed and intended. Seir, Edom, Mount Paran, and Teman are all regional associations for the movement of Yahweh from this mysterious residence, not providing a location for the actual site of the god's point of departure.

Nothing in the old poetry suggests any sense that Yahweh was first worshiped in the southern desert by peoples known to traverse it or occupy its habitable margins, whether Midianites or Edomites. Any effort to unravel the early history of Yahweh may work from non-biblical evidence to propose such a connection, but the Bible itself neither intends this nor suggests it. Yahweh is no more originally "from" Sinai and Seir than Zeus is "from" Olympus or Baal is from Ṣapan.

It remains to explain why Yahweh would have such a mysterious residence in the territory south of Israel and Judah. Somehow Yahweh is at home in the wilderness far from Israel's settled domain, and this is linked to an idea that Israel itself had connections to such back country, as seen with the reference in Deut 2:1–4 to living for some time at the edge of Seir. As we have it, the idea is invoked by kings to support their power. By the motif of journey from the south, Yahweh is not anchored to Samaria, which all understand to be a new capital, and Israel itself embraces peoples beyond the highland north, where old Israel appears to have been situated. The question becomes why the kings of Israel highlighted this aspect of Yahweh's character and where such an idea could have originated. Whatever the answer, it does not derive from Yahweh's first actual worship by peoples of the named regions – at least, not based on any biblical evidence.

5

The Name Yahweh

In support of a Midianite Hypothesis, long-standing interpretation of both prose and poetic biblical texts has found in them reflections of Yahweh's origins outside Israel and Judah among desert peoples that once lived to the south. I have concluded in Chapters 3 and 4 that while both sets of material reflect a persistent and perhaps surprising sense of kinship with such pastoralist neighbors, the texts do not indicate that these were the first peoples to worship Yahweh. Before weighing the biblical material, I undertook in Chapter 2 to reexamine the oldest evidence brought to bear on the name Yahweh, the Yhw3 component of "Shasu-land" in Egyptian geographical lists from the 14th and 13th centuries. This evidence places us among just such a population evoked by the Bible, though without a particularly southern location, and yet Yhw3 does not name a god, at least by its primary and only explicit application.

As argued in Chapter 2, Yhw3 is one of the constituent parts making up what the Soleb scribes designated "Shasu-land." By analogy to two later Egyptian texts that offer a category to classify Shasu units, Papyrus Anastasi VI and Papyrus Harris I (Chapter 2), such parts would be defined as "families" (*mhwt*), which on a larger social scale could be called "tribes."[1] In Papyrus Anastasi VI and Papyrus Harris I, "the tribes

---

[1] I have avoided use of the term "tribe" as a primary category, in spite of its natural English match to the phenomenon in view. Anthropologists have debated its utility, with some rejecting it entirely (Kuper 1982), even as the term received a new lease on life in more recent work, manifest notably in Khoury and Kostiner (1990). In previous work, I have generally reserved use of "tribe" for textual evidence where it offers the best translation for specific words, such as Biblical Hebrew *šēbeṭ* and in the context of kinship-based social

of the Shasu" are identified with Edom and Seir, regions that may be inhabited by named peoples but that are not themselves social or political entities. Egypt would not go to war with "Edom" or make a treaty with it.[2] These two texts present Edom and Seir as populated with Shasu groups, pastoralist "families" or "tribes," unnamed because they matter only as a set. By identifying Yhw3 with the Egyptian category of the "family," I do not intend to strip away any potential territorial aspect. What matters to my analysis is that no matter the relationship between people and land, each of the proper names constituting "Shasu-land" represents a social and political body, a group that acted together in conflict with Egypt and that Egypt understood to have been defeated. On the temple columns at Soleb, each trussed prisoner was matched with a name, one captive to represent an enemy whole. Trbr, Yhw3, Smt, and Pyspys were the individual Shasu entities confronted and conquered. As such, I call them "peoples," and in this sense, Yhw3 identifies a "people," whatever the source and character of the name.

This conclusion from the Egyptian evidence offers occasion to revisit an old chestnut from the study of biblical religion: interpretation of the name Yahweh as a verb. The Bible itself shows the antiquity of the effort in Exodus 3, where the author acknowledges, even plays with what to the readers was the obvious form of the divine name as a finite verb. Modern biblical scholarship has grappled with its etymology to the point of ridicule. The nature of the question changes, however, when a deity is no longer the object of our quest. Does it make sense in historical and linguistic terms for the name of what I am calling a "people," a named social and political entity that was probably defined by imagined kinship in some unknown relationship to land, to have taken its name from the

---

organization in evidence from early second-millennium Mari, two old West Semitic words, *gayum* and *li'mum*, both of which I translate as "tribe." All three of the words I cite here are applied as leveling units to constitute some larger whole, like the *šibṭê yiśrā'ēl* ("tribes of Israel") in Gen 49:16 and Deut 33:5. As part of my work on Mari, see the section, "Using the Word 'Tribe'" in Fleming (2004: 26–33); and on Israel, "Tribe and State" (2012a: 183–85). For Porter (2012), the problem with "tribe" as conceptual category is rooted especially in its opposition to the "state" and to social complexity or sophistication generally, so that tribes end up attached to a long list of inaccurate stereotypes, from egalitarian organization to inability to sustain concerted collective action and tendency toward militaristic aggression (9–10). Applied by Egyptian outsiders, the term *mhwt* ("families, tribes") for plural organizing units of the Shasu people would fit the pattern of my translation as "tribe" in Mari evidence and in the Bible.

[2] Aside from the reference to Shasu "families" there in the Papyrus Harris I, two Ramses II texts refer to the "mountain" of Seir: a stele from Gebel Shaluf and an obelisk from Tanis (Ahituv 1984: 169). Edom appears only with the one Shasu mention (90).

prefixed form of a verb – *y-h-w-(vowel)*? And in the specific case of this name and setting, is origin in a personal name the most likely explanation for such a verbal derivation?

In the larger flow of my investigation into "Yahweh before Israel" this question is significant but not essential. The Shasu entities called Trbr, Smt, and Pyspys were just as much "peoples" by the same definition, likewise with the likelihood of kinship conception, yet lacking names with possible prefixed verbal form (*y-*). If Yhw₃ is a noun, its political character remains the same, and the implications of my analysis in Chapter 2 remain unchanged. Nevertheless, the question of Yahweh's name has both attracted attention and provoked frustration over generations, and I find that the common interpretation as a verb succeeds better in the framework of a Shasu people than when approached directly as a divine name. Moreover, certain debates over possible origins for the god Yahweh turn on conclusions regarding direct derivations for the divine name, when it is unlikely that the name first belonged to deity.

YAHWEH AS A VERB

Long before modern historical consideration of Yahweh as a deity once distinct from the biblical "God" (Elohim or El), the fact of the name itself attracted inquiry. With only one true God to imagine, the individuality of the name could perhaps hold its significance in its meaning, if this could be divined. The Bible itself showed ancient awareness of the problem, with which the writer toys in Moses' encounter at the mountain in Exod 3:14, discussed in Chapter 3. With its opening *y-*, the name *Yhwh* suggests the form of a finite verb, one marked by prefixes and suffixes for person, gender, and number, in this case resembling a third-person masculine singular verb from a root *h-w/y-w/y*. While the original vowels of the divine name cannot be reconstructed with certainty, the first syllable would have been pronounced *Yah-*, as in the exclamation of praise, Hallelu-Yah, where the shortened or "hypocoristic" form resembles what we find in sentence names from Iron Age Israel and Judah. One indication of the Israelite rather than Judahite presence at Kuntillet ʿAjrud at the end of the 9th century is the spelling of the Yahweh element as *-yw* rather than *-yhw*, so */yāw/* for */-yāhū/*.[3] Vocalization of the first syllable as *yā(h)-* in

---

[3] At Kuntillet ʿAjrud, the donor of the great stone basin, whose name would match the biblical "Obadiah," is rendered *ʿōbad-yāw* (KA 1.2); cf. *šamaʿ-yāw* (KA 1.1) as donor of a smaller stone vessel, and other names with shortened Yahweh elements.

the exclamation of praise and in personal names meant that late monarchic or post-monarchic Jewish scribes could not read the divine name as a simple (G/qal) form of the Hebrew verb "to be" in its biblical vocalization (cf. *yihyeh*). Nevertheless, a biblical scribe could have Yahweh play on the name by telling Moses, "I will be what I will be . . . you may tell the Israelites, 'I-Will-Be sent me to you'" (Exod 3:14). The form written here three times as *'hyh* is given this future sense just before, when Yahweh promises Moses, "Indeed I will be with you" (3:12) and it is most natural to keep the same meaning in the naming play in this context, without trying to make of the name a universal statement about God.[4]

In modern evaluation of biblical and Israelite religion through the past two centuries and more, the interpretive question gained a historical dimension, wondering where the god Yahweh could have come from, if the name were not assumed a revelation to Israel without precedent. The availability of newly discovered evidence for the ancient languages and writing from the larger region opened up previously inaccessible analytical avenues, soon accompanied by another flood of explanatory literature.[5] By the time Frank Moore Cross published *Canaanite Myth and Hebrew Epic* in 1973, he could introduce his own meticulous treatment by reference to the antiquity of the undertaking and the bewildering diversity of its results: "The discussion of the meaning and origin of the name Yahweh constitutes a monumental witness to the industry and ingenuity of biblical scholars. Fortunately, there is no space to review it here" (60). In both the sentiment and his eventual solution, Cross followed his teacher Albright (1968: 168), who had observed not long before that, "The long debate over the original meaning of the name *Yahwêh* shows no sign of abating, and the most incredible etymologies are still advanced by otherwise serious scholars."

I likewise shy away from immersion in the question of etymology, which I consider an inadequate basis for understanding Yahweh before

---

[4] Observe that I refer to the meaning in this context, not the etymology of the name in broad historical terms. Exodus 3:14 has attracted endless comment, and the interpretive choices are considerable. I do not attempt here to engage that discussion, which is not necessary to the issues confronted in this chapter.

[5] Again, though the debate is complex and fascinating, it is not essential to the argument here and I refer readers to the works cited below, including van der Toorn's general article on "Yahweh" in *DDD* (1999).

Israel.[6] Nevertheless, the strong possibility, even probability, that Amenhotep III's Yhw3 attests the same name long before Israel's god revives the question of how to understand it on its own terms, which I have argued to be different from the common view. Above all, the debate over the form and origin of the name has always been cast as explanation of a divine designation, a divine name. With the Bible and Israel in view, Yhw3 of Shasu-land has sometimes been interpreted in some direct relation to a divine name, but this presupposes the biblical interest and is in no way indicated by the Egyptian text and context. What we have explicitly is a subdivision of "Shasu-land," an indigenous name recorded from people the Egyptians identified as Shasu, whose organization the Egyptians stereotyped as tribal or family based. If we allow the Egyptian evidence to be our point of departure for exploration of Yahweh before Israel, then the name Yhw3 requires explanation as an identifier of people, setting aside the question of deity. This task simplifies the problem of the name's character and interpretation. Above all, in the company of other Semitic Shasu names, this one (alone) suggests derivation from a finite verb with *y*- prefix and an initial root consonant as H (pronounced /h/).[7] As observed above, my conclusions regarding the social and political character of the Yhw3 entity remain the same regardless of how we interpret the name, but the frequent interpretation of Yahweh in verbal terms would require cautious reconsideration if the name began as a people, not a deity.[8]

---

[6] Lewis (2020b: chapter 6) reviews the question in some detail, concluding that "the consensus of scholarship is certainly correct that *yhwh* represents a verbal form with the *y*- representing the third masculine singular verbal prefix of the verb *hyh* 'to be'." The first point of evidence for Lewis is Exod 3:14. Note the recent proposal by Dewrell (2020) to seek a different verb, *hwh* as "to destroy."

[7] Note that Egyptian had a rich selection of laryngeal consonants, including three that are rendered with variations of H that compare to Semitic /h/, /ḥ/, and /ḫ/; and a fourth, of uncertain pronunciation, rendered as /ẖ/ (Hoch 1997: 8). The identification of /h/ is therefore a precise match to the Hebrew consonant.

[8] Note the careful effort by Tropper (2017) to interpret the divine name Yahweh as a *qatl*-type noun form, like Ba'l(u) and Hadd(u), from an original **yahwa*, with the final short vowel lengthened secondarily. Aside from potential objections to Tropper's reasoning, he is working with the divine name as such, and the question is transformed substantially if we approach the Egyptian evidence on its own terms, as intended here. Görg (1976; 2000) offers one set of alternative possibilities, as already noted. Thomas Schneider (personal communication) considers the verbal interpretation most likely, but he wonders about place names such as the Yarmuk and Yabboq Rivers. I have not pursued the potential etymologies, but both names could derive from verbs.

PERSONAL NAMES AND PEOPLES

In the realm where early West Semitic languages were spoken, it was common for peoples to be identified by what would otherwise be understood as personal names. The phenomenon crosses time beyond what is relevant to our examination of Yhwȝ, which is first attested in the early 14th century, so that the roots of the name itself may go back to the 15th century and the context for the naming type is the mid-second millennium.[9] With this time frame in view, names from the el-Amarna letters (14th century) and other late second-millennium texts are noteworthy, but by far the largest number of available West Semitic names comes from the "Old Babylonian" period in Mesopotamia and especially the 18th century. Further, this assemblage of early second-millennium West Semitic or "Amorite" names includes types that have been compared directly to the *yhw-* base.

In the ancient Near East, many individuals bore theophoric personal names, constructed from a designation of deity plus some further element, by way of request to, appreciation of, or identification with that god.[10] Cities and towns were not generally named this way, and so kingdoms identified by their capitals like Babylon and Aššur also do not belong to this group.[11] It appears that where a human personal name has been

---

[9] For the same pattern in first-millennium Aramean group names, see for example Yaši-il and similar Ya-prefixed names (Younger 2016: 737, etc.). Ahituv (1984) lists a number of geographical or people names from New Kingdom Egyptian sources. Two of these take the form of full theophoric personal names: Ya'qub'ilu (200) and Yašup'il (201), both of which he imagines to be in the Beqa' Valley or further north. Other *y*-initial names that Ahituv does not identify as cities include Yanṣita (198), perhaps in the Beqa' Valley; and Yas'apa/'As'apa (201), perhaps on the Plain of Acco. Knohl (2017) identifies Ya'qub'ilu as a clan that could be linked to Israel by way of Jacob, providing a vehicle to get the name Yhwh to the people of the Bible.

[10] This further element could take the form of a noun, an adjective, or a verb, in each case joined to a divine name in a way that offers a declaration or request. As one example, see the divisions offered by Pruzsinszky (2003) in her study of Emar personal names. The group with verbal predicates consists mainly of thanksgivings ("Danknamen," 131). In her Emar sample, two thirds of this type place the verb before the divine name. Most often the verbs are in preterite (past) tense. For the group that Pruzsinszky classifies as West Semitic, the same pattern applies, with *ya-* prefixes still most often indicating simple past forms (203).

[11] This does not mean that towns or villages could not take names with verbal form, though this could suggest origin in a personal name. As just one example in a context with second-millennium West Semitic names, note Yabliya in the vicinity of Tuttul on the Euphrates River; see ARM I 20, published as LAPO no. 455, with comment on the name, in Durand (1997–2000: 2:28–29). Also note Yasaddi-el in ARM XIV 27:7 (LAPO

applied to a population, it is thus identified in a way that requires no royal head or single settled center. This does not mean that the population must then be considered "tribal." This is a contested category that evolutionary social theory has placed in a hierarchy of simple to complex development: as Elman Service (1975) conceived it, from band to tribe to chiefdom to state.[12] Such names do evoke kinship-based social organization, as if a whole people could be understood by a single family name and ideal ancestor, though the range of use may be more diverse than theoretical models have suggested.[13] For instance, the generalized tribal construction proposed by Evans-Pritchard involved "segmented" subdivisions that are

---

no. 996), a fixed site (village?) in the northern part of the Mari kingdom; and Yaqqim-Ida in ARM III 13:25 (LAPO no. 691), in the Terqa district of the Mari kingdom. Both of these names are based on Durand's collations and require reading with the LAPO text.

[12] See also Fried (1975). The category of the tribe is reconsidered without the specific evolutionary framework in the volume edited by Khoury and Kostiner (1990). Two efforts to apply tribal terminology in ancient Near Eastern context are found in Fleming (2004: 26–33); and Porter (2012: *passim*).

[13] Since the time of Service and Fried, evolutionary interpretations of society have commonly treated "tribe" and "state" as opposed categories, with the tribe a more primitive form that is necessarily lost with progress to more complex organization. For example, Yoffee (1988) calls the principal non-urban peoples in the Mari evidence "ethnic groups," with deference to the developmental scheme. One practical definition, driven more by observed patterns than schematic expectation, is found in Khoury and Kostiner (1990: 5): "*Tribe* may be used loosely of a localized group in which kinship is the dominant idiom of organization, and whose members consider themselves culturally distinct (in terms of customs, dialect or language, and origins); tribes are usually politically unified, though not necessarily under a central leader, both features being commonly attributable to interaction with states." Yet this formulation still carries with it some expectation that we already know what the "tribes" are that we are examining. Working from the analysis of pastoralism in ancient society, Porter (2012) undertakes to rework our definitions from the foundations. She begins with summary of the common view: "animal husbandry and mobility both preclude the accumulation of differentials in wealth that leads to social stratification and that in turn leads to complexity. Mobility also constrains social interactions and organization so that to be pastoralist is essentially to be tribal. And tribe is always something other than the state" (9). In beginning to define an alternative, Porter observes (57), "The main point to make, though, is this: if the tribe – or any social grouping for that matter – is not bound by biology, then it is the tribe at some level that *chooses* what defines it, whom it lets in, and whom it does not, and these choices are both flexible and contingent. This point also applies to descent." Therefore, "genealogies should not be understood as reified social structures but as opportunities to create certain kinds of relationships"; "no tribe, or any other social group, is bound by a single set of delimiting relationships but consists rather of a series of relationships, these being, in the case of the ancient world, kinship, descent, residence, shared subsistences, tradition, and ritual (among other possibilities), that may be regarded as a web of integrative structures that form a system or network that is open-ended" (58).

impossible to identify in any number of groups that would otherwise fit his tribal society.[14]

One prominent example from early second-millennium Mesopotamia is the Yamutbal or Emutbal people, identified with Andarig in the Sinjar region east of the Habur River and in the takeover of Sumerian Larsa by Kudur-mabuk and sons.[15] Emutbal is a contracted form of Amorite Yamut-bal, which means something like "The lord has died," another group name that derives from an individual man's personal name.[16] We cannot be sure that this population ever had a single king or leader, and we have no evidence of its formal division into significant segments.[17] If the Yamutbal were "tribal," they were neither part of some demonstrable larger unity nor the umbrella for affiliated tribes within them. At least we

---

[14] This work is famously based on a study of the Nuer in Africa (Evans-Pritchard 1940); for discussion of this work and its influence on contemporary archaeology and historical reconstruction, see Porter (2012: 45–52).

[15] During the reign of Zimri-Lim at Mari, "the land of the Yamutbal" (*māt Yamutbalim*) defined the people ruled by kings from the capital of Andarig, south of the Jebel Sinjar between the Habur and Tigris Rivers (Fleming 2004: 122); see ARM X 84:24; XXVI 383:7; 432:8′; XXVIII 172:8′–9′. In the preceding period of Samsi-Addu, ruler of upper Mesopotamia more broadly, we find the *māt Razamâ Yamutbalim* (ARM II 18:7), where Razamâ is another town east of Andarig, closer to the Tigris River. For more on the Yamutbal, see Miglio (2014: 83–85, 167–87, etc.). These two bodies of evidence have not generally been treated together, even though the match of population names is evident. Steinkeller (2004) works from the third-millennium Sumerian evidence forward, as defined by the city of Mashkan-shapir, which began to come into its own with the fall of Ur ca. 2000. An Emutbal tribal ruler named Kudur-mabuk took the city, which became a co-capital of the Larsa-based kingdom under Kudur-mabuk's sons Warad-Sîn and Rîm-Sîn until Hammurabi of Babylon defeated the kingdom. Rather than treat the arrangement between the two cities of Mashkan-shapir and Larsa in this period as a union of separate sovereign states, Steinkeller (36) concludes that "the kingdom of Kudur-mabuk (and similarly that of his predecessors at Larsa, going probably as far back as the beginning of the dynasty) was a dimorphic one, combining two different and quite separate entities: a tribal state of the Emutbala within which was embedded the sovereign state of Larsa." Porter (2012: 315–18) takes up Steinkeller's vision of a single polity ruled by the Emutbal leader Kudur-mabuk and reconceives it according to her distinct notion of how pastoralist and settled dimensions of a population were integrated into one social fabric, including the more northern Yamutbal known from the reigns of Samsi-Addu and Zimri-Lim in the Mari texts.

[16] Streck (2000: 180); with comment on the pattern of writing without indication of the middle laryngeal *'ayin* (250–51).

[17] The Yamutbal stand in some relation to the Sim'alites ("Sons of the Right Hand"), who are the people of Zimri-Lim, the last king at Mari. Neither is represented as a subset of the other; see the letter A.1098, cited by Villard (1994: 297 and n.33); translated with comment in Fleming (2004: 81–82); and Miglio (2014: 83–84).

have no evidence for this.[18] Nevertheless, identification as Yamutbal did serve to relate people across distance, without necessary function as a single political entity and yet with potential significance as a political body, as when the king at the city of Andarig could define his realm as the "land of the Yamutbal."[19] In cases like this, Yamutbal was not identified by territory itself even as it could be attached to a "land" (*mātum*) to define a combination of people ruled and the space occupied. Note that in the cuneiform, evidence for the political landscape of the early second millennium is especially in the Akkadian language, which expressed particular conceptions of how population related to land, a question that arose in Chapter 2 in relation to the Egyptian idea of a "Shasu-land" (*tȝ šȝśw*). The Yamutbal name itself, along with other similar examples, was apparently West Semitic, and we do not know the indigenous terminology that delineated political space in these dialects.[20]

For the purposes of biblical study, the lead example is Israel itself, as *yiśrā'ēl*, "May El contend" or "El has contended." Whatever the earliest character of Israel, it took its name from that of a man – not meaning by this the biblical story of Jacob. By far the oldest non-biblical reference to Israel appears in a monument honoring Egypt's pharaoh Merenptah (ca. 1207), where it keeps company with three Canaanite cities claimed

---

[18] In this one case, we cannot insist that the name Yamutbal was understood to be the original ancestor of the whole people; it could also represent a leader. Leonard-Fleckman (2016: 49) identifies the related Aramean/Syrian terminologies of the "House of X" and "Sons of X" as language by which the Assyrians engaged antagonists in their westward expansion, each a "population attached to a particular leader or ancestor 'X' in the Assyrian annals." The point at stake is that we do not know whether the writers even imagined the names to indicate ancestors, just because the Bible proposes this in Genesis, possibly an etiological effort not implied in the names themselves.

[19] With the "time-space distantiation" of Anthony Giddens in the background, Porter (2012: 63) defines the importance of (pastoralist) mobility for ancient social relations: "Not because pastoralists are tribal, but because the practices of kinship, among other things, facilitate the extension of both time and space so that those who are physically apart may remain conceptually together." See especially Giddens (1984).

[20] On the complex character of the Akkadian term *mātum* in Mari-period evidence, see Fleming (2004: 114–32). In Akkadian, the word *erṣetu(m)*, cognate to Biblical Hebrew *'ereṣ* and in this way unlike it, never refers to social and political entities. In early second-millennium writing of Sumerian, by then most likely a purely scribal language, the Akkadian word *mātum* could be rendered with Sumerian kalam, but in earlier Sumerian, kalam referred only to "our land," to Sumerian-speaking polities themselves. The separate word kur ("highland") could also identify a political entity, but it was applied only to non-Sumerians, conceived as inhabiting the high country, away from the Mesopotamian river-plain.

as victims at war: Ashkelon, Gezer, and Yanoam. In contrast to the city determinative applied to the three known towns, Israel is marked to indicate a people not defined by city center.[21] The determinative does not show a "tribe," and nothing in the Egyptian designation anticipates division into constituent parts as tribes.[22] In the Bible, the earliest definition of Israel by plural "tribes" (*šēbeṭ*) may be in the core sayings of Jacob's blessings, where "Dan shall judge his people as one of the tribes of Israel" (Gen 49:16).[23] This includes the peoples north of the Jezreel Valley and may reflect the integrative program of the 9th-century kingdom, not relevant to older Israel.[24]

Like the Mesopotamian Yamutbal, Israel was defined as a body without reference to city or ruler, carrying the name of an individual man while lacking the accoutrements of imagined tribal structure. Even in the ancestral system of Genesis, there is some ambiguity of reference to what would become "Israel." According to the finished text, Jacob is given the name Israel after wrestling a "man" identified with God (Gen 32:29), but he retains his original name as the text continues.[25] A case can be made that in the birth narrative for Jacob's household in Genesis 29–30, the audience awaits the birth of Joseph to represent itself, a people identified by the name "Joseph" (Fleming 2020). Without the context of the larger Jacob–Joseph narrative, the brothers and half-brothers as Jacob's sons would not be equated with Israel but would explain a landscape of family at various distances, all as potential allies or enemies, like Esau as Jacob's twin. In Ps 80:2, Israel is paired with and thus closely linked to Joseph rather than to Jacob, however we are to understand this Joseph identity.[26] The identification of Israel with Jacob appears to serve the interests of the

[21] On this much-discussed detail, see the description in Hoffmeier (1996: 29–30); and the appropriately cautious interpretation in Niccacci (1997: 91).

[22] The determinative does not appear to be related to the category of "families" represented by the term *mhwt*, as found with the Shasu divisions.

[23] Whatever the precise delimitation of the oldest poem in Genesis 49, it should not include the first four sons, who appear in the precise order of their birth in Gen 29:31–35, and it should include the six short sayings for Zebulun, Issachar, Dan, Gad, Asher, and Naphtali in 49:13–21. This shorter core was proposed by Macchi (1999); cf. Fleming (2012a: 86–90). Note also the use of the phrase in Deut 33:5, as observed in Chapter 4.

[24] This matter is discussed in Chapters 3 and 4, including reference to the forthcoming articles on greater Israel and little Israel by Lauren Monroe and Fleming, forthcoming in *Hebrew Bible and Ancient Israel*.

[25] See the discussion of the "*ʾîš* theophany" in Hamori (2008: 13–25).

[26] Lauren Monroe is working on the character of the "House of Joseph" in the Hebrew Bible, with interest in disentangling it from the secondary genealogy that equates it with Ephraim and Manasseh.

northern kingdom in its expansive mode, bringing these peoples into the
entity ruled by Omri and Ahab, however the vision may reach forward or
back in time.

Working from these two examples, we see that individual personal
names can represent peoples not defined by city center or royal rule. It
may be too restrictive to call these "tribal" names, because the early
evidence does not display the larger structures often envisioned for such
systems. Likewise the names do not decisively designate ancestors.
Nevertheless, the form of a human name does render the group in question an extended family, a conceptual clan, even as its actual scope may be
greater than what theorists bent on defining types may mean by that term.

SHORTENED PERSONAL NAMES AND NAMES FOR PEOPLES

Even in the ancient setting of biblical writing, peoples – as opposed to
cities – could be conceived in ancestral terms, taking their names from an
imagined forebear. The account of Joseph and his brothers in Genesis
29–30 explains every group by its relationship to the one son of Rachel,
each eponymous son by another of three women. Genesis as a whole is
occupied by genealogy, interpreting Israel's background by layered ancestral schemes. It is difficult to measure the historical foundations for this
ancient approach to identity through ancestry. How many names of
peoples actually derived from individual men?[27] Various lines of evidence
point to the conception of group names in ancestral terms. Names with
full two-part theophoric form, like the Yamutbal of Mesopotamia and
Israel of the Levant, take a form that is ubiquitous among individual
personal names. Other examples from Arabia and its vicinity include the
Bible's Ishmael and the North Arabian Adbeel from the 8th century BCE,
known as both a group and an (unrelated) individual (Eph'al 1984:
215–16). Such names for peoples demonstrate the possibility of origin
in theophoric personal names. Other traditions for group naming emphasize connection by imagined kinship expressed by the phrase "children
of" or "house of," the former manifest in the biblical Bene Ammon for

---

[27] One indication of a "patriarchal" social framework in the ancient Near East is the
identification of groups by male rather than female names. For thoughtful consideration
of how the Bible preserves important lines of social division defined by mothers rather
than fathers, see Chapman (2016), with notable discussion of the Genesis genealogies,
including the mothers of Jacob's various sons in Genesis 29–30 (43–44). The groups
themselves, however, are still named by male ancestors.

Ammonites and the latter in Syrian Aramaic-speaking polities such as the Bit-Adini.[28]

These last two naming forms also show, however, that identity by descent need not assume a named individual as ancestor, or that such a person of reference must be father of all. The House of David (Bet-David) and Syrian Bit-Agusi took their names from kings (Dion 1997: 229; Leonard-Fleckman 2016). In the later context of ancient Saba' in Yemen, Korotayev (1993: 60) observes that whereas more than half of personal names take the two-part form of sentences, "the overwhelming majority of the clan names are simple (e.g. ĠDBM, BT', GDNM)." Instead of taking simple personal names, the Sabean "clans" are designated Banū Qurayn, Banū Hamdān, and so on (Children of Qurayn, Children of Hamdan). Yet the Arabian group names, whether in the south or elsewhere, do not begin with *y-*, as found in the verbal prefix for masculine subjects, a form that is ubiquitous in second-millennium Semitic personal names. In contrast, second-millennium group names generally lack the "House of" form and frequently begin with the *y-* of prefixed verbs. If such names did not originate in personal names of individuals, they nonetheless suggest verbs.

In the Mari evidence from the 18th century BCE, systematic listing yields a remarkable number of these:

- The five peoples of the Yaminites are the Yariḫû, the Yaḫrurû, the Amnanû, the Rabbû, and the Uprapû, all rendered in their adjectival forms as "the Yariḫeans," "the Yaḫrureans," etc.[29] The first two of these names take the form of finite verbs.[30]
- The subdivisions of the Sim'alites, who together form a complementary pair with the Yaminites to account for the mass of such peoples in ancient Syria during this period, include: the Yabasu, the Kaṣûm,

---

[28] On the "House of X" political category, see Younger (2016); Leonard-Fleckman (2016); Dion (1997).

[29] The long vowel marked by circumflex reflects the gentilic -ī- contracted to the case ending for the masculine plural nominative.

[30] Note that the divisions of the Yaminites are called *li'mum*, a category that appears to be distinct to this association of Syrian populations (Fleming 2004: 43–63). A large portion of peoples across ancient Syria defined themselves in the early 18th century by the complementary pair, "Sons of the Left Hand" (Sim'alites) and "Sons of the Right Hand" (Yaminites), integrating mobile pastoralist and settled farmers into connected social and political entities that could take on the character of full-fledged kingdoms, with their attendant administrative engines. For extended citation of the French work that stands at the center of Mari studies, where the main body of evidence is found, see Durand (1997–2000); Charpin (2004); and Fleming (2004).

the Amurrum, the Abi-nakar, the Yumaḫammu, the Ibal-Aḫum, the Mannapsu, the Wer'ûm, and the Niḫadûm. At least the two-element names clearly derive from personal names, though the prefixed verbal forms are general absent.[31]

- Two city-centered kingdoms south of the Jebel Sinjar, east of the Habur River, are identified with distinct peoples: the city of Kurdâ with the Numḫâ people; and the city of Andarig with the Yamutbal people. The Numḫâ and the Yamutbal shared grazing lands with the Sim'alite people of the Mari king Zimri-Lim.[32]

- Among other kingdoms identified with separate peoples as having a city center and a "land" (*mātum*) of a certain group, one of the largest was Aleppo and "the land of Yamḫad."[33] The smaller city of Talḫayûm, in the upper part of the western Habur River drainage, was the capital of "the land of the Yapturite" (*māt Yapturim*), apparently the name Yaptur rendered nominally.[34]

- One of the large peoples of the Sutû, a category identified with long-range mobility and pastoralism like the Shasu in the Egyptian texts, is called the Yaḫmamû, a gentilic adjective derived from the name Yaḫmam.[35]

In this early second-millennium setting, there were many more names with simple verbal form than full theophoric names with separate subject. It is important to keep in mind that unlike physical features such as the Yarmuk River, these group names define people, so that if the names reflect verbs, the question is how such names in verbal form would have originated without connection to individual personal names. So far as Yhw3 of Shasu-land likewise may take the prefixed verbal form, it is worth lingering over the type. Given the early 14th-century date of the Amenhotep III text, the Mari archives provide by far the largest

---

[31] These divisions are called *gayum*, cognate with Biblical Hebrew *gōy*, even where they may be organized into two larger sets (Fleming 2004). The adjectival gentilic forms are less easily applied, and I render the names without them. The name Yabasu may not reflect a verb. Note some uncertainty regarding how the Sim'alite categories are related with one text that organizes them under two headings as Yabasu and Ašarugayum (A486+; see Durand 2004).

[32] This is stated explicitly in Mari's A.1098, cited above, with references.

[33] ARM I 6:11; IV 6:6; XXVI 365-bis:3.

[34] ARM XIII 144:4; cf. I 19+:11; see Fleming (2004: 122).

[35] In ARM XIV 78 (LAPO no. 929), the governor of the Saggaratum district cites a message from the king at Mari with instructions to sell three intercepted travelers to the Sutû people, "either the Yaḫmamû or the Almutû."

repository of West Semitic personal names that could illuminate the Shasu group, so that Mari-based comparison is no mere convenience.

YAHWI- IN AMORITE PERSONAL NAMES

The first systematic study of Amorite personal names was that of Herbert Huffmon in 1965, still a basic reference. More recently, the key work is Streck (2000), conceived especially as an investigation of Amorite language by way of West Semitic personal names. The contributions of these two specialists are central to any consideration of the cuneiform evidence. Huffmon (1965: 130–35) provides a separate discussion of "hypocoristica," or shortened names, which are not limited to sentence names with verb plus divine subject.[36] He concludes that "obvious imperfect verb elements occurring separately can be listed here, apart from a corresponding full name, since there is no doubt that such a full name is possible" (131). This is the type in question with Yhw₃ of Shasu-land. He elaborates:

> The simplest hypocoristic name is formed by merely omitting one of the elements. The names thus formed are sometimes found without any suffix, even vocalic. In this regard, they resemble many divine names and geographic names. Most of the Mari examples are imperfect verb forms; all are masculine . . .

Examples include: *I-ba-ás-si-ir, Ya-a-ar, Ya₈-ab-na-aḫ, Ya-aḫ-zi-ib, Ya-an-ta-qi-im, Ya-a-pa-aḫ*, and *Ya-aḫ-ta-mar* (132).[37]

When considered in the company of the Amorite evidence, Yhw₃ of Shasu-land in the early 14th-century Egyptian list shares the form of peoples named by simple verbal form, with their possible interpretation as shortened personal names. Study of the Shasu name generally moves directly to the divine, assuming reference to the god later attached to Israel and leapfrogging the question of how to understand a human political entity on its own terms. This risks anachronism, forcing the familiar framework for the name Yahweh back onto much older evidence that lacks any indication of divine reference.[38] In the Mari material, none of the various peoples named by finite

---

[36] Casting a wider net with less precise reference to sources and minimal comment, see Gelb (1980).

[37] This list could be extended by browsing the indices published with texts that appeared since 1965. Note Streck's discussion of hypocoristic names with suffixes /īya/, /āya/, and /ya/ (350–55).

[38] I would include in this anachronism the recent synthesis by Römer (2015: 38): "In these texts *Yhw₃* seems to be a geographic term (referring to a mountain?) and perhaps also a divine name. The explanation of this duality might be that the god of a certain place could come to be identified with that place and thus take its name from that place."

verbal forms is known to be equated with a deity. By the logical sequence proposed here, the 14th-century Yhw₃ must be explained as a subdivision of the Shasu before and without assumed reference to the god Yahweh of Israel. It is much more likely that the divine name Yahweh derives from the Shasu group without divine association than that the Shasu group already related to the eventual Israelite god.

This framing of the naming question removes the divine from immediate consideration in calculating the character of the form Yhw₃. If the name reflects a prefixed verb, would such a verb have stood on its own, without relationship to a personal name, or would it have been shortened (hypcoristic) from a human sentence-name? Here, the Amorite personal names studied by Huffmon (1965) and Streck (2000) are particularly significant because they include specific verbal elements that could relate to the Shasu group, with debated interpretation.

Earlier work on the Amorite personal names took for granted that some fraction of them were constructed with the verbal root *hwy*, "to be, become," like the verb *hyh* in Biblical Hebrew.[39] There has been one key objection, by Michael Streck, who reevaluated Amorite personal names as a whole in 2000 and as part of this work published the separate conclusion (1999) that all the *Ya-wi-* and *Ya-aḫ-wi-* elements in these names must be understood to reflect the same root *ḥwy*, "to live."[40] Streck was concerned with the etymology and origin of the divine name Yahweh, but his argument has similar effect for consideration of Yhw₃ of Shasu-land, because the Egyptian writing preserves the particular phoneme /h/ (versus /ḫ/). Two issues are prominent: the need to find onomastic parallels in other languages from the region; and the question of whether all the names with these two spellings can or must incorporate the same verb. If Streck is correct that these are all forms of the verb "to live," then the Amorite personal names must be set aside as useful to any interpretation of the name Yhw₃. It is not necessary that the Shasu name be derived from a verb "to be"; only that the Amorite evidence include some verb with the first root as *h* and two weak consonants to follow.

---

[39] Along with Huffmon (below), this is the reading of Gelb (1980: 19): HWJ as "to be, to become, to desire"; cf. von Soden (1966: 179); Weippert (1976–80).

[40] Note that although Akkadian preserves only /ḫ/ as a laryngeal consonant, and /ḫ/ would not be written with -Ḫ- in syllabic writing, the conventions for writing West Semitic "Amorite" (*amurrû*) allow this match. Akkadian preserves no /h/, as in Yhw-, and this renders more difficult the search for the verb *hwy* ("to be, become") in second-millennium West Semitic.

In his volume on Amorite personal names, Huffmon (1965: 71–73) gathers and evaluates a set of names that he understands to incorporate verbs probably derived either from the root *ḥwy*, "to be, become," or the root *ḥwy*, "to live." The relevant names from his listed assemblage include:[41]

- *Ya-wi*-DINGIR: ARM II 68:15; VII 227:8′; VIII 5:21; 11:35; IX 291:ii 29; also XIV 126:10; XXII 57B iii′:13′; 262 vi:9; 264:22′; 328 v:25; XXIII 235 ii:10; iii:6; 345 seal; XXIV 8:2; 164:4; 233 ii:49; 234 i:16; XXV 48:4; 135:6; XXVIII 40:2; A.2226:12′–13′ (*M.A.R.I.* 7, p. 184); T.282:28 (*FM* I, p. 36 n.18); *FM* VII 35:6–7; *FM* IX 2:17; M.8251, sender of letter (Guichard 2003: 211); ARM XXXI 158 (silver vases offered); *FM* XI 180 (sender of letter); M.11215, in ARM XXXII, p. 359; M337+:7 (Durand 2010); A.1008 (Villard 2001: 74–76)
- *Ya-wi-i-la*: ARM II 66:10; also *FM* V, p. 167 n.651, reference to seal of Yawi-ila; *Ya-wi-i-lu*, *FM* IX 37:32; *Ya-wi-i-li*, *FM* IX 37:16, 33
- [*Y*]*a-wi-ú-um*: ARM IX 289:6; also XXIII 451:14; and *Ya-wi-um*, XXII 167:12; XXIII 449:12
- *Ya-wi-*ᵈ*D*[*a-gan*]: ARM VII 200:14; XXIV 247 ii:17; also *Ya-wi-*ᵈ*Da-gan*, M.5754:15 (*M.A.R.I.* 8, p. 759 n.47; *FM* IV, p. 49 n.298); *FM* VI 48:15
- *Ya-wi-ya*: ARM VII 215:5
- *Ya-aḫ-wi*-DINGIR: ARM VII 215:5[42]
- *Ya-aḫ-wi-na-si*: ARM VI 200:10; also XXII 105:1″; M.6700:18 (ARM XXX, p. 447); M.7244+ARM XXII 104:45 (ARM XXX, pp. 417–18)

To these may be added the following from more recent publications:[43]

- *Ya-wi-*ᵈIŠKUR (Yawi-Addu): ARM XIV 102:12, 22; 103:11′; XXII 170 r.10; 289:7; XXVII 63:7, 11, 14; cf. *FM* III 140:7 (restored, as *Ya-wi-*ᵈ[IŠKUR]); *FM* XI 121 (a high official)
- *Ya-wi-E-ra-aḫ*: ARM XXI 339; 370; XXIV 32:9; 258:3

---

[41] Texts from volumes published after Huffmon are marked "also." I have gathered these myself, and the list is by no means complete.

[42] This reading is suspect by its isolation – it comes from Huffmon's citation. Bottéro's edition proposes *Ia₈-aḫ-wi-El!*, a spelling not otherwise attested in any of the Yawi-/Yaḫwi- names from Mari.

[43] This listing cannot be considered complete. It is assembled from perusing the name indices from more recent Mari publications and from the Archibab online reference site.

- *Ya-aḫ-wi-a-šar*: ARM XXIII 579:4; XXIV 13:6; 272:4; *FM* VI 35:7; 36:3; 40 v:30
- *Ya-aḫ-wi-*^dIŠKUR: ARM XXIII 86:7; M.12169 (ARM XXX, pp. 441–42; broken, restored comparing M.6481)
- *Ya-aḫ-wi-um*: ARM XXII 327:13; XXIII 448:13; 450:13
- *Ya-ḫu-wa-qa-ar*: ARM XXV 488 rev.3 [44]

Huffmon (1965: 71) considers that the names with *ya-aḫ-wi* probably derive from *ḥwy*, "to live," in a form that he interprets as a causative. The larger number of names based on *ya-wi* could then be taken as variants of the longer spelling, but similar names in other Semitic languages suggest the viability of the root *ḥwy*, "to be, become" (72). Akkadian personal names with the verb *bašû*, "to exist," occur in both basic G-stem and causative Š-stem forms.[45] Ugaritic and Phoenician have semantic correspondents with the root *kwn*.[46] The most serious potential objection to Huffmon's interpretation would be demonstration that the same individual is represented by both spellings, and this is clearly the case in one set of material published since 1965. ARM XXIII (1984) 448–51 are four textually interrelated lists of clothing and complex bows delivered to outsiders at the Mari court under the supervision of Mukannišum within a period of one week (Zimri-Lim year 3 [previously 2'], month 11, days 15, 20, 21, and broken). All four include variants on the same provision

---

[44] Also note the names in La-, with a separate precative particle (listed in Huffmon, with many more published since).

[45] Huffmon cites Stamm (1939: 135, 145, 148–49, 218), for examples.

[46] At Ugarit, consider the following, taken from the individual listings in del Olmo Lete and Sanmartín (2000: 2:525–26): *ykn* (CAT 4.55:20; 4.141 I 15; etc.; syllabic *ia-ku-nu/ni*; *ia-ku-un-ni*; *ya-ku-un-ni*); *ykn'il* (CAT 4.86:15; 4.165:12; syllabic *ia-ku-un*-DINGIR, CAT 4 182:20; etc.); *ykn'm* as place name (CAT 4.49:7; etc.; syllabic ^{uru}*ia-ku-na-me*, PRU 4 65:13' + 67:5'; ^{uru}*ia-ku-na-'-mu*, PRU 6 111:3; ^{uru}*ia-ku*-SIG₅, PRU 3:190:13'; 6 80:3; etc.). The last spelling suggests reading as /*Yakūn-na'mu*/, "What is pleasant has come to be" (or "has been put in place"). Note also the hypocoristic, *ykny* (CAT 4.635:22). For the verb see the entry for /*k-n*/, in the G-stem, "ser (estable), haber" (1.219). For the Phoenician, see Krahmalkov (2000: 232–34), *K-N* I, qal, 1. BE; 2. EXIST; 3. BELONG to, HAVE, POSSESS; 4. BE IN OFFICE; 5. ENDURE, LAST; 6. LIVE, RESIDE; 7. BE OBLIGATED to do something. It is evident that the verb overlaps with Biblical Hebrew *kwn* and Akkadian *kânu*, "to be firm, set in place." Usage as "to be" and "to exist" are clustered in Phoenician royal inscriptions, including KAI 24 (Kilamuwa/Zinjirli, late 9th century) and KAI 26 (Karatepe bilingual, late 8th century). Krahmalkov lists two personal names from this root: *yknšlm* (YAKON-SALŌM, "May Salōm/Peace prevail!"; and *ykln*, for *ykn'ln** (YAKIN-'ALLŌN, "God establish!," "God has created"). Compare Hoftijzer and Jongeling (1995: 1:493–94), *k-w-n*₁ for Old Canaanite, Phoenitican, and Punic; qal verb as 1) "to be, to exist, to happen"; 2) "to be + predicate."

of clothing to five men from Yamḫad (Aleppo), with the same items and names rendered with divergent spellings. The third Yamḫadean is Ya(ḫ) wium, written *Ia-aḫ-wi-um* (448:13; 450:13); *Ia-wi-um* (449:12); and *Ia-wi-ú-um* (451:14). Regardless of other usage, this group of texts proves that no fixed separation can be established between names with "to live" and "to be" according to the presence or absence of -(*a*)ḫ-.[47] This possibility that both writings can represent the same verb and meaning provides one part of Streck's argument against the relevance of the Amorite names for understanding the divine name Yahweh, because all of these names may be taken to use the verb "to live" (*ḥwy*).

Nevertheless, patterns that align attested spellings and particular names suggest the possibility that two verbal roots may be in play. Yawi-il(v) is almost universally written with *Ia-wi-*.[48] Yawi-Dagan and Yawi-Eraḫ occur only without -*aḫ*-,[49] while Yaḫwi-ašar and Yaḫwi-nasi are written with it.[50] Both verbal elements taken separately may be associated with the storm god Addu, and the Yawi- form occurs with two more major deities in Dagan and the moon god Eraḫ. Neither form, especially the common Yawi-name, can be limited to use with "the god" (DINGIR or *i-la*), whatever that name represents.[51] It does not seem, in any case, that the element applies only to Ilu (El) as "The God" known from later Ugarit. The element never indicates a god, and it cannot be invoked as direct evidence for what would become the god of Israel.[52]

---

[47] I identified this set from my own gathering of names from the Mari volumes; Streck (1999: 39) identified exactly this group with the same observation of the implications for Huffmon. It is nevertheless not obvious from this group which verb is represented; Streck himself (38) observes that in the orthography of Amorite personal names, the laryngeal consonants /ʾ/, /h/, /ḥ/, /ʿ/, and /ġ/ can all be written by ∅- and by Ḫ-, with the example for / ḥ/ of *Iš-ma-a-da* for /ʾIšmaʿ-hadda/ from *Yašmaʿ; and *Si-ik-ri-ḫa-da* for /Śikrī-hadda/. The writing itself is therefore not decisive in deciding whether any of the *Ya-wi-* or *Ya-aḫ-wi-* names could reflect the root *ḥwy*.

[48] The one possible exception is in ARM VII 215:5, listed above, with irregular spelling, perhaps to distinguish a different name (and verb).

[49] Durand (1995: 183) takes Eraḫ as an alternative for Yaraḫ, attested at Ugarit as Yariḫ or Yarḫu, the West Semitic name for the moon god.

[50] While both verbal elements may be found with the storm god, it could be significant that the pattern of divergent elements also varies by use of divine names as opposed to titles. Dagan and Eraḫ occur with Yawi- as divine names, while -ašar and -nasi are not listed by Durand as divine names and appear rather to be titles: "May the cared-for live" (*CAD* s. v.*ašru* B, "taken care of," in personal names); and "May the elevated one(?) live."

[51] Durand (1995: 154) concludes that there is no god "El" in the early second-millennium evidence from Mari, but that the element in names represents "el Dios indiferenciado."

[52] There is one unusual name that goes without comment in its publication: *Ya-ḫu-wa-qa-ar* in ARM XXV 488 rev.3. While the form of this name is unique in the set, the structure is

At this point we must recall that the task at hand is not to explain the form or meaning of the divine name Yahweh but rather to explore the possibility that Yhwȝ of Shasu-land could have originated as an abbreviated personal name. Streck's objection would apply to both the divine name and the Shasu name, but the potential application of evidence from second-millennium personal names becomes more direct for the latter as a people. Above all, Streck (1999: 41) finds that the problem with the root *ḥwy* in Amorite names is the lack of secure onomastic parallels, rejecting Huffmon's comparison of Akkadian names with *ibašši-* and Ugaritic/Phoenician *kwn*, whereas such parallels do exist for *ḥwy*, "to live."[53] The strict point is important to observe: we do not have demonstrated cases of alphabetically written personal names constructed from the verb *ḥwy*.

In spite of this lack, which indeed does not apply to the verb *ḥwy*, it is difficult to remove the substantial onomastic evidence from cuneiform Akkadian, Ugaritic, and Phoenician, where all of these northern Semitic languages represent ideas related to existence or being (established) with different verbs. Even with different verbal roots, these do offer at least overlapping semantic parallels that cannot simply be dismissed, especially as representing Semitic languages that lack the verb *ḥwy*, "to be" or "become." Given the limited spelling of *Ya-wi-* with *ilu* (the god) and the god Dagan in the West Semitic names from Mari, it is noteworthy that at Late Bronze Age Emar in northwestern Syria, we find the Akkadian name *Ibašši-ilī*, which Pruzsinszky renders, "Mein Gott ist (da)" and the Akkadian/West Semitic *Ikūn-Dagān*, "Dagān ist zuverlässig."[54] In spite of Pruzsinszky's rendering of the verb *kwn* as "to be trustworthy, sure," use of the root in Ugaritic shows that the meaning of "to be in place" can come to serve as simply "to be." Ugaritic attests the personal name *ykn-'il* (syllabic *ia-ku-un*-DINGIR, for /*yakūn-ilu*/, "The God was (i.e. showed himself) in place," so available to act, perhaps in providing the named son. The same meaning applies to Emar's Ikūn-Dagan and Yakūn-Ra. In the end, notwithstanding Streck's objection that there are no "parallel"

---

consistent with the others: Yaḫu- is the verbal element ("may he live"), and -waqar is the subject, as "the precious one." See *CAD* s.v. *aqru* (c) precious, valuable; 5' persons; including in personal names with many examples.

[53] Streck (1999: 42) gathers these from Ugaritic (*yḥṣdq*; *yḥmn*, *yḥšr*); Phoenician (*yḥwmlk*); Hebrew (*yiḥy-'il* and *yiḥw-'il*; *yiḥy-Yah*); Aramaic (*yḥyy*); and Minaic (South Arabian) (*tḥy*, *tḥyw*).

[54] See Pruzsinszky (2003: 132, 134); the Akkadian prefix for the verb *kwn* is also found with the West Semitic *ya*- in *ia-ku-un-Ra*, "Ra(šap) hat sich zuverlässig gezeigt!" (209).

personal names with the verb *ḥwy*, the evidence for that verb in the second millennium is extremely thin because of the limited alphabetic evidence and Ugarit's preference for a different root to express "being," and it is therefore appropriate to seek semantic parallels for this early period.[55] While the identification of the verbal root in the Amorite names with and without the *-ḫ-* remains impossible to prove with certainty, the parallels with contemporary Old Babylonian Ibašši-DN and the later second-millennium parallels from the verb *kwn* show the viability of a West Semitic root *ḥwy*, "to be, be evident," for at least some portion of these Amorite names. Von Soden (1966: 179) came to this conclusion long ago based on the Babylonian parallel.[56] Further, the names Ya(ḫ) wium and Yawiya show actual short forms of these names.

Returning to the Shasu-name Yhw₃ in Egyptian evidence, the form alone suggests a prefixed verb from a root *ḥwy/w*, whether related to Hebrew *hyh* or originating in a homonymous root, and whether or not derived from a personal name. The *Ya-* prefix would reflect the same West Semitic language group evaluated by Huffmon and Streck in early second-millennium cuneiform evidence, a verbal form that would be found with all western Semitic speakers of the mid-second millennium as well, north and south. As already concluded by Huffmon and von Soden, semantic parallels do exist, and the fact that the prefixed verb form would be quite common in individual personal names would offer a substantial basis for explaining the Shasu-name this way. So far as the Egyptian evidence reflects a people present around 1400 BCE, the name would be even older in its application to any individual, and the chronology of the Amorite evidence suits the historical conditions. It is significant, however, that the type does not remain the common possession of West Semitic speakers in the later second millennium.

THE PERSONAL NAME WITHOUT DIVINE CONCERN

In general, resort to the Amorite personal names has served explanation of the divine name Yahweh, which I have carefully set to one side in this

---

[55] Albright (1968: 169) observed that the root *ḥwy* does not appear in the second millennium outside the Amorite corpus, only to become prominent in Hebrew and Aramaic of the first millennium. The examples cited by de Moor (1997: 327) are not likely to derive from this verb.

[56] "Wir dürfen gewiss annehmen, dass der Sinn der kanaanäischen *Ia(ḫ)wi*-Namen dem der akkadischen *Ibašši*-Namen genau entspricht"; "Jahwe: 'Er ist, Er erweist sich'." See Stamm (1939: 135) for the Akkadian examples and the larger context.

chapter's investigation. Von Soden affirmed the possibility of a simple G-stem (biblical Hebrew qal) interpretation of the name, partly in response to the new work of Huffmon, who represented his teacher Albright in preferring a causative reading, as "may he create."[57] Lewis (2020b) appears likewise to favor the G-stem, as an "archaic *yaqtil*" type.[58] Cross (1973: 63) had argued on philological grounds that the *ya* (*ḥ*)*wi-* verbal element would not likely preserve an old West Semitic *yaqtul* past, though even Huffmon did not consider this point decisive. In the end, Cross expected Yahweh to have origins in "The God" Ilu/El, and he found the origin of the verbal name in a liturgical formula with the "(heavenly) hosts" (*ṣĕbā'ôt*) as created object (65–66). Similarly, de Moor (1997: 334) embraced the entire Amorite name Yahwi-il as a relic of a longer formula that would read as something like, "He is the God of the fathers" – a figure to be identified with El.

Karel van der Toorn (1999: 914) weighs carefully the grammatical character of the name Yahweh with particular reference to the Amorite evidence, observing that the name must somehow be a third masculine singular imperfect verb form. The "Amorite names are the semantic equivalent of the Akkadian name Ibašši-ilum."[59] From this starting point, however, his analysis is guided entirely by the need to explain Yahweh as divine name. Van der Toorn observes that a god may be identified by the verbal forms of human personal names, like Ikrub-El from Mari. As shown by Marten Stol (1991) in his study of Old Babylonian personal names, these names appear to originate as deified ancestors.[60] This

---

[57] Against the analogy of Babylonian names with *ušabši*, von Soden (1966: 182) observes that in Akkadian, the verb *bašû* is only used in the causative for plants and animals, against *banû* ("to build") for creation of humans.

[58] Kitz (2019: 213) concludes similarly: "Today scholars accept that the Barth–Ginsberg law is not a factor in Amorite. When this is coupled with the doubtful existence of the West Semitic H-stem at this time, the identification of *yahwa* as nothing other than a G-stem, imperfective /a/ theme-vowel *yaqtal* becomes a likely prospect." Schneider (personal communication) observed the likelihood that Yhwȝ was vocalized /yahwa/, though it could also have been rendered /yahwe/, so that both *yaqtal* and *yaqtil* vocalization types could be possible.

[59] This is the very name found in the texts from Late Bronze Age Emar in Syria.

[60] Consider Ikrub-El (Yakrub-El), Ikšudum, Ikūnum, and Iqūlam (Stol 1991: 203). "The best solution is to assume that deceased members of a family, as 'patriarchs' or 'ancestors', could acquire this status under circumstances not known to us. Similarly, in a cloistered community of priestesses, Amat-Bēltani considered the priestess Bēltani as her 'matriarch'." Further, "Some readers may observe that these personal names could be kings (a Sumerian tradition)" (204), but no such kings are known for these names. It seems rather that they represent family gods (205).

reasoning could lead to the conclusion that Yahweh also began as the name of an ancestor, as in the first edition of de Moor's volume on "Yahwism," but,

though theoretically possible, it is difficult to believe that the major Israelite deity, venerated in a cult that was imported into Palestine, was originally a deified ancestor. Though such gods are known, they are never found in a leading position in the pantheon. Their worship tends to remain local, as an ancestor is of necessity the ancestor of a restricted group (van der Toorn, 914).[61]

When we shift the object of inquiry to Yhw₃ of Shasu-land in the Soleb inscription of Amenhotep III, and we set aside any consideration of deity in that name as reading back from a later phenomenon without demonstrable connection to the early Shasu, the likeness to personal names stands more simply. The problem is not whether a major deity could be identified by a human ancestor but rather whether a people could be identified by a human personal name, a straightforward question with straightforward answer: yes, and fairly often. Although the Shasu category is Egyptian, as is the later perception that such people were organized by "families" (*mhwt*), these groups occupied a realm in which names for peoples need not be drawn from cities or settlements and could take such form. Understood this way, the difficulty shifts to explaining how the name for a people could come to be attached to a deity that eventually identifies the "god of Israel" (e.g. Judg 5:3, 5).[62] If the Egyptian Yhw₃ indeed represents the same name as Israel's Yahweh, in historical continuity, then it is unlikely that the name itself demands explanation in divine terms. This means also that efforts to explain Yahweh as derived from a liturgical formula for El, as elaborated by Frank Cross from the work of his teacher Albright, bypass the identification of the Shasu group with a human personal name and cannot convince.[63] Likewise, if the

---

[61] In the first edition of his work on Yahweh (1990: 244–5), de Moor observes that divine names of *yqtl* form in the "Canaanite world" are generally "lower deities, mostly deified ancestors." The full personal name from such an ancestor would most likely have been *yhw-'il* (his form), whether for the person or carried forward as the whole divine name.

[62] For the title as such, see the systematic study by Stahl (2020).

[63] "I pointed out a good many years ago that *Yahweh* appears as the first element of other names of obvious liturgical origin such as *Yahwê Ṣebā'ôt*" (Albright 1968: 171). The original idea goes back to Albright (1924), where the second part of the piece is on "The Name *Yahweh*" (370–78). Also, Albright addresses here the semantic parallels from Akkadian *bašû* and West Semitic *kwn*, already proposing a causative interpretation of the divine name with intent that resembles Egyptian ideas of a god creating "that which exists" (377–78).The connection to *Yahwê Ṣebā'ôt* was inspired by the occasion to write a review of a book on the title, so that he combined his previous idea of Yahweh as a

Egyptian evidence does apply to the historical roots of the god Yahweh, the question of how a people gave its name to a deity must take priority over questions of Yahweh's early character, whether as senior figure like "The God" El or young warrior of the storm like Haddu/Baal. We turn next to Yahweh himself, working from the conclusion that Yhw₃ of Shasu-land was a people named in unsurprising form by a shortened personal name.

causative verbal form with the second element as object, "He brings armies into existence" (1948: 380). I have these references thanks to the draft of Ted Lewis's forthcoming book on "God" (2020b). I had not realized the degree to which Cross (1973: 65–66) was simply elaborating the interpretation of his teacher.

6

The People of Yahweh

By my reading of the Egyptian evidence, Yhwӡ is one unit in a coalition of forces that Egypt claimed to have fought and defeated, so as to represent each by a bound prisoner with a distinct label. Together with Trbr, Smt, and Pyspys, Yhwӡ belonged to a "Shasu-land," not a self-given identity but an Egyptian way to characterize the associated groups and to locate them spatially by a logic that is opaque to us beyond the connection of the mobile pastoralist Shasu with land not occupied by the cities of Canaan and their small subordinate kingdoms. This analysis is intended to embrace a range of possible relationships to the "land" that the Egyptians attributed to this connected Shasu population, but the identification of each individual name with a body of people appears unavoidable. These are not topographical features or gods or sacred places unless they gave their names to the Shasu units thus designated. I find no evidence that in the early 14th century, a Shasu-land was restricted to the southern region later identified with Edom and Seir, though a southern location would not affect the larger interpretation of Yhwӡ as a Shasu group, which I define as a "people."

Returning to the essential choices at the start of this volume, I also conclude that the Yhwӡ name is very likely in historical relationship to the god Yahweh (*Yhwh*). The phonological match of the first three consonants is exact, leaving only the concluding -*h* that marks a final long vowel in Hebrew. Equally important is the social and geographical context, with Yhwӡ a major constituent of a West Semitic-speaking population that inhabited the less populated margins of the Levant. The problem is that the Egyptian evidence gives us no reason to identify Yhwӡ with a god, and our only reason to do so would be connection with the famous first-millennium deity that is our object of interest. If we conclude that the historical relationship between the earlier Shasu name and the later divine name is real, then how do we explain the transformation from one to the other? With this chapter I consider how the Bible's "people of Yahweh" (*'am Yhwh*) could represent a link between the deity and the older occurrence of Yhw₃ to name a Shasu group. The larger social and political context for such alignment of deity and people will be reserved for Chapter 7.

If Yhw₃ of Shasu-land does represent the same name later identified with the god of the Bible, including both the kingdoms of Israel and Judah, and this name is not assumed already to be divine, then we must consider how a back-country people gave its name to a god. The prospect is immediately daunting and cannot be expected to have a secure solution, since it is well known that the evidence is limited. After the two related Egyptian lists, the next non-biblical reference to the name is found in the 9th-century Mesha inscription from Moab, which assumes the Greater Israel of the Omrides and considers Kamosh and Yahweh to be opposing gods in a conflict of kingdoms.[1] It is possible that the rich biblical attestation of the divine name includes texts or associations that are older than Mesha and the Omrides, but these are not easy to identify with general agreement, especially taking into account the caution of many European scholars.[2]

YAHWEH IN THE MESHA INSCRIPTION

The Mesha stela celebrates the victories by which the king of Moab secured his realm from a capital in Dibon, including the eviction of the neighboring kingdom of Israel from key centers. While the basic exchange between the two kingdoms is clear enough, the conflict and its participants can too easily be universalized in a way that equates all the elements: Moab as monarchy ruled by Mesha and Kamosh as god of Moab;

---

[1] See first of all the articles gathered in Dearman (1989). In the context of a larger study on Moab, see Routledge (2004: chapter 7 on "Mesha and the Naming of Names"). For up-to-date bibliography, see the recent pieces by Becking (2017) and Schade (2017).

[2] One example of such caution is Konrad Schmid (2012a: 51), who excludes "*extensive* literary production" from the 10th century in both Israel and Judah, tying this to the emergence of "states." "Accordingly, in the tenth to eighth centuries B.C.E. we cannot speak of anything more than the 'beginnings' of Old Testament literature." Schmid does not date any particular text within this span, so that the Mesha inscription would be roughly as old as anything in the Bible.

Israel as monarchy ruled by Omri and his son; and Yahweh as god of Israel. Even as we move to biblical evidence for Yahweh before Israel this oldest non-biblical reference to the clear divine name warrants a closer look.

In first-person voice, Mesha reports the anger of the god Kamosh against "his land" (*'rṣh*), so that he allowed Omri king of Israel to dominate Moab "for many days" (lines 4–6). Before launching into the details, the king boasts, "I looked (victoriously) upon him and upon his house, and Israel disappeared completely and for good" (line 7).[3] The point of departure for Mesha's campaign is the fact that Omri had taken possession of "the land of Mehadaba," using the same category (*'rṣ*) that defined Moab (lines 7–8), and this is what Kamosh restored to Mesha (lines 8–9). Three settlement-focused victories follow, before Mesha turns to his building achievements: over 'Aṭarot, Nebo, and Yahaṣ (lines 10–21). Israel is mentioned once by name in connection with each of the three sites: the king of Israel "built" (so, fortified) 'Aṭarot and Yahaṣ (lines 10–11, 18–19); and Kamosh tells Mesha, "Go take Nebo from Israel" (line 14). Yahweh appears only in connection with Nebo, the only town that Mesha empties by sacred slaughter (*ḥrm*), after which he "took from there the vessels of Yahweh and dragged them before Kamosh" (lines 17–18).[4]

We read these lines imagining from the Bible that Yahweh is something like a "national god" for Israel, just as Kamosh appears to be here for Moab, so that Israel's defeat is equally Kamosh's defeat of Yahweh. Something like this equation does seem to be intended: Israel is indeed bested by taking Nebo, along with other sites, and the final ritual act of presenting Yahweh's sacred objects to Kamosh declares the subordination of the shrine to the Moabite god in a way that is only possible because of Israel's defeat. Yet we should hesitate to assume that we have adequate knowledge of the context. Mesha never claims that Yahweh was introduced to Nebo only with Omri and Israel, and sacred sites tend to persist in time. It is possible that the sanctuary for Yahweh at Nebo preceded Omri's arrival. Indeed Yahweh of the Mesha text is aligned with Israel and its Omride kings, and the biblical and other inscriptional evidence

---

[3] The intensifying effect of the infinitive absolute with the verb *'bd* can be understood to refer to Israel's removal from the land claimed by Moab, not implying the destruction of that kingdom.

[4] On the ritual procedure undertaken here and its relationship to South Arabian and biblical expectations, see Monroe (2007).

confirms Yahweh's identification with Israel in the 9th and 8th centuries. Yet the worship of Yahweh at Nebo need not have required rule by Israel and incorporation into an entity by that name. Just as the "men of Gad" (*'š gd*) are understood to have occupied "the land of 'Aṭarot" from time gone by (line 10), Yahweh may not be a new arrival, though both the Gadites and Yahweh are defeated by Moab.[5] If the Yahweh shrine at Nebo went back to time before Omri, then it could reflect worship that was not tied to Israel. In such a reconstruction, Yahweh at Nebo would also be "before Israel," established without reference to Israel by name, even as that people had long existed in the highlands west of the Jordan River.

THE PEOPLE OF YAHWEH

The Mesha inscription attests directly to the existence of a Yahweh sanctuary at Nebo in Jordan, thus raising the possibility that Yahweh could have been worshiped in this eastern region before incorporation into the polity named Israel. Yhw₃ of the Shasu-land confronts us with the name as a people set back from Canaan, whether south or east. I have argued that Egypt's notion of a Shasu population concentrated in the southern spaces of Edom and Seir only characterizes the late 13th and 12th centuries in the later stages of their Levantine rule, after the period that produced the Shasu-land list of names. If this earlier "Shasu-land" was not located in or limited to that more southern region, Nebo and territory east of the Jordan River and the Dead Sea need not be excluded from land potentially identified with the Yhw₃ group.

Is it possible that the Bible could preserve any recollection that the divine name could once have been identified with a "people," a unified population that could act as a body, whatever its relationship to land? In Biblical Hebrew, two terms most often categorize the political landscape as perceived by the writers: *'ām* and *gōy*, conventionally translated "people" and "nation," respectively, but not absolutely distinguishable.[6]

---

[5] In Num 32:34, the Gadites ("children of Gad") are said to have rebuilt a list of towns identified with Og of Bashan, including names familiar from the Mesha inscription: Dibon, 'Aṭarot, Aroer, and more. There is a connection between Gad and 'Aṭarot, though it is not specific, as in the Mesha text.

[6] Note that the word *gōy* goes back to the West Semitic noun *gayum*, which in texts from early second-millennium Mari applies to subdivisions of some larger population, like the Hebrew *šēbeṭ* as "tribe" in a larger entity, especially Israel (Fleming 2004: 50–58). Within

Although Israel can be a "holy *gōy*" (Exod 19:6) or hope to be a "large *gōy*" (Exod 32:10), the plural *gōyîm* commonly represents the mass of all other peoples.[7] Similarly, the plural *'ammîm* can identify "the peoples of the land" as in Ezek 31:12, where these match the "many peoples" (*gōyîm rabbîm*, v. 6), first to seek the shade of the imperial Assyrian cedar and then to abandon it when cut down. Yet most often, when "our people" are in view, the writers choose *'ām*, and even in the cited texts from Exodus, the selection of *gōy* seems comparative, locating Israel as one among the many. When we are told that the *'ām* is at war, as with Israel against the Philistines under Omri, translators often render it as "army" or "troops," both of which call up institutions not represented by the term.[8] It is the "people" that fight because the word indicates the mustered population, representing all its parts and participating in the decision to do battle.

Although neither *'ām* nor *gōy* is generally attached directly to a proper noun to identify a named people, the word *'ām* occasionally offers such a qualifier. "The people Israel" (*hā'ām yiśrā'ēl*) split into warring factions to choose between Omri and Tibni as king (1 Kgs 16:21).[9] As a genitival construction, "the people of Israel" (*'am yiśrā'ēl*) with Absalom are defeated by "the servants of David" (2 Sam 18:7), and "the people of Aram" (*'am 'ărām*) are promised exile in Amos 1:5.[10] We find "all the

the Syrian division of kinship-defined peoples into Yaminites and Sim'alites, apparently southwest and northeast of the Euphrates River, only the units of the Sim'alites were identified by their own people as *gayum*. During an earlier period, under the rule of Samsi-Addu, the Yaminites and Sim'alites as whole populations could each be considered a *gayum*, viewed from outside. The word *'ām* has equally early West Semitic roots but appears to have begun not as an explicit group but as reference to an emblematic figure to whom a lineage can be traced. Durand (1997–2000: 3:553) translates *'ammum* (written *hammum*) by the French "aïeul" ("forefather").

[7] For example, in Hos 8:8, 10, Israel is measured by its place "among the *gōyîm*," including the great power of Assyria.

[8] Where the *'ām* appears in 1 Kgs 16:15 and 16, encamped at Gibbethon, it is the "army" in the New American Bible and the New International Version, and it is the "troops" in the Jewish Publication Society translation, the Revised Standard Version, and the English Standard Version.

[9] See also Josh 8:33 and Ezra 9:1.

[10] Aside from the pairing with "all the people of Judah" (next note), the phrase only occurs with Israel in Ezra 2:2 and Neh 7:7, to introduce the long list of "the number of the men of the *'am yiśrā'ēl*." In the Chronicles version of Assyrian taunts during the campaign of Sennacherib, his servants speak "Judahite" in the hearing of "the people of Jerusalem" (2 Chr 32:18).

people of Judah" with emphasis on full participation, as in crowning Azariah king (2 Kgs 14:21).[11]

More often, Israel – never Judah – is named with indirect reference to Yahweh, as when Amos has the god proclaim doom on "my people Israel" (*'ammî yiśrā'ēl*).[12] This construction merges the identification of Israel as a "people" (*'ām*) with Yahweh as its god, reminiscent of the title that declares Yahweh the "god of Israel" (*'ĕlōhê yiśrā'ēl*), a combination that Stahl (2020) attributes first to the Omride kings of Israel in the 9th century.[13] Yahweh memorably identifies Israel as "my people" (*'ammî*) in the opening exchange of Hosea 1, and it may be automatic to associate this Hebrew word with the divine name, yet the specific phrase, "the people of Yahweh" (*'am Yhwh*) is quite rare. One of the occurrences, after the call for Deborah and Barak to "awake" in the original opening of the Song of Deborah (Judg 5:12–13), comes from one of the oldest compositional units in the Bible, which I have argued to be older than the reference to Yahweh from Seir and Edom in the opening hymn (5:4–5). Moreover, "the people of Yahweh" in Judg 5:13 introduce a list of groups that fight together against "the kings of Canaan" (v. 19) in the Kishon Valley, along with four more who are criticized for non-participation (vv. 14–18). This old poem puts us in a position to consider with remarkable precision what "the people of Yahweh" were understood to be in this one context. From the beginning of my exposition and with detailed elaboration in Chapter 4, I have proposed what I know to be a new interpretation of the Song's compositional history, whereby verses 2–11 constitute a "revision through introduction" (Milstein 2016). The essential implication of this conclusion, and the observation that inspired it, is that "Israel" and Yahweh as "god of Israel" are secondary to the poetic battle account in verses 12–22/23, so that the appearance of the *'am Yhwh* in verse 13 is "before Israel" in lacking definition in relation to it. This old mention of "the people of Yahweh" may suggest an explanatory framework that could relate the early first-millennium god to the older Shasu group.

---

[11] The same phrase then appears in 2 Chr 26:1 for Uzziah, the same ruler, though the Greek has "all the people of the land." See also 2 Sam 19:41, followed by "half the people of Israel," to accompany David; and Jer 25:1, 2; 26:18, for the recipients of prophecy. In Ezra 4:4, "the people of the land" try to discourage "the people of Judah."

[12] Amos 7:8, 15; and 8:2; see also Josh 11:23 ("his"); 1 Kgs 8:33 ("your"); etc. These listings are not exhaustive.

[13] Stahl identifies the initial "God of Israel" as El, based on the long-observed occurrence of El (or *'ēl*) in the people-name and on the cult epithet linked to Shechem, "El, God of Israel" (*'ēl 'ĕlōhê yiśrā'ēl*) in Gen 33:20.

In a rare construction to which we will return in the final chapter, considering the context for understanding Yahweh's early character, one other god and people are joined in this way in two related texts that display no consciousness of comparison with the *ʿam Yhwh*. The text brings together the combination familiar to us from the 9th-century Mesha inscription, where Kamosh is the particular god who brings victory to the king of Moab. In what Levine (2000: 123–25) calls the "Heshbon Ballad" of Num 21:27–30, attached to the short account of victory against Sihon king of the Amorites, a poetic fragment recalling Heshbon's defeat sets in parallel "Moab" and "the people of Kemosh" (*ʿam kĕmôš*, v. 29). A variant of the same text is picked up in Jeremiah's oracle against Moab (Jer 48:45–46). According to Num 21:28–29a, before the poem is aligned with the preceding prose for passing by Moab and fighting the Amorites, Sihon and Heshbon belong to Moab, and neither this nor any other biblical text explains who defeated them or when. "The people of Kemosh" therefore appear an old traditional category, with another named god entering the Bible without complaint of illegitimacy or idolatry, caught up in memory of military defeat. "The people of Yahweh" should likewise be old and traditional, not a later monarchic or post-monarchic construction, and all the biblical occurrences of the phrase warrant systematic attention.

THE TEN ʿAM YHWH TEXTS

"The people of Yahweh" as *ʿam Yhwh* occur only ten times in the Bible.[14] Five of these are concerned entirely with the people as the possession of Yahweh, serving him, supplied by him, and ruled by him. These are broadly later than and secondary to the others, conceptually derivative and theological, regardless of how individual texts are dated. In Ezek 36:20, Yahweh is provoked into action on behalf of his own name, which has been defamed by other nations who say, "These are the people of Yahweh, and (now) from his land they have departed." The land (*'ereṣ*) in question is Yahweh's so that he himself is its ruler. Yahweh responds with similar sense of personal insult in Zeph 2:10, where he sets himself against Judah's enemies, who "scorned and vaunted themselves over the people of Yahweh of Hosts."

---

[14] Brendon Benz and I developed a preliminary analysis of this terminology in Benz and Fleming (2016). Benz's portion of the paper focused on the texts outside the Song of Deborah, and my discussion here owes much to his effort and insight.

Three portrayals of the Israelites in time long past are preoccupied with the congregation gathered to worship and the proper modes for expression, with interest in prophecy and priestly service. Numbers 11:29 belongs to the account of Yahweh's spirit falling on Israel's seventy elders (v. 25), so that even the two who stayed behind in camp are equally empowered (v. 26). When Joshua complains about these two, Moses replies, "Would that all the people of Yahweh were prophets, that Yahweh would bestow his spirit upon them!"[15] In Numbers 17, the issue is priestly leadership, following a revolt identified in verse 5 with Korah. Moses has Eleazar recast the rebels' firepans to plate the altar, and the people respond bitterly, "You have brought death on the people of Yahweh" (v. 6). Yahweh abruptly strikes the assembled community with plague, which Aaron turns away after thousands of deaths by performing rites of expiation (vv. 12–14). Finally, in the era of Eli, the mishandling of offerings by his sons finally provokes a warning from the aged priest: "Indeed, not good is the report that I am hearing the people of Yahweh spreading" (1 Sam 2:24).[16] All three of these texts are widely considered late, probably after the fall of Judah, when the people of Yahweh were identified entirely by worship.[17]

This leaves only five more occurrences of the *'am Yhwh*, two of them in the Song of Deborah (Judg 5:11, 13).[18] The other three all join "the

---

[15] For translation of the verb *ntn* ("to give") with *'al* ("on") as "bestow," see Levine (1993: 314).

[16] The text is badly jumbled; see the discussion in McCarter (1980: 81–82).

[17] While Numbers 17 is classically Priestly (Levine 1993: 67, 428–32), chapter 11's prophetic concern represents something else. This was once understood as JE and somehow older (Levine, 52), but it is now commonly considered an expansion after the exile. Carr (2011: 267–68) observes the counterpart to the leadership question in Deut 1:9–18, which suggests "a harmonizing expansion adapted to its context, placing a story of the spreading of Moses's spirit near the departure from Sinai," not Priestly and post-Deuteronomistic, contributing to the vision of a consistently rebellious people. 1 Sam 2:24 appears to be part of relatively later material in 2:12–26, reinterpreting the generic plural of verses 12–17 to suit the two named sons of chapter 4 and anticipating both the prophecy against the house of Eli in 2:27–36 and (in verse 26) Samuel's place in the temple from chapter 3. Kratz (2005: 174) includes explanations for the death of Eli's sons in a post-exilic and Priestly expansion.

[18] Note that the Masoretic reading separated *'ām* from *Yhwh* in separate parts of the paired elements in Judg 5:13, with Yahweh alone as the subject of the verb in the second half of the line. Modern commentators and translators appropriately restore the connection, which persisted in early Hebrew and Greek manuscripts. The JPS translates, "The LORD's people won my victory over the warriors"; and Smith (2014: 255), "May the people of Yahweh rule for me over the warriors!"

people of Yahweh" to Israel, with the latter always in the second position, each combination presenting unique details: 2 Sam 1:12; 6:21; and 2 Kgs 9:6. While the dates of composition are beyond reach, the very rarity of the *'am Yhwh* phrase, along with the contrast of these uses to the worshiping congregation displayed in the other five texts, suggests that we are not dealing with the stereotyping hand of writers with large-scale composition in view. Also, the distinct treatment of the phrase in these three texts may relate to the historical sequence portrayed, not to provide dates of composition but to suggest an idea of changing political conditions. 2 Samuel 1 addresses the death of Saul; 2 Samuel 6 the establishment of David; and 2 Kings 9 the anointing of Jehu – all three defined by leadership of Israel without reference to Judah.[19] There is something to be gained by considering the texts in sequence.

2 Samuel 1:11–12 records a lamentation over Saul and Jonathan that is described by a unique combination of phrasing, not picking up any specific language or ideas from the account of Saul's death in 1 Samuel 31.[20] The larger frame holds in tension David's conflict with the Amalekites in 1 Samuel 30 (cf. 2 Sam 1:1) and the apparent assumption that the Amalekite who slew Saul at the king's request served with Israel.[21] On its own, the lament portrays diverse political players divided

---

[19] On David as king of Israel in the 2 Samuel literary tradition, with rule over "Judah" reflecting a very late stage of revision, see Leonard-Fleckman (2016: 137–40).

[20] For detailed discussion of 2 Sam 1:12 and its context, see Stahl (2020).

[21] Note that no priests are involved; only David and his "men." McCarter (1984) considers 2 Sam 1:1–16 a unified account from the History of David's Rise, which he understands to be a very old document from close to David's reign. Hutton (2009: 272–73) develops a more complex version of this approach, including the combined prose narrative and poetic lament from 1:1–27 in his HDR₂, a composition from late in David's own reign that accounts for David's rule in place of Saul. 2 Sam 2:11–12 is frequently included, with verses 1–4, in the older material from this chapter (cf. Willi-Plein 2005; Adam 2008). Kratz (2005: 179) reads the whole chapter as very late, part of a redactional effort to explain the death of Saul as necessary to the establishment of David. The evident independence of the lament described in verses 11–12 suggests a distinct narrative, as proposed in Willi-Plein and envisioned by McCarter with his discussion of two interwoven tales. The notion that the Amalekite offered David the crown of Saul (v. 10), with David's reference to Saul as "the anointed of Yahweh" (v. 14), jumps the gun on David as king of Israel. On the one hand, this statement ignores (and has no need of?) David's initial rule over Judah from the next chapter, while on the other hand it could be read as part of a thread that connected Saul as "anointed" king over Israel (1 Sam 24, cf. 26) and David's anointing to be king in 2 Sam 5. The question is how early such a construction would be. For the analysis undertaken here, the date is not crucial, but it is important to establish whether verses 11–12 offer an account of David's response to Saul's death that is not dependent on other biblical treatments.

between the living and the dead, as subject and object of mourning. David honors the dead by tearing his clothing, and he is imitated by "all the men who were with him" (v. 11), a variant of the common representation of David's company in the older narrative material.[22] None of these has any connection to Israel or even to Yahweh. The object of their honor consists of two individuals and two groups:

They mourned and wept and fasted until evening for [*'al*] Saul and for Jonathan his son and for the people of Yahweh [*'am Yhwh*] and for the house of Israel, because [*kî*] they had fallen by the sword.[23]

However we translate the final phrase, introduced by the malleable conjunction *kî*, the point is that it applies equally to all four preceding objects of mourning, in grammar and in sad fact. Further, the four objects are treated as separate entities, connected three times by "and" with repetition of the preposition *'al* after each one. From this context alone, we cannot tell what exactly is intended by the *'am Yhwh*, but it does not overlap with the *bêt yiśrā'ēl* that follows. Somehow, Saul and Jonathan led two allied bodies, with only one defined by Yahweh. We will return to the question when we have examined the remaining four texts.

The next occurrence is textually doubtful but still worth examination. In 2 Samuel 6, after David has secured his rule by seizing Jerusalem as a new capital and by defeating the perennial Philistine enemy (ch. 5), the king identifies himself with Yahweh by bringing "the ark of God" (6:2, etc.) into the city in celebratory procession, himself at its head. In what may be considered an elaboration on the ritual narrative of 6:1–15, David's wife Michal, the daughter of Saul, complains about his exhibition (vv. 16, 20) and is rebuked in return. The Masoretic Text (MT) and the

---

[22] Leonard-Fleckman (2016: 156–63). This picture is introduced in 1 Sam 22:1–2 and continues into the stories of David's doings before becoming king of Israel (e.g. 2 Sam 2:13, etc.).

[23] The Greek has "the people of Judah" in place of "Israel." This yields a phrase only found with "all the people of Judah" who make Azariah/Uzziah king in 2 Sam 14:21 (2 Chr 26:1). Replacement of "Yahweh" with Judah, spelled with the same first three letters (*yhw-*), appears to reflect consciousness of the peculiar combination of two separate entities, solving the problem by introducing Judah as a group separate from Israel. Nothing in this part of the David story indicates the recognition of Judah as any part of Saul's activity, including the battle at the time of his death. Note also the "house of Israel" terminology, which refers to the people as a whole, not the monarchic line from Saul (see Leonard-Fleckman 2016: 18, with citations).

Greek Codex Vaticanus (LXX^B) present vastly different texts, and "the people of Yahweh" are only in the MT:[24]

MT: Before Yahweh who chose me over [lit. 'more than', *mē*] your father and
          over all his house to command me chief [*nāgîd*] over ['*al*] the people of
          Yahweh, over Israel, and I will perform [*śḥq*] before Yahweh.
LXX^B: Before the Lord [=Yahweh] I will dance. Blessed be the Lord [=Yahweh],
          who chose me over your father and over all his house to appoint me
          leader for his people, for Israel. And I will perform [παιξομαι, for Hebrew
          śḥq] and dance before the Lord [=Yahweh].

McCarter, whose meticulous textual criticism still stands out, prefers the Greek text and suggests that the scribe's eye skipped from the first Yahweh to the second, though this would not affect the variation between "over the people of Yahweh, over Israel" and "for his people, for Israel." It is difficult to decide whether a translator saw nothing special in the *'am Yhwh* and translated loosely or whether the MT added it. If the latter, then the rare phrase must have had a textual inspiration, and for rule by a king of Israel, this could only be the next text, 2 Kgs 9:6. "The people of Yahweh" in 2 Sam 6:21 are equated with Israel as the body ruled by a king, in contrast to the separate entity in 2 Sam 1:12.[25]

2 Kings 9:1–14 recounts how Elisha sent a deputy to anoint Jehu king over Israel, to replace the house of Omri. The first part of the narrative is focused on Elisha and his "young man," the instructions for the anointing and what to say, and their execution at Ramoth-gilead (vv. 1–6). Elisha tells the man to say, "Thus said Yahweh: I have anointed you as king over Israel" – and the prophet follows this with, "and then you shall open the door and flee, and not wait" (v. 3). The deputy does as he is told, but he elaborates considerably in verses 7–10a before finally "opening the door" at the end of verse 10. This added material ruminates on "the house of Ahab," Jezebel and the prophets, and the previous houses of Jeroboam and Baasha, embedding the anointing in the larger narrative of two kingdoms in a way absent from the basic anointing exchange so that it is possible to imagine revision in one or more stages.[26] In broader

---

[24] I translate particularly literally in order to display the difficult Hebrew wording.

[25] A few manuscripts render the phrase, "over the people of Yahweh and over Israel," so that these are distinct. Given that the text is so uncertain, with focus on Yahweh's single selection of David as king, it may be that this separation was influenced by 2 Sam 1:12, Judg 5:11, and 13, or both, rather than representing an ancient recollection of real distinction.

[26] In the case of the prophets Elijah and Elisha, I am inclined toward a more parsimonious reading of the old material for these figures, since so much of the Elijah material appears to be developed from that of Elisha, with reference to a broader biblical horizon that

composition-building terms, this introduction to Jehu's coup has no connection to the collection of Elisha stories that represent an essential center for the tradition of a miracle-working prophet in Israel. So far as the youth who carries the message is attached to Elisha, the text is linked to 1 Kgs 19:15–17, where Elijah is instructed to perform three story-binding anointings, the last two for Jehu and Elisha. Since three different figures – Elijah, Elisha, and the youth – are associated with Jehu's anointing, it is difficult to be sure how an original story or text may have been adjusted for service to a larger narrative, though the Elijah attribution appears to take credit for what 2 Kings 9 assigns to others.

When the words of Yahweh are spoken in verse 6, the man adds our *'am Yhwh*, which had not been part of the instruction in verse 3: "Thus said Yahweh: I have anointed you as king over the people of Yahweh, over Israel." Nothing separates the two, so that the first becomes a description of the second. Given the unusual nature of the phrase, its absence from Elisha's instructions, and the fact that nothing in this text provides it a distinct identity, it may be added by awareness of another text.[27] The two texts that offer a distinct political character for the people of Yahweh are 2 Sam 1:12 and Judges 5. Without such reference it is not clear how the expansion illuminates the commanded anointing to rule Israel.

The last two instances of "the people of Yahweh" appear in Judg 5:11 and 13, straddling and so binding the introduction to the Song and its introduction. In verse 11, we are told, "Then the people of Yahweh went down to the gates," to arrive before the call to Deborah and Barak in verse 12 and therefore to serve as the summoning body. The last introductory reference to Israel just occurred in verse 11a, part of a blessing on Yahweh in verses 9–11 that appears to be cast in Deborah's voice. By representing the assembled allies as a body, "the people of Yahweh" provide a collective to issue the call in verse 12, which must shift from

---

includes the twelve tribes of Israel as Jacob and the monotheistic imperative in 1 Kings 18. In his general treatment of the biblical history, Kratz (2005: 166–67) describes the assimilation of Elijah and Elisha into one type, with 2 Kgs 9:3 and 6 part of a program to present them both as representatives of the word of God.

[27] I have not found discussion on this detail, which should be addressed in commentaries on 1 and 2 Kings. I could imagine such addition at either an earlier or later date, even as part of the core composition, though this change would make it aware of the other narrative – outside the account of two kingdoms that begins in 1 Kings 12, in either case. The Jehu account could simply be independent of the other "people of Yahweh" texts, but if the elaboration reflects knowledge of them, this would suggest a relatively later date.

Deborah to those who want leaders. Yet the sequence of action makes little sense. If "gates" are involved, they can only be the imagined gates of Taanach and Megiddo, where the battle takes place according to verse 19. No fortified city is mentioned as any part of the alliance against the kings of Canaan, so that we cannot explain a location for assembly. Further, the account of combat depicts no city siege, instead presenting pitched battle on the plain, where horses' hoofs can pound (v. 22) and river waters can flood (v. 21). The end of verse 11 thus shows itself a seam that binds the opening hymn in verses 2–11a to the core battle account of verses 12–22/ 23.

Without the introductory hymn to Yahweh and its bridge to the coming call, verse 12 on its own needs no subject; it brings rousing urgency to the battle to come:

> Awake, awake, Deborah! Awake, awake, chant a song!
> Arise, Barak! Take your captives, son of Abinoam!

Between the introductory call and the list of allies that begins in verse 14, victory is anticipated in the name of Yahweh by the people who fight in his name, as the *'am Yhwh* (v. 13).

> Then shall the survivor rule over the lofty,
> shall the people of Yahweh rule for me over the mighty.[28]

For this reversal to occur, Deborah and Barak must "awake" and answer the call to action. Between this peculiar pair of female and male leaders and the list of participant groups, "the people of Yahweh" identify the whole, the alliance led, the confederacy to profit from victory. Although some have removed verse 13 as an elaboration from the battle account that is clearly introduced in verse 12 and carried forward in verse 14, it may be that the very priority of a woman in leadership is best explained in combination with the god Yahweh. Deborah is nowhere identified as a

---

[28] The choice of vocabulary is striking, with its opposition of the single *śārîd* as one who survives battle (e.g. Josh 8:22) or death in the family (Job 20:21) and two varieties of the socially prominent as the object of domination or governance (verb *rdh*). A *śārîd* is a person without a people (Job 18:19). On reading the verb *rdh* ("to rule") rather than *yrd* ("to go down"), see Coogan (1978: 148 n.35), "We interpret these forms as qal imperfects of *rdh*; both the MT vocalization and LXX^A seem to support such a reading. (See further Albright, "Earliest Forms of Hebrew Verse," *JPOS* 2 [1922] 76, n.6.) *rdh* is ordinarily followed by the preposition *b*, as in v. 13b; *l* is used as a variant in v. 13a. (Similar variation between *b* and *l* is found in vv. 15–16.) There is, of course, a play on the verb *yārad* which is used in vv. 11 and 14." Smith (2014: 255) also reads this verb; for *yrd*, see for example Soggin (1981: 82).

"prophet" as in the prose account (4:4), but that title may offer explanation for an authority understood as only possible in the unity under the
divine name.

As portrayed especially in Judg 5:13, the people of Yahweh in the Song
of Deborah are not ruled but rather led, rallied to fight a common foe,
with potential allies left to make their own choices, having only the curse
of Yahweh to motivate the reluctant – to no universal effect. They are
promised self-governance (so, the verb *rdh*), freedom from the mighty
who would dominate them individually. Although Yahweh is identified
powerfully and repeatedly with Israel as such in the opening hymn, this
people of Yahweh in verse 13 is to be understood without reference to the
unifying name of Israel. The one thing that unites those who join Deborah
and Barak, according to the *'am Yhwh* in verse 13, is that name. If we
were to read the battle account in verses 12–22 alone, with Yhw3 of
Shasu-land in mind, we might not even recognize *Yhwh* as a god; rather,
we could imagine something like "the Yahweh-people," syntactically not
so different from what Egypt envisioned as "Shasu-land" (*t3 šʒśw*).[29]
I draw attention to the likeness in syntax in order to underscore the
similarity of constructions. Nevertheless, in the Song of Deborah, especially as joined with the curse by Yahweh in verse 23, though also
informed by the myriad references to the divine name in the poem and
beyond, it is scarcely possible to read the phrase as anything but an
alliance headed by a deity. Nevertheless, the conceptual distance between
"Yahweh-people" and "people of Yahweh" is not great, and with this
use, the Song of Deborah brings us closest to a trace of how one of the
ancient Shasu peoples could have given its name to a god.

THE PEOPLE OF YAHWEH APART FROM ISRAEL: JUDGES 5:13

In the stream of analysis launched by Albright's identification of old
biblical poetry, the Song of Deborah was easily regarded as pre-
monarchic, to locate somewhere in the 12th or 11th centuries.[30] Unlike

---

[29] In biblical prose, it appears that the appositional reading of *'ām* is marked by the definite
article, so "the people Israel" (*hā'ām yiśrā'ēl*) in 1 Kgs 16:21; cf. Josh 8:33; Ezra 9:1.
Poetry cannot be assumed to use the definite article, which would not in any case have
been part of the second-millennium language (so, Ugaritic).

[30] See the discussion in Chapter 3. Note an early exception in Ahlström (1986: 80).
Although we approach the text and argumentation differently, my overall sense of how
the Song of Deborah relates to history resembles that of Mark Smith, who treats the text
carefully and at length in *Poetic Heroes* (2014), chapters 8 and 9.

other poems now found in the Pentateuch, which are bound up in one way or another with origins stories that have not maintained such early dating, Judges 5 treats a conflict in the land between settled participants on both sides, without reference to conquest and settlement. "The kings of Canaan" (v. 19) remain in place without expectation of expulsion, and those who fight against them are equally established. This is no origins story. It has likewise long been observed that Judah and the south are missing from the peoples under consideration. This absence could be attributed to the northern setting of the conflict, but the poem's own concern for commitments not kept because of distance indicates a deeper removal; Reuben and Gilead stay home in the east, while Dan and Asher do likewise from the north. Among the ten peoples listed and judged faithful or failing in verses 14–18 we find many familiar from the standard biblical tribes, yet Gilead and Machir are known names never classified as "tribes" (*šēbeṭ* or *maṭṭeh*). Although Benjamin appears, it is subordinated to Ephraim, which in turn has its "root in Amalek" (v. 14; see Daniels 2018).[31] The entire landscape of Judges 5 is occupied with the eventual northern kingdom in terms completely unaware of kings.

And yet we must acknowledge that these conclusions are based above all on the battle described in verses 14–22, for the allied peoples in verses 14–18 and for the kings of Canaan in the northern lowlands as an abiding presence, not to remove and replace but to keep at bay. The Jael episode offers little social-political orientation except repetition of Sisera as individual leader (vv. 20, 26, 28) and the image of this man as ruler at an urban center, with his mother waiting at a window (vv. 28–30). It is the introduction that gives pause. While those who fight and lead are repeatedly plural, they are never named as separate political entities, deciding or declining as such to fight. As already observed, they are repeatedly what the battle account never calls them: Israel. "The people" who come forward as the poem begins are the unshorn warriors "in Israel" (v. 2);

---

[31] The alternative text lacking *lamed*, "in the valley" (*b'mq*) would avoid the problem of imagining an intimate relationship between Ephraim and Amalek, which is the enemy of Israel in Exod 17:8–16, the last verse of which promises enduring conflict. See the discussion and citations in Smith (2014: 229). In the second half of the line (v. 14a), the literal reading also presents no obstacle except assumptions derived from other biblical texts: "after you, Benjamin, among your peoples." The one significant concern is the duplication of the *mem* in what otherwise looks like the noun *'ām*, "people." Later Biblical Hebrew sometimes duplicates the *mem* in plurals (e.g. Neh 9:22, 24), and this appears to be a poetic biform rather than an unrelated noun.

in the face of blocked routes for travel, the village muster ceased "in Israel" (v. 7); without the appearance of Deborah to lead as mother "in Israel" (v. 7), not one of forty thousand was armed with shield and spear "in Israel" (v. 8); the singer sets his (or her!) heart with "those counted of Israel" (v. 9), the same mass that comes forward in verse 2; and the victories of Yahweh are the victories of "his villages in Israel" (v. 11).[32] In the introduction, Israel is collective, but it is always unified, acting, suffering, choosing, succeeding, or failing as one. This is not at all the image of the battle account. Though indeed the hymn has a distinct purpose in the finished composition, it has imposed a unity on the whole that was not in the battle account, and it has done so under the name Israel, with Yahweh now "the god of Israel" (vv. 3, 5).

In its casting of the battle account peoples as "Israel," the opening hymn assumes a far-flung nation that reaches far north of the Jezreel Valley with Issachar, Zebulun, Naphtali, Dan, and Asher, as well as east of the Jordan River with Reuben and Gilead. Even the David collection most often uses the name Israel with more modest intent, to match the smaller scope of Israel as associated with Saul.[33] It remains an open historical question when an entity called Israel was first identified with such extended geography, but it is certain that Omri and Ahab established a kingdom on this scale. The Mesha inscription, from the mid-9th

---

[32] On the *pĕrāzôn* village collective in verses 7 and 11, see Chapter 4. For villagers rather than warriors, see Stager (1988: 224–25), followed by Schloen (1993: 22). Outside the two appearances in verses 2 and 9, the hitpa'el of the verb *ndb* occurs in the Bible otherwise in late texts from Chronicles, Ezra, and Nehemiah, where it reflects individual choice rather than obligation. The plural participle captured in the phrase, *ḥōqĕqê yiśrā'ēl* would suggest "those who write orders of/in Israel," perhaps out of place in a setting before monarchy and another indication of the royal production envisioned by Stahl for the introductory hymn.

[33] In geographical terms, there is little specific sense of David's Israel outside of the Absalom sequence. He takes Jerusalem, said to be inhabited by (non-Israelite) Jebusites (2 Sam 5:6), as a new capital, a significant move to the north that suggests the inadequacy of Hebron to serve an Israelite population. We only hear about individual sites in David's domain with the arrival of Absalom, first of all when he kills his half-brother Amnon at Baal-hazor "with Ephraim" (13:23). David's decisive battle against Israel led by Absalom takes place in "the forest of Ephraim" (18:6), which must be reconciled in 17:26 with David's location in Mahanaim (v. 24) by explaining that "Israel and Absalom camped in the land of Gilead," east of the Jordan. On its own, Absalom's defeat would require no involvement of the east, which plays a role only as part of the elaborate account of deceit and delay whereby David escapes Jerusalem with a retinue of loyal supporters (chs. 16–17). Without this geographical extension, chapter 18 alone would seem to leave David in Jerusalem, where he awaits word of battle "between the two gates" (v. 24, cf. v. 4), with Israel and Absalom simply out in the Ephraim countryside north of the city.

century, associates Israel's intrusion into the lands east and north of the Dead Sea with Omri, as if a new thing, with the people of Gad a long-time presence not intrinsically linked to Omri and Israel (see above). Given its mention in the Mesha text, it is noteworthy that the Song of Deborah does not place Gad among the peoples potentially committed to fight against a common enemy in verses 14–18. Perhaps they were not part of the alliance. Lacking any reference to Israelite kings and their centers of power, the introduction to Judges 5 nevertheless betrays monarchic composition by its vision of Israel, a vision that suits – perhaps only – the northern kingdom of the 9th and 8th centuries. It is therefore likely that the Song of Deborah in its finished form was composed in that period.[34] Even as the equation of Israel with the peoples of the battle account assumes the extended kingdom, the very effort to forge this identity, without undermining the tradition of decentralized decision-making, suggests that the finished Song invited what might still be recent incorporation of these peoples into a single Israel. What were once allies are now to be regarded as a permanent unity under royal head, and Judges 5 offers this unity as a reinterpretation of what the allies had always expected. Under Yahweh as "god of Israel," the united Israel will gain the respect of "kings" (v. 3), not the allied "kings of Canaan" who fight at Taanach but an outside audience of individual nations like Israel itself.[35] Along with the contrasts between the hymn in Judges 5 and 8th-century poetry from the biblical prophets, this respect paid to non-monarchic political tradition would suit a time when the incorporation was new, perhaps in the early 9th century.

As envisioned here, the introductory hymn in Judg 5:2–11 was composed to recast an earlier poetic account of battle against Canaan, with Yahweh now "the god of Israel." It is significant for the Midianite Hypothesis and its more recent revisions that Yahweh's advance from Seir and Edom belongs to this monarchic recasting, and its prior use is difficult to assess. The identification of Yahweh as "he of Sinai" and "the god of Israel" in verse 5, shared with Ps 68:9, serves directly the

---

[34] Mark Smith (2014: 232) considers much in the Song to originate in the Iron Age I, but the finished text, with its emphasis on Israel and Yahweh, would date plausibly to the 10th century. Smith offers no connection to Jerusalem and the house of David, so he appears to be thinking of the pre-Omride northern kingdom.

[35] In the Song of the Sea, the people cross into the land in the presence of awed neighbors: Philistia, Edom, Moab, and Canaan (Exod 15:14–16). A similar landscape may be envisioned for Judg 5:3, though with different constituents. For the 9th century, one thinks especially of Aram.

conceptual innovation that rereads an alliance as Israel. Like the divine guardians of kingdoms nearby, Israel's robust warrior god Yahweh would fight for his own, and this seems the attraction of the motif, manifest in Israel with the distinct distant home.[36] David Schloen (1993) explains the conflict depicted in the Song by the travel and trade on display in verse 6, when "travelers and caravans ceased, travelers went roundabout."[37] This too, however, belongs to the unifying political vision of the hymn, not the older account of combat with Canaan. So far as problems in the Jezreel Valley represented an obstacle for Israel in the early 9th century, the obvious antagonist would be Damascus, which the Tel Dan inscription records boasting of its victories against both Israel and Judah.[38]

Interpretation of finished composition in light of extended Israel in the 9th century only sharpens the contrast between the hymn and the battle account in the Song of Deborah. It is impossible to date the battle account of verses 12–22/23 by anything but its substantially different vision of the political landscape, when read alone. For our interest in the people of Yahweh, the date of composition is less important than the portrait of alliance and conflict in Palestine without reference to Israel. Consider the following details:

- Battle is led by Deborah and Barak (vv. 12, 15), two individuals without title, neither one presented as holding solitary authority,

---

[36] In contrast to the long literary texts from Ugarit, the first-millennium alphabetic material offers little detail to illuminate the sacred landscape of divine movements. While we have a substantial corpus of royal inscriptions in Phoenician and Aramaic, only two texts depict the god of king or people fighting on their behalf. In Mesha's third campaign, against the king of Israel at Yahaz, "Kamosh drove him away" (19–20); and in the Damascus stela found at Tel Dan, the king says "Hadad went before me" (A5). Neither Kamosh of Moab nor Hadad of Damascus comes from a sacred mountain or distant land – though these are both royal inscriptions, not hymnic reminiscences. Beyond these texts, it is common to find reference to divine patrons for kings in the first-millennium royal inscriptions.

[37] Schloen accepts without argument a 12th-century date, with the question only how it relates to actual history. For Schloen, the riders on donkeys in verse 10 indicate caravans in verses 6–7. The eastern groups were not affected by a blockade of caravans in the Jezreel Valley and so had no interest in joining the battle. In contrast to the effort to find an Iron Age I context for these verses, the short-lived fortified caravansary at Kuntillet 'Ajrud would indicate some new initiative to support Israelite trade in the southern wilderness during the late 9th century.

[38] For recent bibliography on the historical interest of the Tel Dan inscription, see Knapp (2014). Yifat Thareani (2016) examines the latest archaeological evidence from Tel Dan for its historical implications in relation to the Arameans and the 9th century.

and Deborah both times listed first. Deborah is to sing, and Barak is to fight, so that words precede action, in collaboration. This vocal role for Deborah in itself may suggest a divine basis for her authority, though this is not cast as specifically "prophetic" (versus Judg 4:4).

- Deborah and Barak lead the *'am Yhwh*, the only name offered the gathered whole in verses 12–23. It is only by uniting in alliance that a "remnant" of survivors can defeat the "lofty." The people of Yahweh are not such a beleaguered band; only their constituent groups individually, when left on their own.

- Six named groups ally themselves against a common enemy: first Ephraim, Benjamin, Machir, Zebulun, and Issachar (vv. 14–15a); then repeating Zebulun and adding Naphtali (v. 18).[39] None of these groups is located geographically, so we are left to depend on other biblical references, especially the territorial allotments of Joshua 13–19. All six would be west of the Jordan Rift Valley, with Ephraim, Benjamin, and Machir south of the Jezreel Valley and Zebulun, Issachar, and Naphtali immediately to the north of it.[40]

- Four named groups fail to join forces (vv. 15b–17): Reuben, Gilead, Dan, and Asher. Only these lines give account of geography, mainly to indicate distance. Gilead is "across the Jordan" and Asher is "by the shore of the sea" (v. 17).

- The named groups are never classified as "tribes," and there is no effort to organize them as comparable units of some larger whole. Only one category serves interest in identifying groups of any scale: *'ām*. Along with "the people of Yahweh," for the alliance, Zebulun is an *'ām* as it collectively risks death (v. 18), and Benjamin is counted with Ephraim as "among your peoples" (*ba'ămāmêkā*, v. 14). The category is fluid, applied situationally, and even the form of the noun varies, with the duplicated *mem* in verse 14. Each group is treated as a decision-making entity, so in this sense political. The participants

---

[39] Recognizing the odd repetition, Mark Smith (2014: 256) places verse 18 at the head of the battle scene that continues in verses 19–20. This structural choice is not essential to me.

[40] My count of six does not require any numerical symbolism, perhaps to yield ten overall. Benjamin is part of Ephraim, which could reduce the six participants to five, and the root of Ephraim is "in Amalek," which could somehow contribute to the alliance (Daniels 2018). Daniels (personal communication) wonders whether the Amalekite who came from Saul's "camp" in 2 Sam 1:2, 8, should be understood as part of the "people of Yahweh" element of the force described in verse 12. The fact that David, who was an outsider to Saul's coalition, would have been fighting the Amalekites does not prove them fixed enemies of Israel.

"come down" (v. 14), are "with" Deborah, and "sent" in Barak's footsteps (v. 15); while the recalcitrant "stay" (vv. 16–17), all as units defined by these names.

- All ten appear to be treated as equally accountable to the expectations of alliance, without permission to shirk based on distance or self-interest. In this sense they form a whole, for purposes of mutual defense. There is no indication that they cooperate in any other circumstances or that Deborah and Barak have any role as individual leaders except for military muster in self-defense. Indeed, nothing indicates that Deborah and Barak played this part in any other conflict.

- The enemy is also conceived as an association, in their case as plural "kings of Canaan" (v. 19).[41] The political landscapes of both the 18th-century BCE Mari archives and the 14th-century Amarna letters associate kings with individual city centers, even when allied or ruling dispersed peoples, so it is likely that use of the title envisions collaborating cities, as confirmed by reference to Taanach and Megiddo in locating the battle (v. 19).[42] This association has an individual leader in Sisera (v. 20), who is not given a title but whom the text may take to be the leader among kings, perhaps even at Taanach. By the location of the battle, these kings of Canaan appear to occupy the lowlands of the Kishon/Jezreel Valleys.

- Unlike the final section of the Song, which puts Sisera in a chariot (v. 28), the main battle account pictures only horses (v. 22), without clear indication of whether they belong to the Canaanites, the allies under Deborah and Barak, or both.

This combination of features presents many names familiar from later – and in some cases also earlier – evidence for the region's social and political landscape.[43] Without the interpretive lens of the opening hymn, however, Israel itself is absent. No abiding identity unites the ten named groups as a fixed polity, any more than their enemies are imagined to

---

[41] No category is provided, as with the *'ām*. It is possible that we should distinguish between one-time alliance, as in the Damascus arrangement against Shalmaneser III in the 9th century, and a more durable association under a continuing title. Only the latter would merit designation as an *'ām* ("people").

[42] See below for further discussion of such phenomena in evidence from Mari (Fleming 2004) and in the Amarna material from New Kingdom Egypt (Benz 2016).

[43] By "earlier," I mean names that occur in writing from the Late Bronze Age: Canaan, Taanach, and Megiddo.

represent "Canaan" as an ongoing confederation.[44] By including both those praised and those censured, the set of ten is made some kind of whole, with geographical range that corresponds roughly to the later northern kingdom of Israel at its greater extent. Rather than allowing us to conclude that they are in fact already "Israel," the congruent space shows how later kings were able to extend their realms by following traditional lines of alliance and coaxing or coercing these peoples into permanent incorporation.

Within the battle account of verses 12–22/23, the *'am Yhwh* provides the one general identity for the ten allies, not assumed a permanent polity but bound by ongoing commitment that obliges mutual defense against external threat. So far as we can tell from the context in Judges 5, this identity would be activated only for military need; we are to imagine no regular ritual observance or lasting league, as Martin Noth proposed for his amphictyony.[45] Even for the occasion presented in the Song of Deborah, no sacred location or ritual observance is significant enough to warrant mention. If verse 23 belongs to and concludes the original battle account, it does so by invoking a curse in Yahweh's name, likewise without sacred site.[46] So far as no sacred place of assembly is named, we are left to imagine that such was chosen based on the geography of the crisis, in this case in the vicinity of Tanaach and the Kishon River.

When 2 Sam 1:12 presents the people of Yahweh and the house of Israel as separate bodies that lost fighters in the battle against the

---

[44] Benz (2016: 98–110) identifies the following "multipolity decentralized lands" in the Amarna evidence: the "kings of Nuḫašši" and the land of Amurru in northern Syria; the "kings of Canaan" as a variable category in the Levant; the land of Gina including Megiddo in the Jezreel Valley; and the land of Garu, apparently east of the Jordan River; along with a variety of others listed on page 110. For comparison with Judg 5:19, it is particularly interesting that Canaan itself once accompanies the same collective application to joint kings, in what Moran calls a "passport" (EA 30). A note probably written for the king of Mittani addresses together "the kings of Canaan" as "servants of my brother" – the king of Egypt – requesting safe passage. This does not define a political confederacy or even perhaps an alliance.

[45] Noth (1966); and the early critiques by Mayes (1974) and de Geus (1976).

[46] If Monroe (2019) is correct to read *mērôz* as a common noun for "alliance," verse 23 would find an explanation as an intrinsic part of the poetic battle account, indeed as its conclusion, nicely repeating "curse" to match the repeated call to "awake" in verse 12. In her larger work on Judges 5 and the Deborah texts of chapters 4–5 together, Monroe will grapple further with how to understand what I am calling the "battle account" as genre. The curse would be essential to such evaluation, as would the alliance as such, in a combination that recalls the imprecations of treaty texts. Judges 5:12–23 would both condemn the four groups that failed to appear and somehow contribute to the mainten-ance of commitment – presumably among the rest.

Philistines, it likewise separates the *'am Yhwh* from Israel, in this case without further context. If we consider 2 Samuel 1 and Judges 5 together, and we keep in mind the limited geographical scope of "Israel" as envisioned in the Saul narratives, the account of response to the king's death suggests a division between two elements in what he is imagined to have ruled. Monroe and I propose, as reflected in my contribution to our paired articles on early Israel (Fleming forthcoming), that Ephraim and Benjamin may have been considered distinct from "Israel," though joined to it early (Figures 13 and 14). With Saul himself this may be seen in 2 Sam 2:9, where his son Ishbosheth is said to have ruled "over [*'al*] Ephraim, over Benjamin, and over Israel, all of it." In the Saul narratives, as in the search for his father's donkeys in 1 Sam 9:3–5, he belongs to the southern central highlands of Ephraim and Benjamin, so that "Israel" may come to him as a separate entity, making him ruler of the combination. Understood in light of Judges 5 and 2 Sam 2:9 together, "the house of Israel" in 2 Sam 1:12 would refer not to the whole kingdom but to the entity that made him king, leaving Ephraim and Benjamin part of "the people of Yahweh," to which they also contributed in Judg 5:13–14. The relationship between Saul and the people of Yahweh, as well as their extent, is left unclear. He certainly led them in battle, along with his son Jonathan, against the Philistines as a threat from the lowlands, but we cannot tell whether they are envisioned to accept his rule as king. If so, it may be by personal connection to Ephraim and Benjamin, which in the context of Judg 5:12–22/23 represent only the southernmost participants in the "people of Yahweh." Of course we are not dealing here with history as such but with an unusual characterization of Saul's kingdom embedded in the tale of his death and preserved there, however old or accurate it may be.

In Judges 5:13 and 2 Samuel 1:12, the Bible preserves a role for Yahweh that is closely aligned with the definition of a body of people that acts collectively for special purpose. The "people" identified with Yahweh become one only as they join under this name in mutual defense. Reaching back to the Egyptian evidence, we confront a chronological gap that resembles in some ways the one presented by Israel in the Merenptah stele of ca. 1207, three-and-a-half centuries before the first mention of the kingdom in the year 853 by Assyria's Shalmaneser III (Fleming 2012a: 240–46). Egyptian texts name peoples in the Levant mainly with reference to military confrontation, a fact that in itself shows objects of defeat to be "political" entities, bodies that have fought Egypt under the given name, however they may be organized or governed. In the case of Yhw3 of

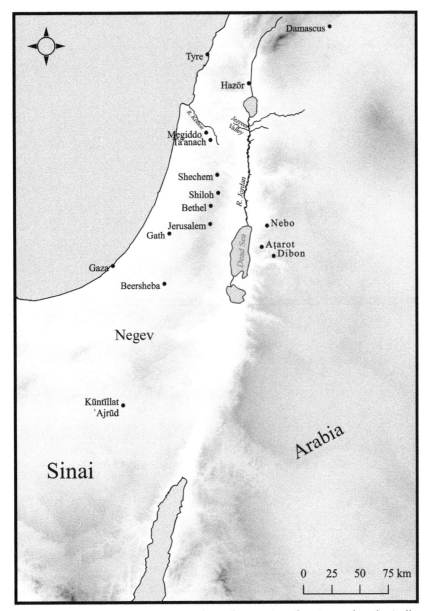

FIGURE 13 The southern Levant in the early Iron Age showing archaeologically known sites
(Map by Kyle Brunner)

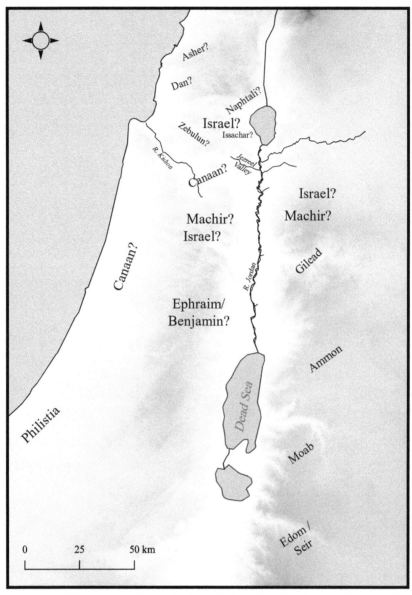

FIGURE 14 The southern Levant in the early Iron Age showing peoples named in the Bible
(Map by Kyle Brunner)

Shasu-land and the Bible's people of Yahweh, both are defined by this same need to do battle.[47]

Aside from a chronological distance that is even greater for Yhw₃ and the *'am Yhwh* than for Israel, the two Egyptian contributions face different obstacles to historical interpretation, with the glaring reality of Yhw₃'s reappearance in the first millennium only as a god. Acknowledging the elusiveness of this crucial transformation, there are lines of likeness that add to the plausibility of identifying the two names. Both would represent large entities gathered to fight an external foe, as Egypt would have been to any peoples they identified as Shasu. We cannot tell the geographical scale or scope of the Shasu group, but by calling the defeated coalition "Shasu-land," the Egyptians have it represent the entire population – unlikely as this may be in a rigorous historical sense. With only four or five named constituents, each of them could be quite large, whether or not the Yhw₃ component would have approached the size and range of the *'am Yhwh* in the Song of Deborah. Nothing makes the comparison intrinsically out of scale. The Egyptian lists accompany images of prisoners and were most likely composed in the aftermath of military conflict. The alliance of independent groups in Judges 5 also resembles what the Egyptians later understood to be the political organization of Shasu peoples by "families" or "tribes" (see above). Even the geographies of the two settings are not incompatible, once we set aside the mistaken inclination to let later Shasu encounters define the earlier ones. The people of Yahweh in Judges 5 would occupy the highlands of central and northern Palestine, straddling inland regions east of the Jordan, territory that the Egyptians associated with Shasu groups.

As for Yahweh himself, the eventual god of Israel, the battle account in the Song of Deborah places him in lands solidly north of Jerusalem. The notion of his residence in Seir and Edom belongs to later revision with its own inspiration and does not locate the people of Yahweh in verse 13 and beyond. It remains important to account for the Bible's tradition of this southern wilderness home for Yahweh, but it has nothing to do with an original setting for his worship by peoples of the south. Until new evidence is discovered, we are left with biblical evidence that supposes, with unsurprising consistency, that

---

[47] In the context of this analysis, Quinn Daniels (personal communication) raised the potential relevance of "the wars of Yahweh" that appear in Num 21:14; 1 Sam 18:12; and 1 Sam 25:28 (see Levine 2000: 92–93). Among these, Num 21:14 stands out for its citation of a geographical description of Moab and the east as from "the Book of the Wars of Yahweh" (*sēper milḥămōt Yhwh*). Such a collection, defined not by Israel but by Yahweh, would align closely with the context for the people of Yahweh in Judg 5:13 and 2 Sam 1:12.

Yahweh was first of all worshiped by inhabitants of the region finally occupied by the kingdom of Israel. The Yahweh sanctuary at Nebo in the Mesha inscription could offer further indication of inland attachment to the god that preceded Israel's arrival. Without any hint of outsider origin and conquest, the Song of Deborah does separate the alliance of ten highland groups from a lowland Canaan. The name Yhwȝ itself, with its connection to Shasu-land, draws consideration of the god's early location toward peoples that Egypt regarded as mobile and dependent on herding.

"YOUR PEOPLE, YAHWEH": EXODUS 15:16

By my reading of the Song of Deborah, the two poetic accounts of Sisera's defeat in verses 12–23 and 24–30 did not identify the victors as Israel or align them with that name and entity. The only collective definition supplied for them occurs in the first of these, focused on the participants in battle and their success against the assembled "kings of Canaan," naming them "the people of Yahweh" as a measure of their commitment to support each other for mutual defense. While the elaboration of the *'am Yhwh* identity is new to this project, the conclusion about the composition and its relation to Israel formed part of my synthetic study of northern kingdom content in the Bible, *The Legacy of Israel in Judah's Bible* (2012). At the time of that work, I left aside one famous text that Albright and others after him have long regarded as ancient: the Song of the Sea in Exodus 15. With its culmination in Yahweh's march to his inherited mountain (*har nāḥălātĕkā*, v. 17) and its language links to Psalms, Isaiah, and more, the Song of the Sea has the feel of Jerusalem, whatever its date of composition, and this would not contribute to a collection of writing transmitted by people from the kingdom of Israel.[48] Also, in vivid contrast to the poems that list Israel's individual peoples or tribes, the Song of the Sea provides the celebrants no name at all, certainly not as "Israel."

Only in returning to the poem in a different context did I recognize the resemblance of its terminology to the collective of the Song of Deborah's

---

[48] I had already reached this conclusion when Stephen Russell began his New York University doctoral dissertation with Mark Smith. Based on independent work, Russell concluded likewise, and his extended treatment of Exodus 15 offers a reference point for recent discussion of the text and content, its Jerusalem connections, and its range of potential compositional dates (2009: 127–76). Russell considers a combination of evidence, including terminology shared by prophetic writing and Psalms from Jerusalem, the lack of specifically northern kingdom ideas for old collective politics, and the geography of the lands that witness the people's movement.

battle account. Yahweh does not travel to his sacred mountain alone: he brings a "people" (*'ām*) with him:

- "the people that you redeemed" (*'ām zû gā'āltā*, v. 13);
- "your people, Yahweh" (*'ammĕkā Yhwh*, v. 16);
- "the people that you purchased" (*'ām zû qānîtā*, v. 16).

In the Song of Deborah, the only collective name provided for the associated groups as a unity is constructed from two elements: "people" and "Yahweh." Sandwiched between the echoing definition as a people bought by its god we find a name by direct address that would only transform "the people of Yahweh" into hymnic form: "your people, Yahweh." Once again we encounter a unified entity, here a group that celebrates its existence as independent from those around it, not by any proper name but only by association with Yahweh as its god. This second poem therefore requires attention as well for the same close alignment of group identity and divine name, a people defined by its god.

The Song of the Sea and Jerusalem

With the Song of the Sea I find myself once again facing a much discussed biblical text, and my purpose is not to engage every controversy and question. The most important issue for historical application is naturally its setting in place and time, which I have undertaken to reevaluate by a fresh reading. In continental Europe today, there is close to consensus that the Song of the Sea is neither old nor historically useful on terms distinct from the prose of Exodus 14. This view is expressed succinctly by Konrad Schmid (2012a: 82):

In its present context the Moses narrative comes to an initial, hymnic conclusion in Exodus 15; however, this psalm (the first in the reading sequence outside the Psalter) appears to contain no ancient traditional material. Pointing to the contrary is the Deutero-Isaianic coloring of the text; in addition, the description and interpretation of the miracle at the sea in Exod 15:8, 13 probably presupposes the Priestly document. Exodus 15 is to be regarded as a literary means, external to the Psalms, to link the Psalter paradigmatically with the first crucial salvation-historical experience of Israel.[49]

Two elements of this analysis represent distinct arguments with different implications. The comparison to Isaiah 40–55 and the Psalms suggests a

---

[49] On the proposed connection between Exodus 15 and Isaiah, see Bartelmus (2004).

Jerusalem location and a date from the 6th century or later, without explaining the narrative source that inspires the poem. It is a separate question whether the Song of the Sea was written with knowledge of the prose that now precedes it, with the walls of water in the Priestly material of Exod 14:22 and 29.

The less compelling of the two arguments is that the Song was composed with awareness of the prose narrative. Aside from the water in verse 8 and the faithful redemption in verse 13, much of the text clashes with what we read in Exodus 14:

- Pharaoh's chariots and men are thrown (verb *yrh*, v. 4) into the sea and sink (vv. 5, 10), not overtaken by flooding waters (14:26) and shaken loose like a bug (14:27). In the Song, they are washed from their means of safe crossing, whether rafts or boats or bridge, by wind-driven waves (vv. 8, 10).
- The beneficiaries of this victory have never been in Egypt. They enter a space reserved for them between four peoples east and west of the highlands along the Dead Sea: Peleset (Philistia), Edom, Moab, and Canaan (vv. 14–16a) – the last appearing to share the lowlands with the Philistines.

As others – outside the current European circle – have already observed, it is at least as easy to explain the prose as a reinterpretation of certain poetic elements from the Song as to force the poem into conceptions of the prose narrative that are not suggested by Exodus 15 when read on its own.[50]

The language shared with Isaiah and Deuteronomy is significant and must be accounted for.[51] This common ground is concentrated in the hymnic dimension of the Song. When specific names are introduced with the context established by them, the shared language is absent: verses 4–5, where Pharaoh and his chariots are identified and defeated; and the terminology describing the four surrounding peoples in verses 14b–15.

---

[50] For example, Cross (1973: 133) saw the prose as dependent on the poetry. On the debate and diverse approaches on both sides, see Stephen Russell (2009: 158–61).

[51] We must nevertheless be cautious in approaching the points of overlap. A substantial majority of the Bible derives from Judah and therefore shows the influence of Jerusalem and its various scribal circles, even so far as these were dispersed after deportation and destruction in 597 and 586, with or without the reestablishment of Jerusalem in the Persian period. To demonstrate direct scribal connection with Jerusalem writing and collection, we need to look for more than just shared vocabulary, such as clusters of terms or similar application and context.

So far as the Song divides into two parts, the defeat of Pharaoh at the Reed Sea in 1b–12, and the leading of a people to Yahweh's mountain home in 13–18, the alignments of language and ideas may be addressed separately for each part.[52]

In the defeat of Pharaoh, verse 2a presents a full match with Isa 12:2 and Ps 118:14, praising Yah "who has become my deliverance." There is some kind of direct literary relationship here, however it is to be explained.[53] Such cross-reference is not typical of the Song, and that fact makes it a weak basis for fixing the setting.[54] Otherwise, the defeat of Pharaoh at sea shares with Psalms and Jerusalem prophets certain notions of divine praise and awe:

- the pilpel of the verb *rwm* ("to exalt," v. 2b) with praise of Yahweh as king (cf. Ps 99:5, 9);[55]
- "the breath of your nostrils" (v. 8) in expression of overwhelming divine power, especially over water (Ps 18:16//2 Sam 22:16; cf. Job 4:9);
- the question "Who is like you among the gods?" resembles similar hymnic inquiries: "Who is a god like you?" (Mic 7:18); "Who is a great god like Elohim (/Yahweh)?" (Ps 77:14); "(Who) compares to Yahweh among the divinities [*běnê 'ēlîm*]?" (Ps 89:7); "Yahweh God of Hosts, who is like you?" (Ps 89:9).

This first part of the Song also derides the confidence of the enemy who counts on subduing a weaker foe. Where the singer can "pursue" (*rdp*) and "overtake" (*nśg*) his enemies in Ps 18:38, the Egyptian enemy counted on this combination in victory (Exod 15:9); an enemy pursues "my soul" so as to overtake the one praying in Ps 7:6 (cf. 143:3).[56] The verb *nšp* ("to blow") occurs only in Exod 15:10 and Isa 40:24, where it

---

[52] Mark Smith (1997: 206–14) makes the same division, with reference to Freedman (1980: 211), emphasizing the corresponding sounds and themes in both parts.

[53] Cross and Freedman (1997 [1975]: 54–56) consider this a later addition; Brian D. Russell (2007: 97–130) argues that the Song of the Sea influenced the other two compositions; cf. Stephen Russell (2009: 139–40).

[54] The waters of the Jordan River stand up like a "dam" (*nēd*) in Josh 3:13 and 16, though the verb there is different from Exod 15:8 (*'md* versus *nṣb*). This is not a full citation as in Exod 15:2a, though the Jordan River image may be inspired by the Song; this image is not found with the walls of water in the prose of Exodus 14.

[55] In Psalm 99, this is linked to "the holy mountain" as Zion (v. 2), not the reference of Exodus 15. This verb also appears in Ps 118:16 and 28, adding to the connection visible in Exod 15:2a.

[56] "Pursuit" of Israel by Egypt is repeated in Exod 14:4, 8, 9, and 23.

applies not to water and waves but to the desiccation of living plants by hot wind.[57]

As a set, these alignments with the language of the Psalms and Jerusalem prophets do not establish a clear date and setting, though they point to a probable connection to that city. The unusual character of the sharp verbal likeness in Exod 15:2a underscores a larger lack of inter-textual connection, a reference between texts. Likewise, these are not the stuff of ideology, reflections of a system of thought that can be delimited historically. That is, the Song does not partake of the emphasis in Isaiah 40–55 on the futility of images or restoration after suffering; there is no presence of Yahweh by *kābôd* or cloud. The character of the connections is related to function and perhaps to institution, or at least in some wider sense to scribal location. By function, I mean the generation of literature for praise and thanksgiving; and by institution, I refer to the Jerusalem temple and the scribes who knew its affairs. Whatever the best termin-ology to describe the features shared by biblical texts from Jerusalem circles, it is clear that the Song's shape as a hymn draws on language familiar to the Psalms collection. The reversal of fate for the overconfident enemy evokes the language of thanksgiving that follows prayer (v. 9). Neither of these aspects demands a specific date, and the text comparisons offer no clear pattern, early or late. Because the Bible preserves examples of similar images and words from texts likely written in Jerusalem, with the special coloring of Yahweh worship there, there is a strong possibility that Exod 15:1b–12 derives from those circles. This set of associations also allows centuries of institutional activity. Against the arguments that the Song of the Sea must have been composed after the two kingdoms, these comparisons are too open-ended for such a conclusion and other contents suggest earlier origins.

Pointing to such an older date and potentially a different setting, the material at the center of the great Egyptian failure stands independent of the Jerusalem writing circle. While the archaic features of grammar and spelling in Exodus 15 may support an early date,[58] it is above all the contrast of its core content to all other biblical writing that calls for

---

[57] The "many waters" of Exod 15:10 appear in the MT of Ps 93:4 for their noise, though the phrase is missing from the Greek and the Syriac, raising the possibility of influence from the Song.

[58] As observed by Stephen Russell (2009: 133), the proposed dates for the Song of the Sea diverge perhaps more widely than for any other biblical text, with Brian Russell still arguing for the 12th century, against the European near-consensus for a post-monarchic composition. Against the argument by Cross and Friedman (1997 [1975]) that the Song's

consideration as old tradition.[59] Two elements stand out in verses 1b–12. First, Egypt's defeat is portrayed in terms that have nothing to do with Israel or Judah, nothing to do with any people at all. No one in particular is present; no battle or conflict takes place. Pharaoh's chariots are overthrown by act of God, crossing a body of water, which if taken literally would mean during preparation for battle, moving forces into place rather than in the midst of battle. The main description in verses 3–7 presents little language shared with the Psalms and Isaiah, and the motif of Yahweh as warrior partakes of an ancient divine ideal shared by Baal at Ugarit and on view in the separate biblical motif of Yahweh marching from the distant south.[60] Likewise the opening verse matches word for word the Song of Miriam in verse 21, except the first person "I will sing" for the command to "sing," none of the contents drawing on demonstrable Jerusalem terminology. Second, Egypt is defeated by Yahweh acting as storm god. Yahweh does not defeat the sea like Baal at Ugarit or Marduk in the Babylonian creation myth, where Yamm and Tiamat are the enemy that stands in the way of the god's rule as king. The sea becomes Yahweh's weapon, collaborating with the force of his winds to swamp and swallow the Egyptian army. Neither of these elements belongs particularly to the Psalms or the Jerusalem prophets.

The second part of the Song is focused on the movement of the "people" into "the encampment of your holiness" (*něwê qodšekā*), a phrase without biblical precedent, not indicating late Jerusalem usage.[61]

---

language is systematically comparable to the Canaanite of Ugarit, Mark Smith considers that the "means of dating by appealing to archaic grammatical features is not a superior criterion, since the standards for dating poetry prior to the eighth-century prophets are poorly attested. The relative chronology offered for poems based on archaic grammatical features rests on the assumption that a density of features provides a reliable standard for dating" (1997: 222–23). Smith does consider that the language of Exodus 15 seems archaic relative to the earliest prophet writing. For a list of the archaic grammatical features, which occur in both parts of the poem, see Kloos (1986: 131–32).

[59] "Tradition" is the category at stake in the old renditions of the Midianite Hypothesis from the late 19th and early 20th centuries, as content picked up by the "authors" whose work and perspectives can be identified in the larger compositions of biblical writing, such as the Priestly "document" of the Pentateuch. Above, Schmid applies the same measure, with his refusal of any "traditional material" in the Song.

[60] Celebration of Yahweh's victory by his "right hand" in Exod 15:6 resembles the sequence in Ps 118:15–16, where this is shouted out. We will return to the question of Yahweh as warrior, below.

[61] The verb *nhl* as "to lead" (pi'el) appears only in writing from such Jerusalem circles (Isa 40:11; 49:10; 51:18; Ps 31:4; 2 Chr 28:19), but the destination combining *nāweh* with holiness has no match, certainly not tied to leading. Nothing requires that the particular verbal use be considered unique to Jerusalem or post-monarchic periods when other

I have followed Stephen Russell in rendering the destination as a "camp," associated with shepherds as in Ps 23:2. In the documentation from early second-millennium Mari, the cognate term *nawûm* defines equally the flocks of mobile pastoralists, the group of herdsmen responsible for them, and their encampments when they settle in one place with their livestock (Fleming 2004: 76 and n.186). Nothing in the poem portrays a single mass in procession, a notion that we only bring to the text from the prose of an exodus out of Egypt. Yahweh "leads" the people (v. 13) so that they "cross" (v. 16, verb *'br*) and are "brought" (verb *bw'*) and "planted" in "the highlands (*hār*) of your inheritance" (v. 17). As with the massed procession, we only perceive a "mountain" like Sinai or Zion by reference to other biblical writing. The people arrive at Yahweh's dwelling (*šebet*), then identified as "a sanctuary" (*miqdāš*) that "your hands gave form" (v. 17), so not human made.[62] The Song of the Sea only describes a space surrounded by four awe-struck peoples and the leaders who might otherwise oppose the people: "the rulers of the Philistines"; "the chiefs of Edom"; "the leaders of Moab"; and "the rulers of Canaan" (vv. 14b–15).[63] If there is an analogy from public worship, it might be the pilgrimage festival, which brings households from every part of a land to some sacred meeting place. As far as we can tell from the poetry of verses 13–18, the people come streaming in from every direction, not as a mass and not even at the same exact time. Like the portrait of Pharaoh's humiliation at sea in the first part of the Song, no other biblical text, poetry or prose, imagines such a summoning to the sacred highlands of Yahweh.

This second part of the Song presents further associations with the language of worship known from Jerusalem. The idea of divine "redemption" (verb *g'l*) is central to Isaiah 40–55, though in this case it is a buying

---

elements of the verse show no such association, including the combination of *nḥh* "lead" with *ḥesed* as instrument.

[62] The verb for the divine construction is the po'lel of *kwn*, "to be firm." In Solomon's repeated prayer of 1 Kings 8, Yahweh's *šebet* is "the heavens" as a whole that represent the same "place of your dwelling." In 1 Kgs 8:39, 43, and 49, the phrase is a genitive construct chain, *mēkōn šibtēkā*, whereas the identification of Yahweh with the "place" is accomplished by the preposition *l*- in Exod 15:17 (*mākōn lēšibtēkā*). From this verbal root for "sitting," the place could equally be for "your throne," and Yahweh is proclaimed king in verse 18. The ruling aspect does not change the sense of "place" as his whole personal domain, like "the heavens" in 1 Kings 8.

[63] The plurals attached to Edom and Moab apply specifically to leadership, so that the same is to be expected for "those who sit" (verb *yšb*), rather than "inhabitants" of Peleset and Canaan. See also Cross (1973: 130).

back from exile to Babylon.[64] In the Psalms, such redemption can be more global, establishing "your people" in the world (Ps 77:16; cf. 74:2).[65] "The peoples shook" in response to Yahweh's rule as king in Ps 99:1, with the same phrase introducing the four peoples of Exod 15:14–15, before Yahweh is proclaimed king in verse 18.[66] Here, both terminology and context in worship align. The writhing expressed by the noun *ḥîl* in verse 14b also "seizes" (verb *'ḥz*) opposing rulers in Ps 48:7, where the *hār* of Yahweh's holiness is definitely a mountain, as "Mount Zion" (vv. 2–3). "The greatness of your arm" also identifies Yahweh's power in Ps 79:11, there as a hope for prisoners. The verb *qnh*, which as a complement to *g'l* as "redeem" points to a financial transaction rather than "creation," appears also in Isa 11:11 and Ps 78:54, raising once again the question of relationship to Exodus 15. As a whole, the pilgrimage of Yahweh's people to his highland dwelling in Exod 15:13–18 is expressed in language much like what we find with Jerusalem worship, though the particular image has no counterpart.

As I understand it, the Song of the Sea has a compositional character quite different from that of the Song of Deborah, and this character makes the poem in Exodus 15 more difficult to date. The Song of the Sea lacks the detailed political geography in the Song of Deborah that sets it apart from so much of the Bible, and the Song of Deborah lacks the considerable verbal continuity with late monarchic and post-monarchic biblical writing from Jerusalem that some take to provide a setting. At the center of Exod 15:1–18 stand paired visions, each contrasting with any other biblical account. Egypt is defeated when Yahweh's winds drive mountainous waves, so that Pharaoh's chariots are tossed into the sea before battle; and an unnamed people assemble at Yahweh's likewise unnamed highland dwelling, traveling without interference from awestruck peoples on all sides. The poem may share in a larger tradition of Egypt's failure and the establishment of some part of the biblical people, or it may have informed later biblical composition, but the text at its center was not informed by any surviving rendition of these themes. I therefore take the Song of the Sea to be biblically old, independent of other composition in its main ideas, even as the similarities to later Jerusalem poetry point to

---

[64] See for example Isa 43:1, "fear not for I have redeemed you"; cf. 49:22, 25, 26.

[65] The language connections in Psalms 74 and 77 raise once again the question of textual relationship, which Brian Russell (2007: 114–16) considers a reinterpretation of the Song. If so, the reproduction of the Song of the Sea in connection with Jerusalem would be confirmed for later dates, whatever else might be its range of use.

[66] For Jerusalem poetry centered on Yahweh as king, see also Pss 93:1; 95:3; 97:1.

transmission in the capital of Judah in the last phase of the kingdom, carried afterward by the community that survived its fall. To my eye, the relationship between Isaiah 40–55 and the Song of the Sea is not direct and indicates no narrow match of setting or scribal circle.

This means that the Song of the Sea originated before the 8th century, when biblical composition begins on a larger scale. Language alone is too slippery a phenomenon to allow more precise dating of early poetry (Smith 1997: 222–23). The parallels to later writing are not superficial, no mere linguistic updating, so that either they reveal work in the late 7th or 6th centuries and beyond or they reflect continuity of scribal creativity with earlier periods. In principle, writing in Jerusalem could go back to the 10th century, given the chronology for two kingdoms that begins with Jeroboam and Rehoboam of separate northern and southern realms, and considering the possibility of a modest Jerusalem capital under David and Solomon.[67] The text offers too few points of reference to allow confidence regarding either its antiquity or its place of composition, also a question for the historical reflection below. Almost certainly, however, the Song of the Sea ended up in Jerusalem, where it may indeed, with Schmid, have been regarded as the prototypical Psalm.

The Song of the Sea and History

Nothing about the Song of the Sea indicates an account of events from a vantage close to the events. The historical interest of the text derives rather from its literary and conceptual independence from the prose accounts of escape from Egypt and crossing the Reed Sea in the book of Exodus. Pharaoh's army suffers its downfall without reference to any people present or participating, and the people who then go to Yahweh's highland home have no connection to Egypt. In juxtaposition, the establishment of the people in the highlands under Yahweh as king is made possible by Yahweh's prior put-down of Egyptian power.[68]

---

[67] Few doubt the existence of a founding king named David or of a capital at Jerusalem in the 10th century, though European scholars decline to imagine any connection between David and Israel. The Song of the Sea does not name Israel, and there is no historical barrier to locating such a composition in Jerusalem during the 10th or 9th centuries. See Carr (2011: chapter 12), on "Early Highland States and Evidence for Literary Textuality in Them."

[68] Stephen Russell was working on his New York University doctoral dissertation under Mark Smith as primary advisor at the same time as I was developing the book that became *The Legacy of Israel in Judah's Bible* (2012a). Our responses to Exodus

Whatever its dates for composition and transmission we must ask what the Song understands of the past when read on its own terms.

The Song of the Sea is an origins story. A people identified by its worship of Yahweh in a space inhabited by Yahweh comes to share this land and enjoy security from its neighbors after Pharaoh's defeat. The Song is the best expression of Ronald Hendel's assertion that the exodus preserves a "cultural memory" of Egypt's domination of Canaan during the dynasties of the New Kingdom.[69] The combination of Egypt as enemy and the origins of the people meant that the Song of the Sea *had* to be embedded in the Moses-exodus narrative. It is possible that the separate story of a "sea" episode originated in the poem and serial efforts to make it fit with the exodus/plague account (Fleming 2015: 485). In specific terms, the Yam Suph "Sea of Reeds" was embedded in the poem, unrelated to any exodus from Egypt or Egyptian geography, and it had to be adapted to Israel's presence in and escape from the land of the Nile.[70]

In the episode at the Sea of Reeds as recounted in the Song, Egypt's army is put out of action without reference to any human enemy, so we cannot picture any military conflict except in prospect. The four peoples named in verses 14b–15 are all groups that have territorial associations, effectively enclosing a particular space to be occupied by the human protagonists. Yet the groups are not identified by cities, and their leaders are plural, not individual kings. All are located in the Levant and benefit from Egypt's defeat. If as Hendel suggests, the poem recalls Egypt's rule in Asia, the removal of Egypt benefits these four as well as Yahweh's own people. Their terror reflects understanding that Yahweh's power is responsible for Egypt's failure, perhaps even that they likewise benefit. Given the actual history of conflicts with the Sea Peoples in the early 12th century, I once wondered whether such a setback could have lain behind the image of defeat at sea, thinking of the naval battle scene at Medinet

---

15 followed distinct lines while maintaining the same sense that Egypt's defeat could as easily be along the southern Levantine coast as at a site closer to Egypt. See Russell's reflections on history in his *Images of Egypt* (2009: 173–76).

[69] As Hendel (2015) acknowledges in his recent discussion of "The Exodus as Cultural Memory," this idea developed in stages (2001; 2005: 8–9). Na'aman (2011) brings a historian's detailed knowledge of New Kingdom Egypt in Canaan to the question of how Egyptian withdrawal could have left an impact on Iron Age populations, as preserved with Israel in the Bible.

[70] This exodus is what Stephen Russell explores as a specifically Israelite and Central Highlands tradition (2009: chapter 2).

Habu.[71] Yet little as the Song displays knowledge of Egyptian history or warfare, it attributes the defeat not to battle but to an act of God that did crucial damage to the primary means by which Egypt projected power into the Levantine lowlands, its chariotry. Even this hymn preserved in first-millennium Jerusalem literature appears, as asserted by Hendel, to recall Egypt's domination and the establishment of a "people" in the highlands after deliverance from this.

The character of the Song as a hymn to Yahweh indicates use in collective worship in a setting where Yahweh could be declared king. As already observed, several Jerusalem Psalms confirm that Jerusalem would suit this feature of Exodus 15, and this royal aspect is one feature that would make the Song at home in the kingdom of Judah and its capital. Further, the geography of Peleset (Philistia), Edom, and Moab frames the southern highlands, as far as the north extent of the Dead Sea, to suit what became the core territory of Judah, rather than Israel further north. "Canaan" in this context may be more coastal than inland. We would seem therefore to have an origins hymn composed at Jerusalem but with no interest in the institutions of that city: the temple and Yahweh's identification with Mount Zion; the Davidic monarchy; and even the city itself. As observed by Mark Smith (personal communication), this lack of interest could speak against a Jerusalem creation. Why produce a cultic "origins story" at Jerusalem without reference to celebrated elements of the city's Iron Age cult?

Based on lines of connection between Exodus 15 and Psalm 78, Smith himself (1997: 225–26) once cautiously linked the Song of the Sea to Shiloh, weighing the possibility "that Exod. 15.17 contains a Shilohite tradition for the divine mountain." He then cites Goldin (1971: 51–55), without advocacy, for the hypothesis that the poem could have been "fashioned as a Shilohite polemic against the southern royal ideology, specifically against the rival Solomonic temple of Jerusalem."[72] Such ruminations illuminate the interpretive situation nicely. Shiloh was destroyed permanently in the 11th century (Finkelstein 2013: 23–27), and it left a reputation that lies behind a variety of stories and story-fragments,

---

[71] For one rendition of this image, which appears in most descriptions of the Sea Peoples, see Dothan (1983: 10); from Nelson et al. (1930: pl. 37); cf. Nelson (1943).

[72] It is common to observe other geographical proposals, including Sinai and Gilgal, none with historically confirmed cult activity of appropriate time and scale (Smith 1997: 224; Stephen Russell 2009: 145–46).

all of which appear to be retrospective.[73] Both Psalm 78, which renders Jerusalem and Mount Zion the heir to Shiloh's earlier prestige (vv. 60, 68–72), and Jeremiah 7, which warns that Jerusalem's temple could follow the fate of Shiloh's shrine (vv. 12–15), display Jerusalem memories of a prior Shiloh sanctuary. These comparisons suggest that an origins story propagated at Jerusalem would recall an older sanctuary for Yahweh, not the temple on Mount Zion. Nothing in Exodus 15 identifies the mountain or its sacred *miqdāš* with Shiloh, and it may be that Psalm 78 and Jeremiah 7 draw on Shiloh lore that was not in the Song-writer's purview.

One solution could be that a writer at Jerusalem intended no specific shrine and allowed the idea of the *hār* as "highland" to take the place of any specific "mountain." Jerusalem and its institutions, as well as anything such a scribe could have known of Shiloh and its priests, may have held no connection for the writer between these and the Egypt miracle. The Song of the Sea looks back to a starting point before all of this. Yet the "people" who inherit the benefits of that divine act of creation are those who proclaim Yahweh king, most probably at the Jerusalem temple. These are a people defined only by their relationship to Yahweh, as "your people, Yahweh," where the crucial act of their establishment is described as *financial* liberation, redemption, and purchase, for movement into the highlands defined as *nāweh* and *hār*, "pasture" and "highland," a space for grazing flocks in the high ridge of the southern Levant.

THE PEOPLE DEFINED BY YAHWEH AND YAHWEH DEFINED BY A PEOPLE

The word "people" (*'ām*) and the name Yahweh are juxtaposed in both the Song of Deborah and the Song of the Sea to describe the whole body still identified with those who still maintain the poem: "the people of Yahweh" (*'am Yhwh*) in Judg 5:13; and "your people, Yahweh" (*'ammĕkā Yhwh*) in Exod 15:16.[74] The two phrases define a relationship between people and deity that is similar enough to warrant consideration

---

[73] In the biblical sequence, the first of these is in Josh 18:8–10, on the division of some territory into seven parts by lot. On this text, with the larger position of Shiloh in view, see Fleming (2018).

[74] Note the vocalization of *'am* with the pathaḥ expected with reading as a bound form, as opposed to the Masoretic *'ām*.

of both texts in connection to the question raised by the Egyptian evidence
for Yhw3 as a subdivision of the Shasu pastoralists, in a list of peoples
placed by Egypt in a defeated "land" of mobile herders. If by far the
oldest attestation of the name attests an inland pastoralist people, not a
god, how could a people give its name to the deity who became the focus
of worship in the two kingdoms of Israel and Judah?

Along with their basic likeness, the combination of Yahweh and people
in the two biblical poems is nevertheless carried out in significantly
different terms. This contrast may be expressed by observing that in the
Song of the Sea, the people are defined by Yahweh, while in the Song of
Deborah, Yahweh is defined by a people – a simplification to be elaborated in what follows. In Exodus 15, Yahweh himself takes two identities,
neither one defined by the people who worship him: he is a storm god like
Hadad/Baal; and he is king like Baal – not of the people but of the divine
world. Measured by the traditions of the region, Yahweh in the Song of
the Sea is indeed god of the storm, as asserted for his origin by Reinhard
Müller.[75] The Jerusalem associations of Exodus 15 locate the celebration
of Yahweh as storm god in that setting, also as observed by Müller, but
they do not explain the character of Yahweh in broader terms and outside
that setting.

The place of Yahweh in the Song of Deborah is at least as old as in the
Song of the Sea, and it supposes a completely different relationship to the
people portrayed. Like the Song of the Sea, the complete Song of Deborah
has been adapted to a monarchic need, this time for the northern kingdom
rather than the one centered at Jerusalem, and Yahweh's march from Seir
and Edom belongs to that adaptation. Even there, the earth drips and
shakes, but this is not the same figure who drives up massive waves by his
winds.[76] I have argued, however, that the opening hymn of Judg 5:2–11

---

[75] In the résumé of his monograph for *The Origins of Yahwism*, Müller (2017: 210–17)
compares the "monolatrous" attitude of certain psalms with what we find associated with
Kamosh and Moab in the 9th-century Mesha inscription. For Yahweh and the storm, he
cites (in this order) Psalm 29; a section of the royal Psalm 97; Ps 18:8–16*; Ps 77:17–20;
and Psalm 65. I name Müller for the interest of his part in the new "Berlin hypothesis" of
Yahweh's origin in the immediate neighborhood of Israel as a Hadad-like storm god, but
the identification is a commonplace (cf. van der Toorn 1999: 916).

[76] Smith (personal communication) observes that in the Baal myth from Ugarit, the storm
god also "marches" before opening the window in his new palace. In CAT 1.4 VII, having
struck down Sea (Yamm) and thus gained right to rule the gods as king and having won
permission from El to set up this rule with a palace, Baal goes from town to town, taking
them into his domain. By the verb *'ḥd* ("to take"), Baal is recognized as lord of each
settlement that makes up his realm, not a conquest but a recognition. (This non-military

refashions an older battle account that did not share its identification of the assembled groups as Israel. In this older poem, they fought as "the people of Yahweh" (v. 13), and if Yahweh had any other role it was to curse those who failed to join (v. 23). In contrast to Exodus 15, Yahweh does not win the battle for these allied groups; only "the stars fought from heaven" (Judg 5:20). This is not proof that Yahweh belongs only to the later adaptation of an original battle poem.[77] On the contrary, it is evidence for the relationship between Yahweh and the people in the Song of Deborah, as contrasted with the Song of the Sea. In Judg 5:12–22/23, Yahweh is defined by the people. He is not a king; he is not a warrior; and he is not a storm god.[78] Indeed, the function of Yahweh as deity is to bind the allies who fight under his name, and if the curse against *mērôz* (v. 23) belonged to the same older composition, it would present Yahweh in the same terms, active only as judge against any who fail to keep their commitments.

In the Song of Deborah, "the people of Yahweh" are an alliance for mutual defense, in this case against a corresponding alliance called "the kings of Canaan," also not named for a city but unlike the constituents of the Yahweh-people, defined as a coordinated set of individual rulers, with the term *melek* likely assuming separate cities.[79] None of the constituents of the people of Yahweh is defined by a city and there is no reference to

---

implication is elaborated in Smith and Pitard 2009: 663.) This combination of movement and (potential) rain is here the general result of Baal's new authority as king rather than an individual movement toward battle on behalf of a protected people.

[77] See especially Mark Smith (2014: 245); with others before him including Soggin (1981: 97).

[78] The battle account of Judg 5:12–22/23 has no interest in Yahweh's activity in the actual conflict, in contrast to the image of his going to war for Israel in verses 4–5. As part of the revision through introduction (Milstein 2016), verses 4–5 insert Yahweh directly into the battle as if to remedy a perceived lacuna in the program of the received poem. Of course he must have fought directly for the people, since they defeated the kings of Canaan as "the people of Yahweh."

[79] This is true for the *mātum* alliances of the Mari evidence: Ida-Maraṣ, Zalmaqum, and Šubartum (Fleming 2004: 124–8); cf. Brendon Benz's "Multipolity Decentralized Lands" in the Late Bronze Age evidence from el-Amarna (2016: 95–110). In Akkadian, the *mātum* as "land" defines a major political body with a territory that includes more than a single settlement, so an acknowledgment of and interest in extended geographical space, at the same time as it describes only people, never land without population or a region that could be inhabited by different political entities. In practice, a *mātum* is a "king-dom," or rather the population ruled by one or more kings as a united realm. In the context of Judg 5:12–22/23, "Canaan" is rendered such a united political entity by the definition of a set of kings that fight under that name, however temporary such a coalition may have been in reality.

"kings" among them.[80] Deborah and Barak serve to lead them into battle, jointly and without title; otherwise the group leadership is always plural, identified only with those who came (Machir, Zebulun, and Issachar), not with those absent. As an alliance, this people of Yahweh consists of collectives on all levels in a mode that in other contexts would be taken to indicate kinship-based social organization of the sort represented also by the "families" or "tribes" (*mhwt*) of the Shasu in Egyptian conception. Geographically, the alliance stands entirely north of Jerusalem, with Ephraim and Benjamin, perhaps along with Amalek, the southernmost contributor. Its members straddle the Jordan River, with Reuben and Gilead to the east, and they likewise straddle the Jezreel Valley, with the main body of concerned peoples to its north, in Zebulun, Issachar, and Naphtali, for all that the more distant Dan and Asher stay aloof.[81] Yet without the anachronistic recasting as Israel in the introductory hymn, the people of Yahweh named in verse 13 are "before Israel" in the sense that Israel is in no way identified with them, either as a participant or to name the whole, and we have no reason to force the name Israel onto the assembly of these far-flung groups.

The "people" in the Song of the Sea are equally distinct from Israel in that the name has no significance for the poem. The text cannot be dated securely, but if we locate it at Jerusalem with royal psalms that suggest the period of monarchy, the name of this southern kingdom is elusive before it appears as Judah in the late 8th century.[82] We cannot assume that the name Israel had any connection to the people who worship Yahweh in the Song when read independently of its secondary prose context. Indeed one significant ramification of reading the poem as if composed from the prose is that we would thereby bring all the categories and assumptions of that narrative into the poem, when the text by itself leaves us in a different conceptual world. Unlike the Song of Deborah, the Song of the Sea has no concern for alliance and likewise none for names. Only the god matters. Although we do encounter a "people" defined entirely by Yahweh, the character of that people as a social or political entity is

---

[80] This is one problem with reading *mērôz* as a city with "inhabitants" (see Monroe, forthcoming), along with the absence of any evidence for such a geographical name.

[81] We cannot be certain that the geography of these peoples matches what is indicated by other biblical writing, including the territorial allotments of Joshua 13–19, but there are no obvious problems except with the difficult people of Dan, who are associated with ships and the sea (cf. Stager 1989).

[82] See Fleming (2012a: 23); Leonard-Fleckman (2016: 231–32). Judah is listed in an Assyrian tribute list in 734; see text no. 11 in Cogan (2008: 56).

obscure. The combination of terminology in the Song of the Sea suggests some relationship to "the people of Yahweh" found as an alliance in the more northern setting of the Song of Deborah, but Exodus 15 stands at greater remove from any political reality. Was the *'am Yhwh* identity available also to groups in the southern highlands of the kingdom based at Jerusalem? We cannot tell from this evidence. At least this Jerusalem text warns us not to apply the details of Judges 5 too narrowly to the combination of Yahweh and people, as if this were the only configuration of its historical use. In the Song of the Sea, Yahweh is the god who grants the land of a particular "people," and he is the divine king who rules the people and the space they occupy.

YAHWEH THE GOD AND YHWȝ THE PEOPLE

Contemporary scholarly interest in the Shasu name Yhwȝ follows especially its potential relationship to the later god Yahweh. Certainly this is true for my undertaking here. Yet so far as the god is our object, we must keep a clear view of the distinction between the oldest evidence for Yahweh as divine name and anything else of potential relevance. The earliest inscriptional mention of the god Yahweh is in the Mesha inscription from about 840, with references to Yahweh of Teman and Yahweh of Samaria from Kuntillet 'Ajrud near 800, unless some go back further into the 9th century (Schniedewind 2017). In their finished forms, we cannot place either the Song of Deborah or the Song of the Sea at much older dates with confidence. The battle account in Judg 5:12–22/23, however, directly indicates an earlier setting before kings, and the recollection of Egypt's defeat in Exodus 15 hearkens back to an origin in a landscape that could be much different from that of the worshipping people.

When we consider this cluster of inscriptional and biblical evidence together, not attempting to extend it further into the Bible, we find Yahweh attached to the capitals of both 9th-century kingdoms, at Samaria and Jerusalem. In the tradition of Yahweh coming from Seir and Edom in Judg 5:4–5, he is "the god of Israel," probably our oldest evidence for the equation that comes to be global in the Bible (Stahl 2020).[83] In making the disparate allies of battle against Canaan a single

---

[83] Ted Lewis (personal communication) draws attention to the parallel Jerusalem title, "Holy One of Israel" (Williamson 2001), which would have followed a different path to combination with "Israel," which also would have occurred after the fall of the

Israel, however, the Song of Deborah reads the ambitions of the monarchy back onto older times, probably from the 9th-century Omrides (Stahl 2020). It is not likely that Yahweh as God of Israel and Yahweh of Samaria provide a way back into the earliest available character of this deity.

The Song of the Sea offers a different view of Yahweh, as windy storm god and king, indistinguishable from – and perhaps taking over – the character of Baal-Hadad. This Yahweh rules from the highlands, evidently in the space enclosed by Edom and Moab to the east and Peleset (Philistia) and "Canaan" to the west, but he is capable of stirring up the waters of a "Reed Sea" large enough to drown an army. He does not go to war from the distant south, like the God of Israel in Judg 5:4–5. By his resemblance to Baal, Yahweh of Exodus 15 looks too like a major Levantine deity to give confidence that he must take this form in other contexts, especially given the contrast with all levels of the Song of Deborah. Yahweh of Exodus 15 may assume worship at Jerusalem, though neither city nor temple holds any interest for the poem, leaving us to wonder what other settings could be imagined or in view. In this respect, the Song of the Sea contrasts with Psalms 97 and 99, which locate Yahweh's rule at Zion.[84]

In the same cluster of inscriptional and biblical evidence for the god Yahweh, we find a countercurrent that recalls the larger pattern from the search for this divine name. Yahweh has long seemed to come from off the grid of gods known to the region, in contrast to El and Baal, Asherah and Ashtart/Astarte. This made the Midianite Hypothesis of origin among desert peoples intrinsically attractive. Even without the Midianites and Kenites or interpretation of early poetry as proving Yahweh's southern origin, the name is absent from the religious geography of the urban Levant – as could be said for Kamosh of Mesha and the Moabites.[85] While Yahweh's association with the south does not

---

northern kingdom. Williamson dates the oldest instances in Isaiah (30:11, 12, 15; 31:1) to the circumstances of Sennacherib's invasion in 701. The "Holy One" title could have been associated with El and (then) Yahweh at Jerusalem without the Israel addition.

[84] Pss 97:8 and 99:2; note that Psalm 93 does not make explicit reference to Zion or Jerusalem, and it shares with Exodus 15 an emphasis on Yahweh's ability to roil the sea (93:3–4).

[85] One apparent exception would be Yau-bi'di, king of Hamath near the year 720, perhaps with Azri-Yau from the same setting slightly earlier, ca. 738 (Younger 2016: 492–99; cf. Dalley 1990). I would be inclined to explain any real worship of Yahweh at Hamath as deriving from origin in Israel and a political relationship with that kingdom.

settle a specific location for the origin of his worship, it does display non-urban affinities and a geographical orientation very different from that provided by the high mountains of Lebanon, Syria, and Anatolia. In the material from Judg 5:4–5 shared with Ps 68:8–9, the only geographical name is Sinai, not as mountain and not linked to exodus or law-giving but surely in the southern wilderness, as indicated by all its other literary connections.[86] By worship as Yahweh of Teman, the occupants of the Israelite outpost at Kuntillet 'Ajrud acknowledged the same southern interest of Yahweh, even as they represented the kingdom of Israel's own interests in and projection of power into that very region. This name demonstrates no special cult among peoples native to the region. The introductory hymn in the Song of Deborah locates Yahweh's southern interest in Seir and Edom, still in the back country far from Israel, sharing a perception already found in late 13th- and 12th-century Egypt that pastoralists mainly inhabited the south.

Two other elements of the early evidence point inland without specifying the south. The Mesha inscription identifies Yahweh with Israel in a way that may too quickly be matched with Kamosh and Moab. Because Kamosh is presented in terms so familiar to biblical conceptions of divine anger and beneficence, we can forget that only the Moabite god has such character in this text. The vessels of Yahweh are available for appropriation because of Israel's defeat, but the text never identifies Yahweh with Israel as such or with its kings. Location of a shrine at Nebo east of the Jordan River raises the possibility that Yahweh was worshipped there before Omri made it part of his kingdom. Such an eastern location aligns with the geography of Reuben and Gilead in the Song of Deborah, where these two represent the uncooperative eastern contingent (Judg 5:15–17).

With its political landscape devoid of Israelite kings, the battle account in the Song is the one biblical text that appears demonstrably older than the 9th century, at least in its institutional assumptions. I have argued that "the people of Yahweh" in verse 13, after the call to Deborah and Barak that opens the battle account, identify the participants without reference

---

[86] In a doctoral seminar at New York University, Noam Cohen developed the possibility of reading Sinai as a divine epithet rather than a place, reading with the Masoretic grammar of a gloss in the phrase *zeh sînāy*, which would still leave Sinai in the south. This solution would be more consistent than Michael Fishbane's notion (1985: 54–55) of a reference to the "mountains" of Judg 5:4. Smith (2014: 237 and n.13) objects that such a reading leaves a tension between the singular demonstrative pronoun and the plural referent as "mountains" (*hārîm*); another problem is the fact that *zeh sînāy* appears in both texts as part of the base version while only Judges 5 includes the mountains.

to Israel. This reading includes Yahweh in what I understand to be older than Exodus 15 and its storm god king, older than the God of Israel and Sinai, Seir, and Edom in Judg 5:4–5 and Ps 68:8–9. This relative antiquity does not provide an origin for Yahweh but it draws attention to a tradition that defines Yahweh by allied peoples in a social construction characteristic of kinship-based systems. Where the Midianite Hypothesis with its various iterations has looked south, this people of Yahweh brings us closer to Israel, not identified with it at the time of composition but encompassing groups that would come to be drawn into the kingdom of Israel, thus explaining how Yahweh could be brought into Israel based on existing relationships. At the same time, the Song of the Sea, with its probable Jerusalem composition and southern highland people, warns us not to restrict Yahweh's geography to suit the Song of Deborah alone. Yahweh of Judg 5:12–22/23 is a basis for political solidarity, a god who could unify allies to fight without being a war god. It is the stars that fight for the allies and the Kishon River that carries off their enemies.

Up to this point I have framed an account of Yahweh in early evidence entirely from biblical texts and first-millennium alphabetic inscriptions. Of course this textual base could be expanded, yet this small set supplies the essentials.[87] In developing my analysis, I have made one further piece of potential evidence an engine for new thought, a point of reference for both reconsideration of the Midianite Hypothesis and construction of new possibilities. This is the Egyptian identification of a Yhwȝ subunit of Shasu-land in the early 14th century. Because the later rendition of the Shasu-land list begins with what is often identified as Seir, also one of the places in Judg 5:4, this much older Egyptian evidence has been treated as confirmation of the renovated Midianite Hypothesis, proving that the name Yhwȝ literally belongs to the southern wilderness, whatever it might mean in the Shasu context. Aside from the geography, the framework of borrowing by "Israel" from peoples foreign to it may often be taken for granted. In Chapter 2, I expressed deep doubt about the location of "Shasu-land" in the distant south, as if identical to Edom and Seir of later Egyptian texts. More crucial, however, is my identification of Yhwȝ as a unit of Shasu-land, so what I have called a "people," a category that focuses on a social and political body that acts under the given name, whatever its relationship to physical land. The Yhwȝ people were one of

---

[87] For an extensive collection of evidence relevant to Yahweh, see the forthcoming work of Theodore Lewis on "God" (2020).

four or five major components of the entire Shasu country as encountered by Egypt in the early 14th century. In offering a new interpretation of the Egyptian Shasu evidence, not focused on the south as such, I nonetheless accept the likelihood that this Yhwȝ stands in historical lineage with the later divine name so that the relationship must be explained. Correspondingly, Yhwȝ of Shasu-land would be by far the oldest evidence for the name, even where it explicitly names a people, not a god, and this makes it a good starting point for positive construction of an interpretation of Yahweh before Israel.

My analysis of "Yahweh before Israel" grapples with shards of a past that is largely lost to us. Thanks to Egypt's presence in Asia during the late second millennium, we have Yhwȝ of Shasu-land from the early 14th century and Israel from the late 13th, along with the Amarna letters for Egypt's vassals in Canaan from the mid-14th century and assorted texts that treat the kingdom's activities in the region. When it comes to names and identities, whether of peoples or of gods, we appropriately rely on texts, and the Egyptian sources for this early period only provide names for consumers of information foreign to them, necessary only to record the details of military adventures and travel. Egyptian geography was a mix of indigenous designations, Egyptian commonplaces with precise reference, and stereotyped generalities, including the "Shasu" of our interest. It should be no surprise that we lack so much of the region's geography as it would have been perceived by its own inhabitants. Likewise, the gap between earliest mention of the god Yahweh and Yhwȝ of Egyptian reference should not be surprising, both for its length in time and its contrast of types. There is bound to be much between these that we cannot explain.

The central question remains: How could the name of a people become the name of a god? Others have observed that divine names can sometimes take the form of human theophoric personal names, like Ikrub-El, Ikšudum, and others from cuneiform writing.[88] Johannes de Moor has already interpreted Yahweh as an abbreviated form of *Yahweh-El, "May El be present," "probably the divine ancestor of one of the

---

[88] See Stol (1991: 203): "Some of these names not only look like personal names but actually are names used by human beings ... Here, we are confronted with something new in Assyriology: down-to-earth human beings being presented as gods. The best solution is to assume that deceased members of a family, as 'patriarchs' or 'ancestors,' could acquire this status under circumstances not known to us."

proto-Israelite tribes."[89] Van der Toorn (1999: 914) considers this intrinsically implausible:

... though theoretically possible, it is difficult to believe that the major Israelite deity, venerated in a cult that was imported into Palestine, was originally a deified ancestor. Though such gods are known, they are never found in a leading position in the pantheon. Their worship tends to remain local, as an ancestor is of necessity the ancestor of a restricted group.

Keeping in mind the obstacles intrinsic to work with such limited data, any exploration of the space between Yhw3 of Shasu-land and Yahweh the god must consider the conditions and process that would be required. First, I underscore the social continuity between the Shasu people and the "people of Yahweh" in the Song of Deborah. What the Egyptians call "Shasu-land" is their interpretation of a coalition consisting of the listed names, which I understand as "families" or "tribes" (*mhwt*) based on texts that envision Shasu divisions this way. Such alliance of collectives resembles markedly what is depicted in the Song of Deborah. Further, the Song's definition of the alliance as the *'am Yhwh*, which could be rendered the "Yahweh-people" as well as "the people of Yahweh," identifies deity with human community so closely that without the curse of verse 23 and the larger biblical text we could imagine *Yhwh* to represent a social-political entity, a "people."

If Yhw3 of Shasu-land was a people, and the name does stand behind the later god Yahweh, then we would have to imagine that at some point, for some population identified with the Yhw3/Yhw(h) name, the people understood themselves to have as a divine patron a god so fully identified with them as to share their name. As will be explored in the concluding chapter, there is some evidence for the identification of a community by a divine name taking the form of a personal name, evidenced by Yasaddi-el in the Mari documentation. For the substantial scale of such a Yahweh people we would have to turn to Ashur of the early second millennium, naming collective city and deity equally. This interpretation of the name would not imagine the name as a family "ancestor" any more than Ashur must be the ancestor of the Upper Mesopotamian city. The name in question would identify the people before it was understood to correlate also to the god whose concerns corresponded perfectly with that people.

---

[89] See the 1990 edition of de Moor's *Rise of Yahwism* (244); in the 1997 version, de Moor explains the name as ultimately pointing to El himself, so giving up what could be seen as a narrowly construed derivation.

Yhwȝ of Shasu-land would identify such a people without reference to deity, and the eventual god Yahweh should not be identified with all Yhw(h) people going back to their beginning. This would be a secondary and specific development.

Finally, the appearance of a god Yahweh in association with a Yhw(h) people is to be understood as separate from Israel. For all that scholars remind us regularly that Israel in the Merenptah stela is designated a people rather than a city, with an Egyptian determinative different from those for Ashkelon, Gezer, and Yanoam, Israel is in no way associated with the Shasu, who make no appearance in the text.[90] So far as both Israel and Yahweh are already mentioned in Egyptian evidence, they suggest different realms. Yhwȝ was one of the Shasu peoples, a name that was intelligible only in relation to these back-country herding groups. Israel was associated with three Canaanite cities of the accessible low-lands, on and near the Mediterranean in the case of Ashkelon and Gezer, perhaps in the Jordan River Valley for Yanoam.[91] Given the location of the lesser Israel of Saul (and David) in a more limited highland space adjacent to the Jezreel Valley, joined to Ephraim/Benjamin to its south (Fleming forthcoming), Merenptah's Israel most easily lay somewhere in the same space – a contrast to where Egyptians expected to find the Shasu. Closer to the time of Merenptah, the revised list for Shasu-land from the 13th-century reign of Ramses II appears to give first place to Seir, in the southern inland. If El and so Elohim was a (if not "the") god of Israel going back as far as Merenptah, then Yahweh appears to represent a second dimension of the population that came to be included in the large kingdom.

In this respect, Yahweh's background before Israel becomes crucial to the separate question of what lay behind the Israelite kingdom itself. Although it is standard to speak of "Israelite origins," or as Avraham Faust (2006) defined it, "ethnogenesis," the biblical evidence alone, with its trove of individual group names, suggests that "Israel" was only one in a landscape of peoples that came to define the large kingdom. Philip Davies usefully distinguished between "historical Israel" and "biblical Israel" (Davies 1992), but in fact, "historical Israel" in strict terms

---

[90] See the earlier discussion of the Merenptah reference; the Shasu make no appearance in the text, either in the odd Asian elaboration with Israel at the end of the stele or in any connection to the Libyan concerns of the main text. As I understand both terms, Israel is not to be regarded as a Shasu name in the way developed by Na'aman (2011).

[91] For review of the evidence and previous literature, along with a novel interpretation of his own, see Na'aman (1977).

appears to have grown substantially under its early rulers, so that groups not originally connected with that name were later incorporated. By the sheer complexity of its layered record, the Bible provides the best available evidence for this historical transformation and what may have belonged to its earlier stages. Yahweh reflects one part of that external reality.

The Early Character of the God Yahweh

After respectful consideration of Amorite evidence for personal names with the Yaḥwi-/Yawi- verbal element, Karel van der Toorn (1999: 914) concludes that "though theoretically possible, it is difficult to believe that the major Israelite deity, venerated in a cult that was imported into Palestine, was originally a deified ancestor." Gods that originated as human ancestors tend to be worshiped locally, for a restricted group. Having declined this possibility, van der Toorn turns to other composite names, such as Rakib-'el (Charioteer of El) or Malakbel (Messenger of Bel), which represent subordinates to the great gods. Albright, Cross, Dijkstra, and de Moor all proposed explanations that identify Yahweh with El, a deity of unassailable prominence, but van der Toorn (915) finds it unexpected to have the proper name of a major god replaced by an activity attributed to him. More deeply, with two different divine names in play and contrasting associations, the very notion of an original identification raises doubt.

In the end, as van der Toorn weighs the possibilities, Yahweh's storm god associations offer better prospects. This is based in part on the Bible's notion of conflict with Baal (1999: 916),[1] and also on images of rain: the clouds dripping water at Yahweh's advance from Seir in Judg 5:4–5; and the clouds, water, and thunder that accompany him in Ps 18:12–14. Mark Smith also follows the analogy of Haddu/Baal, less for the storm than for his standing at

---

[1] Van der Toorn cites Mettinger (1990). Since van der Toorn, the decisive rejection of the Midianite Hypothesis by Christoph Levin and others has likewise identified Yahweh as a storm god: Levin (2000); Müller (2008). In support of a local central highlands origin in something like this mode, see also Köckert (2001); Pfeiffer (2017). Note that Römer (2015: 34) prefers a storm-oriented etymology for Yahweh as "he who blows."

Ugarit as a younger-generation warrior god, which Smith assigns to the second level of a regional pantheon both at Ugarit and in pre-monarchic Israel, where El and his consort Asherah would occupy the "first tier."[2] "Like Baal in the Ugaritic pantheon, Yahweh seems to be an outsider warrior-god who makes his way to the top of the pantheon" (Smith 2004: 106). Both Baal at Ugarit and Yahweh in Israel increased in importance, tending to over-shadow El, at least in some contexts. With van der Toorn, Smith approves Mettinger's conclusion that Yahweh was first a southern storm god, and then he asks how such a conclusion would suit the southern terrain. In contrast to the climate in the northern Levant, the region of Seir and Edom that is on view in the Song of Deborah has much lower annual rainfall:

> Judges 5:4–5 reflects a god that provide[s] rains, but does this rain necessarily reflect the standard repertoire of a coastal storm-god, or does the passage reflect the storm and flash floods of desert areas? And if the rain does reflect the natural rains associated with a coastal storm-god, then might the depiction in Judges 5 reflect a secondary adaptation of the god's presentation to the coastal-highland religion? Battle and precipitation may have been features original to Yahweh's profile, but perhaps Yahweh's original character approximated the profile of Athtar, a warrior- and precipitation-producing god associated with mostly inland desert sites with less rainfall.
>
> (2001a: 146)

Smith wonders whether the constant comparison with Ugarit has made El and Baal the measure of Yahweh's "original profile" in a way that leads us to miss other aspects from the southern setting. The particular features of Yahweh that render him a storm god like Baal/Hadad, such as the violent lightning of Psalm 29, may be secondary. This secondary align-ment with the prestigious storm gods of Damascus and the early first-millennium Phoenician cities is what Christoph Levin, Reinhard Müller, and others are attributing to Yahweh's original character.[3]

IN SEARCH OF ANALOGY

The approach that I have set out in the preceding pages demands a fresh accounting of Yahweh's early character, defined by options different from

---

[2] Smith lays out this interpretive scheme in *The Origins of Biblical Monotheism* (2001a: 45–53), in sections on "The Divine Council and Its Four Tiers"; and "Israel and the Tiers of the Pantheon." See also his discussion of pre-monarchic Israel in *The Memoirs of God* (2004: 106–7).

[3] This last formulation reflects comments by Smith on a previous manuscript of this book, once more a constant point of fruitful dialogue.

the above. In the Egyptian lists, Yhw3 of Shasu-land indicates the divine name's older identification with a social and political entity. This need not be associated with the south in particular, but more importantly, the "origins" of Yahweh will not be explained by separating "Israel" from some source that is external and foreign to it. El is most likely the first "god of Israel," and Israel of the early Iron Age coexisted with groups that came to be included in the later Iron Age kingdom by that name. Equally, I do not find Yahweh's associations with rain or storm to be demonstrated as original to his worship. Left to the evidence for the divine name alone, conclusions about Yahweh's first profile seem highly tentative, even when based on a much wider sampling of the primarily biblical material than I have undertaken. I start from the Egyptian evidence. Once Yhw3 is identified as a group within a larger Shasu population organized by kinship-based structures, what the Bible and common parlance would call a "tribe," the name of that people derives most easily from an abbreviated personal name, not necessarily as an ancestor, yet certainly conceived in relation to a single person, in familial or kinship terms.

The "origin" of Yahweh remains obscure – geographically, conceptually, and historically. We know neither where to locate the Yhw3 people of what the Egyptians called Shasu-land nor how such a group related to geographical space. They need not have appeared in only a single, circumscribed territory.[4] We do not know how a people could have given its name to a god and what the relationship of the first god Yahweh may have been to a community that worshiped him – though the discussion of South Arabia and Moab, below, aims to define a context for such connection. Was Yahweh one of several gods significant to his first worshipers, and how would Yahweh have related to any others in play? Further, we cannot date Yahweh's first appearance as a god and explain the circumstances that would have provoked such a development. There is

---

[4] Working to break down models by which mobile pastoralists are isolated from "urban and agricultural society," Anne Porter (2009) proposes that kinship ties could form the basis for integrating long-range herding with settled farming in single communities, as illustrated in part by the Yamutbal at Andarig in the Mari evidence and the Emutbal at Larsa. For Porter, the appearance of such names across distance can indicate contemporary relationship, not just transfer of names by migration. In the case of the name Der, she proposes – provocatively – that the name well known from the Balih River and then near Mari also shows a social link to downstream Mesopotamia by its appearance east of the Tigris. Even if the last example has another explanation as a geographical homonym, the connection between Der of the Balih and Der along the Euphrates is solid, and Porter's interpretation in a single time and social fabric opens up important possibilities for understanding the appearance of the same names in more than one place.

no reason to insist that the Yhw₃ people worshiped a god named Yahweh from the moment of their inception; the form of the name as the verbal element in a type familiar to second-millennium Amorite language accounts for Yhw₃ as a human identity without reference to divinity.

The Great Gods of Mesopotamia

In spite of the obstacles that render futile any search for Yahweh's specific origins, Yhw₃ of Shasu-land and its identity as a people provide important constraints for understanding who the god was understood to be before he had to be explained in relation to El or Baal. Van der Toorn's characterization of ancestor gods as unacceptably limited by their narrow interest must be weighed cautiously. Let us begin with two of the most prominent political gods of Mesopotamia, to reconsider the notion that major deities must originate in a major divine type.

Marduk is known first of all as the god of Babylon, whatever his origins, and this early significance for a specific population did not keep him from becoming one of the great gods of ancient Mesopotamia, with the rise of the Old Babylonian kingdom and the spread of Babylonian influence on writing and religion.[5] In late third-millennium and early second-millennium Mesopotamia, Enlil held special authority among the gods as their leading authority without clear connection to the powers of nature. We cannot rule out historical scenarios for the increased importance of a given god because its original type strikes us as inadequate to such transformation. At 18th-century Mari, Itur-Mer was identified with the city in a way that cannot be described as having "restricted scope" (van der Toorn), in that he was invoked to represent the capital as such in combination with Dagan as regional god of the Euphrates River.[6] Mari's political and religious history never developed along lines that gave Itur-Mer the lasting visibility of Marduk, but though the god Itur-Mer takes the form of a full personal name, this does not represent a type that prevented such prominence.

---

[5] The most important work on Marduk, focused on the second millennium BCE, is Sommerfeld (1982; cf. 1987–90). For a recent review of Marduk's character, see Brisch (2016). The "original" character of Marduk appears to be as obscure as that of Yahweh. He has an early association with incantations, partly through an eventual identification with the god Asalluḫi, but it is not clear whether this connection preceded that alignment.

[6] Itur-Mer is called "king of Mari," with a particular role in presiding over oaths (Durand 1995: 160–61). Nakata (2011) calls him "the second most important deity of the kingdom of Mari" based on his pairing with Dagan as the divine assistance essential to the realm's survival.

Another analogy may be found in Aššur, the god of the city by the same name. As particularly bound to a single urban settlement, Aššur resembles Marduk and Itur-Mer with an obvious difference: deity and city share the name. Like Marduk, Aššur came to lead a pantheon and to hold similar importance, though the singular identification of divine and city name contributed to rendering the god less easily embraced by other communities in contact.[7] Already in the earliest second millennium, as attested in the letters found at Kanesh in ancient Anatolia, Aššur was still just an important merchant town and its god a divine embodiment of its population.[8] Although the god Aššur has been interpreted as originally defined by place, perhaps even a visible feature of the city site, there is no basis for separating city and god in the evidence for the earliest second millennium.[9]

If we reach back further, however, the primacy of Aššur as god of the city Aššur is at least uncertain. A dedicatory plaque from the late third-millennium ruler Ititi, preserved centuries later in the Ištar temple at Aššur, suggests the particular importance of the goddess for his success: "Ititi, the ruler, son of Ininlaba, dedicated (this object) from the booty of Gasur to the goddess Ištar."[10] The Ištar temple at Aššur goes back to the early third millennium, in the Early Dynastic period.[11] According to Beate Pongratz-Leisten (2015: 115–16), "Finds from the Sumerian period in the same temple prove that Ištar's cult preceded the cult of the god Aššur

---

[7] For systematic investigation of the "Aššur" identity as it is transformed between the early and later parts of the second millennium, see Valk (2018). In the context of the Assyrian merchant community that straddled the city of Aššur and the Anatolian city of Kanesh, see also the discussion of "Old Assyrian Collective Identity" in chapter 3 of Highcock (2018).

[8] "The very fact that the city shares its name with its patron deity further blurs the boundaries between human flesh, divine flesh, and the city, and earlier Assyrian royal inscriptions are often inconsistent in their use of the divine determinative (DINGIR) and place determinative (KI), conflating god and city" (Highcock 2018: 128–29). Highcock illustrates this observation by a collection of the spellings preserved in the inscriptions of Erišum I (20th century).

[9] See the long note 322 in Highcock (2018: 129), where she addresses this question in relation to specific orthographies. The later king Šamši-Adad I demarcates sharply his own identity as "governor of Aššur" with the divine determinative for Aššur as deity and Aššur the place as "my city." She concludes, "I would argue that this outsider consistency supports the argument that native Assyrian rulers did not conceive of the city and the god as entirely separate entities as evidenced by their purposefully ambiguous writings of Aššur." For the notion that this identification of city and god was secondary to the old *numen locus*, see Lambert (1983).

[10] See the translation and discussion in Pongratz-Leisten (2015: 105–7).

[11] Bär (2003a, 2003b); and Meinhold (2009). Pongratz-Leisten (2015: 115) comments, "Ištar's central role in the cultic life of Aššur is evident by the Early Dynastic period, notably in the discovery in the Ištar temple of a relief plaque that depicts her naked in a frontal position, which is similar to her representation on the much later Hasanlu bowl." Valk (2018: 106) observes that the nearby cities of Nineveh and Arbela had early primary cults for Ištar as well.

by at least a millennium."[12] The interest of this process for Yahweh is the fact that city appears to have existed before its collective community was given divine expression as a god by the same name. So far as Yhw₃ of Shasu-land was a people not evidently identified with deity, the temporal priority of community to god would apply to both Aššur with city and Yahweh with people.

It is fruitless to attempt characterization of the original Marduk or Aššur as senior or younger generation deities. In Babylonian conception, the great gods, including Marduk as divine sponsor of the city as such, call and command kings, endow them with gifts of wisdom and strength, and may even provide sweeping help, but they do not come to battle on the king's behalf.[13] For the Assyrian kings, we do not see reference to direct divine accompaniment in battle until the period of expansion in the late second millennium, and it is Ištar who goes at the head of the army.[14] The gods Marduk and Aššur support the rulers of their respective cities not from any particular divine specialty but because this is the role of such a patron god of a particular population, and the glory of that support grows with the people's success. Neither began, so far as we can tell, as a young warrior god like Ninurta in Mesopotamia or Haddu/Baal as envisioned in Ugaritic literature. Both end up like El, as "heads" of pantheons, dominant over all other gods. Yet the same could be said for Yahweh, without explaining his early nature.

South Arabia and Moab

In her 2007 article on "war-*ḥērem* traditions" and "national identity," Lauren Monroe assembles a set of features attached to written accounts of sacralized annihilation of a defeated enemy. She finds these in only three sets of data: the 9th-century Mesha stele from Moab; a South Arabian text from the end of the 8th century (also BCE); and parts of

---

[12] In a single text from the Ur III period (late third millennium), the name of the city is written with determinatives for both deity and place (the governor Zarriqum, text A.o.1003.2001 in Grayson (1987). The oldest levels for the Aššur temple at the site only go back to the beginning of the second millennium (Haller and Andrae 1955: 9–14; cf. Valk 2018: 105–7).

[13] This conclusion follows from the collected royal inscriptions of the early second millennium (Frayne 1990).

[14] See the commemoration of rebuilding the palace at Aššur under Tukulti-Ninurta I (13th century), *KAH* II, no. 58.

the biblical material, especially in Joshua 8. The commonalities are extensive and precise (2007: 335):

- large-scale destruction especially by fire;
- at least a segment of the population killed and consecrated to deity;
- resettlement focused on the empty towns left by the destruction;
- erection of a cult installation.

Seeking an explanation for the geographical and social pattern that includes only these three settings, Monroe proposes a particular alignment of "people, land and god" that accompanies what she identifies as a "tribal, inland Palestinian setting with cultural connections extending into the South Arabian peninsula" (341). I begin with Monroe's piece because the same combination of settings pertains to our pursuit of Yahweh as god in relation to Yhw₃ as an earlier people.

Moab shows features of politics and religion that align with South Arabian evidence beyond the *ḥērem* investigated by Monroe. The written evidence from South Arabia, which now appears to go back as early as the 11th or 10th century BCE and which continues through the first millennium, is massive compared to the Northwest Semitic of the Levant and remains a relatively untapped resource for biblical scholars.[15] With my comments on society and religion I only scratch the surface of material that is entirely new to me. It is clear, however, that the role of religion and the forms of its practice in politics and society open up vistas that begin to suggest a context for how god and people may relate in their naming and in the familial bonds that connect them.[16]

Christian Robin (2012: 12) describes the category of gods that serve and are based on political and social organization as "institutional," and

---

[15] Stein (2011: 1042) counts roughly ten thousand published South Arabian inscriptions in "monumental" script, mostly on stone, including about 1,500 dedicatory texts and 800 building inscriptions. In recent years these have been augmented by texts in "minuscule" script, written on wooden sticks and palm-leaf stalks, with ¹⁴C dates that push dates from the late 8th century back to the 11th or 10th. In one study of the minuscule texts in a Leiden collection, Stein (2015) reviews 380 texts in Sabaean, Minaean, or undifferentiated South Arabian, breaking these down into legal/economic, letters, scribal exercises, and cult praxis.

[16] The character of South Arabian religion as embedded in society has been a particular concern of Christian Robin (e.g. 2012, 2018). I thank Robert Hoyland for pointing me in the right direction in acquiring a beginning familiarity with this material. John Huehnergard sent me to the new work on the minuscule texts and the South Arabian language by Stein. My ideas here represent only lines of potential application, with an outsider's appreciation of how much I have not fully grasped and how much more the material demands.

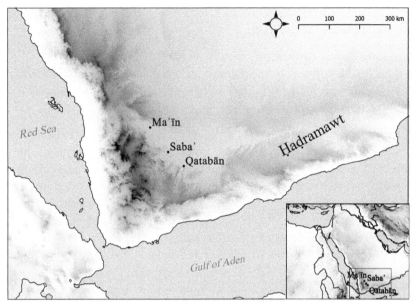

FIGURE 15 South Arabia in the first millennium BCE
(Map by Kyle Brunner)

it is at this level that we find the comparisons relevant to the Bible's
"people of Yahweh" and the older Yhw3 people of Shasu-land. Each of
the South Arabian polities with such large-scale structures can be called a
"kingdom," like Mesha's Moab and unlike the "people of Yahweh" in
the Song of Deborah, and the religious elements of this public domain
have as one purpose to bind the king into a larger social and political
fabric.[17] The best documented of these is Saba', but Ma'īn is equally old,
followed by Qatabān and Ḥaḍramawt (Figure 15). In the context of the
South Arabian kingdoms, what may be called "tribes" or "communities"
(Avanzini 2016: 57) are completely integrated into the settled landscape,
with territorial associations that could be fit into the lines of monarchic
rule. "Nomads" lived on the margins of these kingdoms, not as an

---

[17] Avanzini (2016: 49–57) addresses this large scale of South Arabian political formation as
"states," in an analysis that could be taken to confirm Anne Porter's (2012) insistence
that tribe and state cannot be relegated to separate levels of evolutionary development,
though Avanzini uses both terms without hesitation. For Avanzini, the "state" has three
bases: the god, the king, and the tribe.

essential part of them, and wealth was generated especially by trade.[18] The roots of potential mobility in these kinship structures may be visible in what Avanzini translates as the "lineages" into which the large "tribes" are divided, using a word for "tent" that is familiar from Biblical Hebrew (*'hl*).[19]

RES 3945, which Monroe discusses for its reference to the "war-*ḥērem*," offers one Sabaean example of a larger pattern in the set of South Arabian gods with a political function that integrates the ruling right of kings with communal/collective identities. The gods include Almaqah of Saba', 'Amm of Qatabān, and Sayīn of Ḥaḍramawt. I follow here Robin's 2018 study of this political-religious type, which makes 'Amm and Qatabān the point of reference while emphasizing the pattern. In each of the major South Arabian kingdoms, the great god ("grand dieu") was always a major deity, though 'Athtar was consistently preeminent, and local communities could regard other gods as having equal or higher status. The roles of Almaqah for Saba' and 'Amm for Qatabān applied specifically to each people as a kingdom, in a kind of alliance of communities in agreement to royal rule.[20]

At Qatabān, 'Amm is both the "great god" of the kingdom and "the ancestor of an ensemble of groups called the 'Descendants of 'Amm'" (*wld 'm*).[21] For Robin, "There is little doubt that the 'Descendants of 'Amm' are a vast coalition of communes constituted by Qatabān and led by its king."[22] We know that the "Descendants of Almaqah" assembled annually to worship the god at the capital of Marib, and a similar practice

---

[18] Given my experience with the integration of mobile pastoralist and settled agricultural populations in the kingdoms of the Mari landscape, I wonder whether there is more to discover in the social arrangements of the South Arabian kingdoms. Perhaps the Arabian desert environment led to a sharper separation of pastoralists from the settled space, with an economic contribution smaller than what could occur in early Mesopotamia.

[19] Avanzini (2016: 58) observes that individuals are identified first by patronym (or of "an ancestry"), then by "sub-lineage" as *'hl* or *ḏ* ("belonging to," the relative pronoun), then by "lineage" (*'hl*), and finally by community or tribe (*s²'b*).

[20] Robin (2018: 97–98) observes that while three cult places were consecrated to Almaqah at the Sabaean capital of Marib, in the mountain "communes" of the kingdom, which were governed by autonomous "princes" (*qyl*), only three of twelve had Almaqah as the lead god.

[21] Robin (2018: 104), "l'ancêtre d'un ensemble de groupes appelés la 'Descendance de 'Amm'."

[22] "Il ne fait donc guère de doute que la 'Descendance de 'Amm' est une vaste coalition de communes constituée par Qatabān et dirigée par son roi." Robin uses the French category of the "commune" for the building blocks of a collectively constructed society, from the French structure of the truly local communities from which all larger governmental administration is built.

is likely with 'Amm at Qatabān (2018: 105). Qatabanian inscriptions from the 6th to the 1st century identify the king as *"mukarrib* of Qatabān and of (all) the Descendants of 'Amm," and where some renditions add more groups, these seem to be as members of the *wld 'm* (106). Robin concludes (134),

> The "Descendants of 'Amm" probably designate, originally, the ensemble of groups for which 'Amm was the great god. When they are mentioned for the first time, in the great inscription of Yatha''amar at Ṣirwāḥ (end of the 8th c. BCE), they are an alliance of small kingdoms organized and led by the king of Qatabān. Thereafter, the contours of the descendants of 'Amm seem to merge with those of the kingdom of Qatabān, which would have progressively annexed these small kingdoms.[23]

Approaching the South Arabian setting as an outsider familiar with the social patterns and history of the Levant and greater Mesopotamia, I am struck by the kinship terminology embedded in both the collective "Descendants of 'Amm" and the divine name itself, cognate with Hebrew *'ām*. Robin renders this as "(paternal) uncle" (103), consistent with common interpretation of the old Semitic word, but Durand (1997–2000) may translate it better as the more sweeping "forefather" (French "aïeul"). Robin wonders whether 'Amm could be a way of naming a god whose old designation is forgotten, and whether or not this is true, the term belongs to human kinship and recalls the fact that Almaqah of Saba' and other South Arabian gods bear names that suggest human sentence-names.[24] Each kingdom consists of allied groups conceived as the "descendants" of the god that unifies them under such rule, a mechanism that identifies the combined people of Qatabān or Saba' as the literal family of the binding deity. In each case, the terminology of the *wld 'm* and the *wld 'lmqh* is old, visible in the earliest documentation for Qatabān and Saba'. This indicates that the kings latch onto conceptions that already exist, and the role of these political/"institutional" gods would appear to derive from unity under divine "descent" that already served the associated groups. The "Descendants of 'Amm" would then have been such before kings.

None of the South Arabian evidence offers a case like Aššur, where the names of god and people are equated. We do encounter, however, a

---

[23] I translate "se confondre" ("to confuse") as "merge," with reference to the outlines of the collective.

[24] See also 'Aranyada' of Našq (e.g. Stein 2015: 206; cf. Arbach 2011: 191); Yada'ismu of Haram (Mathieu-Colas 2017). I have not encountered an interpretation of the name Almaqah, written with initial aleph (*l'l*).

structure that envisions a deep alignment of the two as kin, where the people are the family of the god, who is what Ryckmans (1989: 162) calls a "mythical ancestor." So far as Yhw₃ of the Egyptian evidence was one of the major Shasu groups, and some centuries later we find a god Yahweh with the same name, the South Arabian notions of political unity from divine descent could provide a framework for imagining how divine name and political definition as unified "people" could be connected. In the context of the Sabaean text RES 3945, with its sacred cleansing of town populations, the destruction is devoted "to Almaqah and to Saba'," treating the Saba' people as inseparable from the god Almaqah, as recipients of such offering (Ryckmans 1989). The same categorical alignment of god and people to receive offering appears in the 9th-century Mesha inscription, where similar slaughter is devoted "to Kamosh and to Moab" (line 12; cf. Ryckmans 1983: 15; Beeston 1985). Although we have much less documentation for Moab, this combination suggests a similarity of political and religious conception that includes the "war-*ḥērem*" investigated by Monroe (2007).

In the Mesha inscription, the king's first military successes, over the towns of 'Aṭarot and Nebo, are recounted with parallel structures that highlight the alignment of the details from each element. Only the second victory, over Nebo, celebrates the despoiling of a sanctuary for Yahweh, and this is the battle that concludes with *ḥērem* slaughter "for Ashtar-Kamosh" (line 17). The victory over 'Aṭarot also results in annihilation of the inhabitants, though it is described with different terminology, in this case "for Kamosh and for Moab," yielding the South Arabian parallel.[25] In their comment on line 12, Donner and Röllig (1968: 175) appreciated the force of this combination in an "offering" (*Darbringung*) to both god and people: "Note that Moab here is apparently listed next to Kamosh as a divine numen."[26] Beeston (1985: 143) finds that the pairing here and in South Arabian texts like RES 3945 need not divinize the people, and he takes the phrase as "a legal technicality referring to the Sabaean national

---

[25] The reading of Mesha line 12 is the subject of debate, with Lemaire (1987) proposing to read *hyt* ("to be") for what has been an imponderable noun *ryt*. Schade (2017) argues at length from his own examination of the stele and the squeezes taken from the object before its modern damage that *ryt* is the correct reading (cf. Zevit 2012). South Arabian attestation of a noun *ryt* for "claim" or "obligation" would produce some version of "offering" when addressed to a god, as already concluded by Donner and Röllig (1968).

[26] "Beachte, dass מאב hier neben Kamoš offenbar als göttliches Numen aufgeführt wird." In their discussion of *ryt* in line 12, Donner and Röllig were aware of and applied the South Arabian use of the term.

entity as a whole." Perhaps the detail provided by Robin (2018) can both account for the distinction of people from deity and explain the shared posture as beneficiaries of a single sacred act. In hypothetical reconstruction of the situation at ʿAṭarot, Moab would represent the groups that unified under Mesha's rule as king, having an identity that preceded monarchy. Moab, by analogy to the South Arabian kingdoms, would be "the descendants of Kamosh."

Against this backdrop, it is significant that in the Bible, the only other "people" constructed by identification with a god is the *ʿam kĕmôš* ("people of Kemosh"), set in parallel with "Moab," the kingdom on the east side of the Dead Sea (Num 21:29; Jer 48:46). By further comparison with the detailed South Arabian material, Moab as the "people of Kemosh" would be the counterpart of "the descendants of ʿAmm" or "the descendants of Almaqah," identified directly with the god based on an underlying notion of kinship.[27] Rather than reflecting ordinary representations of "national gods" in a broadly Near Eastern or even Levantine formulation, "the people of Kemosh" and "the people of Yahweh" in the Bible point to a more particular intersection of politics and religion.[28] For the peoples of Moab in Jordan, of South Arabia, and perhaps those who were eventually incorporated into the kingdoms of Israel and Judah, unity with their individual "great gods" made them literal family. In a social setting no longer requiring the mobility of their lineage "tents" (*ʾhl*), the South Arabian expression of such a relationship could be called "tribal," where this term helps see structural likeness, in contrast to the city-based collectivity of Aššur. Such tribal social organization appears to stand behind the older Shasu people called Yhwꜣ.

Great Gods and Divine Character

Investigations of early "Israelite" religion must grapple immediately with the ubiquity of two divine names: Yahweh (or Yhwh) and Elohim ("God"). Now that the simple form El is richly documented in late second-millennium writing from Ugarit, much can be said of El's

---

[27] Such divine kinship is often associated with kings in the ancient Near East, even with biblical kings from the line of David, as expressed in Ps 2:7, "He said to me: You are my son."

[28] For the idea of the "national god," see, for example, Albertz (1994: 97–98). It is almost unfair to cite individual scholars, as if this were a flaw, though the category is problematic. The term is partly a convenience, much as it deserves further qualification and testing.

character as father and leader of gods, whose very name as "The God" renders him "great." The harder question has been how to characterize Yahweh as a deity distinct from El. By considering the great gods of Babylon and Assyria on one hand and the political gods of South Arabia and Moab on the other, I have weighed analogies that do not place primary significance on job descriptions that are imagined to be original to each deity. What makes each god "great" for the people in question is his (in these cases) identification with the people bound to him.[29] With the South Arabian setting as one particularly apt parallel, I am arguing that Yahweh's early standing as the primary deity for a substantial people was based on the same framework of binding groups with common interests into a single political whole. This notion requires a shift of orientation as we consider how Yahweh relates or compares to other major gods. Understood this way, every likeness to a major type is likely to be secondary, attached to Yahweh or similar figures as an extrapolation from his basic centrality to his own people. Such secondary matching of character is visible in the war-*ḥērem* of Mesha, which is carried out for Ashtar-Kamosh, identifying the unifying god Kamosh with the dominant deity of the inland regions.[30]

In concrete terms, the question of divine character plays out in discussion of Yahweh as comparison with El and Baal, the pantheon head and the young warrior, as well as with storm gods young and old. I do not mean to undertake a developed history of early religion like Smith's *Early History of God* (1990) or Day's *Yahweh and the Gods and Goddesses of Canaan* (2000), both of which are concerned to locate Yahweh among the other gods of the region and time. Aside from the evidence from the southern Levant and South Arabia, the most successful of great gods from Mesopotamia counter the objection that a deity rooted in identification with a limited people could not emerge as a major god. The actual histories of gods like Marduk and Aššur demonstrate otherwise. With growth of social scale and developing political structures it is natural for a god identified with a particular people to be transformed in the process. At least in the case of Yahweh it appears that we must imagine such a background.

---

[29] Although there are major goddesses identified with cities, such as the Lady of Gubla (Byblos) and Athena of Athens, the type is most often male. Robin (2018: 94) observes that in the South Arabian material, the leading god of each kingdom's "pantheon" is always a god, never a goddess.
[30] See above, with 'Amm and Qatabān, for 'Athtar in South Arabia.

YAHWEH, EL, AND ISRAEL

In the framing hymn for the Song of Deborah, the writer makes explicit how to envision Israel's religious world: its trials came at a time when "they chose new gods" (v. 8), when Yahweh was "the god of Israel" (vv. 3, 5).[31] Given that Yahweh is only identified with Israel in this new introduction, the peculiar comment about "new gods" (or, "a new god") is best understood as the alternative, before the coining of the later stereotype as "other gods" (*'ēlōhîm 'ăḥērîm*) but with similar intent. The title in Judg 5:3 and 5 appears to make Yahweh the political god, the deity that unifies a kingdom, for Israel, like Kamosh for Moab in the Mesha inscription.[32] In the Song of Moses, the assignment of gods to peoples is attributed to the "olden days" (*yōmōt 'ōlām*, Deut 32:7),[33] "when Elyon made allotments to the nations [*gōyīm*], when he divided up humanity [*běnê 'ādām*], he set the territories of the peoples ['*ammîm*] by the number of the gods – indeed, the share of Yahweh was his people, Jacob was his surveyed portion" (vv. 8–9).[34] Deuteronomy 32:7–9 and

---

[31] The phrase, "they chose *'ēlōhîm ḥădāšîm*" is unique in Biblical Hebrew and has provoked consideration of alternatives to the obvious translation. Mark Smith leaves the question open, rendering the phrase, "It (Israel) chose new leaders/gods(?)" (2014: 254). BDB s.v. *ḥādāš* concludes that the text is corrupt, citing a list of early commentators.

[32] I am avoiding the "national god" category. In modern conception, the term "nation" is tied up with "nation states" as bounded and mutually recognized sovereign political entities. In older usage, the notion of nations rubbed shoulders with races in what modern discourse has translated into ethnicity. It is not evident that sovereign polities like Israel and Moab under kings are adequately described as "nations" or their identities as "national," but when the problem is acknowledged, the application is at least intelligible. With focus on the alignment created by addition of the introductory hymn to the Song of Deborah, Michael Stahl (personal communication) is considering the category of "kingdom god." This would work nicely with the South Arabian evidence as well. It would remain to decide what to call such a deity as a unifying figure before formulation of monarchy.

[33] Tigay (1996: 302 and n.41) comments on the authority of elders, "the custodians of historical tradition in a predominantly oral culture" (cf. Job 8:8–10).

[34] It has become almost universal to prefer the Greek and Qumran reading of verse 8 as "sons of gods," so "divine beings," or effectively, simply "gods." While the Jewish Publication Society translation stays with the Masoretic reading, "in relation to Israel's numbers," Tigay in his accompanying commentary explains the better sense of the "divine beings," which he interprets as "angelic" (1996: 302–3). While the text has commonly been included in the Bible's archaic poetry, it displays features that have led to a variety of qualified later dates, still generally preexilic, at least in American scholarship. For the voluminous comment, see Sanders (1996); and Leuchter (2007). Ki-Eun Jang (2017) proposes that Deuteronomy 32 belongs to the circle of Jerusalem-based prophet writing that generated the books of Isaiah and Jeremiah.

Judg 5:2–11a share a world thus divided into kingdoms with particular gods to represent them, a world that suits the political innovations of both Israel's Omride kings and Moab's Mesha.[35] For both biblical texts, the god of Israel (or Jacob) is Yahweh. Judges 5 has no concern for the other deity who might be linked to Israel: "The God" El, or Elohim, who bears the same name as Ugarit's divine patriarch, Ilu.[36]

In Deuteronomy 32, the reader is expected to equate Yahweh with Elyon, so that the same god both assigns nations to divinities and keeps the best for himself, but in the segment on its own Elyon evokes El, who could be understood to superintend the process as a distinct deity and make the special assignment to Yahweh.[37] Although Yahweh may easily be seen as Israel's divine lord, "God" (Elohim or El) is just as present in biblical writing. The ancestor narratives of Genesis gather lore for sacred sites linked by various titles to El: El Elyon at Salem/Jerusalem (14:19–20); El ʿOlam at Beersheba (21:33); El Bethel at Bethel (31:13); and El God of Israel at Shechem (33:20).[38] In the Priestly scheme for explaining the special status of Moses, Yahweh only revealed his proper

---

[35] Routledge (2004: chapter 7) proposes that Mesha's conception of Moab is new, effectively constituting a permanent kingdom in new terms. Smith (2001a: 48–49) underscores the "family view of the divine arrangement of the world," by which Deut 32:8–9 shows "Israelite polytheism that focuses on the central importance of Yahweh for Israel within the larger scheme of the world, yet this larger scheme provides a place for the other gods of the other nations in the world."

[36] I render this with the definite article because Ugaritic lacked its separate designation, and the name appears to require the specification. Biblical Hebrew sometimes preserves the definite article in the occasional rendition as both *hāʾēl* (e.g. Gen 31:13; 35:1, 3; 46:3; 2 Sam 22:31, 33, 48; Ps 68:20, 21; 77:15) and *hāʾĕlōhîm* (e.g. Gen 5:22, 24; 6:9, 11; 44:16; Deut 7:9; Judg 6:36, 39; 7:14; 2 Sam 2:27; 6:7). For *hāʾĕlōhîm* there are many more instances even for the name with definite article in independent use; other cases include the name with article in phrases or attached to names like Yahweh, where the nominal meaning as "the god" is significant (see BDB s.v. *ʾĕlōhîm* 3).

[37] For El and Deut 32:7–9, see Greenfield (1987: 554), followed by Smith (1990: 11). In returning to this text, which is so obviously central to his ongoing historical study of religion, Smith moves from treating Elyon and Yahweh as separate gods in Deut 32:8–9 (2001a: 48–49, 156–57) to an acknowledgment of their identification in the finished text (2004: 152). While the lines do preserve "the old notions of the divine family and its world theology," nonetheless "it is evident that the author of this poem, even with the reading 'number of the divine sons,' evidently understood Elyon and Yahweh to be one and the same god, the god of Israel, for the poem goes on to refer to the other gods as 'no-gods' (v. 17, NRSV 'not God'), and to describe Yahweh as the only god (v. 39). It is clear that for this author there really are no other gods." For discussion of all the biblical evidence for El Elyon, see Lewis (2020b: on "El Worship" in chapter 4), who identifies the oldest text as Num 24:16, in the Balaam poetry.

[38] In his discussion of "ʾĒl Epithets in Patriarchal Narratives," interacting with Alt (1929; 1953: 1–78), Cross (1973: 46–60) reviews the relevant material in Genesis.

name to this special intermediary, and to suit the pattern of assembled associations in Genesis, he appeared to Abraham, Isaac, and Jacob as El Shadday.[39] Beyond such explicit references to the name of The God, scholars mining especially the mass of material from Ugarit have identified much of Levantine El's character in the epithets and affinities of the biblical God, even when named as Yahweh.[40] It seems clear that the religion reflected in the Bible is saturated in ideas of El, so deeply that there survives little tension between the once separate identities of Yahweh and The God.[41]

Inscriptional evidence is not adequate to resolve the early history of how Yahweh and El "converged," to use Mark Smith's terminology, into one deity.[42] The Mesha inscription from Moab (ca. 840) already associates the kingdom of Israel with Yahweh, whose vessels are dragged before Kamosh after the fall of Nebo (lines 17–18), though it is never stated directly that Yahweh plays the same role for Israel as does Kamosh for Moab, governing its destiny for good or ill and guiding its king to victory. Perhaps slightly later, depending on the range of dates for the inscriptional evidence, the various inscriptions from Kuntillet ʿAjrud include several that invoke Yahweh, either by identification with Samaria, capital of the northern kingdom of Israel, or with Teman, oriented to this southern site (see above). If blessings are offered in the name of Yahweh and "his asherah" together, the combination would assume the identification of Yahweh and El, no matter the specific intent of the second

---

[39] In Jacob's poetic blessing for Joseph, the name El is invoked twice together as "El of your father" and El Shadday (Gen 49:25), if we read with several MSS, the Samaritan Pentateuch, and the translations against the MT. For discussion of this verse with special weight to its separation from the altar set, see Cross (1973: 52–60). Cross argues that these truly represent El as known at Ugarit, not just local deities as imagined by Alt, who did not have access to this new evidence when he made his important early observation.

[40] The above references to Greenfield and Smith are two. Cross (1973) was a major contributor in the material just cited, and in larger terms, Smith (1990) and Day (2000) include whole chapters devoted to Yahweh and El.

[41] Tiele (1872 [1882: 283]) already knew El as a Canaanite god from Phoenician inscriptional sources. He identifies El of the Syrians and of the Hebrews, later named Yahveh by the latter, the residue of a primitive monotheism, obscured and altered through time by the multiplicity of divine personifications, perpetuated in El Shadday of the Hebrews and El Elyon of Melchizedek.

[42] My focus here is on "how" this occurred. Certainly Kuntillet ʿAjrud text 4.2 and Habakkuk 3 display the equation, as remarked by Lewis (personal communication). Michael Stahl (2020) would envision the equation of Yahweh and El in the introduction to the Song of Deborah, some time in the 9th century, when Yahweh is made "god of Israel," a setting in the northern kingdom that would be shared by the Kuntillet ʿAjrud material. The earliest identification of the two names could be older still.

figure; derivation from the consort of El underlies the pairing in any case.[43] By the reading of Lewis (2020a), the literary text KA 4.2 uses both names with reference to the same deity.[44] Slightly later still, sometime in the 8th century, two sets of writing on plaster from Deir 'Alla record visions of Balaam by the "utterance" of El (Combination 1:1–2).[45] Deir 'Alla is east of the Jordan River, just north of the Jabbok River, not far from Succoth, within the kingdom of Israel during any period when it incorporated eastern territory.[46] The plaster texts are not in Hebrew and only the geography and date would locate them in Israel, but the presence and prominence of El, without concern for Yahweh, display the persistent centrality of El in this region as a god unto himself.[47]

All of this inscriptional evidence from the 9th and 8th centuries relates to the kingdom of Israel, in spite of its varied locations. Although Deir 'Alla suggests that El could persist without reference to Yahweh, and Mesha shows

---

[43] The argument over the precise meaning of "his asherah" in the Kuntillet 'Ajrud texts has continued to the point of shedding little new light. For a sensible and thorough review at a relatively early stage, see Emerton (1999). If we read the term as "sanctuary," the entire association with Asherah would be removed and this evidence irrelevant to the question of El and Yahweh.

[44] See the discussion of this text with Judges 5 and Psalm 68 in Chapter 4.

[45] This is the translation of Baruch Levine in COS (2.142); see also his extensive discussion of the Deir 'Alla texts in the second volume of his Numbers commentary (2000: 241–75). The dates for these texts are problematic, given their discovery in context that may just follow the fall of Israel in 720. Mark Smith (1990: 139) responds to Levine's proposal that the Deir 'Alla texts reflect the worship of El in the region of Israel east of the Jordan River: "Two questions surrounding this interpretation involve genre and date." The literary tradition could predate monarchic Israel; and the inscription may be a copy of an older text.

[46] See, for example, the maps of the northern kingdom in Rainey and Notley (2006): "The rise of Omri" (197); "Israel and Judah invade Moab" (205); "The wars of Amaziah and Jehoash" (216); "Israel and Judah in the days of Jeroboam II and Uzziah" (219).

[47] On the historical setting of the inscriptions, see the recent discussion of Schüle (2017: 72–73). The Iron Age II level of the site appears to have been destroyed by an earthquake, the geological evidence for which indicates one in about 750 and one in the decades before that. For the texts themselves, Schüle observes that "The cursive script initially gave some scholars reason to believe that this was an inscription from the late 8th or even early 7th cent. BCE. The grammar and syntax on the other hand seem much more archaic compared to inscriptions from the second half of the 9th and the first half of the 8th century BCE. The radiocarbon dating, which may be the most reliable tool in this regard, suggests a date in the second half of the 9th century BCE" (72). This date then places Deir 'Alla in the chronological company of the writing on plaster at Kuntillet 'Ajrud. On the language, for all its problems, Schüle reviews the diagnostic details under the rubric of early Aramaic, concluding that "if one had to pick one category to describe the language of the plaster inscription, it would have to be Aramaic" (78). Given the historical context for the involvement of the Damascus-based kingdom in the region and Jeroboam II's probable rule in the east, it appears that the text represents a local tradition that follows the public religious practice of neither kingdom (75).

Yahweh as a god present in land held by Israel without concern to relate him to El, KA 4.2 shows that the drawing together of the two deities was under way in this period. None of this material allows us to define precisely either Yahweh's relationship to Israel or even whether there was any single "god of Israel" in the 9th and 8th centuries, though Nebo's Yahweh in the Mesha text and Yahweh of Samaria at Kuntillet 'Ajrud suggest a political connection, different in each case. In the end, we have only the Bible to help us guess how Yahweh related to Israel before the Omride kingdom. The same is certainly true for the kingdom centered at Jerusalem.

It is not my purpose to examine all of this biblical evidence. With Yahweh as "god of Israel" evidently secondary to the battle account in the Song of Deborah, the Bible lacks compelling proof of this identity before the 9th century.[48] Israel itself must be carefully distinguished within the larger tapestry of peoples eventually named under this banner, so that no specific religious affiliation with the name Israel will explain the religious connections of these other groups.[49] Mark Smith has long endorsed the conclusion that the first "god of Israel" was El, as the deity in the personal name *yiśrā'ēl*.[50] So far as this may prove true, it would underscore the need to understand Yahweh's arrival in terms separate from Israel by name even where this god could have played a long-standing role in the affairs of other peoples who were integrated into the large kingdom in (or by) the 9th century. This is what I have suggested by my analysis of the *'am Yhwh* in Judg 5:13 and 2 Sam 1:12 (Chapter 6).

In the end, the positions of El and Yahweh in literal Israel (the named entity) before the 9th century remain to discern. It is plausible that both deities held significance, though the details remain obscure. The relationship between geography and politics remains a question throughout, and one way to explore the problem is through names associated with early worship. In what follows, I begin with "Israel" itself and then consider individual sites that may be relevant to evaluating El and Yahweh as gods with large group interest before the 9th century. What follows is not exhaustive but more an investigative foray.

---

[48] This is the conclusion of Michael Stahl (2020: chapter 2).

[49] For our ongoing work on the named political landscape, with interest in what the Bible preserves, see Monroe and Fleming (2019); Monroe (forthcoming); and Fleming (forthcoming).

[50] See his section 7.5, "Was El Israel's Original God?" in Smith (2001a: 142–45). In his forthcoming compendium on "God," Lewis (2020b) reaches the same conclusion (chapter 4, "El Worship"). For Stahl (2020), the strongest evidence is not the name "Israel" itself but the title "El, god of Israel" in Gen 33:20.

The Name Israel

If "the god" in *yiśrā'ēl* is indeed El and not the generic "god" of many such personal names, this would establish a particular link between El and Israel that goes back to the origin of the people's identity and is therefore essential, whether or not it requires a single "god of Israel."[51] Such a connection would go back at least to the late 13th century, when Israel appears in the Merenptah stela and when The God (Ilu/El) is attested at Ugarit and beyond. In this relationship, Israel would have no unique claim on El but would rather claim participation in the interests of the major deity. At the moment when Israel received its name, no role for Yahweh need be supposed.

Shechem

El appears to have had a sanctuary in the central highlands at Shechem, a town bearing a name that had been attached to a "land" that represented one of Lab'ayu's several bases in the 14th-century evidence from el-Amarna.[52] Judges 9 preserves a tale defined by Shechem as a town, without reference to Israel or its peoples, concerned with the destruction of the settlement and its tower, which housed "the temple of El-Berith," El of the Bond (v. 46).[53] Genesis 33:20 records Jacob's construction of an altar at Shechem in the name of El Elohe Yisra'el, "El, the god of Israel."[54] According to 1 Kings 12, Rehoboam son of Solomon lost Israel to Jeroboam at the time of an assembly of leaders at Shechem.

---

[51] It is not automatic that the *ilu/'ēl* element in theophoric personal names must represent a deity called "The God." This element is common in Akkadian names, where a first-person suffix may not always be indicated to distinguish "my god." In the onomasticon from Late Bronze Age Emar in northern Syria, where we find no identifiable cult for a separate god Ilu/El, note the names Ilu-abu, Ilu-bani, Ilu-bitu, Ilum-ma, Ilu-malik, and Ilum-aḫu; as well as names with verbal predicates, Ir'am-ila, Irbi-ilu (in Pruzsinszky 2013). The use of the *ilu* element to represent a "personal god" goes back to the third millennium (Di Vito 1993).

[52] "The land of Shechem" (not the city as such) appears in EA 289 with reference to the rule of Lab'ayu. Benz (2016: chapter 6) reconsiders this text in the context of all evidence for Lab'ayu in the el-Amarna correspondence, concluding that "Lab'ayu and his family operated in and around the territory associated with Piḫilu" (186), with influence that extended into the highlands.

[53] On this passage and the god, see Lewis (1996). Benz (2016: chapter 11) discusses Judges 9 in relation to the archeological finds at Tel Balâṭah, where a *temenos* is to be distinguished from the town. The location of the tower in relation to the main city is debated.

[54] See the discussion of Gen 33:20 in Stahl (2020: chapter 2).

For reasons that are never elaborated, Rehoboam must go to this site to receive Israel's collective approval, so that he cannot be its king until they make the choice. Together, these three biblical texts suggest a collective political tradition at Shechem that was identified with Israel by name, under the divine supervision of El. Both the altar name in Gen 33:20 and the temple for El-Berith in Judg 9:46 mark association with El, and the "bond" (or "covenant") in the divine title may involve alliance between human parties as well as an alliance with the god. Yahweh plays no role in these texts.

According to the narrative for the two kingdoms, Jeroboam made Shechem his capital but then moved it to Tirzah, so that Shechem dropped from sight almost as soon as Jerusalem split off as the center of a separate realm.[55] Regardless of how 1 Kings 12 is to be dated it appears that any significance held by Shechem in Israel did not last beyond the 10th century.

The "Bull Site" and Mount Ebal

Lauren Monroe and I conclude that earliest (so our "little") Israel was located north of Ephraim in the central highlands, perhaps straddling the Jezreel Valley and reaching across the Jordan River in its more northern section (Fleming forthcoming). Shechem would have been at the southern extent of this space. Excavations in the modern highlands have yielded little secure evidence for substantial sacred sites in the Iron Age I, and it is noteworthy that the two most prominent examples are situated in this likely location for Israel, between Shechem and the Jezreel/Kishon Valleys. These are the "Bull Site," named for the bronze figurine found in a walled-off area on a high ridge east of Dothan (Mazar 1982); and the construction on the flank of Mount Ebal, which in spite of much appropriate caution about hasty matches with the curses recounted in Deuteronomy 27, really does look like a sacred enclosure.[56]

---

[55] The reference to Jeroboam at Shechem appears only in the bridge from the tale of how the two kingdoms were separated to the account of Jeroboam's offenses at Bethel, in 1 Kgs 12:25. It is possible that this solitary line only reflects Jeroboam's association with the narrative for Israel's collective action at Shechem, without demonstrating that the site ever served as capital of Israel. In 1 Kgs 14:17, Jeroboam is assumed to be at Tirzah, without reference to any prior move.

[56] Hawkins (2012) describes exhaustively both the sacred parallels and the problems with alternatives: village; farmstead; commercial center; house; and watchtower. In rejecting the most serious of these, as a watchtower, he returns to Zertal's (1986–87) objections: no evidence for an Iron I fortification network; location not set to watch roads; no defensive wall; architecture not as a tower; and the central structure not a foundation for something above it. Dever (2017: 159–60) calls the identification "controversial" but

Both of these sites stand at a distance from any settlement and, as Mazar (1982: 37–38) observes, while the "Bull Site" is several kilometers from Dothan and other larger towns, several small Iron Age I villages were nearby, and this could have served as a central ritual gathering place for those settlements. Of the two sacred sites, Ebal is much more elaborate and may have served a larger circle, perhaps with the service of a particular priest. Neither location supplies clear evidence of the god worshiped there, but in the context of Israel and Shechem, the first candidate would be El. Evaluated in relation to gender and generation, the figurine's form as a mature bull would suit that god (Fleming 1999).[57]

Accepting the difficulty both of locating the Israel name in the Iron Age I and of establishing definite interest in specific deities, it would be easy to imagine that from its obscure beginnings through the end of the second millennium, the political god identified with Israel was El. There is no reason to exclude the worship of other gods, male and female, and Yahweh could have been among them. One obstacle remains our ignorance of what population identified itself with Israel and of whether groups with other names also considered themselves part of Israel, and on what terms. Still weighing the biblical traditions of worship in the highlands, two more sites warrant consideration for their potential political significance, both to the south of Shechem, Mount Ebal, and the "Bull Site."

Shiloh

For the Iron Age between the 12th and 10th centuries, the Bible offers one intriguing location that excavation has left unconfirmed. Shiloh, between Shechem and Bethel in the highlands north of Jerusalem, is portrayed in

endorses a sacred interpretation. "A large subrectangular boundary wall enclosed an area of about one acre, in which the only structure was a large stone podium surrounded by a low enclosure wall, approached by a sort of ramp, and featuring two adjacent courtyards." Without denying the interpretations as a "farmstead" or "watchtower," and in spite of the ritual oddity of finding the bones of fallow deer, Dever concludes, "Nevertheless, some cultic functions may be surmised."

[57] The drive to incorporate images into the study of Israelite religion has moved the field into important new areas; see above all, Keel and Uehlinger (1998). Seeking a balance between the incorporation of this data and the need for certainty about names, Lewis (2020b: chapter 5) comments, "Iconography complements texts, it cannot replace them." In particular, there is the danger of misidentification – even between representations of humans versus gods. Based on detailed review of images from excavated sites, Lewis concludes that human figures from the Late Bronze Age certainly do not fit a young warrior god but cannot be identified securely as El. The figurine from the Iron Age I "Bull Site" offers the "best candidate for a theriomorphic representation of Israelite El."

biblical writing as active only during the period of Israelite settlement before monarchy.[58] The site appears with Joshua and makes its exit with Eli at the beginning of 1 Samuel, after which it drops from view without reference to its destruction, which only appears outside the primary narrative.[59] In spite of Seow's (1989) argument that the Shiloh sanctuary exhibited El imagery, all of the biblical traditions surrounding Shiloh associate it with Yahweh.[60]

- Joshua divides territory there "before Yahweh" (Josh 18:8–10);
- Israel gets wives for Benjamin at the annual "pilgrimage [*ḥāg*] of Yahweh" (Judg 21:19);
- Eli serves "the temple of Yahweh" (1 Sam 1:9);
- the sons of Eli offend Yahweh (2:12–17);
- Samuel is apprenticed to Eli in service of Yahweh (chs. 1–3);[61]

[58] Shiloh was excavated in the 1980s under the direction of Israel Finkelstein (see Finkelstein 2013: 49–50). Radiocarbon dates place the destruction of Shiloh in the late 11th century, which Finkelstein places a century before the time of the Gibeon-Bethel plateau sites that have been linked to a kingdom of Saul. Regardless of the controversy surrounding Iron Age chronology, this distance in time is substantial.

[59] For all the biblical references to Shiloh in the context of the site's first appearance in Joshua 18, see Fleming (2018). The texts include Joshua 18; Judges 21; 1 Samuel 1, 2, and 4; and Psalm 78 for the tent shrine. The prophecies against the Jerusalem temple in Jeremiah allude to Shiloh's end as a precedent (7:12–14; 26:6). In Gen 49:10, the problematic "until Shiloh comes" in the saying for Judah does not represent a secure reference to the city.

[60] Seow devotes a long opening section (1989: 11–54) to Shiloh, building on a legacy of linkages that envisioned biblical knowledge of actual practice at Shiloh, a knowledge that is difficult to establish with confidence when the site itself was irrecoverably destroyed in the mid-11th century. He begins with the title "Yahweh of Hosts," which had long been associated with Shiloh based on 1 Sam 1:3, 11; and 4:4. Cross's (1973) explanation for the name Yahweh as abbreviated from a ritual title for El, associated with creating the heavenly "host," provides one important connection between Shiloh and El. In 1 Samuel 1, Hannah's husband is Elqanah, bearing an El-name with the verb "to create" or "to acquire" that appears with El in connection with Salem (for Jerusalem) in Gen 14:18. Psalm 78 recalls the destruction of the Shiloh shrine as prelude to establishment of Jerusalem, in a text replete with references to El and Elyon. Such features highlight the connection between Jerusalem and the idea of past worship at Shiloh, but they are inadequate to demonstrate the identity of the god who may have been worshiped at Shiloh itself, or even to prove a particular connection to El rather than Yahweh in later scribal memory.

[61] The connection of Samuel to Shiloh appears to be secondary and impossible to read as foundational tradition; see, for example, Römer's "Deuteronomistic story of Samuel" in 1 Samuel 1 (now read as pertaining to Samuel); 2:18–21; 3*; and 7:5–17, in which Samuel leads a transition from the period of judges to the time of kings (2005: 138).

- the narrative of the ark's loss in chs. 4–6 alternates between identifying it with Yahweh and Elohim;[62]
- the reference to God abandoning the tabernacle at Shiloh in Ps 78:59–60 belongs to a section of the book that rendered Yahweh as Elohim;[63]
- and in Jeremiah Yahweh recalls what he did to "my place" at Shiloh (7:12).

This collection means that Shiloh is not among the El shrines set up by the ancestors according to the book of Genesis, with its anticipation of various sites of later religious importance, including Bethel, Jerusalem, and Shechem.

It is difficult to evaluate this collection of Shiloh tradition in historical terms. The Eli material is particularly diverse and includes the unexpected and archaic account in 1 Samuel 1 of a true "temple" (*hêkāl*) with annual pilgrimage festival – like the one in Judges 21 (Milstein 2016: 190–91). I have argued (Fleming 2018) that Josh 18:8–10 preserves the citation of a tradition that some unnamed land was divided by lot at Shiloh in the presence of Yahweh, with seven parts distributed to unnamed recipients – not the "tribes" from the finished list of twelve in the book's exhaustive land allotment. These three texts suggest the oldest conceptions of an early sacred site and the activities accruing to it, each account divorced entirely from other biblical norms for cultic performance and narrative frame. Perhaps Jeremiah 7 and 26, along with Psalm 78, maintain the real memory of an ancient destruction, though excavation has not confirmed it. The remaining texts from the start of 1 Samuel may be later and more artificial in their construction. One burden of 1 Samuel 1–4 is to explain the removal of any authority from an Elide priesthood generally, which is cast as unnumbered plural "sons of Eli" in 2:12–17, when read without the preparation of two names from 1:3.[64]

Monroe and I have proposed that Ephraim may have maintained a distinct identity within the kingdom of Israel, displayed in the geography

---

[62] See the "ark of God" in 4:4, 13, 17, 18, 19, 21, 22; 5:1, 2, 7, 8, 10; 6:3; the "ark of Yahweh" in 4:3, 6; 5:3; 6:1, 8, 11, 15, 18, 19, 21; 7:1.

[63] For the "Elohistic Psalms" see Hossfeld and Zenger (2003; 2005: 4–5). Note the opening of Psalm 82 as an example, where Elohim takes his stand in the assembly of the gods, clearly taking the place of Yahweh.

[64] In her continuing work on the Ark Narrative in its context in 1 Samuel 1–6, Jaime Myers concludes that these "sons of Eli" are also relatively late in the construction of the section, present in order to be replaced by Samuel.

for Ishbosheth's rule (2 Sam 2:8–9) and in Hosea (Fleming forthcoming), and an indication that it was not included in earlier Israel. One implication of such a historical scenario would be that Shiloh would be outside Israel of the Late Bronze and Iron I periods, near the center of the Ephraim/Benjamin highlands, between Shechem and Jerusalem.[65] It is noteworthy (Monroe forthcoming) that while Israel by name is absent from the battle account in Judg 5:12–23, the combination of Ephraim and Benjamin leads the praised participants in the "people of Yahweh." The first royal centers depicted for a kingdom of Israel before division into two are located at Gibeah and Jerusalem, close to each other in the southern part of this Ephraim/Benjamin space. Here, the history is hard to determine when we have only the Bible for names and political formations, but it is striking that these first remembered kings were located outside Israel in the same highland region shared by Shiloh and Bethel.

The biblical texts treating Shiloh highlight a further conceptual problem in projecting later names and definitions back onto earlier time and space. It is common to divide the land of the Bible, and indeed of Yahweh, by the two kingdoms of Israel and Judah, north and south. Shiloh is a point of reference for the Jerusalem temple as remembered at the end of Psalm 78 and in Jeremiah 7 and 26, indicating a connection that crosses the boundary between the two kingdoms. The tale of Eli and Hannah in 1 Samuel 1 may go back to the birth of Saul before transfer to Samuel, and the "temple" at Shiloh (*hêkāl*, v. 9) is tied to worship of "Yahweh of Hosts" (*Yhwh ṣĕbā'ôt*, v. 11), both expressions attached to Yahweh at Jerusalem.[66] The association of Yahweh with Shiloh, for all its location north of anything belonging to the kingdom of Judah, requires

---

[65] Finkelstein (2013: 50) considers that with the lack of any Iron Age II or later presence at Shiloh, the sanctuary tradition cannot be taken to reflect some such practice. "Thus, one cannot escape the conclusion that there was a strong memory in late-monarchic Judah of an early devastated cult place at Shiloh. This could have been one more orally transmitted, genuine north Israelite tradition that reached Judah with northern refugees after the conquest of Israel by the Assyrians or a northern etiological tradition that was based on an acquaintance, in monarchic times, with a large ruin at the site."

[66] For 1 Samuel 1 and Saul, see the recent argument in Milstein (2016: 185–89), with literature going back to Hylander (1932). For the Jerusalem temple as *hêkāl*, see Solomon's construction in 1 Kgs 6:3 (etc.) and Isaiah's call (Isa 6:1). The title appears throughout both Isaiah (e.g. 1:9, 24; 5:7, 9; 6:3, 5) and Psalms with Jerusalem reference (e.g. 24:10; 80: 5, 8; 89:9). For discussion and bibliography, see Mettinger (1999) and Stahl (2020: chapter 3.3).

consideration of Jerusalem as well, at least as a place where Shiloh traditions were treasured and maintained.[67]

Jerusalem

Van der Toorn (1993) has argued that Yahweh became the god of Israel under Saul, a hypothesis that raises the question of what god or gods were identified with monarchic Israel before the two kingdoms of the late 10th and 9th centuries.[68] The historical reconstruction of political circumstances before the two kingdoms is itself fraught, with so much biblical narrative devoted to Saul, David, and Solomon and so little external data.[69] Two elements from the biblical books of Kings may provide more substantial historical evidence, beyond the particulars of individual stories. The chronology for the rulers of Israel and Judah as companion kingdoms is detailed and interwoven, roughly confirmed in some cases by Egyptian, Mesopotamian, and other inscriptional material.[70] Even as the chronology continues through the end of Judah in the early 6th century, possibly with updates, to indicate a later systematic document, its precise accounting for both kingdoms in relation to each other puts the starting point of this recollection of parallel realms in the late 10th century. It would seem that by that date Jerusalem really was the capital of a separate southern kingdom.

---

[67] Stahl (2020: chapter 3) concludes, "1 Samuel 1*'s interest in Shiloh and the Benjaminite hero Saul, combined with the positive parallels that the text draws between Shiloh and the Jerusalem temple, may suggest that 1 Samuel 1* was composed, or at least reworked, by a Benjaminite community living in or affiliated with Judah/Jerusalem after the fall of the kingdom of Israel." I would consider the specific identification of Saul with Benjamin to be secondary to, or one thread within, the Saul traditions, but Benjamin people could indeed have been responsible for preserving Saul lore into the Judah kingdom and its aftermath.

[68] Van der Toorn (1999: 918) locates "the national temple of the Saulide state" at Gibeon, where Solomon goes to receive Yahweh's blessing (1 Kgs 3:4). Although the identity of a first Jeroboam is sometimes doubted, the precisely calibrated chronology for two paired kingdoms reaches back specifically to Jeroboam and a son Nadab (1 Kgs 14:20) and Rehoboam and his son Abijam (14:21, 31), who would occupy the end of the 10th century.

[69] Only the Tel Dan inscription names David, in the later 9th century, in association with the southern of the two kingdoms. Archaeology has yielded rich material evidence, but proof of how this aligns with biblical names and narrative is always a delicate matter, in danger of leaning on the Bible's content, whether to confirm, to recast, or to disprove it.

[70] For discussion of the Kings narrative in relation to first-millennium royal inscriptions, see Na'aman (1999) and Parker (2006). Although the handling of the late 10th-century Egyptian campaign by Shoshenq is debated for its detail, this already appears to reflect some kind of source. Then we have Assyrian references to the Omrides, Mesha, and Tel Dan, and finally the 8th-century Assyrian annals starting with Tiglath-pileser III.

A second item of evidence for the early importance of Jerusalem may be the temple for Yahweh, which plays an elaborate part in narrative from the late monarchy, as in the account of reading prophecy there in Jeremiah 36.[71] The question is when the Yahweh temple would have been built, if not by Solomon as imagined elaborately in 1 Kings 6–7.[72] No biblical tradition for the Jerusalem temple suggests an alternative, except perhaps the later effort in Chronicles to credit David with key preparations (1 Chronicles 28–29). So far as Melchizedek and "Salem" in Gen 14:18–20 anticipate Jerusalem, the city is associated with the ancient worship not of Yahweh but of El Elyon as "creator of heaven and earth." In biblical writing, Jerusalem was the possession of Jebusites when David seized it as a new capital after "the tribes of Israel" made him king (2 Sam 5:1, 6–8), shifting his center of power northward from Hebron. Worship of Yahweh at Jerusalem is linked to David by a ritual tradition for entry of the ark into the city in 2 Samuel 6.[73] A separate account of David's support for Yahweh worship at Jerusalem has him buy land from a Jebusite as part of reconciliation following the king's census and resulting plague (2 Samuel 24). Neither of these texts makes a direct connection to the temple finally built by Solomon (Russell 2017: 17), and the enduring result is not that specific institution but rather the association of David's rule with Yahweh.

[71] In the books of Kings, after the account of the temple's construction under Solomon in 1 Kings 6–7, it appears in the following texts: as competition for Bethel (1 Kgs 12:27, 32); stripped of wealth given or lost to outsiders (Shishak, 1 Kgs 14:26; Jehoash of Israel, 2 Kgs 14:14; Tiglath-pileser III, 2 Kgs 16:8; Sennacherib, 2 Kgs 18:15–16); a place for cultic reforms (Asa, 1 Kgs 15:15; cf. Josiah); where Jehoiada kept Joash (2 Kings 11), who made systematic repairs (2 Kings 12); construction of the Upper Gate by Jotham (2 Kgs 15:35); new altar made by Ahaz (2 Kgs 16:10–18); place of Hezekiah's prayer (2 Kings 19); Manasseh's renovations (2 Kgs 21:4–7); Josiah's reconstruction and reform (2 Kings 22–23); destruction by Babylonian forces (2 Kings 25). Dubovsky (2015) works from a cautious premise, not engaging the alternatives, that Solomon was responsible for building a temple to Yahweh in Jerusalem in the 10th century. The identifications of specific episodes of "despoliation" (41–47) perhaps offer a thread of administrative continuity that reaches back to the late 10th century with Shishak/Shoshenq.

[72] Finkelstein and Silberman (2006) emphasize what archaeology cannot confirm, with the Jerusalem Temple Mount entirely inaccessible to excavation ("Who Built the Temple?" in chapter 5). They wonder whether the renovations portrayed under Joash could reflect a complete new construction from a smaller previous edifice, not doubting that a capital would have included a temple.

[73] As noted above, the text begins by naming the object "the ark of The God" (v. 2) and alternates between definition by Elohim and by Yahweh. The festival itself is for Yahweh, however (vv. 5, 14, 16, 17), and it is Yahweh who strikes down Uzzah for touching the ark (v. 7).

Just as David had to take Jerusalem from Jebusites to make it his capital, and he entered the city as a foreign invader, the narratives of Samuel and Kings envision Yahweh as a new arrival there, with David and his family. The main description of Solomon's temple construction begins directly with the business at hand, not concerned with what came before.[74] These texts understand the worship of Yahweh to have come to Jerusalem with its founding kings. Should we imagine a different history? The 9th-century Tel Dan inscription names the Jerusalem-centered kingdom "the House of David," evidently recalling a founding figure to match the biblical king. If David and Solomon did not establish Yahweh as the unifying political god for the realm centered at Jerusalem, we must imagine a later figure, probably no later than Asa, whose son Jehoshaphat ("Yahweh has judged") ruled after him in the early 9th century (1 Kgs 15:24).[75] In search of such an alternative, the political role of Yahweh at Jerusalem, binding a people to its king, would have to have bypassed David as founder and arrived before the Omrides built the north into a major power. Such a solution is possible, though any effort to reconstruct the 10th and early 9th centuries at Jerusalem requires much guesswork. Whenever Yahweh became essential to the Jerusalem capital, this religious innovation may have involved assimilation to a major god who dominated the site before David, whether El or another deity. No matter the specific political history, Jerusalem is likely to have been central to the encounter of El and Yahweh.

Yahweh before Omri

Keeping in mind the hypothesis of a "people of Yahweh" distinct from early Israel, an alliance of peoples beyond yet potentially overlapping Israel and its northern highland center, Yahweh would likely have played a substantial role in the region before Omri and Ahab. In order to

---

[74] The building account is framed by Solomon's exchanges with Hiram of Tyre, with references to David and Yahweh's promises to him as known from 2 Samuel 7 (1 Kgs 5:15–19; 6:12). Dubovsky (2015: 101) acknowledges the proposal by Rupprecht (1977) that Solomon's temple may have represented the rebuilding of a Jebusite shrine.

[75] Jerusalem is considered in some circles to belong only to a separate southern kingdom without having been the capital of Israel under David and Solomon. See, for example, Kratz (2005: 170–86); Fischer (2004); Wright (2014). One principal object of Leonard-Fleckman's *House of David* (2016) is to reverse this account, understanding the biblical accounts in 1 and 2 Samuel to begin with David as eventual king of Israel and only to add his rule over Judah at a late stage in literary development. My considerations regarding Jerusalem's importance to the worship of Yahweh could be adapted to either approach.

subsume peoples like Issachar, Zebulun, and Naphtali of the north or Gad of the east into the kingdom of Israel, the 9th-century kings would have embraced Yahweh as the particular "god of Israel" whether or not this god held significance for earlier Israelite kings. It appears that both Yahweh and El had political roles in the region. El may be represented in Israel's name, and collective Israel was defined in relation to El at Shechem; and however else he may have been present in the region, Yahweh undergirded an arrangement for mutual self-defense that reached a larger space to the north, the south, and inland.

Nothing indicates or requires that Yahweh was a god of the El type, either the head of a pantheon (however small) or a senior deity. Equally, this social-political landscape requires no hierarchy with El as head and Yahweh in a second tier. The "convergence" (Smith 1990) of Yahweh with El may make most sense in the early stages of monarchy associated with the two kingdoms that the Bible calls Israel and Judah, whether or not a real Saul, David, or Solomon played a part in the arrival of royal institutions. Like Aššur at the city by that name, Yahweh may naturally have assumed the dominant role once a larger social and religious world came into play, and his identification with El may have resembled the eventual equation of Aššur with Marduk and Enlil in the ambitious Assyrian kingdom. Alone, however, the god whose name goes back to the Yhw3 people of Shasu-land would not have derived from "The God" known to Ugarit.

YAHWEH THE YOUNG

The discovery of Ugarit and its alphabetic cuneiform transformed all understanding of religion in the land that became Israel. One long poetic narrative is devoted to Baal (Ba'lu) as storm god, the older expression of the first-millennium Hadad (Haddu), and the leading deity in this text is El (Ilu), patriarch of all gods and head of a divine assembly.[76] Although it

---

[76] Mark Smith has become the essential point of reference in discussion of this "Baal Cycle" through his commentary and related studies; see Smith (1994); Smith and Pitard (2009). Smith's *Origins of Biblical Monotheism* (2001a) works from the religion of Ugarit toward that of Israel and the Bible; and Smith was the appropriate person to serve as bridge between old and newer generations in recounting the history of Ugarit applications in his *Untold Stories* (2001b). Before Smith, his teacher Marvin Pope (1955) wrote the essential treatment of "The God"; and Cross's *Canaanite Myth and Hebrew Epic* (1973) defined the Canaanite mainly by reference to Ugarit. Along with Smith, see also Day (1985) and Lewis (1989). This represents only a selection.

is acknowledged that the gods of Iron Age peoples across the Levant may never have been organized into such pantheons as we encounter in major northern cities and kingdoms of the Late Bronze Age, Iron Age polytheism is still commonly approached in hierarchical terms with Ugarit as a reference point.[77] In this framework, if Yahweh is not regarded as a manifestation of El, he is most often understood to have begun as a warrior of the younger type seen in Baal at Ugarit or Ninurta in second-millennium Babylonia.[78] Working from the role of Elyon as a separate leading god in Deut 32:8–9 and Psalm 82, Mark Smith (2001a: 49) reconstructs the situation as follows:

From the perspective of this older theology, Yahweh did not belong to the top tier of the pantheon. Instead, in early Israel the god of Israel apparently belonged to the second tier of the pantheon; he was not the presider god, but one of his sons. Accordingly, what is at work is not a loss of the second tier of a pantheon headed by Yahweh. Instead, the collapse of the first and second tiers in the early Israelite pantheon likely was caused by an identification of El, the head of this pantheon, with Yahweh, a member of its second tier.

As with Yahweh and El, the non-biblical evidence allows no convincing conclusion regarding Yahweh's early or "original" character, and interpreters find themselves sifting what may be older writing from the Bible. In Psalm 29, Yahweh is celebrated as a simple storm god, battering the mountains of Lebanon and Sirion with his thundering "voice."[79] It is clear that Yahweh thus replaces Hadad or Baal, although it is not obvious when and against what religious background,[80] and we cannot assume that the text preserves an original divine character rather than a secondary claim with expansion of divine powers.[81] The geography of Psalm

---

[77] This hierarchy is explicit in the four "tiers" of Mark Smith's "divine household" (2001a: 54–58), though this analysis partakes of a trend in applications of non-biblical evidence to the religion on display in the Bible.

[78] I have already addressed the identification of Yahweh with El and the conclusion that Yahweh was first a storm god. My reference to "manifestation" flirts with current fascination with how multiple divine identities were understood by those who worshiped gods by related titles. See Sommer (2009); and a response by Smith (2012b), developed further in his 2016 book. See also the useful yet conceptually difficult exploration by Allen (2015). The nuances of the ideas and terminology are not essential to my discussion here.

[79] On Yahweh replacing "Baal of Lebanon" in particular in Psalm 29, see Smith (2016: 90).

[80] Michael Stahl (personal communication) favors the 9th century, with Israel confronting Damascus and its god Hadad in competition to the east, and forms of Baal associated with the powerful coastal kingdoms of Tyre and Sidon.

[81] Cross (1973: 151–52) describes the psalm as "an ancient Baʻl hymn, only slightly modified for use in the early cultus of Yahweh" – borrowed in the 10th century. Smith

29 spans the northern domain familiar to Hadad and the "wilderness of Kadesh" that evokes the southern movements of Israel in the wilderness – unless this is the old Syrian site between Damascus and Hamath.[82] In the overlapping texts for Yahweh's advance in Judg 5:4–5 and Ps 68:8–10, water is drawn from the sky in both, as the earth shakes. Unlike Psalm 29, however, Yahweh has no "voice" and the paired earth and sky stand for all creation, each part responding to his power. The hymn that opens the Song of Deborah celebrates the certainty of Yahweh's victory, guaranteed by his overwhelming presence, and Psalm 68 likewise lauds his supremacy. He brings rain as provision (vv. 10–11), just as he brings justice to the vulnerable (vv. 6–7), so that Yahweh is left the particular god of neither storm nor justice.

It does not appear that fighting for a people necessarily makes a "war god." At least, such a conclusion must depend on details beyond the basic granting of military victory by the power of a people's primary deity. In the Kurkh Monolith, Shalmaneser III declares that he defeated the Syrian people of Bīt-Adīni because "the fear of the splendor of Aššur, my lord, overwhelmed them"; and against a larger coalition, "with the fierce weapons which Aššur, my lord, gave, I fought with them."[83] Likewise, Kamosh not only commands Mesha to attack Nebo (line 14), but he also "restored" the land of Mehadaba to Moab (line 9) and "drove out" the king of Israel before Mesha at the town of Yahaṣ (line 19).

In the case of Yahweh and the two kingdoms, it remains difficult to know whether Yahweh would have been assigned such power before the expanded scale of Omride rule, and we have no evidence for the military

(1990: 15) considers the fragment for Yahweh coming from the south in Judg 5:4–5 and Psalm 29 both to "use imagery characteristic of Baal to describe Yahweh as the divine warrior fighting to deliver Israel." These texts show that the need to disentangle Yahweh from Baal was only "a problem of the monarchic period." Ringgren (1966: 71) asserts that the psalm "demonstrates that Canaanite elements have contributed to the development of the conception of God. These traits, however, could not simply have been ascribed to Yahweh if points of contact were not already present in his original nature." This method cannot be applied to the "convergence" (Smith) of all divine capacities in Yahweh.

[82] Cross (1973: 155) renders this line, "Yahweh makes the Holy Desert to writhe," avoiding the geographical problem that would be created by a southern proper noun. For Kadesh in the south, see Gen 16:14; 20:1; Num 13:26; 20:1, 14, 16, 22; 33:36, 37; Deut 1:46; 32:51; Judg 11:16, 17. With the northern orientation toward the mountains of Lebanon and Syria, one thinks of the Kadesh in Syria in the great battle between Egypt and Hatti in the 13th century (Tell Nebi Mend, destroyed in the 12th century; cf. Parr 1997).

[83] The translations are from Lawson Younger (COS 2.261–62).

ideology of Jerusalem from the late 10th and early 9th centuries. Nothing in the Bible offers secure confirmation in either case. As new rulers of a single kingdom of Israel, Saul and David are cast as fighting under Yahweh's command, but the texts as we have them may be colored by the expectations of later monarchy and beyond.[84] The particular cluster of biblical poems with Yahweh's advance from the south suggests association with the larger Israel of the 9th and 8th centuries and it is possible that this combination of devoted warrior deity and march from a distant residence was new to that period. So far as the Song of Deborah may be the oldest example, Judg 5:4–5 would nevertheless reflect a 9th-century setting in its equation with the geographical range of the battle account, and its assertion that Yahweh is "god of Israel" represents a shift from El as the initial bearer of that title. Perhaps such political gods were understood to have their remote residences from which they came to the rescue of their peoples.[85] At least we must consider explanations that are innovative rather than ancient and traditional.

Returning to the model of younger-generation gods like Ugarit's Baal, storm gods are not intrinsically excluded from leadership of a larger pantheon. The leading god of the major kingdom at Aleppo in the early second millennium was the storm god Addu, and the principal deity of the Hittite kingdom in Anatolia was likewise defined by power of the storm.[86] After the transformation of northern Syria and southern Anatolia at the end of the Bronze Age, the kingdoms of the region generally revered a storm god as primary deity.[87] In the first millennium,

---

[84] By this caution I do not mean to deny the possibility of earlier connection between Yahweh and Israel's first kings, but the biblical texts may not provide unfiltered access to the 10th century. In his proposal that Yahweh became the national god of Israel through Saul, van der Toorn (1993: 528) identifies the army as the primary vehicle for religious practice in the circle of the king; it is hard to be sure whether such details preserve memory from the time of the ancient king.

[85] I use the phrase "political gods" with awareness of Robin's "institutional" category for the deities that bind king to people in the South Arabian polities. Michael Stahl (personal communication) is considering the category of "kingdom gods" for a type that would also include city-based monarchy, in place of "national gods."

[86] The ultimate reference for all matters related to Near Eastern storm gods is Schwemer (2001). For Aleppo, see section 5.1 (211–37); and for the Hittites, see chapter 6 on syncretism in upper Mesopotamia and northern Syria.

[87] There has been a flood of new evidence, with particular importance for a realm named "Palastina" with capital at Tell Tayinat and power at Aleppo. For two new stelae with storm god images and texts from Arsuz, dated to the late 10th century, see Dinçol et al. (2015) and the literature cited; cf. Bunnens (2006); Hawkins (2011). Dinçol et al. (75) observe that "The Storm-god is depicted on almost every stele that has been recovered from the area of Syria and southern Anatolia."

when the smaller western domains of Syria and the Levant were often identified with particular representative deities like Yahweh of Israel and Kamosh of Moab, the kingdom of Aram centered at Damascus gave the storm god Hadad this special place.[88]

POLYTHEISM WITHOUT PANTHEON

It is impossible to examine the emergence of Jewish monotheism, against the backdrop of religion in Israel and Judah, without considering the involvement of more than one god.[89] Even the names El and Yahweh most likely derive from different deities, and efforts to explain Yahweh from an epithet of El give pause by their very simplification of divergent divine names into worship of one god (or God) to suit the eventual biblical norm.[90] The Bible itself acknowledges the worship of other gods, right through the end of the two kingdoms, but regards this worship as infidelity to Yahweh and entanglement with foreign figures and practices, not proper to the people themselves.[91] In this study of Yahweh before Israel, I conclude that the divine name did not originally pertain to El and that we must grapple with the reality of two key gods underlying the single God of late monarchic Judah and Judaism. Beyond

[88] See the Tel Dan inscription, as well as the Hazael Booty inscription *COS* 2.40A. Contrast Baal-shamayn for the kingdom of Hamath in the Zakkur inscription (COS 2.35). Lipiński (2000: 626) distinguishes the Arameans of Syria for their placement of Hadad at the head of their pantheon, in contrast to the Chaldean Arameans of southeastern Mesopotamia.

[89] So, Mark Smith's *Early History of God* (1990); John Day's *Yahweh and the Gods and Goddesses* (2000); van der Toorn's "Yahweh" and the whole *DDD* project (1999).

[90] Van der Toorn (1999: 917) addresses the major contributors with respect and caution, yet with notable hesitation: "Speculations about the original identity of Yahweh with El need to be critically examined, however. There are problems concerning both the nature of the identification, and the divine type to which Yahweh belongs. It is insufficiently realized that, at the beginning of the Iron Age, El's role had become largely nominal. . . . This fact explains why there are no traces of polemics against El in the Hebrew Bible. It can therefore be argued that the smooth identification of El as Yahweh was based, not on an identity of character, but on El's decay." Smith (above) shares the sense of two different divine types to go with the separate names, but he starts from the texts that treat Yahweh and Elyon as separate deities, with Elyon presiding (Deut 32:8–9 and Psalm 82).

[91] Deuteronomy 7:3–4 prohibits marriage with the previous inhabitants of the land because this will lead to the worship of "other gods," and 2 Kgs 17:7–20 explains the dismantling of Israel by religious failure, understood as imitating the peoples around them (v. 13). Such worship of other gods is distinct from the abiding critique of the people's worship of their own god Yahweh, as in Amos 5, whether with practices considered anathema or joined to social failures. In the structure provided for the history of the two kingdoms in 1 Kings 12/14–2 Kings 25, the primary (and original) criticism has to do with the worship of Yahweh at sites other than Jerusalem, especially at Bethel by the northern kingdom.

the two dominant names for God, the Bible's repeated complaints against goddesses called Asherah or Ashtoreth and, perhaps more than anything, iconographic evidence, suggest the persistence of female deities in religion of the region.[92] Other lesser deities may also have received attention.

If we are dealing with a variety of gods, it would be natural to call this "polytheism," and the body of gods as a whole is commonly termed a "pantheon." Reconstruction of the divine community in the world of the Bible and Israel is a matter of restoring a fabric from a few threads. Even where we think we have a glimpse, we are in danger of overgeneralizing from a particular setting. Do we assemble a collection of divine names, or potential names? When we add the evidence of images, how many of these locate the individual figures in relation to a whole? Are we to understand the divine community known to individual families and households to match what was recognized by the political leadership of towns or kingdoms – and would the gods of Israel and Judah have been the same, considered as whole divine communities?

The Near Eastern models for our analysis of Israelite polytheism tend to reflect large polities with correspondingly large scale. Even Ugarit, our most convenient "Canaanite" reference, was a wealthy city incorporated into the mighty Hittite kingdom, as was the more recent and less well-known Syrian site of Emar. Beyond any concern for numbers, the scribes of these Syrian cities composed long lists of individually named deities who had to receive attention. At Emar, the longest of these attended the celebration of a major public event called the *zukru* festival with what would have been over a hundred named recipients of special offerings, one for each shrine or figure worshiped in the city.[93] Ugarit attests nothing this long, but separate lists of divine names served a similar purpose to account for all the offerings provided on a single ritual occasion (del Olmo Lete 1999). The *zukru* festival list from Emar is given a hierarchy by the assignment of offerings in three tiers, with decreasing

---

[92] There is a world of detail behind this statement. Early studies include Olyan (1988); and Ackerman (1992). For the Ishtar-like goddess 'Athtart, see Ornan (2001); and for Asherah in the context of goddesses identified with spinning and weaving, see Ackerman (2008). For these last two, I have selected for their particular interest rather than as overviews.

[93] See my edition and study in Fleming (2000a: chapter 3), for Emar VI.3 373. A monograph-length study of all the *zukru* evidence from Emar has now been completed by John Thames in his 2016 Johns Hopkins doctoral dissertation.

quantities for the larger number of sites.[94] In general, the Ugaritic lists follow no strict sequence and attempt no visible hierarchy, but there are patterns that suggest prestige or importance for the occasion in view.[95] In the all-inclusive religious interest of these two cities' Hittite overlords, the numbers mount into the hundreds, though the presentations reflect the particular ritual purposes of each setting and are highly variable. There is no authoritative "pantheon" of Hittite gods but rather all sorts of pantheon cross-sections.[96]

Returning to the threads of our reconstructed Israelite polytheism, how do they fit the warp and woof of such assemblages? On one hand, the variety of the lists and combinations from each site warn against imagining a single and fixed system. In this respect, Lowell Handy's (1994) framework of "bureaucracy" is too rigid even where the texts show a powerful administrative concern. Yet the image of the family household taken up by David Schloen and Mark Smith, grounded as it is in the language of the ancient texts, leaves the possibility of enormous variation between divine "families."[97] If the number of gods in play depends in every case on the human community on hand, the "pantheon" will vary accordingly. It is not clear from any source for Israel and Judah whether we should expect their assemblages of gods to compare even with the numbers from Emar or Ugarit. Each of those lists accompanies a specific occasion at which the indicated divine names would receive an offering, to suit their participation in the public affairs of the people gathered. Would there have been such a collection of shrines and figures in

[94] Other lists of divine names in the Emar documentation are shorter and lack the effort at system. The second longest list is Emar VI.3 378, which is related to the *zukru* list.

[95] The Ugaritic lists vary between twenty and forty entries. Del Olmo Lete (321) observes certain patterns, including: Ilu (El) and Ba'lu (Baal) come first in this order, with varied forms; the order does not follow what we might expect from the myths, perhaps reflecting "patronage and cult specialization"; there are particular offerings to gods identified by Ugarit and Aleppo.

[96] For a sense of the whole, which is frankly overwhelming, see the encyclopedic study by Haas (1994). Note the pertinence of different categories for organizing deity: super-regional gods; gods from specific regions not originally Anatolian, versus old Anatolian gods; gods identified with animals or vegetation; protective deities; clusters of gods into pairs, triads, or even groups of nine and twelve; pantheons associated with individual cities; gods joined for the great temples at the capital Ḫattuša; the special rock temple at Yazilikaya.

[97] See Schloen (2001), especially chapter 14, on "The House of 'Ilu: Canaanite Gods and Human Society"; and Smith (2001a), chapter 3, on "The Divine Family."

Jerusalem and Samaria of the two kingdoms?[98] If so, how many of them would have been dedicated to named individuations of Yahweh or El? And with this last question, we are caught up in the morass of debate over divine embodiment and identity.

Were there then Israelite "pantheons"? The word "pantheon" carries with it assumptions of order and even hierarchy that need not apply equally to all situations with plural gods.[99] In the case of Yahweh and El, it may be illuminating to reevaluate their religious framework without the burden of a potentially mismatched category. Two features of "pantheons" tend to attach to Near Eastern religion generally and to reconstructions of pre-monotheizing religion in Israel and Judah. Both of these find expression in Mark Smith's characterization of Israelite polytheism in his *Origins of Biblical Monotheism* (2001a), where he presents them as elements of the divine family, citing David Schloen with approval as an alternative to Lowell Handy. First, there is hierarchy – not of a palace administration but of a household – divided as Smith sees it into four "tiers" as at Ugarit:

1) Ilu (El) and Athiratu (Asherah) stand at the head, as ruler and consort in general assembly.[100] These are first of all father and mother, and their authority follows the pattern of a family.

2) Next come the "royal children," once named "the seventy sons (children)" of Athiratu (CAT 1.4 VI 46), and possibly also called "the great gods" (CAT 1.124:1–2). Most of the major deities encountered at Ugarit would be found here, including Anat, Athtart, Shapshu, Yarih, Shahar, and Shalim. In spite of his outsider status, Baal comes into the pantheon at this level, requiring Ilu's approval to become "king" of the gods. Some of these gods are identified with the natural world and its effects.

3) A third tier would be defined by service to the other gods, so that the craftsman deity Kothar-wa-Ḫasis belongs here, though his narrative role is substantial. To my eye he is not part of the divine

---

[98] DeGrado (2018: chapter 3) envisions just such objects as lying behind the rhetoric in Isa 10:5–15, with the threat that Assyria could do to Jerusalem what it had already done to Samaria, "kidnapping" its gods.

[99] I appreciate the caution with which Robin (2012) applies the term only to political assemblages, in his discussion of "institutional" deities: "Je reserve l'appellatif 'panthéon' pour cet ensemble de divinités recevant un culte collectif et public" (13).

[100] This list follows Smith (2001a: 45–46). Smith observes that the four levels proposed here are confirmed by the scenes of divine assembly in the Baal myth (CTA 1.2 I and 1.4 III) and in the Kirta tale (CTA 1.15 II). See first of all, Smith 1984.

household and in Smith's construction a visitor, representing the possibility of outsiders rather than a hierarchical element.

4) The final level pertains to minor deities who appear in the retinues of major gods.[101]

A second trait of pantheons is bound up with the first in treatments of Ugarit and the background to Israelite religion: a "divine council," as reflected in the assemblies of gods depicted in Ugaritic myth and various lists (Smith 2001a: chapter 2). Both El and Baal have particular circles surrounding them that appear to represent subsets of the whole divine community, conceived as distinct households or courts. The ideal number for the assembled community would seem to be the seventy of Athirat's children, present to celebrate Baal's reign as king, where they are equally called "his brothers" (*'aḫḫ*) and "his kin" (*'a[r]yh*). At Emar, it is intriguing to find the same number outside of literary use in the ritual instructions for the *zukru* festival, where it contradicts the longer count of individual shrines to receive offerings.[102]

When it comes to a pantheon of gods, as manifest in the offering lists from Emar and Ugarit or the meeting scene cut into the rock shrine at Yazilikaya for the great Hittite kingdom, the presentations themselves do not break down the gods into tiers of the sort proposed by Smith, and the ordering of the gods serves the occasion.[103] To apply the common Near

---

[101] For his understanding of Mesopotamian pantheons, Smith relies considerably on Mullen (1980).

[102] It seems that the list of recipients refers to shrines, not to "gods" as such, if the number 70 is consciously smaller than the count for distribution. This could point away from interpretation of every titled deity as a separate "god," as in the debate over "divine multiplicity" (see Allen 2015). At Emar, the number 70 is defined not as "sons" or children of the leading god, who would be Dagan, but as "all the gods of Emar," the land with its city center (Emar VI.3 373:39). In this ritual context, the 70 gods receive concrete offerings by just this number, 70 lambs to provide one each – in concept, probably not to match all the shrines listed later in the text. This set of 70 may correspond to the group offerings to "the assembly of the gods" in List A from Ugarit (*pḫr 'ilm* or ^d*pu-ḫur* DINGIR^{meš}), as a single line item.

[103] I find artificial the definition of a third tier to suit the craftsman Kothar, though the point of his outsider standing is taken. In his systematic treatment of god lists and offering lists, del Olmo Lete (1999: 308) calls his List A (alphabetic cuneiform Ugaritic KTU/CAT 1.148; 1.47; 1.148:1–9; and ordinary cuneiform Akkadian RS 20.24) "the principal or canonical list," with Kothar (*kṯr*) written in the cuneiform rendition as ^d*É-a* (Ea), the Mesopotamian god of crafts, magic, and cleverness. This list yields 33 entries to produce a "pantheon" (his term) that "does in fact include the group of principal gods of Ugarit, exactly as they appear in myth and the official cult (KTU 1.148 = RS 24.643:1–9). It represents a mythologizing expansion which tends to make organic distinctions between

Eastern phenomenon to the gods of Israel and its kin, we really face a simple division between El as head and the body of gods who make up his household or assembled community. This brings us back to the two texts that provide Smith's point of departure for biblical recollection of Israelite polytheism: Deut 32:8–9 and Psalm 82. Both texts distinguish Elyon ("Most High") as above a body of gods defined as his "sons" in a notable echo of Ugarit's "sons of Ilu." Likewise, both assign Yahweh a role that belongs to those "sons" rather than to Elyon, though the separate relationship of Yahweh to Elyon as separate gods is never clear.

Yet the two texts present a vision of the gods as a whole that is unknown from any ancient writing, that a single "highest" god has distributed rule of individual lands or peoples to an array of gods below him, one each, to account for the entire world. According to Deut 32:8–9:

> When Elyon made allotments to the nations [*gōyīm*],
> when he divided up humanity [*běnê 'ādām*],
> he set the territories of the peoples ['*ammîm*] by the number of the gods
> – indeed, the share of Yahweh was his people,
> Jacob was his surveyed portion.[104]

In strict terms, it would appear that there are no more gods than nations, since the "boundaries" of the latter have been assigned to match the "number" of the former.[105] Whether we are dealing with El at Ugarit or Dagan at Emar, the circle of gods follows no political lines. If we are to take the mythic world of Ugarit's Baal text to represent the entire cosmos, not bounded by Ugarit or any other human polity, the gods nevertheless have no particular attachment to the earth's domains, certainly not distributively. In Psalm 82, "God" (for Yahweh) accuses "the assembly of El" of failure to govern justly (v. 1), perhaps suiting a vision similar to the one more explicit in Deut 32:8–9, where each god has responsibility for

the gods and at the same time to assimilate other foreign pantheons within its own religious framework, from the multiple cultural influence which affected Ugarit: Amorite, Hurrian, Hittite, Sumerian and Akkadian" (310). Kothar also appears in List B (311), gods of the month Ḫiyaru (KTU 1.148:23–45; RS 26.142) and List C (312), KTU 1.102 and 1.139:13–19. In what del Olmo Lete calls a "litany" of names for prayer (316), with a preference for compound forms, we find the full Kothar-wa-Ḫasis (KTU 1.123:9 and 28). See also the full Kothar-wa-Ḫasis in the magical incantation texts KTU 1.100 and 1.107 (322).

[104] See above for comment on the text, with "sons of God/gods" for "sons of Israel" in verse 8.

[105] Nothing indicates that this "number" should be taken as 70. I am aware of no text that attaches this number to the peoples of the world.

one people.[106] In a declaration of judgment, these "gods" who were "sons of Elyon" are destined to die like humans (vv. 6–7).

Because these two texts stand so awkwardly in the company of the Bible's monotheism, they appear archaic and thus available to generalize for early Israelite religion, yet they portray a peculiar and highly specific divine world. Smith calls what we find in Deut 32:8–9 and Psalm 82 a "world theology" (2001a: 49). "This worldview was cast as the patrimonial household in Deuteronomy 32: each god held his own inheritance, and the whole was headed by the patriarchal god." Meanwhile, "The author of Psalm 82 deposes the older theology." For Smith, this tolerance of many gods was only possible with the understanding that they would not impinge on Israel's experience, a notion no longer possible after the arrival of Assyrian world power. The picture of an authoritative divine head distributing the nations of the whole world among the gods, however, resists explanation in terms of old regional religious traditions, and the novelty of the notion suggests innovation.

It may be better, therefore, to approach Deut 32:8–9 as a new application of the ancient idea of El and sons. The idea in itself was familial, with El's circle conceived as an extended household, a combination of the political and the social that was normal to the second millennium.[107] Indeed the filial language of both texts, with the "sons of gods/God" (*běnê 'ĕlōhîm*) in the Qumran text for Deut 32:8 (Tigay 1996: 546 n.2) and the "sons of Elyon" in Ps 82:6, preserves a much older conception of a divine family. Yet in both contexts, a single god, called Elyon, wields authority over the entire world in a way that is closer to imperial, a perspective difficult to imagine before the Assyrian conquest.[108] In Deuteronomy 32, the possibility of separating Elyon as divine head from a family of lesser gods derives from this heritage, but the assignment of nations to gods is political and administrative, the act of a world-ruler in patrimonial mode. And the context here is political, when "nations" are in view.[109] In verses 8–9, playing with the generational division of a distant age, Yahweh takes the role of Elyon and keeps Israel for himself

---

[106] This is Smith's reading (2001a: 48), and it makes sense of the complaint about responsibility for justice that is difficult to understand in the context of Israel alone.

[107] Elyon "allots" (verb *nḥl*) shares to every "nation" (*gōy*), like a father to every son, yet the authority behind such a world-inclusive family is as absolute as that of a head of household, in the old "patrimonial" political mode (Schloen 2001).

[108] This is not the "monotheistic" idea of Levine (2005), but it supposes a similar dynamic.

[109] Likewise the deposed judges of Psalm 82 exercised their legal responsibilities as appointed governors (*śārîm*, v. 7).

(Smith 2004: 152). Both the world oversight and the equation of Yahweh with Elyon may be understood not as prior traditions but as belonging to the setting of the author.

The assignment of gods to nations brings up images of the Assyrian provinces and vassals of the 7th century or even the satrapies of the Achaemenids, after the fall of Jerusalem. Smith is correct to find here a remarkable survival of Canaanite religious categories and also to conclude that this represents evidence for the continuity of Israel's religious tradition with its larger neighborhood. Yet whatever its historical origin and range, the polytheism of Deut 32:8–9 and Psalm 82 resembles nothing Canaanite that we know – not in the specific sense of a single divine authority who governs the landscape of kingdoms and peoples by distribution of them to individual gods. We should therefore consider alternatives to reading them as vestiges of early Israelite conception. It is notable that Frank Cross (1973: 106–109) read the 6th-century manifesto of Isaiah 40–55 through the lens of the divine warrior known from Baal at Ugarit, with victorious procession in chapter 40 accompanied by recollection of Yahweh's defeat of Rahab and the dragon Tannin (51:9–11). For Cross, the time after Judah's defeat brought a "recrudescence of myth" (135), and it may be that the rise of what seemed one-world power inspired new explanations of Yahweh's place in that world, explanations that hearkened back to old notions of El and his children, never lost and now given new form.

The divine council or assembly of gods finds other expression in biblical texts that portray Yahweh or God in heaven with a supporting cast of heavenly beings. One of the most vivid examples of this picture occurs in the prose introduction to Job, where "the adversary [*haśśāṭān*]" joins Yahweh with "the divine sons [*bĕnê hā'ĕlōhîm*]" for conversation that ends in Job's virtues (1:6–8). This text is widely understood to come from after the time of the kingdoms.[110] Creation of humanity in Gen 1:26 "in our image," addressing the community of the heavens, launches the Priestly document of Pentateuchal composition, also not likely a monarchic text. The vision of the prophet Micaiah in 1 Kgs 22:19–22, where a spirit from "the host of heaven" volunteers to enter Ahab's prophets and lie through them, may likewise not reflect an old Israelite religious vision. At the least, the tale belongs explicitly to the sphere of kings, with its

---

[110] For example, Konrad Schmid (2012a: 154) places the finished book in the Persian Period (154), observing the reference to the Neo-Babylonian "Chaldeans" in 1:17 and the need to work mainly from references to other biblical texts (Schmid 2007).

image of a heavenly court, and the subordinate "host" lined up to the right and left of Yahweh on his throne.[111] Unlike the unusual scenes from Deut 32:8–9 and Psalm 82, none of these portraits of the heavens places Yahweh among the masses, below a separate El or Elyon. These all leave the gods – or divine offspring – as the circle of Yahweh's servants.

So far as the biblical texts just discussed offer refractions of a polytheistic system, they all do so through the prism of one-world rule in a conceptual universe made possible only by the imperial line from Assyria to Babylonia to the Achaemenids in the late 8th through 4th centuries. Given these historical and political bounds, it is not possible to reconstruct the earlier polytheism of Israel, Judah, and their antecedent peoples from such materials. What would we find if we could see the divine community of this landscape before the arrival of foreign empire? Certainly El and Yahweh would have represented distinct gods, both of them attested in non-biblical inscriptions – Deir 'Alla, Kuntillet 'Ajrud, and Mesha – as well as biblical poetry that probably comes from similarly early dates. None of this evidence puts them into relationship, however, so that we are left largely ignorant of how this was handled in different settings. All the evidence from antiquity warns against overly rigid generalization, and the solutions may have varied, even in early times. Before kings and their administrations, collective action would have followed the lines of social organization, whether by individual settlements or in collaborations ordered by kinship or other notions of association. Where the social settings did not demand strict hierarchy and assignment of relationships, the gods would likewise not have been set in order. Just as Schloen's vision of patriarchal political authority requires too much construction as concentric circles around a single head, the same variety of social configuration would have applied to the gods.[112] All this would have played out in a polytheistic religious world, but in the decentralized social and political landscape of the early southern Levant, the idea of pantheon is more likely to lead astray than to guide.

So far as Yahweh of the allies in Judg 5:13 took his name from a people once identified by the Egyptians as part of Shasu-land, it is impossible to know when and exactly how this occurred, as well as what other gods

---

[111] Noam Cohen (2018) proposes that the scene in heaven is a secondary elaboration of the prophecy, when the original text simply has Micaiah prophesy victory for Ahab and then be rebuked for lying, so that Ahab will go to his doom regardless.

[112] On Schloen's *House of the Father* (2001), see my reflections in Fleming (2002), where I develop the observation made here.

were worshiped by such a people. By the logic of a deity sharing the name of a human community, joined to the leading role later attributed to Yahweh in Israel, we could conclude that no other god held higher standing attendant to the succor or specific support guaranteed by that bond. Yet divine rank is intelligible only as defined in relationship with other gods, and we dare not assume that some earliest Yahweh had either to shoulder aside El or to submit to him in order to enjoy his own position. At present, we cannot know and we may benefit by considering the possibility of a religious framework without divine assembly and without the hierarchy of a pantheon. Even if many gods were perceived to inhabit a sky full of stars and the many niches of their natural world, do we know that they gathered to act as one or that they had a king? When Yahweh came on the scene, was it taken for granted that he had to be fitted into a pantheon with El as head? Perhaps, but I wonder whether we have relied too much on the structures of major kingdoms to reconstruct the religion of small towns and a back country beyond.

YAHWEH BEFORE, AND ALONGSIDE, ISRAEL

As observed in beginning this reconceptualization of Yahweh, I have undertaken both a negative and a positive task. Negatively, we must set aside the Midianite Hypothesis of Yahweh's first worship among people foreign to an unambiguous "Israel," brought in by way of desert contacts. Neither the biblical nor the Egyptian evidence supports this idea, whether in its geography or in its expectation that Yahweh came into Israel by way of groups that were never part of it. Positively, the essential starting point for identifying the background of Yahweh must be the Yhw3 subdivision of Shasu-land in the list from Egypt's king Amenhotep III. As such a unit of the Shasu encountered by Egypt in the early 14th century or before, Yhw3 would be one of several large groups both identified with the "land" of that population and mobile within it. In later times, the Egyptians called the divisions of the Shasu population "families" or "tribes" (*mhwt*), a designation that can maintain a relationship to space. Among the Shasu groups or "peoples," only Yhw3 begins with /y/, as would a Semitic prefixed verb, and when approached in the kinship terms of the Egyptian *mhwt*, the form of the name is not difficult to explain as derived from a human personal name. We are then left to account for how a deity could take the name of a people – not necessarily an "ancestor" – and to consider the characteristics of such a deity when measured against the gods who dominated the region for centuries, especially El and Baal (Hadad).

Equally, we must locate Yahweh in a political and social landscape not simply defined by "Israel" and peoples foreign to it. Israel in its largest scope was defined especially by the unity and geographical extent of the northern kingdom in the 9th and 8th centuries. Before this time, Israel was smaller and limited to a space identified especially with the highlands north of Ephraim, possibly including adjacent population further to the north and east. The *'am Yhwh* in the Song of Deborah included groups with no connection to Israel when the battle account of Judg 5:13–22/23 was first composed. In the context of that conflict, the majority had no such Israelite identity. At least, belonging to Israel was irrelevant to participation with the "people of Yahweh." When I insist that Yahweh in the early days was not an Israelite god, this is not just because he was not identified with Israel. Israel itself was a different and more limited entity in the early days of Yahweh. Against various models, Yahweh was not a god or a name taken from El, and the Egyptian context for Yhw₃ as people suggests no reason to treat him as once a young warrior or storm god. All of these associations, however archaic, came afterward. When the god identified with a people had to stand and be counted among a circle of major gods, as that people likewise took its stand in a larger world, he could not cede such powers to anyone.

In the end, the best analogies for thinking about Yahweh before Israel come from South Arabia, where new inscriptional evidence allows detailed knowledge of political structures and the ritual practices integrated with them. If we must imagine early Yahweh to have had a profile, this should follow the pattern of the Sabaean Almaqah and the Qatabanian 'Amm. These do not appear to have been defined first of all by a place in the natural world, as storm gods or as celestial gods of moon or stars. In their political function, binding people to kings, they became divine leaders, yet they were not intrinsically the primary authorities or patriarchs in the divine world – unlike El of Ugarit. If any single god held such prestige in South Arabia, it appears to have been 'Athtar (Robin 2018: 96). This prestige may be displayed already in the 9th-century Mesha inscription for Moab, where the recipient of the war-*ḥērem* is Ashtar-Kamosh. This equation is secondary to Kamosh in the same way as Yahweh's identification with El, which becomes visible only with the kingdoms of Israel and Judah. If the manifestation of Yahweh's power in Judg 5:4–5, with shaking mountains and dripping sky, recalls 'Athtar more than Hadad, as suggested by Smith (2001a: 146), then this text could be aligning Yahweh with 'Athtar – secondarily – just as Kamosh is aligned with Ashtar in the Mesha text.

The power of Almaqah and 'Amm derived from their complete identification with the people they unified and protected. The peoples of Saba' and Qatabān were their family, "the descendants of Almaqah" and "the descendants of 'Amm." Kamosh and Moab appear to have reflected the same pattern, and the Bible's "people of Kemosh" (Num 21:29; Jer 48:46) may represent the same kind of bond. So then, also, would the "people of Yahweh" with Yahweh the god.

Before Israel, and then alongside it, Yahweh was the god of people without kings, allied as occasion required, to fight any deemed a common enemy. Without reference to Israel, the political alignment of people with deity on display here is typical of the inland, preserved in evidence from Moabite Jordan and southern Arabia. Yahweh seems not to have begun as a god of cities, whether the lowland centers controlled by Egypt or the old highland strongholds of the Bronze Age, like Jerusalem. The question of Yahweh's own "early history," to paraphrase Mark Smith (1990), has always been a tantalizing one in its own right. With this interpretation of the evidence, I underscore Yahweh's contribution to understanding the social and political threads that are represented by ancient names, names that scatter as we trace their threads back in time, only braided together in secondary formations. These are the "glimpses of history in a divine name."

Bibliography

Ackerman, Susan. 1992. *Under Every Green Tree: Popular Religion in Sixth-Century Judah*. Atlanta, GA: Scholars Press.

2008. "Asherah, the West Semitic Goddess of Spinning and Weaving?" *JNES* 67: 1–29.

Adam, Klaus-Peter. 2008. "Erzählerwertung und Geschichtsverständnis in den Samuelbüchern (1 Samuel 31, 2 Samuel 1; 11; 18)." Pp. 131–80 in Adam (ed.), *Historiographie in der Antike*. Berlin: de Gruyter.

Adrom, Faried, and Matthias Müller. 2017. "The Tetragrammaton in Egyptian Sources: Fact and Fiction." Pp. 93–113 in Jürgen van Oortschot and Markus Witte (eds.), *The Origins of Yahwism*. Berlin: de Gruyter.

Ahituv, Shmuel. 1984. *Canaanite Toponyms in Ancient Egyptian Documents*. Jerusalem: Magnes/Leiden: Brill.

2008. "The Sinai Theophany in the Psalm of Habakkuk." Pp. 1:225–32 in Chaim Cohen et al. (eds.), *Birkat Shalom: Studies in the Bible, Ancient Near Eastern Literature, and Postbiblical Judaism Presented to Shalom M. Paul*. Winona Lake, IN: Eisenbrauns.

Ahituv, Shmuel, Esther Eshel, and Ze'ev Meshel. 2012. "The Inscriptions." Pp. 73–142 in Ze'ev Meshel, *Kuntillet 'Ajrud (Horvat Teman): An Iron Age II Religious Site on the Judah-Sinai Border*. Jerusalem: Israel Exploration Society.

Ahlström, Gösta W. 1986. *Who Were the Israelites?* Winona Lake, IN: Eisenbrauns.

Albertz, Rainer. 1994 (German 1990). *A History of Israelite Religion in the Old Testament Period. Volume 1: From the Beginnings to the End of the Monarchy*. Louisville, KY: Westminster John Knox.

Albright, William F. 1922. "The Earliest Forms of Hebrew Verse." *Journal of the Palestine Oriental Society* 2: 69–86.

1924. "Contributions to Biblical Archaeology and Philology." *JBL* 43: 363–93.

1944. "The Oracles of Balaam." *JBL* 63: 207–33.

1945. "The Old Testament and Canaanite Language and Literature." *CBQ* 7: 5–31.

1948. Review of B. M. Wambacq, *L'épithète divine Jahvé Seba'ôt: Étude philologique, historique et exégétique*, 1947. *JBL* 67: 377–81.

1950. "The Psalm of Habakkuk." Pp. 1–18 in H. H. Rowley (ed.), *Studies in Old Testament Prophecy*. Edinburgh: T. & T. Clark.

1950–51. "A Catalogue of Early Hebrew Lyric Poems (Psalm LXVIII)." *HUCA* 23: 1–39.

1968. *Yahweh and the Gods of Canaan: A Historical Analysis of Two Contrasting Faiths*. Garden City, NY: Doubleday.

Allen, Spencer L. 2015. *The Splintered Divine: A Study of Ištar, Baal, and Yahweh Divine Names and Divine Multiplicity in the Ancient Near East*. Berlin: de Gruyter.

Alt, Albrecht. 1929. *Der Gott der Väter*. Beiträge zur Wissenschaft vom Alten und Neuen Testament.

1953. *Kleine Schriften zur Geschichte des Volkes Israel*. Munich: Beck.

Amzallag, Nissim. 2009. "Yahweh, the Canaanite God of Metallurgy?" *JSOT* 33: 387–404.

Anderson, James S. 2015. *Monotheism and Yahweh's Appropriation of Baal*. London: T. & T. Clark.

Anthony, Flora B. 2016. *Foreigners in Ancient Egypt: Theban Tomb Paintings from the Early Eighteenth Dynasty (1550–1372 BC)*. London: Bloomsbury.

Arbach, Mounir. 2011. "Qui a construit le rampart de Nashshān l'actuel as-Sawdā' (Yémen), au VIIIe siècle avant J.-C.?" *Semitica et Classica* 4: 187–92.

Armstrong, Karen. 1993. *A History of God: The 4,000-Year Quest of Judaism, Christianity, and Islam*. London: William Heinemann.

Astour, Michael C. 1979. "Yahweh in Egyptian Topographic Lists." Pp. 17–33 in Manfred Görg and Edgar Pusch (eds.), *Festschrift Elmar Edel*. Bamberg: M. Görg.

Avanzini, Alessandra. 2016. *By Land and Sea: A History of South Arabia before Islam Recounted from Inscriptions*. Rome: "L'Erma" di Bretschneider.

Baden, Joel S. 2009. *J, E, and the Redaction of the Pentateuch*. Tübingen: Mohr Siebeck.

2012. "The Continuity of the Non-Priestly Narrative from Genesis to Exodus." *Biblica* 93: 161–86.

Bär, Jürgen. 2003a. *Die ältesten Ischtar-Tempel in Assur*. Saarbrücken: Saarbrücker Druckerei und Verlag.

2003b. "Sumerians, Gutians and Hurrians at Ashur? A Re-examination of Ishtar Temples G and F." *Iraq* 65: 143–60.

Barstad, Hans. 2007. "Can Prophetic Texts Be Dated? Amos 1–2 as an Example." Pp. 21–40 in Lester L. Grabbe (ed.), *Ahab Agonistes: The Rise and Fall of the Omri Dynasty*. London: T. & T. Clark.

Bartelmus, Rüdiger. 2004. "'Schriftprophetie' ausserhalb des corpus propheticum – eine unmögliche Möglichkeit? Das Mose-Lied (Ex 15,1–21) als deutero-jesajanisch geprägtes 'eschatologisches Loblied'." Pp. 55–82 in Friedhelm Hartenstein et al. (eds.), *Schriftprophetie: Festschrift für Jörg Jeremias zum 65. Geburtstag*. Neukirchen–Vluyn: Neukirchener.

Beaux, Nathalie, and Nicolas Grimal. 2013. *Soleb VI. Hommages à Michela Schiff Giorgini.* Cairo: Institut français d'archéologie orientale.

Becking, Bob. 2017. "A Voice from across the Jordan: Royal Ideology as Implied in the Moabite Stela." Pp. 125–45 in Christoph Levin and Reinhard Müller (eds.), *Herrschaftslegitimation in vorderorientalischen Reichen der Eisenzeit.* Tübingen: Mohr Siebeck.

Beeston, A. F. L. 1985. "Mesha and Ataroth." *Journal of the Royal Asiatic Society* 117: 143–48.

Ben-Yosef, Erez. 2010. "Technology and Social Processes: Oscillations in Iron Age Copper Production and Power in Southern Jordan." University of California at San Diego PhD.

Benz, Brendon C. 2016. *The Land before the Kingdom of Israel: A History of the Southern Levant and the People Who Populated It.* Winona Lake, IN: Eisenbrauns.

Benz, Brendon C., and Daniel E. Fleming. 2016. "The People of Yahweh and Early Israel." Society of Biblical Literature Annual Meeting.

Berman, Lawrence M. 1998. "Overview of Amenhotep III and His Reign." Pp. 1–25 in David O'Connor and Eric Cline (eds.), *Amenhotep III: Perspectives on His Reign.* Ann Arbor, MI: University of Michigan Press.

Berner, Christoph. 2010. *Die Exoduserzählung: Das literarische Werden einer Ursprungslegende Israels.* Tübingen: Mohr Siebeck.

2017. "'I Am Yahweh Your God, Who Brought You Out of the Land of Egypt' (Exod 20:2): Reflections on the Status of the Exodus Creed in the History of Israel and the Literary History of the Hebrew Bible." Pp. 181–206 in Jürgen van Oortschot and Markus Witte (eds.), *The Origins of Yahwism.* Berlin: de Gruyter.

Beyerle, Stefan. 1997. *Mosesegen im Deuteronomium: Eine text-, kompositions-, und formkritische Studie zu Deuteronomium 33.* Berlin: de Gruyter.

Biella, Joan Copeland. 1982. *Dictionary of Old South Arabic: Sabaean Dialect.* Chico, CA: Scholars.

Blenkinsopp, Joseph. 2008. "The Midianite-Kenite Hypothesis Revisited and the Origins of Judah." *JSOT* 33: 131–53.

Blum, Erhard. 1984. *Die Komposition der Vätergeschichte.* Neukirchen–Vluyn: Neukirchener.

1990. *Studien zur Komposition des Pentateuch.* Berlin: de Gruyter.

2002. "Die literarische Verbindung des Erzvätern und Exodus: Ein Gespräch mit neueren Endredaktionshypothesen." Pp. 119–56 in J. C. Gertz et al. (eds.), *Abschied vom Jahwisten: Die Komposition des Hexateuch in der jüngsten Diskussion.* Berlin: de Gruyter.

2006. "The Literary Connection between the Books of Genesis and Exodus and the End of the Book of Joshua." Pp. 91–96 in Thomas B. Dozeman and Konrad Schmid (eds.), *A Farewell to the Yahwist? The Composition of the Pentateuch in Recent European Scholarship.* Atlanta, GA: Scholars Press.

2013. "Die Wandinschriften 4.2 und 4.6 sowie die Pithos-Inschrift 3.9 aus Kuntillet 'Aǧrūd." *ZDPV* 129: 21–54.

Boorer, Susanne. 2016. *The Vision of the Priestly Narrative: Its Genre and Hermeneutics of Time.* Atlanta, GA: Scholars Press.

Boree, Wilhelm. 1930. *Die alten Ortsnamen Palastinas.* Leipzig: Eduard Pfeiffer.

Brisch, Nicole. 2016. "Marduk (God)." http://oracc.iaas.upenn.edu/amgg/listofde ities/marduk/ in *Ancient Mesopotamian Gods and Goddesses*. Oracc and the UK Higher Education Academy.

Bryan, Betsy M. 1998. "Antecedents to Amenhotep III." Pp. 27–62 in David O'Connor and Eric H. Cline (eds.), *Amenhotep III: Perspectives on His Reign*. Ann Arbor, MI: University of Michigan Press.

Budde, Karl. 1882. "Das hebräische Klagelied." *ZAW* 2: 1–52.

1899 (German 1905). *The Religion of Israel to the Exile*. London: G. P. Putnam's Sons.

1912. *Die altisraelitische Religion*. Giessen: Alfred Töpelmann.

Bunnens, Guy. 2006. *A New Luwian Stele and the Cult of the Storm-God at Til Barsib – Masuwari*. Leuven: Peeters.

Carr, David M. 1996. *Reading the Fractures of Genesis: Historical and Literary Approaches*. Louisville, KY: Westminster John Knox.

2011. *The Formation of the Hebrew Bible: A New Reconstruction*. Oxford: Oxford University Press.

forthcoming. *Commentary on Genesis 1–11*. Oxford: Oxford University Press.

Cathcart, Kevin J. 2011. "The Earliest Contributions to the Decipherment of Sumerian and Akkadian." *Cuneiform Digital Library Journal* 1: 1–12.

Chapman, Cynthia R. 2016. *The House of the Mother: The Social Roles of Maternal Kin in Biblical Hebrew Narrative and Poetry*. New Haven, CT: Yale University Press.

Charpin, Dominique. 2004. "Histoire politique du Proche-Orient amorrite (2002–1595)." Pp. 25–480 in *Mesopotamien: Die altbabylonische Zeit*. Göttingen: Vandenhoeck und Ruprecht.

Childs, Brevard. 1974. *The Book of Exodus: A Critical, Theological Commentary*. Philadelphia: Westminster.

Cline, Eric H. 1998. "Amenhotep III, the Aegean, and Anatolia." Pp. 236–50 in David O'Connor and Eric Cline (eds.), *Amenhotep III: Perspectives on His Reign*. Ann Arbor, MI: University of Michigan Press.

Cline, Eric H., and David O'Connor (eds.). 2006. *Thutmose III: A New Biography*. Ann Arbor, MI: University of Michigan Press.

Cogan, Mordechai. 2008. *The Raging Torrent: Historical Inscriptions from Assyria and Babylonia Relating to Ancient Israel*. Jerusalem: Carta.

Cohen, Noam. 2018. "A Prophecy of Doom as Requested: The Role of Micaiah in 1 Kings 22." New York University graduate seminar paper.

2019. "Written in Stone: Inscribed Stone Vessels and the Sanctity of Kuntillet 'Ajrud." New York University graduate seminar paper.

Coogan, Michael D. 1978. "A Structural and Literary Analysis of the Song of Deborah." *CBQ* 40: 143–66.

Cortese, Enzo. 1990. *Josua 13–21: Ein priesterschriftlicher Abschnitt im deuter-onomistischen Geschichtswerk*. Göttingen: Vandenhoeck und Ruprecht.

Cross, Frank Moore. 1962. "Yahweh and the God of the Patriarchs." *HTR* 55: 225–59.

1966. "The Divine Warrior in Israel's Early Cult." Pp. 11–30 in Alexander Altmann (ed.), *Biblical Motifs: Origins and Transformations*. Cambridge, MA: Harvard University Press.

1968. "The Song of the Sea and Canaanite Myth." *Journal of Theology and the Church* 5: 1–25.

1973. *Canaanite Myth and Hebrew Epic*. Cambridge, MA: Harvard University Press.

1988. "Reuben, the Firstborn of Jacob: Sacral Traditions and Early Israelite History." *ZAW* 100: 46–66.

1998. *From Epic to Canon: History and Literature in Ancient Israel*. Baltimore: The Johns Hopkins University Press.

Cross, Frank Moore, and David Noel Freedman. 1948. "The Blessing of Moses." *JBL* 67: 191–210.

1997 (1975). *Studies in Ancient Yahwistic Poetry*. Grand Rapids, MI: Eerdmans.

Dalley, Stephanie. 1990. "Yahweh in Hamath in the 8th Century BC: Cuneiform Material and Historical Deductions." *VT* 40: 21–32.

Daniels, D. Quinn. 2018. "The Politics of the Song of Deborah: The Enduring 'Root' of Ephraim in Amaleq (Judg. 5:14a)." Society of Biblical Literature Annual Meeting.

Daniels, Peter T. 1995. "The Decipherment of Ancient Near Eastern Scripts." Pp. 81–93 in Jack M. Sasson (ed.), *Civilizations of the Ancient Near East*. Four volumes; New York: Charles Scribner's Sons.

Davies, Philip R. 1992. *In Search of "Ancient Israel."* Sheffield: Sheffield Academic Press.

Day, John. 1985. *God's Conflict with the Dragon and the Sea: Echoes of a Canaanite Myth in the Old Testament*. Cambridge: Cambridge University Press.

2000. *Yahweh and the Gods and Goddesses of Canaan*. Sheffield: Sheffield Academic Press.

Dearman, J. Andrew (ed.). 1989. *Studies in the Mesha Inscription and Moab*. Atlanta, GA: Scholars Press.

DeGrado, Jessie. 2018. "Authoring Empire: Intellectual Engagement with the Neo-Assyrian Empire in the Bible." University of Chicago PhD.

Dever, William G. 1981. "The Impact of the 'New Archaeology' on Syro-Palestinian Archaeology." *BASOR* 242: 15–29.

2001. *What Did the Biblical Writers Know and When Did They Know It?* Grand Rapids, MI: Eerdmans.

2003. *Who Were the Early Israelites and Where Did They Come From?* Grand Rapids, MI: Eerdmans.

2005. *Did God Have a Wife? Archaeology and Folk Religion in Ancient Israel*. Grand Rapids, MI: Eerdmans.

2017. *Beyond the Texts: An Archaeological Portrait of Ancient Israel and Judah*. Atlanta, GA: Society of Biblical Literature.

Dewrell, Heath D. 2020. "Yahweh the Destroyer: On the Meaning of יהוה." In Christopher Rollston (ed.), *Biblical and Ancient Near Eastern Studies in Honor of P. Kyle McCarter*. Atlanta, GA: Society of Biblical Literature.

Dijkstra, Meindert. 1988. "The Statue of SR 346 and the Tribe of the Kenites." Pp. 95–97 in Matthias Augustin and Klaus-Dietrich Schunck (eds.), *"Wünschet Jerusalem Frieden": Collected Communications to XIIth*

Congress of International Organization for the Study of the Old Testament, Jerusalem, 1986. Frankfurt am Main: P. Lang.

Dinçol, Belkıs et al. 2015. "Two New Inscribed Storm-God Stelae from Arsuz (İskenderun): ARSUZ 1 and 2." *Anatolian Studies* 65: 59–77.

Dion, Paul-Eugène. 1997. *Les araméens à l'Âge du Fer: Histoire politique et structures sociales.* Paris: J. Gabalda.

Di Vito, Robert A. 1993. *Studies in Third Millennium Sumerian and Akkadian Personal Names: The Designation and Conception of the Personal God.* Rome: Pontifical Institute.

Dobbs-Allsopp, F. W. 2015. *On Biblical Poetry.* Oxford: Oxford University Press.

Donner, Herbert, and Wolfgang Röllig. 1968. *Kanaanäische und aramäische Inschriften. Band II: Kommentar.* Wiesbaden: Harrassowitz.

Dothan, Trude. 1983. *The Philistines and Their Material Culture.* New Haven, CT: Yale University Press.

Driver, S. R. 1911. *The Book of Exodus.* Cambridge: Cambridge University Press.

Dubovsky, Peter. 2015. *The Building of the First Temple: A Study in Redactional, Text-Critical and Historical Perspective.* Tübingen: Mohr Siebeck.

Durand, Jean-Marie. 1995. "La religion en Siria durante la época de los reinos amorreos según la documentación de Mari." Pp. 127–533 in G. del Olmo Lete (ed.), *Mitología y Religión del Oriente Antiguo II/1: Semitas Occidentales (Ebla, Mari).* Barcelona: Editorial AUSA.

———. 1997–2000. *Documents épistolaires du palais de Mari.* Three volumes; Paris: Éditions du Cerf.

———. 2004. "Peuplement et société à l'époque amorrite (I): Les clans Bensim'alites." Pp. 111–97 in Christophe Nicolle (ed.), *Amurru 3: Nomades et sédentaires dans le Proche-Orient ancient.* Paris: Éditions Recherche sur les Civilisations.

———. 2010. "Des dieux, un ministre et un coquin." Pp. 63–72 in Dahlia Shehata, Frauke Weiershäuser, and Kamran V. Zand (eds.), *Von Göttern und Menschen: Beiträge zu Literatur und Geschichte des Alten Orients. Festschrift für Brigitte Gröneberg.* Leiden: Brill.

Edel, Elmar. 1966. *Die Ortsnamenlisten aus dem Totentempel Amenophis III.* Bonn: Peter Hanstein.

———. 1980. "Die Ortsnamenlisten aus dem Totentempeln von Aksha, Amarah und Soleb." *BN* 11: 63–79.

Edel, Elmar, and Manfred Görg. 2005. *Die Ortsnamen in nördlichen Säulenhof des Totentempels Amenophis III.* Wiesbaden: Harrassowitz.

Emerton, John A. 1999. "'Yahweh and His Asherah': The Goddess or Her Symbol?" *VT* 49: 315–37.

Eph'al, Israel. 1984. *The Ancient Arabs: Nomads on the Borders of the Fertile Crescent, 9th–5th Centuries B.C.* Jerusalem: Magnes.

Evans-Pritchard, E. E. 1940. *The Nuer.* Oxford: Clarendon.

Fairman, H. W. 1939. "Preliminary Report on the Excavations at 'Amārah West, Anglo-Egyptian Sudan, 1938–9." *Journal of Egyptian Archaeology* 25: 139–44, pls. xiii–xvi.

Faulkner, Raymond O. 1962. *A Concise Dictionary of Middle Egyptian.* Oxford: Griffith Institute.

Faust, Avraham. 2006. *Israel's Ethnogenesis: Settlement, Interaction, Expansion and Resistance*. London: Equinox.

Finkelstein, Israel. 1988. *The Archaeology of the Israelite Settlement*. Jerusalem: Israel Exploration Society.

2013. *The Forgotten Kingdom: The Archaeology and History of the Northern Kingdom*. Atlanta, GA: Society of Biblical Literature.

2017. "Major Saviors, Minor Judges: The Historical Background of the Northern Accounts in the Book of Judges." *JSOT* 41: 431–49.

2019. "First Israel, Core Israel, United (Northern) Israel." *NEA* 82: 8–15.

Finkelstein, Israel, and Nadav Na'aman. 2005. "Shechem of the Amarna Period and the Rise of the Northern Kingdom of Israel." *IEJ* 55: 172–93.

Finkelstein, Israel, and Neil Asher Silberman. 2001. *The Bible Unearthed: Archaeology's New Vision of Ancient Israel and the Origin of Its Sacred Texts*. New York: Simon and Schuster.

2006. *David and Solomon: In Search of the Bible's Sacred Kings and the Roots of the Western Tradition*. New York: Free Press.

Finkelstein, Israel, and Thomas Römer. 2014a. "Comments on the Historical Background of the Jacob Narrative in Genesis." *ZAW* 126: 317–38.

2014b. "Comments on the Historical Background of the Abraham Narrative: Between 'Realia' and Exegetica." *HBAI* 3: 3–23.

Fischer, Alexander A. 2004. *Von Hebron nach Jerusalem: Eine redaktions-geschichtliche Studie zur Erzählung von König David in II Sam 1–5*. Berlin: de Gruyter.

Fishbane, Michael. 1985. *Biblical Interpretation in Ancient Israel*. Oxford: Clarendon.

Fleming, Daniel E. 1999. "If El Is a Bull, Who Is a Calf? Reflections on Religion in Second-Millennium Syria-Palestine." Pp. 23*–27* in B. A. Levine et al. (eds.), Frank M. Cross Festschrift, *Eretz-Israel* 26.

2000a. *Time at Emar: The Cultic Calendar and the Rituals from the Diviner's Archive*. Winona Lake, IN: Eisenbrauns.

2000b. "Mari's Large Public Tent and the Priestly Tent Sanctuary." *VT* 50: 484–98.

2002. "Schloen's Patrimonial Pyramid: Explaining Bronze Age Society." *BASOR* 328: 73–80.

2004. *Democracy's Ancient Ancestors: Mari and Early Collective Governance*. Cambridge: Cambridge University Press.

2009. "Kingship of City and Tribe Conjoined: Zimri-Lim at Mari." Pp. 227–40 in Jeffrey Szuchman (ed.), *Nomads, Tribes, and the State in the Ancient Near East: Cross-Disciplinary Perspectives*. Chicago: Oriental Institute.

2012a. *The Legacy of Israel in Judah's Bible: History, Politics, and the Reinscribing of Tradition*. Cambridge: Cambridge University Press.

2012b. "People without Town: The '*apiru* in the Amarna Evidence." Pp. 39–49 in Rebecca Hasselbach and Na'ama Pat-el (eds.), *Language and Nature: Papers Presented to John Huehnergard on the Occasion of His 60th Birthday*. Chicago: Oriental Institute.

2015. "Living by Livestock in Israel's Exodus: Explaining Origins over Distance." Pp. 483–91 in Thomas E. Levy, Thomas Schneider, and William

H. C. Propp (eds.), *Israel's Exodus in Transdisciplinary Perspective: Text, Archaeology, Culture, and Geoscience*. Cham: Springer.

2018. "The Shiloh Ritual in Joshua 18 as Origin of the Territorial Division by Lot." Pp. 311–37 in Christoph Berner and Harald Samuel (eds.), *Book-Seams in the Hexateuch I: The Literary Transitions between the Books of Genesis/ Exodus and Joshua/Judges*. Tübingen: Mohr Siebeck.

2020. "Joseph and His Allies in Genesis 29–30." In Christopher Rollston (ed.), *Biblical and Ancient Near Eastern Studies in Honor of P. Kyle McCarter*. Atlanta, GA: Society of Biblical Literature.

forthcoming. "The Bible's Little Israel: Textual Inclusions in a Later Matrix." *HBAI*.

Fleming, Daniel E., and Sara J. Milstein. 2010. *The Buried Foundation of the Gilgamesh Epic: The Akkadian Huwawa Narrative*. Leiden: Brill.

Foley, John Miles. 1991. *Immanent Art: From Structure to Meaning in Traditional Oral Epic*. Bloomington, IN: Indiana University Press.

Frayne, Douglas. 1990. *Old Babylonian Period (2003–1595 B.C.): Early Periods, Volume 4*. Toronto: University of Toronto Press.

Freedman, David Noel. 1980. *Pottery, Poetry and Prophecy*. Winona Lake, IN: Eisenbrauns.

Freidenreich, Aron. 2019. "Reconceptualizing the Relationship between P and Non-P: A Study of the Dynamic Interaction between the Priestly and Non-Priestly Narrative Texts of the Pentateuch and Their Mutual Development." Union Theological Seminary PhD.

Freud, Liora. 2008. "The Date of Kuntillet ʿAjrud: A Reply to Lily Singer-Avitz." *TA* 35: 169–74.

Fried, Morton H. 1975. *The Notion of the Tribe*. Menlo Park, CA: Cummings.

Fritz, Volkmar. 2006. "The Complex of Traditions in Judges 4 and 5 and the Religion of Pre-state Israel." Pp. 2:689–98 in Aren Maier and Pierre de Miroschedji (eds.), *"I Will Speak the Riddles of Ancient Times": Archaeological and Historical Studies in Honor of Amihai Mazar on the Occasion of His Sixtieth Birthday*. Two volumes; Winona Lake, IN: Eisenbrauns.

Gadot, Yuval. 2019. "The Iron I Settlement Wave in the Samaria Highlands and Its Connection with the Urban Centers." *NEA* 82: 32–41.

Gardiner, Alan. 1997. *Ancient Egyptian Onomastica. Three volumes*; Oxford: Oxford University Press.

Garr, W. Randall. 1992. "The Grammar and Interpretation of Exodus 6:3." *JBL* 111: 385–408.

Gelb, Ignace J. 1980. *Computer-Aided Analysis of Amorite*. Chicago: The Oriental Institute.

de Geus, C. H. J. 1976. *The Tribes of Israel: An Investigation into Some of the Presuppositions of Martin Noth's Amphictyony Hypothesis*. Assen: van Gorcum.

Ghillany, Friedrich (as Richard von der Alm). 1862. *Theologische Briefe an die Gebildeten der deutschen Nation*. Two volumes; Leipzig: Otto Wigand.

Giddens, Anthony. 1984. *The Construction of Society: Outline of the Theory of Structuration*. Berkeley: University of California Press.

Giveon, Raphael. 1964. "Toponymes oust-asiatiques à Soleb." *VT* 14: 239–55.
1971. *Les bédouins Shosou des documents égyptiens*. Leiden: Brill.

Goedicke, Hans. 1992. *Problems concerning Amenophis III*. Baltimore: Halgo.
1994. "The Tetragrammaton in Egyptian?" *Society for the Study of Egyptian Antiquities* 24: 24–27.

Goldin, Judah. 1971. *The Song of the Sea: Being a Commentary on a Commentary in Two Parts*. New Haven, CT: Yale University Press.

Görg, Manfred. 1976. "YHWH – ein Toponym?" *BN* 1: 7–14.
2000. "YHWH – ein Toponym? Weitere Perspektiven." *BN* 101: 10–14.

Gottwald, Norman. 1979. *The Tribes of Yahweh: A Sociology of the Religion of Liberated Israel, 1250–1050*. Maryknoll, N.Y.: Orbis.

Grabbe, Lester L. (ed.). 2007. *Ahab Agonistes: The Rise and Fall of the Omri Dynasty*. London: T. & T. Clark.

Grandet, Pierre. 1994. *Papyrus Harris I*. Cairo: Institut français de l'archéologie orientale.

Grayson, A. K. 1987. *Assyrian Rulers of the Third and Second Millennium BC (To 1115 BC). The Royal Inscriptions of Mesopotamia: Assyrian Periods, Volume 1*. Toronto: Toronto University Press.

Grdseloff, Bernhard. 1947. "Edôm d'après les sources égyptiennes." *Revue de l'histoire juive en Égypte* 1: 69–99.

Greenfield, Jonas. 1987. "The Hebrew Bible and Canaanite Literature." Pp. 545–60 in Robert Alter and Frank Kermode (eds.), *The Literary Guide to the Bible*. Cambridge, MA: Harvard University Press.

Gressmann, Hugo. 1913. *Mose und seine Zeit: Ein Kommentar zu den Mose-Sagen*. Göttingen: Vandenhoeck und Ruprecht.

Guichard, Michaël. 2003. "Lecture des *Archives Royales de Mari*, Tome XXVIII: Lettres royales du temps de Zimrî-Lîm." *Syria* 80: 199–216.

Haak, Robert D. 1992. *Habakkuk*. Leiden: Brill.

Haas, Volkert. 1994. *Geschichte der hethitischen Religion*. Leiden: Brill.

Hadley, Judith M. 1993. "Kuntillet 'Ajrud: Religious Centre or Desert Way Station?" *PEQ* 125: 115–24.

Hainesworth. John Bryan. 1968. *The Flexibility of the Homeric Formula*. Oxford: Clarendon.

Haller, Arndt, and Walter Andrae. 1955. *Die Heiligtumer des Gottes Assur und der Sin-Šamaš-Tempel in Assur*. Berlin: Gebr. Mann Verlag.

Halpern, Baruch. 1983. "The Resourceful Israelite Historian: The Song of Deborah and Israelite Historiography." *HTR* 76: 379–401.

Hamori, Esther J. 2008. *"When Gods Were Men": The Embodied God in Biblical and Near Eastern Literature*. Berlin: de Gruyter.

Handy, Lowell. 1994. *Among the Host of Heaven: The Syro-Palestinian Pantheon as Bureaucracy*. Winona Lake, IN: Eisenbrauns.

Hartenstein, Friedhelm. 2017. "The Beginnings of YHWH and 'Longing for the Origin': A Historico-Hermeneutical Query." Pp. 283–307 in Jürgen van Oortschot and Markus Witte (eds.), *The Origins of Yahwism*. Berlin: de Gruyter.

Hawkins, J. D. 2011. "The Inscriptions of the Aleppo Temple." *Anatolian Studies* 61: 35–54.

Hawkins, Ralph K. 2012. *The Iron Age I Structure on Mt. Ebal: Excavation and Interpretation.* Winona Lake, IN: Eisenbrauns.

Heltzer, Michael. 1981. *The Suteans.* Naples: Istituto Universitario Orientale.

Hendel, Ronald S. 2001. "The Exodus in Biblical Memory." *JBL* 120: 601–22.

2005. *Remembering Abraham: Culture, Memory, and History in the Hebrew Bible.* Oxford: Oxford University Press.

2015. "The Exodus as Cultural Memory: Egyptian Bondage and the Song of the Sea." Pp. 65–77 in Thomas E. Levy, Thomas Schneider, and William H. C. Propp (eds.), *Israel's Exodus in Transdisciplinary Perspective: Text, Archaeology, Culture, and Geoscience.* Cham: Springer, 2015.

2017. "God and the Gods in the Tetrateuch." Pp. 239–66 in Jürgen van Oortschot and Markus Witte (eds.), *The Origins of Yahwism.* Berlin: de Gruyter.

Herzog, Ze'ev. 2002. "The Fortress Mound at Tel Arad: An Interim Report." *TA* 29: 3–109.

Hiebert, Theodore. 1986. *God of My Victory: The Ancient Hymn in Habakkuk 3.* Atlanta, GA: Scholars Press.

Highcock, Nancy A. 2018. "Community across Distance: The Forging of Identity between Aššur and Anatolia." New York University PhD.

Hoch, James E. 1997. *Middle Egyptian Grammar.* Mississauga, ON: Benben.

Hoffmeier, James K. 1996. *Israel in Egypt: The Evidence for the Authenticity of the Exodus Tradition.* Oxford: Oxford University Press.

Hoftijzer, J., and K. Jongeling. 1995. *Dictionary of the North-West Semitic Inscriptions.* Two volumes; Leiden: Brill.

Holzinger, Heinrich. 1900. *Exodus.* Kurzer Hand-Commentar zum Alten Testament; Tübingern: Mohr-Siebeck.

Horowitz, Wayne, and Takayoshi Oshima. 2002. "Two More Cuneiform Finds from Hazor." *IEJ* 52: 179–86.

2006. *Cuneiform in Canaan: Cuneiform Sources from the Land of Israel in Ancient Times.* Jerusalem: Israel Exploration Society.

Hossfeld, Frank-Lothar, and Erich Zenger. 2003. "The So-Called Elohistic Psalter: A New Solution for an Old Problem." Pp. 35–51 in Brent A. Strawn and Nancy R. Bowen (eds.), *A God So Near: Essays on Old Testament Theology in Honor of Patrick D. Miller.* Winona Lake, IN: Eisenbrauns.

2005. *Psalms 2: A Commentary on Psalms 51–100.* Minneapolis: Fortress.

Houtman, Cornelis. 1996. *Exodus.* Two volumes; Kampen: KOK.

Huffmon, Herbert B. 1965. *Amorite Personal Names in the Mari Texts: A Structural and Lexical Study.* Baltimore: The Johns Hopkins Press.

Hunt, Patrick N. 1991. "Mount Saphon in Myth and Fact." Pp. 103–15 in Edward Lipiński (ed.), *Phoenicia in the Bible: Proceedings of the Conference Held at the University of Leuven on the 15th and 16th of March 1990.* Leuven: Peeters.

Hutton, Jeremy M. 2009. *The Transjordan Palimpsest: The Overwritten Texts of Personal Exile and Transformation in the Deuteronomistic History.* Berlin: de Gruyter.

2010. "Local Manifestations of Yahweh and Worship in the Interstices: A Note on Kuntillet 'Ajrud." *JANER* 10: 177–210.

Hylander, Ivar. 1932. *Der literarische Samuel-Saul Komplex (I Sam 1–15): Traditionsgeschichtlich untersucht.* Leipzig: Harrassowitz.

Jacob, Benno. 1922. "Mose am Dornbusch: Die beiden Hauptbeweisstellen der Quellenscheidung im Pentateuch, Ex 3 und 6, aufs Neue exegetisch geprüft." *Monatschrift für Geschichte und Wissenschaft des Judentums* 66: 1:11–33; 2:116–38; 3:180–200.

Jang, Ki-Eun. 2017. "How Did Deuteronomy 32 Become the Song of Moses?" Paper, Society of Biblical Literature Annual Meeting.

Jeremias, Jörg. 2017. "Three Theses on the Early History of Israel." Pp. 145–56 in Jürgen van Oortschot and Markus Witte (eds.), *The Origins of Yahwism.* Berlin: de Gruyter.

Kawashima, Robert S. 2004. *Biblical Narrative and the Death of the Rhapsode.* Bloomington, IN: Indiana University Press.

Keel, Othmar. 2006. *Die Geschichte Jerusalems und die Entstehung des Monotheismus.* Göttingen: Vandenhoeck und Ruprecht.

Keel, Othmar, and Christoph Uehlinger. 1998. *Gods, Goddesses, and Images of God in Ancient Israel.* Minneapolis: Fortress.

Khoury, Philip S., and Joseph Kostiner. 1990. "Introduction: Tribes and the Complexities of State Formation in the Middle East." Pp. 1–22 in Khoury and Kostiner (eds.), *Tribes and State Formation in the Middle East.* Berkeley: University of California Press.

Killebrew, Ann E. 2005. *Biblical Peoples and Ethnicity: An Archaeological Study of Egyptians, Canaanites, Philistines, and Early Israel 1300–1100 B.C.E.* Atlanta, GA: Scholars Press.

Kitz, Anne Marie. 2019. "The Verb **yahway.*" *JBL* 138: 39–62.

Kloos, Carola. 1986. *YHWH's Combat with the Sea: A Canaanite Tradition in the Religion of Ancient Israel.* Leiden: Brill.

Knapp, Andrew. 2014. "The Dispute over the Land of Qedem at the Onset of the Aram-Israel Conflict: A Reanalysis of Lines 3–4 of the Tel Dan Inscription." *JNES* 73: 105–16.

Knohl, Israel. 1995 (Hebrew 1992). *The Sanctuary of Silence.* Minneapolis: Fortress.

2017. "Jacob-el in the Land of Esau and the Roots of Biblical Religion." *VT* 67: 481–84.

Knott, Elizabeth. 2018. "Mari's Ištar Rituals and the Politics of Divine Multiplicity in the Age of Warring Kings." New York University PhD.

Köckert, Matthias. 2001. "Die Theophanie des Wettergottes in Psalm 18." Pp. 209–26 in Thomas Richter et al. (eds.), *Kulturgeschichten: Altorientalische Studien für Volkert Haas zum 65. Geburtstag.* Saarbrücken: Saarbrücker Druckerei und Verlag.

Korotayev, Andrey. 1993. "Bayt: Basis of Middle Sabaean Social Structure." *Rivista degli Studi Orientali* 67: 55–63.

Kozloff, Arielle P. 2012. *Amenhotep III: Egypt's Radiant Pharaoh.* Cambridge: Cambridge University Press.

Kozloff, Arielle P., and Betsy M. Bryan. 1992. *Egypt's Dazzling Sun: Amenhotep III and His World.* Cleveland: Cleveland Museum of Art.

Krahmalkov, Charles R. 2000. *Phoenician–Punic Dictionary.* Leuven: Peeters.

Kratz, Reinhard G. 1997. "Erkenntnis Gottes im Hoseabuch." *ZThK* 94: 1–24.
2005 (German 2000). *The Composition of the Narrative Books of the Old Testament.* London: T. & T. Clark.

Kuenen, Abraham. 1861–65. *Historisch-kritisch onderzoek naar het ontstaan en de verzameling van de boeken des ouden verbonds.* Three volumes; Leiden: Akademische Boekhandel van P. Engels.

1869–70 (English 1874–75). *De godsdienst van Israël tot den ondergang van den Joodschen staat.* Three volumes; Haarlem: A. C. Kruseman.

Kuper, Adam. 1982. "Lineage Theory: A Critical Retrospect." *Annual Review of Anthropology* 11: 71–95.

Lambert, Wilfrid G. 1960. *Babylonian Wisdom Literature.* Oxford: Clarendon.
1983. "The God Aššur." *Iraq* 45: 82–86.

Lawrence, Beatrice J. W. 2017. *Jethro and the Jews: Jewish Biblical Interpretation and the Question of Identity.* Leiden: Brill.

Leclant, Jean. 1962. "Fouilles et travaux en Égypte et au Soudan, 1960–1961." *Orientalia* 31: 322–38.

1963. "Fouilles et travaux en Égypte et au Soudan, 1961–1962." *Orientalia* 32: 184–219.

1964. "Fouilles et travaux en Égypte et au Soudan, 1962–1963." *Orientalia* 33: 337–404.

1965. "Les fouilles de Soleb (Nubie soudanaise): quelques remarques sur les écussons des peuples envoûtés de la salle hypostyle du secteur IV." Pp. 205–16 in Siegfried Schott (ed.), *Göttinger Vorträge vom Ägyptologischen Kolloquium der Akademie am 25. und 26. August 1964.* Göttingen: Vandenhoeck und Ruprecht.

Lees, Susan H., and Daniel G. Bates. 1974. "The Origins of Specialized Nomadic Pastoralism: A Systemic Model." *American Antiquity* 39: 187–93.

Lemaire, André. 1987. "Notes d'épigraphie nord-ouest sémitique." *Syria* 64: 205–16.

2007. *The Birth of Monotheism: The Rise and Disappearance of Yahwism.* Washington, DC: Biblical Archaeology Society.

Lemche, Niels-Peter. 1991. *The Canaanites and Their Land: The Tradition of the Canaanites.* Sheffield: Sheffield Academic Press.

Leonard-Fleckman, Mahri. 2016. *The House of David: Between Political Formation and Literary Revision.* Minneapolis: Fortress.

Leuchter, Mark. 2007. "Why Is the Song of Moses in the Book of Deuteronomy?" *VT* 57: 295–317.

Leuenberger, Martin. 2017. "YHWH's Provenance from the South: A New Evaluation of the Arguments Pro and Contra." Pp. 157–79 in Jürgen van Oortschot and Markus Witte (eds.), *The Origins of Yahwism.* Berlin: de Gruyter.

Levin, Christoph. 1993. *Der Jahwist.* Göttingen: Vandenhoeck und Ruprecht.
2000. "Das vorstaatliche Israel." *ZThK* 97: 385–403.

Levine, Baruch A. 1993. *Numbers 1–20: A New Translation with Introduction and Commentary.* New York: Doubleday.

2000. *Numbers 21–36: A New Translation with Introduction and Commentary.* New York: Doubleday.

2005. "Assyrian Ideology and Israelite Monotheism." *Iraq* 67: 411–27.

Lewis, Theodore J. 1989. *Cults of the Dead in Ancient Israel and Ugarit*. Atlanta, GA: Scholars Press.

1996. "The Identity and Function of El/Baal Berith." *JBL* 115: 401–23.

2013. "Divine Fire in Deuteronomy 33:2." *JBL* 132: 791–803.

2020a. "A Holy Warrior at Kuntillet 'Ajrud? Kuntillet 'Ajrud Plaster Inscription 4.2." In Christopher Rollston (ed.), *Biblical and Ancient Near Eastern Studies in Honor of P. Kyle McCarter*. Atlanta, GA: Society of Biblical Literature.

2020b. *The Origin and Character of God: Ancient Israelite Religion through the Lens of Divinity*. Oxford: Oxford University Press.

Lipiński, Edward. 2000. *The Aramaeans: Their Ancient History, Culture, and Religion*. Leuven: Peeters.

Lohfink, Norbert. 1978. "Die Priesterschrift und die Geschichte." Pp. 213–53 in J. A. Emerton (ed.), *Congress Volume: Göttingen 1977*. Leiden: Brill.

Lord, Albert B. 1960. *The Singer of Tales*. Cambridge, MA: Harvard University Press.

Macchi, Jean-Daniel. 1999. *Israël et ses tribus selon Genèse 49*. Göttingen: Vandenhoeck und Ruprecht.

Martin, Mario A. S., and Israel Finkelstein. 2013. "Iron IIA Pottery from the Negev Highlands: Petrographic Analysis and Historical Implications." *TA* 40: 6–45.

Mathieu-Colas, Michel. 2017. "Divinités arabes préislamiques." www.mathieu-colas.fr/michel/Classes/Divinités_arabes.pdf.

Mattingly, Gerald L. 1992. "The Cultural-Historical Approach and Moabite Origins." Pp. 55–64 in Piotr Bienkowski (ed.), *Early Edom and Moab: The Beginning of the Iron Age in Southern Jordan*. Sheffield: J. R. Collis.

Mayes, A. D. H. 1974. *Israel in the Period of the Judges*. Naperville, IL: A. R. Allenson.

1981. *Deuteronomy*. Grand Rapids, MI: Eerdmans.

Mazar, Amihai. 1982. "The 'Bull Site': An Iron Age I Open Cult Place." *BASOR* 247: 27–42.

1990. *Archaeology of the Land of the Bible 10,000–586 B.C.E.* New York: Doubleday.

McCarter, P. Kyle. 1980. *1 Samuel: A New Translation with Introduction, Notes and Commentary*. Garden City, NY: Doubleday.

1984. *2 Samuel: A New Translation with Introduction, Notes and Commentary*. Garden City, NY: Doubleday.

McNutt, Paula M. 1999. "In the Shadow of Cain." *Semeia* 87: 47–53.

Meek, Theophile James. 1920. "A Proposed Reconstruction of Early Hebrew History." *American Journal of Theology* 24: 209–16.

Meinhold, Wiebke. 2009. *Ištar in Aššur: Untersuchungen eines Lokalkultes von ca. 2500 bis 614 v. Chr.* Münster: Ugarit-Verlag.

Meshel, Ze'ev. 2012. *Kuntillet 'Ajrud (Ḥorvat Teman): An Iron Age II Religious Site on the Judah-Sinai Border*. Jerusalem: Israel Exploration Society.

Mettinger, Tryggve N. D. 1990. "The Elusive Essence: YHWH, El and Baal and the Distinctiveness of Israelite Faith." Pp. 393–417 in Erhard Blum et al. (eds.), *Die Hebräische Bibel und ihre zweifache Nachgeschichte (Festschrift Rolf Rendtorff zum 65. Geburtstag)*. Neukirchen–Vluyn: Neukirchener.

1999. "Yahweh Zebaoth." Pp. 920–24 in van der Toorn, Bob Becking, and Pieter W. van der Horst (eds.), *The Dictionary of Deities and Demons*. Leiden: Brill.

Meyer, Eduard. 1881. "Kritik der Berichte über die Eroberung Palästinas (Num. 20,14 bis Jud. 2,5)." *ZAW* 1: 117–46.

1906. *Die Israeliten und ihre Nachbarstämme: Alttestamentliche Untersuchungen*. Halle: Max Niemeyer.

1912. *Der Papyrusfund von Elephantine: Dokumente einer jüdischen Gemeinde aus der Perserzeit und das älteste erhaltene Buch der Weltliteratur*. Leipzig: J. C. Hinrichs.

Miglio, Adam E. 2014. *Tribe and State: The Dynamics of Innternational Politics and the Reign of Zimri-Lim*. Piscataway, NJ: Gorgias.

Miller, Patrick D. 1971. "Animal Names as Designations in Ugaritic and Hebrew." *UF* 2: 177–86.

Milstein, Sara J. 2010. "Reworking Ancient Texts: Revision through Introduction in Mesopotamian and Biblical Literature." New York University PhD.

2016. *Tracking the Master Scribe: Revision through Introduction in Biblical and Mesopotamian Literature*. Oxford: Oxford University Press.

Molendijk, Arie L. 2000. "The Heritage of Cornelis Petrus Tiele (1830–1902)." *Nederlands Archief voor Kerkgeschiedenis / Dutch Review of Church History* 80: 78–114.

Monroe, Lauren. 2007. "Israelite, Moabite and Sabaean War-herem Traditions and the Forging of National Identity: Reconsidering the Sabaean Text RES 3945 in Light of Biblical and Moabite Evidence." *VT* 57: 318–41.

2019. "'For They Did Not Come to the Help of Yahweh': Reconsidering the Curse of *mērôz* in Judges 5:23." Paper, Colloquium for Biblical Research.

forthcoming. "On the Origins and Development of 'Greater Israel'." *HBAI*.

Monroe, Lauren, and Daniel E. Fleming. 2019. "Earliest Israel in Highland Company." *NEA* 82: 16–23.

de Moor, Johannes C. 1997 (1990). *The Rise of Yahwism: The Roots of Israelite Monotheism*. Revised and enlarged edition; Leuven: Peeters.

Morris, Ellen F. 2005. *The Architecture of Imperialism: Military Bases and the Evolution of Foreign Policy in Egypt's New Kingdom*. Leiden: Brill.

Mullen, Theodore. 1980. *The Divine Council in Canaanite and Early Hebrew Literature*. Chico, CA: Scholars Press.

Müller, Hans-Peter. 1966. "Der Aufbau des Deboralieder." *VT* 16: 446–59.

Müller, Reinhard. 2008. *Jahwe als Wettergott: Studien zur althebräischen Kultlyrik anhand ausgewählter Psalmen*. Berlin: de Gruyter.

2017. "The Origins of YHWH in Light of the Earliest Psalms." Pp. 207–38 in Jürgen van Oortschot and Markus Witte (eds.), *The Origins of Yahwism*. Berlin: de Gruyter.

Na'aman, Nadav. 1977. "Yeno'am." *TA* 4: 168–77.

1999. "The Contribution of Royal Inscriptions for a Re-evaluation of the Book of Kings as a Historical Source." *JSOT* 82: 3–17.

2011. "The Exodus Story: Between Historical Memory and Historiographical Composition." *JANER* 11: 39–69.

Nakata, Ichiro. 2011. "The God Itūr-Mēr in the Middle Euphrates Region during the Old Babylonian Period." *RA* 105: 129–36.

Neef, Heinz-Dieter. 2002. *Deboraerzählung und Deboralied: Studien zu Jdc 4,1–5,31.* Neukirchen–Vluyn: Neukirchener.

Nelson, Harold H. 1943. "The Naval Battle Pictured at Medineet Habu." *JNES* 2: 40–55.

et al. 1930. *Medinet Habu I: Early Historical Records of Ramses III.* Chicago: The Oriental Institute.

Niccacci, Alviero. 1997. "La stèle d'Israël: Grammaire et stratégie de communication." Pp. 43–107 in Marcel Sigrist (ed.), *Études égyptologiques et bibliques à la mémoire de Père B. Couroyer.* Paris: J. Gabalda.

Nihan, Christophe. 2007. *From Priestly Torah to Pentateuch: A Study in the Composition of the Book of Leviticus.* Tübingen: Mohr Siebeck.

Noth, Martin. 1966. *Das System der zwölf Stämme Israels.* Darmstadt: Wissenschaftliche Buchgesellschaft.

Nübel, Hans-Ulrich. 1959. "Davids Aufstieg in der frühe israelitischer Geschichtsschreibung." Bonn PhD.

O'Connor, David. 1987. "Egyptians and Libyans in the New Kingdom: An Interpretation." *Expedition Magazine* 29/3: 35–37.

1998. "The City and the World: Worldview and Built Forms in the Reign of Amenhotep III." Pp. 125–72 in David O'Connor and Eric Cline (eds.), *Amenhotep III: Perspectives on His Reign.* Ann Arbor, MI: University of Michigan Press.

2006. "Thutmose III: An Enigmatic Pharaoh." Pp. 1–38 in Eric H. Cline and David O'Connor (eds.), *Thutmose III: A New Biography.* Ann Arbor, MI: University of Michigan Press.

O'Connor, David, and Eric H. Cline (eds.). 1998. *Amenhotep III: Perspectives on His Reign.* Ann Arbor, MI: University of Michigan Press.

del Olmo Lete, Gregorio. 1999. "The Offering Lists and the God Lists." Pp. 305–52 in Wilfred Watson and Nicholas Wyatt (eds.), *Handbook of Ugaritic Studies.* Leiden: Brill.

del Olmo Lete, G., and J. Sanmartín (eds.). 2000. *Diccionario de la lengua ugarítica.* Two volumes; Barcelona: Editorial AUSA.

Olyan, Saul. 1988. *Asherah and the Cult of Yahweh in Israel.* Atlanta, GA: Scholars Press.

van Oortschot, Jürgen, and Markus Witte (eds.). 2017. *The Origins of Yahwism.* Berlin: de Gruyter.

Ornan, Tallay. 2001. "Ištar as Depicted on Finds from Israel." Pp. 235–56 in Amihai Mazar (ed.), *Studies in the Archaeology of the Iron Age in Israel and Jordan.* Sheffield: Sheffield Academic.

2016. "Sketches and Final Works of Art: The Drawings of Wall Paintings of Kuntillet 'Ajrud Revisited." *TA* 43: 3–26.

Otto, Eckart. 1996. "Die nachpriesterschriftliche Pentateuchredaktion im Buch Exodus." Pp. 101–11 in Marc Vervenne (ed.), *Studies in the Book of Exodus: Redaction – Reception – Interpretation.* Leuven: Peeters.

1997. "Forschungen zur Priesterschrift." *Theologische Rundschau* 62: 1–50.

Parker, Simon B. (ed.). 1997. *Ugaritic Narrative Poetry*. Atlanta, GA: Scholars Press.

Parker, Simon B. 2006. "Ancient Northwest Semitic Epigraphy and the 'Deuteronomistic' Tradition in Kings." Pp. 213–27 in Markus Witte et al. (eds.), *Die deuteronomistischen Geschichtswerke: Redaktions- und religionsgeschichtliche Perspektiven zur "Deuteronomismus" – Diskussion in Tora und Vorderen Propheten*. Berlin: de Gruyter.

Parkinson, Richard. 1999. *Cracking Codes: The Rosetta Stone and Decipherment*. Berkeley: University of California Press.

Parr, Peter J. 1997. "Nebi Mend, Tell." Pp. 4:114–15 in Eric M. Meyers (ed.), *The Oxford Encyclopedia of Archaeology in the Near East*. Oxford: Oxford University Press.

van Pelt, W. Paul. 2013. "Revising Egypto–Nubian Relations in New Kingdom Lower Nubia: From Egyptianization to Cultural Entanglement." *Cambridge Archaeological Journal* 23: 523–50.

Pfeiffer, Henrik. 2005. *Jahwes Kommen von Süden: Jdc 5, Hab 3, Dtn 33, und Ps 68 in ihrem literatur- und theologiegeschichtlichen Umfeld*. Göttingen: Vandenhoeck und Ruprecht.

2017. "The Origin of YHWH and Its Attestation." Pp. 115–44 in Jürgen van Oortschot and Markus Witte (eds.), *The Origins of Yahwism*. Berlin: de Gruyter.

Pola, Thomas. 1995. *Die ursprüngliche Priesterschrift: Beobachtungen zur Literarkritik und Traditionsgeschichte von Pg*. Neukirchen–Vluyn: Neukirchener.

Pongratz-Leisten, Beate. 2015. *Religion and Ideology in Assyria*. Berlin: de Gruyter.

Pope, Marvin. 1955. *El in the Ugaritic Texts*. Leiden: Brill.

Porter, Anne. 2009. "Beyond Dimorphism: Ideologies and Materialities of Kinship." Pp. 201–25 in Jeffrey Szuchman (ed.), *Nomads, Tribes, and the State in the Ancient Near East: Cross-Disciplinary Perspectives*. Chicago: The Oriental Institute.

2012. *Mobile Pastoralism and the Formation of Near Eastern Civilizations: Weaving together Society*. Cambridge: Cambridge University Press.

Propp, William H. C. 1998. *Exodus 1–18: A New Translation with Introduction and Commentary*. New York: Doubleday.

2006. *Exodus 19–40: A New Translation with Introduction and Commentary*. New York: Doubleday.

Pruzsinszky, Regine. 2003. *Die Personennamen der Texte aus Emar*. Bethesda, MD: CDL.

Quirke, Stephen G. J. 2001. "Second Intermediate Period." Pp. 3:260–65 in Donald B. Redford (ed.), *The Oxford Encyclopedia of Ancient Egypt*. Oxford: Oxford University Press.

Rad, Gerhard von. 1966. *The Problem of the Hexateuch and Other Essays*. Edinburgh: Oliver & Boyd.

Rainey, Anson F. 1976. "Topographic Problems." *TA* 3: 57–69.

1996. "Who Is a Canaanite? A Review of the Textual Evidence." *BASOR* 304: 1–15.

Rainey, Anson F., and R. Steven Notley. 2006. *The Sacred Bridge: Carta's Atlas of the Biblical World.* Jerusalem: Carta.

Redford, Donald B. 1992. *Egypt, Canaan, and Israel in Ancient Times.* Princeton: Princeton University Press.

2003. *The Wars in Syria and Palestine of Thutmose III: The Foundations of the Egyptian Empire in Asia.* Leiden: Brill.

2006. "The Northern Wars of Thutmose III." Pp. 325–43 in Eric H. Cline and David O'Connor (eds.), *Thutmose III: A New Biography.* Ann Arbor, MI: University of Michigan Press.

Ringgren, Helmer. 1966. *Israelite Religion.* London: S.P.C.K.

Robertson, David A. 1972. *Linguistic Evidence in Dating Early Hebrew Poetry.* Missoula: Mont Scholars Press.

Robin, Christian. 2012. "Matériaux pour une typologie des divinités arabiques et de leurs representations." Pp. 7–118 in Isabelle Sachet and Christian Robin (eds.), *Dieux et déesses d'Arabie: Images et représentations.* Paris: De Boccard.

2018. "Qatabān (royaume de l'Arabie méridionale antique) et son grand dieu 'Amm." *Semitica et Classica* 11: 93–141.

Rofé, Alexander. 2009. *Introduction to the Literature of the Hebrew Bible.* Jerusalem: Simor.

Römer, Thomas. 1990. *Israels Väter: Untersuchungen zur Väterthematik im Deuteronomium und in der deuteronomistischen Tradition.* Göttingen: Vandenhoeck und Ruprecht.

2005. *The So-Called Deuteronomistic History: A Sociological, Historical and Literary Introduction.* London: T. & T. Clark.

2006. "Exodus 3–4 und die aktuelle Pentateuchdiskussion." Pp. 65–79 in Riemer Roukema et al. (eds.), *The Interpretation of Exodus: Studies in Honour of Cornelis Houtman.* Leuven: Peeters.

2015. *The Invention of God.* Cambridge, MA: Harvard University Press.

Rost, Leonhard. 1926. *Die Überlieferung von der Thronnachfolge Davids.* Stuttgart: Kohlhammer.

Routledge, Bruce. 2004. *Moab in the Iron Age: Hegemony, Polity, Archaeology.* Philadelphia: University of Pennsylvania Press.

Routledge, Bruce, and Carolyn Routledge. 2009. "The Balu'a Stela Revisited." Pp. 71–96 in Piotr Bienkowski (ed.), *Studies on Iron Age Moab and Neighboring Areas in Honour of Michèle Daviau.* Leuven: Peeters.

Rowley, H. H. 1946. *The Re-Discovery of the Old Testament.* Philadelphia: Westminster.

1950. *From Joseph to Joshua: Biblical Traditions in the Light of Archaeology.* London: Oxford University Press and the British Academy.

(ed.). 1951. *The Old Testament and Modern Study: A Generation of Discovery and Research.* Oxford: Clarendon.

Rupprecht, Konrad. 1977. *Der Tempel von Jerusalem: Gründung Salomos oder jebusitisches Erbe?* Berlin: de Gruyter.

Russell, Brian D. 2007. *The Song of the Sea: The Date of Composition and Influence of Exodus 15:1–21.* New York: Peter Lang.

Russell, Stephen C. 2009. *Images of Egypt in Early Biblical Literature: Cisjordan-Israelite, Transjordan-Israelite, and Judahite Portrayals.* Berlin: de Gruyter.

2015. "The Structure of Legal Administration in the Moses Story." Pp. 317–29 in Thomas E. Levy et al. (eds.), *Israel's Exodus in Transdisciplinary Perspective: Text, Archaeology, Culture, and Geoscience.* Heidelberg: Springer.

2017. *The King and the Land: A Geography of Royal Power in the Biblical World.* Oxford: Oxford University Press.

Ryckmans, Jacques. 1983. "Biblical and Old South Arabian Institutions: Some Parallels." Pp. 14–25 in R. Bidwell and G. R. Smith (eds.), *Arabian and Islamic Studies: Articles Presented to R. B. Serjeant on the Occasion of His Retirement from the Sir Thomas Adam's Chair of Arabic at the University of Cambridge.* London: Longman.

1989. "Le panthéon de l'Arabie du sud préislamique: État des problèmes et brève synthèse." *Revue de l'histoire des religions* 206: 151–69.

Ryholt, K. S. B. 1997. *The Political Situation in Egypt during the Second Intermediate Period c. 1800–1550 B.C.* Copenhagen: Museum Tusculanum Press.

Sanders, Paul. 1996. *The Provenance of Deuteronomy 32.* Leiden: Brill.

Sanders, Seth. 2009. *The Invention of Hebrew.* Urbana, IL: University of Illinois Press.

Schade, Aaron. 2017. "*Ryt* or *hyt* in Line 12 of the Mesha Inscription: A New Examination of the Stele and the Squeeze, and the Syntactic, Literary, and Cultic Implications of the Reading." *BASOR* 378: 145–62.

Schiff Giorgini, Michela. 1965. *Soleb I: 1813–1963.* Florence: Sansoni.

1998. *Soleb III. Le temple: Description.* Cairo: Institut français d'archéologie orientale.

2002. *Soleb V. Le temple: Plans et photographies.* Cairo: Institut français d'archéologie orientale.

2003. *Soleb IV. Le temple: Bas reliefs et inscriptions.* Cairo: Institut français d'archéologie orientale.

Schloen, J. David. 1993. "Caravans, Kenites, and Casus Belli: Enmity and Alliance in the Song of Deborah." *CBQ* 55: 18–38.

2001. *The House of the Father as Fact and Symbol: Patrimonialism in Ugarit and the Ancient Near East.* Winona Lake, IN: Eisenbrauns.

Schmid, Konrad. 2007. "Innerbiblische Schriftdiskussion im Hiobbuch." Pp. 241–61 in Thomas Krüger et al. (eds.), *Das Buch Hiob und seine Interpretationen.* Zurich: Theologischer Verlag.

2010 (German 1999). *Genesis and the Moses Story: Israel's Dual Origins in the Hebrew Bible.* Winona Lake, IN: Eisenbrauns.

2012a (German 2008). *The Old Testament: A Literary History.* Minneapolis: Fortress.

2012b. "Genesis and Exodus as Two Formerly Independent Traditions of Origins for Ancient Israel." *Biblica* 93: 187–208.

Schmidt, Brian B. 2002. "The Iron Age Pithoi Drawings from Horvat Teman or Kuntillet 'Ajrud: Some New Proposals." *JANER* 2: 91–125.

Schmidt, Ludwig. 1976. *"De Deo": Studien zur Literarkritik und Theologie des Buches Jonas, des Gesprächs zwischen Abraham und Jahwe in Gen 18,22ff. und von Hi 1.* Berlin: de Gruyter.

Schneider, Thomas. 2003. *Ausländer in Ägypten während des Mittleren Reiches und der Hyksoszeit. Teil 2: Ausländische Bewölkerung.* Wiesbaden: Harrassowitz.

———. 2007. "The First Documented Occurrence of the God Yahweh? (Book of the Dead Princeton, 'Roll 5')." *JANER* 7: 113–20.

Schniedewind, William. 2004. *How the Bible Became a Book: The Textualization of Ancient Israel.* Cambridge: Cambridge University Press.

———. 2013. *A Social History of Hebrew: Its Origins through the Rabbinic Period.* New Haven, CT: Yale University Press.

———. 2014. "Understanding Scribal Education in Ancient Israel: A View from Kuntillet 'Ajrud." *Maarav* 21: 271–93.

———. 2017. "An Early Iron Age Phase to Kuntillet 'Ajrud?" Pp. 134–46 in Frerick E. Greenspahn and Gary A. Rendsburg (eds.), *Le-ma'an Ziony: Essays in Honor of Ziony Zevit.* Eugene, OR: Wipf & Stock.

———. 2019. *The Finger of the Scribe: The Beginnings of Scribal Education and How It Shaped the Hebrew Bible.* Oxford: Oxford University Press.

Schorn, Ulrike. 1997. *Ruben und das System der zwölf Stämme Israels: Redaktionsgeschichtliche Untersuchungen zur Bedeutung des Erstgeborenen Jakobs.* Berlin: de Gruyter.

Schüle, Andreas. 2017. "Balaam from Deir Allā – A Peripheral Aramean?" Pp. 69–80 in Angelika Berlejung et al. (eds.), *Wandering Arameans: Arameans Outside Syria, Textual and Archaeological Perspectives.* Wiesbaden: Harrassowitz.

Schwemer, Daniel. 2001. *Die Wettergottgestalten Mesopotamiens und Nordsyriens im Zeitalter der Keilschriftkulturen: Materialien und Studien nach den schriftlichen Quellen.* Wiesbaden: Harrassowitz.

Seebass, Horst. 1977. "Die Stämmeliste von Dtn. XXXIII." *VT* 27: 158–69.

———. 1997. *Genesis II: Vätergeschichte I (11,27–22,24).* Neukirchen–Vluyn: Neukirchener.

Seow, Choon-Leong. 1989. *Myth, Drama, and the Politics of David's Dance.* Atlanta, GA: Scholars Press.

Service, Elman R. 1975. *Origins of the State and Civilization: The Process of Cultural Evolution.* New York: W. W. Norton.

Simons, J. 1937. *Handbook for the Study of the Egyptian Topographical Lists Relating to Western Asia.* Leiden: Brill.

Singer-Avitz, Lily. 2006. "The Date of Kuntillet 'Ajrud." *TA* 33: 196–228.

Smith, Mark S. 1984. "Divine Travel as a Token of Divine Rank." *UF* 16: 359.

———. 1990 (2nd edition 2002). *The Early History of God: Yahweh and the Other Deities in Ancient Israel.* San Francisco: Harper and Row.

———. 1994. *The Ugaritic Baal Cycle, Volume I: Introduction with Text, Translation and Commentary of KTU 1.1–1.2.* Leiden: Brill.

1997. *The Pilgrimage Pattern in Exodus.* Sheffield: Sheffield Academic.

2001a. *The Origins of Biblical Monotheism: Israel's Polytheistic Background and the Ugaritic Texts.* Oxford: Oxford University Press.

2001b. *Untold Stories: The Bible and Ugaritic Studies in the Twentieth Century.* Peabody, MA: Hendrickson.

2004. *The Memoirs of God: History, Memory, and the Experience of the Divine in Ancient Israel.* Minneapolis: Fortress.

2009. "What Is Prologue Is Past: Composing Israelite Identity in Judges 5." Pp. 43–58 in John J. Ahn and Stephen L. Cook (eds.), *Thus Says the Lord: Essays on the Former and Latter Prophets in Honor of Robert R. Wilson.* New York: T. & T. Clark.

2012a. "God in Israel's Bible: Divinity between the World and Israel, between the Old and the New." *CBQ* 74: 1–27.

2012b. "The Problem of the God and His Manifestations: The Case of the Baals at Ugarit, with Implications for Yahweh of Various Locales." Pp. 205–50 in Aaron Schart and Jutta Krispenz (eds.), *Die Stadt im Zwölfprophetenbuch.* Berlin: de Gruyter.

2014. *Poetic Heroes: Literary Commemorations of Warriors and Warrior Culture in the Early Biblical World.* Grand Rapids, MI: Eerdmans.

2016. *Where the Gods Are: Spatial Dimensions of Anthropomorphism.* New Haven, CT: Yale University Press.

2017. "YHWH's Original Character: Questions about an Unknown God." Pp. 23–43 in Jürgen van Oortschot and Markus Witte (eds.), *The Origins of Yahwism.* Berlin: de Gruyter.

Smith, Mark S., and Wayne Pitard. 2009. *The Ugaritic Baal Cycle, Volume II: Introduction with Text, Translation and Commentary of KTU/CAT 1.3–1.4.* Leiden: Brill.

von Soden, Wolfram. 1966. "Jahwe: 'Er ist, Er erweist sich'." *WO* 3: 177–87.

Soggin, J. Alberto. 1981. *Judges.* Philadelphia: Westminster.

Sommer, Benjamin D. 2009. *The Bodies of God and the World of Ancient Israel.* Cambridge: Cambridge University Press.

Sommerfeld, Walter. 1982. *Der Aufstieg Marduks: Die Stellung Marduks in der babylonischen Religion des zweiten Jahrtausends v.Chr.* Neukirchen–Vluyn: Neukirchener.

1987–90. "Marduk. A. Philologisch. I. In Mesopotamien." *RlA* 7: 360–70.

Sparks, Kenton L. 2003. "Genesis 49 and the Tribal List Tradition in Ancient Israel." *ZAW* 115: 327–47.

Spencer, Neal. 2014. "Egypt in Kush: Creating a Pharaonic Town in Nubia." Pp. 2–23 in Neal Spencer, Anna Stephens, and Michaela Binder (eds.), *Amara West: Living in Ancient Nubia.* London: The British Museum.

Spina, Frank A. 2005. *The Faith of the Outsider: Exclusion and Inclusion in the Biblical Story.* Grand Rapids, MI: Eerdmans.

Stade, Berhard. 1887. *Geschichte der Volkes Israel,* volume 1. Berlin: G. Grote.

Stager, Lawrence E. 1988. "Archaeology, Ecology, and Social History: Background Themes to the Song of Deborah." Pp. 221–34 in J. A. Emerton (ed.), *Congress Volume: Jerusalem, 1986.* Leiden: Brill.

1989. "The Song of Deborah – Why Some Tribes Answered the Call and Others Did Not." *BAR* 15/1: 50–64.

Stahl, Michael J. 2020. *The "God of Israel" in History and Tradition.* Leiden: Brill.

Stamm, Johann Jakob. 1939. *Die akkadische Namengebung.* Leipzig: J. C. Hinrichs.

Stein, Peter. 2011. "Ancient South Arabian." Pp. 1042–73 in Stefan Weninger et al. (eds.), *Semitic Languages: An International Handbook.* Berlin: de Gruyter Mouton.

2015. "Die altsüdarabischen Minuskelinschriften auf Holzstäbchen in der Sammlung des Oosters Instituut in Leiden." Pp. 193–211 in Iris Gerlach (ed.), *South Arabia and Its Neighbors: Phenomena of Intercultural Contacts.* Wiesbaden: Reichert.

Steiner, Richard C. 1996. "*dāt* and *'ēn*: Two Verbs Masquerading as Nouns in Moses' Blessing (Deuteronomy 33:2, 28)." *JBL* 115: 693–98.

Steiner, Richard C., and Sid Z. Leiman. 2009. "The Lost Meaning of Deuteronomy 33:2 as Preserved in the Palestinian Targum to the Decalogue." Pp. 157–66 in Nili S. Fox, David A. Glatt-Gilad, and Michael J. Williams (eds.), *Mishneh Todah: Studies in Deuteronomy and Its Cultural Environment in Honor of Jeffrey H. Tigay.* Winona Lake, IN: Eisenbrauns.

Steinkeller, Piotr. 2004. "A History of Mashkan-shapir and Its Role in the Kingdom of Larsa." Pp. 26–42 in Elizabeth Stone and Paul Zimansky (eds.), *The Anatomy of a Mesopotamian City: Survey and Soundings at Mashkan-shapir.* Winona Lake, IN: Eisenbrauns.

Stol, Marten. 1991. "Old Babylonian Personal Names." *SEL* 8: 191–212.

Streck, Michael P. 1999. "Der Gottesname 'Jahwe' und das amurritische Onomastikon." *WO* 30: 35–46.

2000. *Das amurritische Onomastikon der altbabylonischen Zeit. Band 1: Die Amurriter. Die onomastische Forschung. Orthographie und Phonologie. Nominalmorphologie.* Neukirchen–Vluyn: Neukirchener.

Taylor, J. Glen. 1993. *Yahweh and the Sun: Biblical and Archaeological Evidence for Sun Worship in Ancient Israel.* Sheffield: Sheffield Academic Press.

Tebes, Juan Manuel. 2006. "Egypt in the East: The Egyptian Presence in the Negev and the Local Society during the Early Iron Age." *Cahiers Caribéens d'Égyptologie* 9: 75–94.

2017. "The Southern Home of YHWH and Pre-Priestly Patriarchal/Exodus Traditions from a Southern Perspective." *Biblica* 98: 166–88.

Thames, John T. 2016. "Ritual Revision and the Influence of Empire: The Politics of Change in the *zukru* Festival of Late Bronze Emar." Johns Hopkins Ph.D.

Thareani, Yifat. 2016. "*Enemy at the Gates? The Archaeological Visibility of the Aramaeans at Tel Dan.*" Pp. 169–98 in Omer Sergi, Manfred Oeming, and Izaak J. de Hulster (eds.), In Search for Aram and Israel: Politics, Culture, and Identity. Tübingen: Mohr Siebeck.

Tiele Cornelis Petrus. 1864. *Die Godsdienst van Zarathustra van haar ontstaan in Baktrië tot den val van het Oud-Perzische Rijk.* Haarlem: Kruseman.

1872 (French 1882). *Vergelijkende geschiedenis von de Egyptische en Mesopotamische godsdiensten: Egypte, Babel-Assur, Harran, Fenicië, Israël.* Amsterdam: P. N. van Kampen; French, *Histoire comparée des anciennes religions de l'Égypte et des peuples sémitiques.* Paris: G. Fischbacher.

1876. *Geschiedenis van den godsdienst, tot aan de heerschappij der Wereldgodsdiensten.* Amsterdam: Van Kampen.

1886–88. *Babylonisch-Assyrische Geschichte.* Two volumes; Gotha: F. A. Perthes.

Tigay, Jeffrey H. 1996. *Deuteronomy: The Traditional Hebrew Text with the New JPS Translation.* Philadelphia: Jewish Publication Society.

van der Toorn, Karel. 1993. "Saul and the Rise of Israelite State Religion." *VT* 43: 519–42.

1999. "Yahweh." Pp. 910–19 in van der Toorn, Bob Becking, and Pieter W. van der Horst (eds.), *The Dictionary of Deities and Demons.* Leiden: Brill.

Tropper, Josef. 2017. "The Divine Name *Yahwa." Pp. 13–33 in Jürgen van Oortschot and Markus Witte (eds.), *The Origins of Yahwism.* Berlin: de Gruyter.

Uphill, Eric. 1967. "The Nine Bows." *Jaarbericht van het Voorasiatisch-Egyptisch Gezelshap Ex Oriente Lux VI* 19: 393–420.

Valk, Jonathan. 2018. "Assyrian Collective Identity in the Second Millennium BCE: A Social Categories Approach." New York University PhD.

Van Seters, John. 1975. *Abraham in History and Tradition.* New Haven, CT: Yale University Press.

1983. *In Search of History: Historiography in the Ancient World and the Origins of Biblical History.* New Haven, CT: Yale University Press.

1994. *The Life of Moses: The Yahwist as Historian in Exodus–Numbers.* Louisville, KY: Westminster John Knox.

de Vaux, Roland. 1969. "Sur l'origine kénite ou madianite du Yahwisme." *Eretz Israel* 9: 28–31.

Villard, Pierre. 1994. "Nomination d'un scheich." *FM* 2: 291–97.

2001. "Les administrateurs de l'époque de Yasmah-Addu." Pp. 9–140 in Jean-Marie Durand and Dominique Charpin (eds.), *Amurru 2: Mari, Ébla et les Hourrites. Dix ans de travaux.* Paris: Éditions Recherche sur les Civilisations.

Watts, James W. 1992. *Psalm and Story: Inset Hymns in Hebrew Literature.* Sheffield: JSOT Press.

1996. "Psalmody in Prophecy: Habakkuk 3 in Context." Pp. 209–23 in James W. Watts and Paul R. House (eds.), *Forming Prophetic Literature: Essays on Isaiah and the Twelve in Honor of John D. W. Watts.* Sheffield: Sheffield Academic Press.

Weinfeld, Moshe. 1987. "The Tribal League at Sinai." Pp. 303–14 in Patrick D. Miller, Paul D. Hanson, and J. Dean McBride (eds.), *Ancient Israelite Religion: Essays in Honor of Frank Moore Cross.* Minneapolis: Fortress.

Weinstein, James M. 1998. "Egypt and the Levant in the Reign of Amenhotep III." Pp. 223–36 in David O'Connor and Eric Cline (eds.), *Amenhotep III: Perspectives on His Reign.* Ann Arbor, MI: University of Michigan Press.

Weinstein, James M., Eric H. Cline, Kenneth A. Kitchen, and David O'Connor. 1998. Pp. 223–70 in David O'Connor and Eric H. Cline (eds.), *Amenhotep III: Perspectives on His Reign.* Ann Arbor, MI: University of Michigan Press.

Weippert, Manfred. 1974. "Semitische Nomaden des zweiten Jahrtausends."
  Biblica 55: 265–80, 427–33.
  1976–80. "Jahwe." *RlA* 5: 251–52.
Weitzman, Steven. 1997. *Song and Story in Biblical Narrative: The History of a
  Literary Convention in Ancient Israel.* Bloomington, IN: Indiana University
  Press.
Westermann, Claus. 1986 (German 1982). *Genesis 37–50: A Commentary.*
  Minneapolis: Augsburg.
Wicksteed, Philip H. 1892. "Abraham Kuenen." *JQR* 4: 571–605.
Williamson, H. G. M. 2001. "Isaiah and the Holy One of Israel." Pp. 22–38 in A.
  Rapoport-Albert and G. Greenberg (eds.), *Biblical Hebrew, Biblical Texts:
  Essays in Memory of Michael P. Weitzman.* Sheffield: Sheffield Academic.
Willi-Plein, Ina. 2005. "I Sam 18–19 und die Davidshausgeschichte." Pp. 138–71
  in Walter Dietrich (ed.), *David und Saul im Widerstreit – Diachronie und
  Synchronie im Weitstreit: Beiträge zur Auslegung des ersten Samuelbuches.*
  Göttingen: Vandenhoeck und Ruprecht.
Wright, Jacob L. 2014. *David, King of Israel, and Caleb in Biblical Memory.*
  Cambridge: Cambridge University Press.
Yoffee, Norman. 1988. "The Collapse of Ancient Mesopotamian States and
  Civilization." Pp. 44–68 in Yoffee and George L. Cowgill (eds.), *The
  Collapse of Ancient States and Civilizations.* Tuxcon: University of Arizona
  Press.
Younger, K. Lawson. 2016. *A Political History of the Arameans: From Their
  Origin to the End of Their Polities.* Atlanta, GA: Society of Biblical
  Literature.
Zertal, Adam. 1986–87. "An Early Iron Age Cultic Site on Mount Ebal:
  Excavation Seasons 1982–1987; Preliminary Report." *TA* 13/14: 105–65.
Zevit, Ziony. 2012. "Mesha's *Ryt* in the Context of Moabite and Israelite
  Bloodletting." Pp. 235–38 in Marilyn J. Lundberg, Steven Fine, and Wayne
  T. Pitard (eds.), *Puzzling Out the Past: Studies in Northwest Semitic
  Languages and Literatures in Honor of Bruce Zuckerman.* Leiden: Brill.

Ancient Near East Index

Scripture Index

Subject Index

For EU product safety concerns, contact us at Calle de José Abascal, 56–1°, 28003 Madrid, Spain or eugpsr@cambridge.org.